STRENGTH OF STRUCTURAL MATERIALS

STRENGTH OF STRUCTURAL MATERIALS

UNDERSTANDING BASIC STRUCTURAL DESIGN

GIUSEPPE DE CAMPOLI, Ph.D., P.E.
City College of the
City University of New York

A Wiley-Interscience Publication

JOHN WILEY & SONS

New York   Chichester   Brisbane   Toronto   Singapore

Library of Congress Cataloging in Publication Data:

De Campoli, Giuseppe.
  Strength of structural materials.

  "A Wiley–Interscience publication."
  Bibliography: p.
  Includes index.
  1. Strength of materials. 2. Structural design.
I. Title.

TA405.D33   1984   620.1'12   84-3569
ISBN 0-471-89082-0

Printed in the United States of America

10 9 8 7 6 5 4 3 2 1

*To Imma, Jiovanni,
and Mario*

PREFACE

This book on strength of structural materials is intended to be the logical continuation of my previous book *Statics of Structural Components: Understanding Basic Structural Design* (Wiley, 1983).

The introductory chapter of the *Statics* book lists the eight basic steps in the design of a typical structure. The study and practice of steps 1 through 4 for statically determinate structures constitute the scope of that book. The reader who is familiar with it will recall these first four steps in the design of structures:

1. Specification of a structural model.
2. Evaluation of the reactions of the constraints.
3. Evaluation of internal forces.
4. Evaluation of cross-sectional properties.

In *Strength of Structural Materials* the next four steps are studied and practiced:

5. Evaluation of internal stresses.
6. Comparison of the internal stresses with their safe limits specified by the building codes.
7. Evaluation of structural deformations.
8. Comparison of the structural deformations with their safe limits specified by the building codes.

In addition, this book aims at expanding the reader's understanding of structural design by resuming the discussion of the reactions of constraints for statically indeterminate structures.

The last chapter of this book returns to a discussion of loads and suggests design criteria for structures in earthquake and hurricane zones.

Throughout there is a concern for the systematic placement of each topic in the general context of structural design. More specifically, the topics are presented in the sequence in which they are used in the practice of structural analysis, that is, according to the eight basic steps. The problems solved and those proposed at the end of a chapter not only focus on that chapter's topic, they often simulate the design process, starting with Step 1, so that the reader each time is able to get a feeling for an actual design problem and is not limited to the challenge of abstract and disconnected tasks. Although for this purpose reference is frequently made to the problems in *Statics of Structural Components*, restatement of data and results of earlier steps avoids the need for continual hopping between the two books.

The approach of each chapter to a given topic generally takes the following form:

An opening discussion of the place and relevance of that topic in structural analysis.

A discussion of the physical aspects of the problem.

A statement of the physical events in equation form.

The numerical operations for the solution of the equation.

Discussion of the results.

Examples and problems.

Such an approach allows an instructor to vary the depth of coverage at will. Instructors of Civil Engineering will probably cover every topic fully. Instructors in Architecture will perhaps limit the discussion to the presentation of a topic and the final formula (a la Harry Parker) although the understanding of the physics of a structural topic is the most valuable part for an architect. Engineers need the final formulas in sizing a great number of structural components. They also need a complete understanding of the physics behind the formulas in order to be in control of the results of their own calculations and of computer outputs. Architects need mostly an understanding of the physical structural behavior. A final formula is useful to them as a summary and a test tool of their understanding.

However, the true understanding of the physical behavior of structures is generated by the derivation of formulas. The mathematical operations for the solution of the equations ought to be viewed as well as positive means of training in clear thinking, careful planning, and making precise specifications—all important qualities for architects and engineers. In these mathematical operations calculus is only used symbolically. The reader never needs to perform an integration or differentiation to follow the text. All the basic mathematical concepts used in the book are reviewed ad hoc.

The final choice of how to use the book of course belongs to the instructors who adopt it. The book's format makes it easy to jump to final formulas and practice with the problems, but the book is best used by following the logical development through which each formula is obtained. Because of these possibilities the book can be useful also to young professionals in engineering and architecture.

In sum, this book may be viewed as a kind of structural primer without which the glossy coatings of current complex methods and techniques of automated analysis flake off. No one who lacks a thorough familiarity with the theories and methods in "statics" and "strength," as set forth in these books, should be entrusted with the responsibility of designing structures of any relevance, preparing inputs for computerized stress calculations, or interpreting and implementing the suggestions of computer output.

GIUSEPPE DE CAMPOLI

New York, New York
July 1984

CONTENTS

STRENGTH OF STRUCTURAL MATERIALS

ONE

INTERNAL STRESSES

Among the internal forces of structures four types are recognized. Their action on a small structural element can be visualized using the example of an accordion and its possible deformations.* These four internal forces are the axial and shear forces and the bending and twisting moments.

Cross-sectional properties indicate the strength and rigidity of a cross section under the action of the internal forces. Indeed they condition the effect of internal forces on structures. Thus the selection of cross-sectional shapes and dimensions is an important step in structural design. Together internal forces and cross-sectional properties are used to obtain the stresses in structural materials.†

Each of the four internal forces produces a different type of stress response on a cross section that is, a different distribution of stresses. Accordingly there are four different states of stress:

Axial Stress, σ_a
Shear Stress, τ_s
Bending Stress, σ_b
Torsional Stress, τ_t

Axial and bending stresses occur at a right angle to the plane of the cross section and parallel to the fibers of the structural material, which these stresses tend to elongate or shorten.

Shear and torsional stresses, both frictional, occur on the plane of the cross section. This can be illustrated by holding a deck of playing

---

*See G. de Campoli, *Statics of Structural Components* (New York: Wiley, 1983), Chapters 1, 4.
† Ibid.

FIGURE 1.1.   **FIGURE 1.2.**

cards, which would represent a small structural element, between the palms of both hands and deforming it as in Fig. 1.1. Friction develops between adjacent cards as the deck deforms. Friction between the cards also develops if the palms of both hands apply a torque to the ends of the deck, and each card rotates with respect to the next (Fig. 1.2).

In this chapter we derive the formulas needed for the quantitative evaluation of internal stresses. The classic notations σ and τ indicating the internal stresses are used in order to avoid the conflict between the notations of the American Concrete Institute and those of the Timber and Steel Construction manuals. In structural analysis equations of equilibrium of the external forces are used to obtain the reactions of the constraints of statically determinate structural elements. Then, equations of equilibrium, written for only a part of a structural element, extending from one end to a typical section S, are used to obtain the internal forces on the section S. The formulas by which internal stresses are evaluated derive from equations of equilibrium written for an individual cross section of a structural element.

1.1. AXIAL STRESSES

The stress distribution on the typical cross section of a structural element such as a cable, which is subject only to axial forces, produces a resultant R equal and opposite to the local axial force P to satisfy the condition of equilibrium of the cross-section in translation. Moreover the resultant is colinear with P to satisfy the condition of equi-

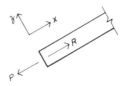

FIGURE 1.3.

librium of the cross section in rotation (Fig. 1.3). The condition of equilibrium in translation, with the x axis tangent to the cable at the typical section, has the form

$$\sum F_x = P - R = 0.$$

The equation of equilibrium of moments on the typical cross section is identically satisfied, which means not only the sum of the moments of P and R about the centroid vanishes but also each moment vanishes because P and R are both on the centroid of the section.

We know from observation that all the fibers of a homogeneous element of a cable extend by the same amount when the element is pulled by two axial forces P (Fig. 1.4). Since all the fibers are made of the same material (i.e., homogeneous cable) and have the same length, there is no possibility that they may be equally extended by different stresses. In summary, the axial stress is identical in each fiber or constant on the cross section.

Considering an elemental area dA on the cross section (Fig. 1.5), the product of the local axial stress σ_a with the area dA is an elemental axial force dF_a. As an infinite number of these forces dF_a act on the cross section, the resultant R is their sum, and since the summation of an infinite number of infinitesimal forces dF_a is an integral

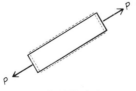

FIGURE 1.4.

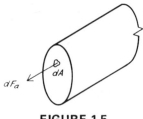

FIGURE 1.5.

$$R = \int_A dF_a = \int_A \sigma_a \, dA,$$

then the equation of force equilibrium on the cross section

$$P - R = 0$$

can be written as

$$P = R = \int_A \sigma_a \, dA,$$

where the integral is calculated over the entire cross-sectional area A. Remembering that the stress σ_a is constant on the cross section, we can write σ_a outside the integral sign. Then

$$P = \sigma_a \int_A dA.$$

The summation $\int_A dA$ of all the infinitesimal areas dA of the cross section is the total area A of the section. Therefore we can conclude

$$P = A\sigma_a$$

from which

$$\sigma_a = \frac{P}{A}.$$

The preceding formula gives the axial stress as a function of the axial force P and the cross-sectional area A. It is evident that A measures the axial strength of the section since for a given value of P, the stress σ_a is large if A is small, and vice versa.

Design Example

The reaction P of a cable measures 24 k. If the cable is made with a steel rod and if the allowable stress in the steel is $\sigma_{all} = 24$ k/in.^{2}, the required section of the rod is given by

$$A = \frac{P}{\sigma_{all}} = \frac{24}{24} = 1 \text{ in.}^2$$

Investigation Example

The cable element of Fig. 1.4 is pulled by axial forces $P = 20$ k. The cable is made of steel rod with a 9/8-in. diameter and a cross-sectional area $A = 1$ in.^{2} The actual stress in the cable is then

$$\sigma_a = \frac{P}{A} = \frac{20}{1} = 20 \text{ k/in.}^2$$

If the allowable tensile stress in the material is equal to or greater than 20 k/in.^{2}, the cable is dimensioned on the safe side.

1.2. BENDING STRESSES

The bending moment M on a typical cross section of a flexural member produces extension of some fibers of material and contraction of others in the direction perpendicular to the cross section. The bending stresses are therefore perpendicular to the cross section, and their distribution includes both positive (tensile) and negative (compressive) stresses (Fig. 1.6). The elemental forces dF_b, which are at each point of the section the product $\sigma_b \, dA$ of the local bending stress σ_b with the elemental area dA, lack a resultant R. If indeed the resultant R existed, it would be the only force perpendicular to the cross section,

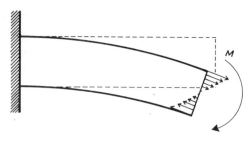

FIGURE 1.6.

and the equilibrium in that direction would be impossible for lack of an opposite force.

The resultant T of the tensile forces dF_b must then be equal to the resultant C of the compressive forces dF_b. T and C are both perpendicular to the section, but they are not colinear since tensile and compressive stresses belong to different regions of the cross section. As equal, opposite and parallel forces, T and C form a system (called couple) without a resultant R but with a moment that is the internal moment M_i of the stress distribution on the section. This moment is called resisting moment M_R when the extreme bending stress on the section equals the allowable stress for a given structural material.

Our objective is to derive a formula for evaluating the bending stresses σ_b. For this purpose we consider an elemental area dA, of a typical cross section subject to bending, located above the neutral axis at a distance z_A from it (Fig. 1.7). The bending stress σ_b pro-

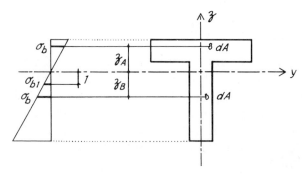

FIGURE 1.7.

duces on dA the elemental force $\sigma_b \, dA$ which has a moment $z_A \sigma_b \, dA$ about the axis of rotation of the cross section, that is the neutral axis, here identified with the y axis of the x, y, z Cartesian reference frame. Similarly an area dA located below the neutral axis at a distance z_B from it contributes an elemental moment $z_B \sigma_b \, dA$ to the moment M_i of the internal stresses. M_i is the summation of all these elemental moments over the cross-sectional area A.

$$M_i = \int_A z_A \sigma_b \, dA + \int_A z_B \sigma_b \, dA$$

Results of experimental tests show that when the structural material is not stressed close to its breaking point, the variation in bending stresses from the top to the bottom fibers of the section is linear, and thus the stress in a typical fiber is proportional to its distance z from the neutral axis. Calling indeed σ_{b1} the stress at the coordinate $z = 1$ (Fig. 1.7), the similarity of the triangles with the bases σ_b and σ_{b1} and with the altitudes z_A and 1 allows us to write

$$\frac{\sigma_b}{\sigma_{b1}} = \frac{z_a}{1}.$$

Thus

$$\sigma_b = \sigma_{b1} z_A.$$

Similarly,

$$\sigma_b = \sigma_{b1} z_B.$$

σ_{b1} is the constant of proportionality which links σ_b to z_A or z_B.
Using the preceding expressions of σ_b, the internal moment M_i has the form

$$M_i = \sigma_{b1} \int z_A^2 \, dA + \sigma_{b1} \int z_B^2 \, dA.$$

Since two integrals on the right side of this expression represent the moments of inertia I_A and I_B, respectively, of the areas above and below the neutral axis about the neutral axis, we have

$$M_i = \sigma_{b1} I_A + \sigma_{b1} I_B.$$

Factoring out σ_{b1} gives

$$M_i = \sigma_{b1}(I_A + I_B) = \sigma_{b1} I,$$

where I is the total moment of inertia of the cross section about the neutral axis.

For the cross section to be in equilibrium, the sum of all moments must vanish

$$\sum M = M - M_i = 0.$$

In other words, the internal moment M_i is equal to the bending moment M. The constant of proportionality between the bending stresses and the z coordinates is then

$$\sigma_{b1} = \frac{M_i}{I} = \frac{M}{I},$$

and the formula for the evaluation of the bending stress is

$$\sigma_b = \sigma_{b1} z = \frac{M}{I} z,$$

where

M = the bending moment on the cross section,

I = the cross section's moment of inertia about the neutral axis,

z = the elevation of the typical fiber on the neutral axis.

It is easy to prove that *the neutral axis of the bending stresses coin-*

cides with the centroidal axis of the cross section. Observing the fact that

$$dF_b = \sigma_b \, dA = \sigma_{b1} z \, dA = \sigma_{b1} \, dQ,$$

one realizes that the elemental forces dF_b are proportional through the constant σ_{b1} to the elemental area moments dQ about the neutral axis. Therefore where the forces dF_b change sign, the area moments dQ must also change sign.

The elemental forces dF_b change from positive to negative (tensile to compressive) through the neutral axis. The area moments dQ turn from positive to negative through the centroidal axis. The centroidal axis and the neutral axis must therefore coincide. Note that the axis that makes the moment of an area vanish is the centroidal axis. Indeed the moment Q of an area A (Fig. 1.8) about an axis y is

$$Q = AZ_A.$$

When the y axis is centroidal ($Z_A = 0$), Q vanishes.

The proportionality between elemental forces dF_b and elemental area moments dQ also suggests that the center of the compressive forces dF_b (point of application of C) is the same as the center of the moments dQ of the elemental compressive areas about the centroidal axis. The distance from the centroidal axis to the center of the moments dQ is obtained from the definition of moment of inertia

$$I = QZ_Q = AZ_A Z_Q$$

which gives

$$Z_Q = \frac{I}{Q}.$$

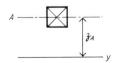

FIGURE 1.8.

Assuming the zone above the neutral axis to be in compression, the z coordinate of C is thus

$$Z_C = \frac{I_A}{Q_A}.$$

The z coordinate of T is similarly given by

$$Z_T = \frac{I_B}{Q_B}.$$

The arm of the internal moment M_i is

$$Z = Z_C + Z_T = \frac{I_A}{Q_A} + \frac{I_B}{Q_B}.$$

Q_A and Q_B are both equal to the maximum value, Q_{max}, of the area moment on the section. Indeed, Q_A or Q_B are reduced by the addition of area moments from the other side of the centroidal axis which have an opposite sign. A more compact expression of Z is then

$$Z = \frac{1}{Q_{max}} (I_A + I_B) = \frac{I}{Q_{max}}.$$

It will be shown that the value of Z is a measure of the shear strength of the cross section.

Example: Investigation of a Flexural Bar

A cantilevered wooden beam made of glued planks spans 3 ft and has the cross-sectional dimensions shown in Fig. 1.9. Find the beam's capacity to carry a load F concentrated at its end with an allowable stress

$$\sigma_b = 1.5 \text{ k/in.}^2$$

Also find the extreme stresses when $F = 0.320$ k.

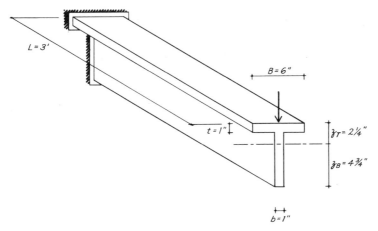

FIGURE 1.9.

Solution.   The fixed end moment is

$$M_{max} = FL = 3F \text{ ft-k.}$$

The cross-sectional properties are obtained as follows:

Flange area

$$A_1 = 6 \text{ in.}^2$$

Web area

$$A_2 = 6 \text{ in.}^2$$

Total area

$$A = \sum A_i = 12 \text{ in.}^2$$

Depth of centroidal axis

$$z_T = \frac{\sum A_i z_{Ti}}{\sum A_i} = \frac{6(0.5) + 6(4)}{12} = 2.25 \text{ in.}$$

Moment of compression area about centroidal axis

$$Q_{max} = bz_B \left(\frac{z_B}{2}\right) = 4.75(4.75)0.5 = 11.3 \text{ in.}^3$$

Moment of inertia of compression area about centroidal axis

$$I_B = \frac{b}{3}(z_B)^3 = \frac{1}{3}(4.75)^3 = 35.7 \text{ in.}^4$$

Moment of inertia of tension area about centroidal axis

$$I_A = \frac{B}{3}(z_T)^3 - \frac{(B-b)}{3}(z_T - t)^3 = \frac{6}{3}(2.25)^3 - \frac{5}{3}(1.25)^3 = 19.5 \text{ in.}^4$$

Total moment of inertia

$$I = I_A + I_B = 35.7 + 19.5 = 55.2 \text{ in.}^4$$

Distance from compressive resultant C to centroidal axis

$$Z_B = \frac{I_B}{Q_{max}} = \frac{35.7}{11.3} = 3.16 \text{ in.}$$

Distance from tensile resultant T to centroidal axis

$$Z_A = \frac{I_A}{Q_{max}} = \frac{19.5}{11.3} = 1.72 \text{ in.}$$

Arm of resisting moment

$$Z = Z_A + Z_B = 3.16 + 1.72 = 4.88 \text{ in.}$$

The extreme fiber stresses are

$$\sigma_b^T = \frac{M}{I} z_T = \frac{12(3F)2.25}{55.2} = 1.47F$$

$$\sigma_b^B = \frac{M}{I} z_B = \frac{12(3F)4.75}{55.2} = 3.11F.$$

Specifying that

$$3.11F = 1.5$$

one obtains

$$F = \frac{1.5}{3.11} = 0.48 \text{ k}$$

When $F = 0.32$ k,

$$\sigma_b^B = 3.11(0.32) = 1 \text{ k/in.}^2$$

$$\sigma_b^T = 1.47(0.32) = 0.47 \text{ k/in.}^2$$

Example: Design of a Rectangular Flexural Bar

The beam of Fig. 1.9 must be built with a rectangular cross section, with width $b = 3$ in. to carry a tip load $F = 0.32$ k without exceeding the allowable stress $\sigma_B = 1.5$ k/in.^{2}

Solution.   With the notation of section modulus

$$S_A = \frac{I}{z_T} \quad \text{or} \quad S_B = \frac{I}{z_B},$$

the bending stresses at the extreme fibers are

$$\sigma_b^T = \frac{M}{S_A}; \quad \sigma_b^B = \frac{M}{S_B}.$$

For a rectangular section with depth H and width b

$$z_T = z_B = \frac{H}{2};$$

$$S_A = S_B = \frac{bH^3}{12}\left(\frac{2}{H}\right) = \frac{bH^2}{6}.$$

In this problem

$$\sigma_b^T = \sigma_b^B = \frac{6M}{bH^2} = \frac{12(0.96)6}{3H^2} = 1.5.$$

from which

$$H = \sqrt{\frac{12(0.96)6}{3(1.5)}} = \sqrt{15.36} \cong 4 \text{ in.}$$

In the formula just derived for the bending stress σ_b and for the arm Z of the internal moment M_i, the cross section was assumed to be symmetric about the plane of action of the bending moment M.

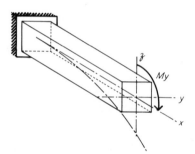

FIGURE 1.10.

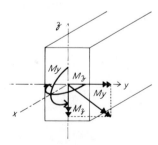

FIGURE 1.11.

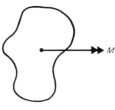

FIGURE 1.12.

This is the plane that contains the bent axis of the structural element shown in Fig. 1.10 as the coordinate plane xz. If M is not acting on a plane of symmetry, but the cross section has two such planes, the moment vector M can be decomposed into two moments, M_y and M_z, each acting on a plane of symmetry of the cross section (Fig. 1.11). Then the bending stresses due to M_y and M_z can be evaluated separately:

$$\sigma_{by} = \frac{M_y}{I_y} z;$$

$$\sigma_{bz} = \frac{M_z}{I_z} y.$$

If M does not act on a plane of symmetry and cannot be decomposed into the two bending moments M_y and M_z because the cross section lacks axes of symmetry (Fig. 1.12), these formulas do not apply any longer. The derivation of suitable formulas for this case is beyond the scope of this book.

1.3.   COMBINATION OF STRESSES DUE TO BENDING MOMENTS ON TWO PLANES OF SYMMETRY OF A CROSS SECTION

The principle of superposition of the effects is applicable in most cases of structural design pertaining to architectural buildings. The bending stresses

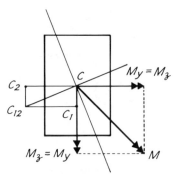

FIGURE 1.13.

$$\sigma_{by} = \frac{M_y}{I_y} z \quad \text{and} \quad \sigma_{bz} = \frac{M_z}{I_z} y$$

independently produced by the simultaneously applied moments M_y and M_z on a cross-section can thus be combined by straightforward superposition. One can assume, for example, that the cross section of a timber spandrel beam (Fig. 1.14) would be subjected to a bending moment M_y due to gravity loads and to a bending moment M_z due to wind loads, for which the extreme values of the bending stresses would be

$$\sigma_b^B = \sigma_b^T = 1.2 \ \text{k/in.}^2,$$

$$\sigma_b^L = \sigma_b^R = 0.3 \ \text{k/in.}^2,$$

where the symbols L and R indicate far left and far right fibers.

According to the principle of superposition of the effects, the stress in the bottom left fiber, which is the extreme compression fiber, has the value

$$\sigma_b^{BL} = \sigma_b^B + \sigma_b^L = -1.2 - 0.3 = -1.5 \ \text{k/in.}^2$$

Similarly, the stress in the top right fiber, which is the extreme tension fiber, has the value

$$\sigma_b^{TR} = \sigma_b^T + \sigma_b^R = +1.2 + 0.3 = 1.5 \ \text{k/in.}^2$$

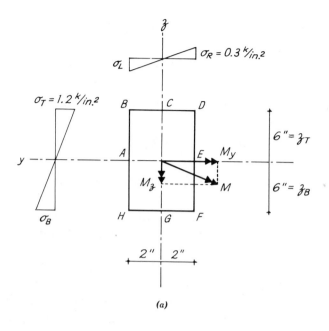

(a)

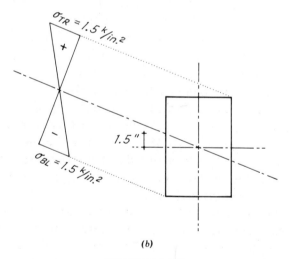

(b)

FIGURE 1.14.

The stress in the upper left corner of the section has the value

$$\sigma_b^{TL} = \sigma_b^T + \sigma_b^L = +1.2 - 0.3 = +0.9 \text{ k/in.}^2$$

The stress in the bottom right corner of the section has the value

$$\sigma_b^{BR} = \sigma_b^B + \sigma_b^R = -1.2 + 0.3 = -0.9 \text{ k/in.}^2$$

It is convenient to consolidate the two separate stress diagrams into one compact diagram. For this purpose the neutral axis of the combined stress distribution must first be traced since the baseline of the total stress diagram must be drawn at right angle to the neutral axis.

In the case of bending on a single plane, the neutral axis (the axis around which the section rotates) coincides with the line of action of the moment vector. For example, the neutral axis of the bending stresses produced by M_y is the y axis, and the neutral axis of the stresses produced by M_z is the z axis (Fig. 1.11). However, when both bending moments M_y and M_z are applied to the cross section, the neutral axis does not coincide with the line of action of the resultant moment vector M. This is demonstrated by applying equal moments M_y and M_z to a cross section (Fig. 1.13).

The moment M_y, by bending the beam, displaces the center C of the cross section to a new position C_1, and the equal moment M_z displaces the center C to C_2. The displacement CC_2 is greater than CC_1 because the moments M_y and M_z are equal while the beam is more rigid vertically than it is horizontally. Thus the resultant displacement CC_{1-2} and the neutral axis which is at right angle to it are not inclined $45°$ on the coordinate axes.

Then the neutral axis and the moment vector M which bisects the fourth yz quadrant are not colinear. Further, to draw the neutral axis, one must reason as follows. The center of the cross section is on the neutral axis since both bending stress diagrams change sign there. If another point of the cross section is found where the total stress vanishes, the neutral axis is identified by the line containing both the centroid and the latter point. Working with the cross section and the stress diagrams of Fig. 1.14a, one recognizes that the fibers along the *GHA* portion of the section's outline are all in compression since from *H* to *A* the compressive stress σ_b^L is compounded with the compressive stresses produced by M_y, and from *G* to *H* the compressive stress σ_b^B is compounded with the compressive stresses produced by M_z. Similarly, one realizes that the fibers along the *CDE* portion of the outline are all in tension. The neutral axis will therefore be in the second and last quadrant of the cross section since the total stress can only vanish on a fiber of the *ABC* or *EFG* part of the cross-sectional outline.

Indeed, the total bending stress vanishes on the fiber of the *AB* part of the outline where the tensile bending stress produced by M_y equals the 0.3 k/in.^{2} compressive stress σ_b^L produced by M_z. Thus the z coordinate of the point on *AB* where the total stress vanishes is given by

$$\sigma_b^L = \frac{\sigma_b^T}{z_T} z,$$

from which

$$z = \frac{\sigma_b^L}{\sigma_b^T} z_T = \frac{0.3}{1.2} (6) = 1.5 \text{ in.}$$

Two points of the neutral axis are now recognizable: one is the center of the section; the other has the coordinates

$$y = -2 \text{ in.} \quad \text{and} \quad z = 1.5 \text{ in.}$$

The neutral axis is thus defined (Fig. 1.14b). The combined stress diagram has its baseline at right angle to the neutral axis and the previously calculated extreme fiber stresses.

The problems with solutions at the end of this chapter further clarify the procedure for the combination of bending stresses due to moments M_y and M_z. The reader is encouraged to practice with the problems without solutions.

1.4. COMBINATIONS OF AXIAL AND BENDING STRESSES

Most columns of building frames receive the reactions of floor beams eccentrically with respect to their geometric axis. Thus the typical cross section of a column is in general subject to an axial force and to two bending moments M_y and M_z (Fig. 1.15). Beams as well are often subject to axial forces in addition to bending moments, as they transfer horizontal forces of wind or earthquake loads from column to column.

The bars of a truss never have pin connections, and the loads of a truss are never concentrated exclusively at the joints, for the self-weight of the bars alone is certainly distributed along the bars. Thus axial forces are always accompanied by bending moments in the bars of a truss.

Arches of course are other examples of structures simultaneously subject to bending moments and axial forces, for a bending-free arch should have the reversed shape of a cable carrying the same loads.

It becomes therefore evident that the combination of axial and bending stresses is the most frequent case to be encountered in structural design. Two different investigative approaches to this case must be used, depending on whether or not the principle of superposition of the effects can be applied.

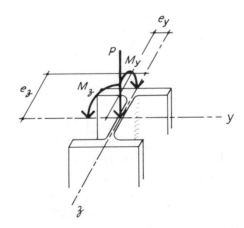

FIGURE 1.15.

1.4.1. Combination of Axial and Bending Stresses by Superposition

When the principle of superposition is applicable, the evaluation of the combined stresses is a straightforward summation of the fiber stresses individually produced by the axial force P and by the bending moments M_y and M_z, regardless of the value of the eccentricities of the axial force P given by

$$e_y = \frac{M_z}{P}, \quad e_z = \frac{M_y}{P},$$

and shown on Fig. 1.15.

Considering, for example, the cross section of the column shown in Fig. 1.16 with the properties

$$A = 46.5 \text{ in.}^2,$$

$$I_y = 1900 \text{ in.}^4,$$

$$I_z = 745 \text{ in.}^4,$$

one obtains the extreme fiber stresses individually produced by the axial force P and by the bending moment M_y:

$$\frac{P}{A} = \frac{300}{46.5} = 6.5 \text{ k/in.}^2;$$

$$\frac{M_y}{I_y} z_{max} = \frac{250(12)7.5}{1900} = 11.8 \text{ k/in.}^2$$

The combined stress diagram is shown in Fig. 1.16, with the extreme values in the far and near fibers

$$\sigma_f = -11.8 - 6.5 = -18.3 \text{ k/in.}^2;$$

$$\sigma_n = 11.8 - 6.5 = 5.3 \text{ k/in.}^2$$

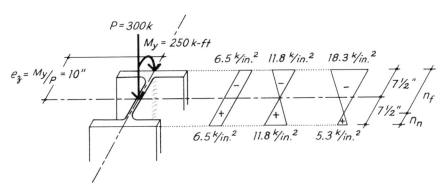

FIGURE 1.16.

The position of the neutral axis is obtained by drawing in scale the combined stress diagram, or numerically with the similar triangles formula

$$\frac{n_f}{d} = \frac{\sigma_f}{\sigma_f + \sigma_n},$$

from which

$$n_f = \frac{\sigma_f}{\sigma_f + \sigma_n} \, d = \frac{18.3}{23.6} \, (15) = 11.63 \text{ in.}$$

If a moment $M_z = 60$ k-ft is also acting on the cross section, it produces the bending stress distribution shown in Fig. 1.17a with its extreme values

$$\frac{M_z}{I_z} \, y_{\max} = 7.5 \text{ k/in.}^2$$

The combination of the individual stress diagrams due to P, M_y and M_z produces the extreme fiber stresses (Fig. 1.17b):

$$\sigma_{lf} = -18.3 - 7.5 = -25.8 \text{ k/in.}^2,$$

$$\sigma_{rn} = 5.3 + 7.5 = 12.8 \text{ k/in.}^2$$

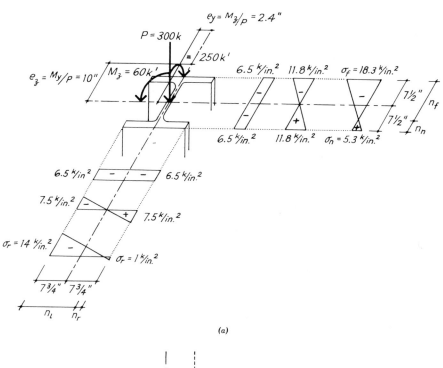

(a)

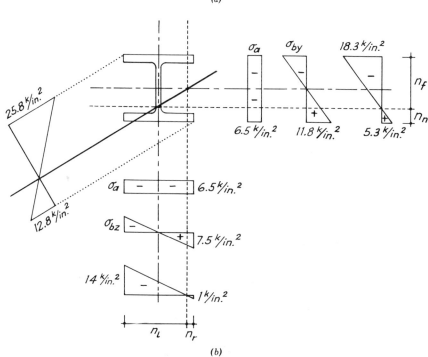

(b)

FIGURE 1.17.

23

It is convenient to consolidate the three stress distributions in one compact diagram. For this purpose the neutral axis must first be traced since the baseline of the combined stress diagram is at right angle to the neutral axis.

If the bending moment M_z temporarily vanished, the neutral axis would be parallel to y at a distance n_f from the far side of the cross section (Fig. 1.17b). This axis would cross z at a point that belongs to the true neutral axis of the stress distribution due to P, M_y, and M_z. Indeed, the bending stress due to M_z also vanishes at this point, which is therefore stress free.

If the moment M_y temporarily vanished, the neutral axis would be parallel to z at a distance n_l from the leftmost fibers of the section (Fig. 1.17b). This axis would cross y at a point which belongs to the true neutral axis. In fact the bending moment M_y does not produce additional stress on this point. With two of its points identified, the neutral axis can now be traced, and the combined stress diagram is drawn on a baseline at right angle to the neutral axis, with extreme fiber stresses

$$\sigma_{lf} = -25.8 \text{ k/in.}^2, \quad \sigma_{rn} = +12.8 \text{ k/in.}^2$$

It should be noted that in Fig. 1.17b the diagram of axial stresses σ_a is shown for convenience next to the diagram of bending stresses σ_{by}, while M_z is being temporarily disregarded, and next to the diagram of bending stresses σ_{bz}, while M_y is being disregarded. Of course the stresses σ_a are only included once in the total stress combination. At the end of this chapter, problems with and without solutions are provided for additional practice with the superposition of axial and bending stresses.

1.4.2. Combination of Axial and Bending Stresses on Cross Sections without Tensile Strength

Structural materials such as unreinforced masonry, unreinforced concrete, and foundation ground have negligible tensile strength. For this reason the principle of superposition cannot always be applied to combine axial and bending stresses on cross sections of structural elements made of these materials. Considering, for example, the contact area between the concrete footing of a column and the foundation ground, one realizes that if the combination of axial and bending stresses produces compression everywhere on the contact area (Fig. 1.18), both the axial force P and the bending moment M act on the entire base of the footing. On this base, with an area A and a section modulus S, P produces the uniform stress P/A and M produces the extreme stresses M/S. The combined extreme stresses, both compressive, are obtained by superposition as

$$\sigma_{\max} = \frac{P}{A} + \frac{M}{S}, \quad \sigma_{\min} = \frac{P}{A} - \frac{M}{S}.$$

If, however, the relative magnitude of the moment M and the axial force P is such that traction should develop between the concrete footing and the foundation ground, an air gap (Fig. 1.19) materializes instead over part of the base area since the ground does not resist tensile stresses, and separation occurs. In this case the stress that P would individually produce on the entire base area and the stress actually produced by P on the partialized area, where P acts simultaneously with M, have different values. It is therefore impossible to obtain the total stresses by simply superposing those individually produced by P and M: the principle of superposition is no longer applicable.

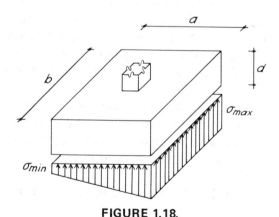

FIGURE 1.18.

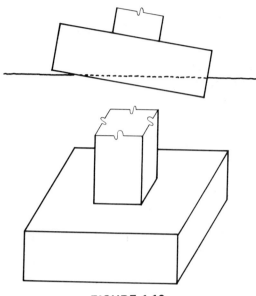

FIGURE 1.19.

Before we can discuss the correct approach for this case, we must present a testing method that is used to determine whether the cross section is entirely or just partially in compression.

1.4.2.1. The Kern Region. The combined stresses due to P and M fall in two ranges: one in which P prevails and all the stresses have the same sign (e.g., negative compression), and one in which M prevails and stresses of both signs are produced on the cross section (Fig. 1.20). In between these two ranges we have the case where one of the extreme fiber stresses is neither positive nor negative. At the two outer ends we find the cases of pure axial stress ($M = 0$) and pure bending stress ($P = 0$).

Using the position of the neutral axis as a feature of the ranges, one could identify the range of stresses without sign change as that in which the neutral axis is out of the cross section at the point of concurrence of the stress diagram with its baseline.

The stress range with sign change is the one with the neutral axis on the cross section.

At the borderline between the two ranges the neutral axis is on the edge of the section.

At the outer end of one of the ranges the neutral axis is infinitely far from the cross section.

Opposite it, at the end of the other range the neutral axis is on the center of the section.

The most appropriate range finder, however, is the eccentricity $e = M/P$.

When $P = 0$, $e = \infty$. This is the case of pure bending.

When P is small with respect to M, the eccentricity is large. Thus large eccentricity identifies the range of stresses with sign change.

When P is large with respect to M, the eccentricity is small, and the combined stresses fall in the range without sign change.

When $M = 0$, $e = 0$. This is a case of pure axial stress.

Intermediate eccentricity is that which makes the combined stress vanish on the outline of the cross section.

The intermediate eccentricities radiating in all directions from the center of the section cover an area called the *kern region* or *inertia kernel*, which is another geometrical property of the cross section, independent of the internal forces or moments actually applied to the cross section.

Once the kern region of a section has been identified, it is possible to foretell whether the combined stress distribution due to P and M falls in the range of stresses with or without sign change.

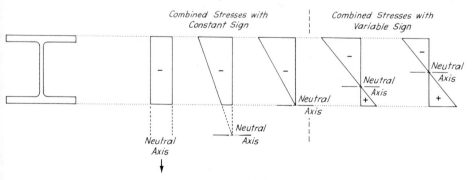

FIGURE 1.20.

If indeed the eccentricity e of the axial force P exceeds, on a given axis, the colinear radius k of the kern region, then the stress distribution changes sign on the cross section.

If e is less than k, the combined stresses all have the same sign.

If $e = k$, the combined stress vanishes on the outline of the cross section.

The intermediate eccentricity k on a given centroidal axis of the cross section (e.g., z) is found graphically or numerically with the following procedure (Fig. 1.21), which is later justified in a note:

The neutral axis of the combined stress distribution is assumed to coincide with a tangent to the cross section's outline, for example, the lower edge of the cross section in Fig. 1.21a.

The radius of gyration ρ_z on the centroidal axis at right angle to the neutral axis is rotated $90°$ to a position CA parallel to the neutral axis.

Next one draws the third side AB of a triangle ABC, of which $CB = z_B$ and the rotated gyrator $AC = \rho_z$ are the first and second sides.

Finally, a segment AD at right angle to AB is drawn from the point A on the y axis to the point D on the z axis.

The segment $CD = k_z$ is the intermediate eccentricity of P on the z axis which produces a combined stress distribution with neutral axis on the edge of the cross section. The intermediate eccentricity k_z is obtained numerically with the aid of the Euclidean theorem applied to the right angle triangle ABD in which the altitude AC divides the base BD in the two segments CB and CD. According to the Euclidean theorem

$$(CD)(CB) = (CA)^2,$$

otherwise stated as

$$k_z z_B = \rho_z^2$$

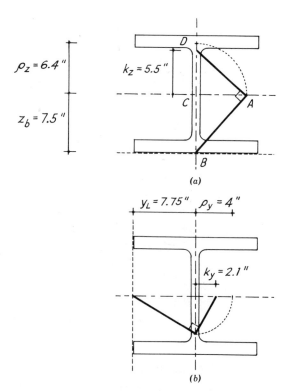

FIGURE 1.21.

from which

$$k_z = \frac{\rho_z^2}{z_B}.$$

For the cross section of Fig. 1.21a which has the properties

$$A = 46.5 \text{ in.}^2,$$

$$I_y = 1900 \text{ in.}^4,$$

$$I_z = 745 \text{ in.}^4,$$

$$z_B = 7.5 \text{ in.},$$

$$y_L = 7.75 \text{ in.},$$

one finds

$$\rho_z^2 = \frac{I_y}{A} = \frac{1900}{46.5} = 40.86 \text{ in.}^2,$$

$$k_z = \frac{40.86}{7.5} = 5.45 \text{ in.}$$

Figure 1.21b shows the analogous graphical procedure to find k_y. Note that, in order to justify this method, one needs to recognize that the elemental force dF, produced on an area dA of the cross section by the local combined stress, is linked to the static moment dQ of dA about the neutral axis by the following linear relation (Fig. 1.22):

$$dF = \sigma \, dA = \sigma_1 n \, dA = \sigma_1 \, dQ$$

where

σ = combined stress on dA due to P and M,

σ_1 = combined stress on fibers at unit distance from neutral axis,

n = distance from dA to neutral axis.

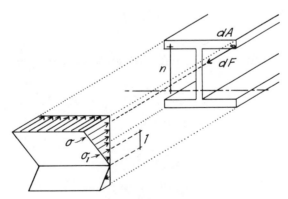

FIGURE 1.22.

The center of the forces dF (the point of application of their resultant R) coincides therefore with the center of the moments dQ. Since R is, for reasons of equilibrium, equal, opposite, and colinear with P, its point of application has the known eccentricity $e = M/P$, which is also the eccentricity of the sum Q of the moments dQ. One can therefore find the neutral axis of the combined stress distribution with the procedure that links the center of the area moments dQ about a given reference axis with the reference axis itself.* This is the procedure applied in reverse in Fig. 1.21 for the determination of the intermediate eccentricity k.

In summary, with the knowledge of the eccentricity $e = M/P$ of the axial force P, one can apply the foregoing procedure in graphical or numerical form for the determination of the neutral axis. By assuming the neutral axis is positioned on the outline of the cross section, one can use the reverse procedure to determine a point on the outline of the kern region. The next two examples provide further practice in both procedures.

Example:　Kern Region of an Annular Cross Section with Outer Radius R and Inner Radius r (Fig. 1.23)

The diametral moment of inertia of the section is

$$I = \frac{\pi}{4} (R^4 - r^4) = \frac{\pi}{4} (R^2 + r^2)(R^2 - r^2).$$

The cross-sectional area is

$$A = \pi(R^2 - r^2).$$

The radius of gyration is

$$\rho = \sqrt{\frac{I}{A}} = \sqrt{\frac{(\pi/4)(R^2 + r^2)(R^2 - r^2)}{\pi(R^2 - r^2)}} = \frac{1}{2} \sqrt{R^2 + r^2}.$$

*See G. de Campoli, *Statics of Structural Components* (New York: Wiley, 1983), Chapter 9.

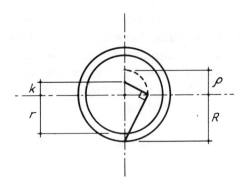

FIGURE 1.23.

The distance from the center to the outline of the section is R. Then the radius of the kern region is

$$k = \frac{\rho^2}{R} = \frac{R^2 + r^2}{4R}.$$

If the inner radius is $r = 0$ (full section),

$$\rho = \frac{R}{2},$$

$$k = \frac{R}{4}.$$

Example: Neutral Axis of the Combined Stress Distribution due to an Axial Force P and to Bending Moments M_y, M_z

This case has already been explored with a different approach (Fig. 1.17b). Here the neutral axis is traced again with the aid of the new procedure as shown by Fig. 1.24. Numerically one obtains

$$\rho_z^2 = \frac{I_y}{A} = \frac{1900}{46.5} = 40.86 \text{ in.}^2,$$

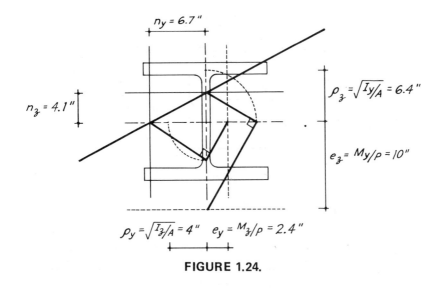

FIGURE 1.24.

$$n_z = \frac{\rho_z^2}{e_z} = \frac{40.86}{10} = 4.09 \text{ in.,}$$

$$\rho_y^2 = \frac{I_z}{A} = \frac{745}{46.5} = 16 \text{ in.}^2,$$

$$n_y = \frac{\rho_y^2}{e_y} = \frac{16}{2.4} = 6.68 \text{ in.}$$

1.4.2.2. Combined Stresses on Partialized Sections. When the eccentricity of the axial force P on the cross section of a pier of unreinforced masonry, or on the contact area of a spread footing on ground, exceeds the intermediate eccentricity k, partialization of the cross section results from the lack of tensile strength in the structural material. The combined stresses due to P and M must be evaluated with an approach other than straightforward superposition.

For the equilibrium in translation and rotation of the partialized section, the resultant R of the combined stress distribution must be equal, opposite, and colinear with the axial force P eccentrically applied. Because of the triangular shape of the stress diagram (Fig.

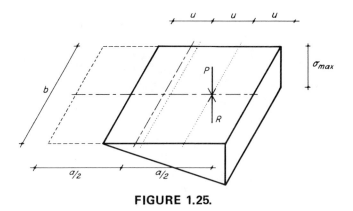

FIGURE 1.25.

1.25), the resultant R has a distance u from the extreme stress σ_{max} which equals one-third of the depth $3u$ of the contact area. The axial force P, which has the eccentricity $e = M/P$, is also at a distance u from the extreme stress σ_{max} since P is colinear with R. The distance u is thus given by

$$u = \frac{a}{2} - e = \frac{a}{2} - \frac{M}{P},$$

and the contact area has the dimensions

$$3ub = 3\left(\frac{a}{2} - \frac{M}{P}\right)b.$$

The average stress on the contact area is

$$\sigma_{av} = \frac{P}{3ub},$$

and the largest stress is

$$\sigma_{max} = 2\sigma_{av} = \frac{2P}{3ub} = \frac{2P}{3[(a/2) - (M/P)]b}$$

Example

The spread footing of a column has a 4 ft × 6 ft base area, and it delivers to the ground a vertical force $P_x = 50$ k and a moment $M_y = 75$ k-ft. The foundation ground can safely carry a stress not exceeding 6 k/ft^2. Investigation of the adequacy of the footing proceeds as follows:

$a = 6$ ft (depth of base area),

$b = 4$ ft (width of base area),

$z_B = z_T = 3$ ft (coordinate of the edge of the area),

$A = ab = 4 \times 6 = 24$ ft^2 (area of base),

$$I_y = \frac{b}{12}(a)^3 = \frac{4}{12}(6)^3 = 72 \text{ ft}^4 \text{ (moment of inertia of base area)}$$

$$\rho_z = \frac{I_y}{A} = \frac{a}{\sqrt{12}} = \frac{6}{\sqrt{12}} = 1.73 \text{ ft (radius of gyration of base area)},$$

$$k_z = \frac{\rho_z^2}{z_B} = \frac{a^2}{12}\left(\frac{2}{a}\right) = \frac{a}{6}$$

$\qquad = 1$ ft (intermediate eccentricity of base area),

$$e_z = \frac{M_y}{P} = \frac{75}{50} = 1.5 \text{ ft} > 1 \text{ ft (contact area is partialized)},$$

$$u = \frac{a}{2} - e_z = 3 - 1.5 = 1.5 \text{ ft (distance from } P \text{ to edge of base)},$$

$$\sigma_{max} = \frac{2P}{3bu} = \frac{100}{3(4)1.5} = 5.6 \text{ k/ft}^2 < 6 \text{ k/ft}^2 \text{ (footing is adequate).}$$

1.5. SHEAR STRESSES

The shear force V and the bending moment M coexist with few exceptions on the typical cross section of a flexural member. The shear force V is indeed the rate of change dM/dx of the bending moment M along the geometric axis x of a flexural member. Shear stresses therefore always accompany bending stresses unless the bending moment is constant. This case occurs, for instance, in the structure in Fig. 1.26, where the load P has a constant distance l from every section of the column.

The shear stresses of short flexural members (e.g., brackets, footings) are often greater than the bending stresses, whereas in long flexural members the necessary limitation of the loads, and their extended arms, produce smaller shear forces V (and shear stresses τ_s) than bending moments M (and stresses σ_b). Thus shear stresses often govern the design of short flexural members, and bending stresses govern the design of long flexural members.

The distribution of frictional stresses τ_s, in the absence of an applied or induced twisting moment, must produce on the plane of the cross section a resultant S equal, opposite, and colinear with the applied shear force V, or the cross section will not be in equilibrium. If indeed S were greater or lesser than V, the section would translate. If S and V were equal and opposite but not colinear, then they would form a couple, and the couple's moment would make the section twist. It is easy to visualize that shear stresses on the planes of the cross sections (which henceforth will be called vertical shear stresses) develop simultaneously with shear stresses between hori-

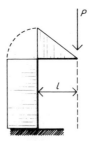

FIGURE 1.26.

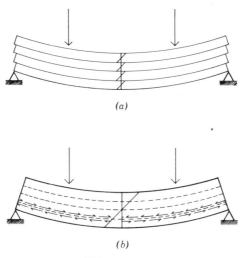

(a)

(b)

FIGURE 1.27.

zontal layers of the structural material. If indeed one observes two flexural members with identical loads, constraints, and geometries but made differently, one by a package of separate planks and one solid, the bending stress distributions over the typical sections of the two members look different, as shown in Figs. 1.27a and b. In the flexural member made of separate planks, the top fibers of the lowest plank shrink, and the bottom fibers of the next lowest plank extend. There is, at the interface between the two planks, a discontinuity of strains and stresses. This discontinuity does not occur in the solid beam, where the planks, so to speak, are glued together. The reason for the different behavior of the two beams is the ability of the glue to carry and therefore permit the development of horizontal shear stresses between the planks, as shown in Fig. 1.27b. These horizontal shear stresses extend to some degree the top fibers of the lowest plank, and they shrink the bottom fibers of the next to lowest plank, thus eliminating the discontinuity.

It can also be shown that at any one point in the structural material, the vertical and horizontal shear stresses have the same magnitude. Indeed, the equilibrium of an infinitesimal cube of structural material (Fig. 1.28) requires that the vertical shear stress on the left face of the cube develop with an equal but opposite stress on the

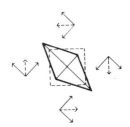

FIGURE 1.28.   **FIGURE 1.29.**

right face (for vertical equilibrium) and that shear stresses, with the
same magnitude of the vertical shear stresses, also develop on the
cube's horizontal faces, with the signs shown in Fig. 1.28 for horizontal and rotational equilibrium. Incidentally, a replacement with
diagonal components of the forces produced on the four faces of the
cube by the shear stresses, shows the reason for the deformation of
the square section of the cube into a rhombus (Fig. 1.29).

If a suitable formula is derived for the evaluation of the shear
stresses between horizontal layers of structural materials, this formula will also give the magnitude of the shear stresses on vertical
cross sections of flexural members. With this objective in mind, we
cut out of a flexural member the infinitesimal parallelepiped shown
in Fig. 1.30.

On the left face of this element the bending moment M produces
bending stresses σ_b. On the right face of the element the different
bending moment $M + dM$ produces the stresses $\sigma_b + d\sigma_b$. Therefore
on an elemental area dA of the parallelepiped's left face and on the
corresponding area dA of the right face, the bending stresses produce
two different elemental forces

$$dF = \sigma_b dA,$$

$$dF' = (\sigma_b + d\sigma_b)\, dA.$$

Assuming M smaller than $M + dM$, the forces dF on the area $\bar{A}$ of the
left face have a lesser resultant L given by

$$L = \int_{\bar{A}} dF = \int_{\bar{A}} \sigma_b \, dA.$$

The forces dF' on the area $\bar{A}$ of the right face have a greater resultant G given by

$$G = \int_{\bar{A}} dF' = \int_{\bar{A}} (\sigma_b + d\sigma_b) \, dA = L + \int_{\bar{A}} d\sigma_b \, dA.$$

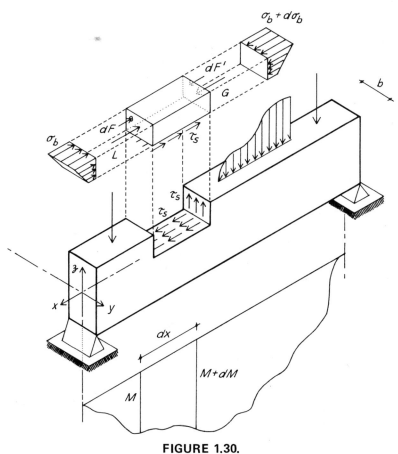

FIGURE 1.30.

For the equilibrium of the parallelepiped in the x direction, the unbalanced force

$$G - L = \int_{\bar{A}} d\sigma_b \, dA$$

must be neutralized by the resultant of the distribution of horizontal shear stresses τ_s on the bottom face of the element. This resultant is the product of the area $b(dx)$ of the bottom face with the stress τ_s.

The equation of equilibrium is then

$$\sum F_x = 0 = G - L - \tau_s b dx,$$

from which

$$\int_{\bar{A}} d\sigma_b \, dA = \tau_s b dx.$$

The infinitesimal increment of the bending stress σ_b in the x direction is

$$d\sigma_b = d\left(\frac{M}{I} z\right) = \frac{d}{dx}\left(\frac{M}{I} z\right) dx = \frac{z}{I} \frac{dM}{dx} dx = \frac{zV}{I} dx.$$

Indeed, z and I are independent on the variable x and treated as constants in the differentiation.

Replacing the foregoing expression of $d\sigma_b$ in the equilibrium equation gives

$$\tau_s b dx = \int_{\bar{A}} z \frac{V}{I} dx dA = \frac{V dx}{I} \int_{\bar{A}} z dA.$$

Indeed, V, I, and dx are independent of the variable of integration z and are treated as constants. Dividing both sides of the equation by $b(dx)$ and using the notation dQ for the moment of the elemental area dA about the neutral axis of pure bending, we obtain the formula for the shear stress τ_s:

$$\tau_s = \frac{V}{bI} \int_{\bar{A}} dQ = \frac{VQ_{\bar{A}}}{bI},$$

where

V = the shear force on the typical cross section of a flexural member,

I = the cross-sectional moment of inertia,

b = the width of the cross section at the level of the bottom face of the parallelepiped,

$Q_{\bar{A}}$ = the moment of the area $\bar{A}$ about the neutral axis of pure bending,

$\bar{A}$ = the area of the terminal section of the parallelepiped.

According to the expression of τ_s obtained here, the shear stress vanishes at the top and bottom of the cross section. If indeed the parallepiped of Fig. 1.30 is as deep as the beam itself, the area $\bar{A}$ of its left or right face coincides with the full cross-sectional area, which lacks moment Q_A about its own centroid.

If the depth of the parallelepiped vanishes, $\bar{A}$, $Q_{\bar{A}}$, and τ_s vanish as well. Thus the formula for τ_s satisfies the physical requirement that the frictional stresses vanish near the top and bottom of the cross section where they would "peel off" the extreme fibers of structural material, a fact denied by experimental evidence.

As the notch of Fig. 1.30 is cut deeper and deeper into the beam, the area $\bar{A}$ of the terminal section of the parallelepiped, its moment $Q_{\bar{A}}$, and the value of τ_s increase. If, however, the depth of the notch exceeds the depth of the centroid, the elemental areas $d\bar{A}$ below the centroid have negative moments $dQ_{\bar{A}}$ because their distance to the centroidal axis is negative. As a result $Q_{\bar{A}}$ decreases and vanishes altogether when the depth of the notch equals the depth of the section. The shear stress τ_s thus has its greatest value on the centroidal axis of a cross section. This value can be calculated with a simplified expression which is

$$\tau_s^{\max} = \frac{VQ_{\max}}{bI} = \frac{V}{b(I/Q_{\max})} = \frac{V}{bZ},$$

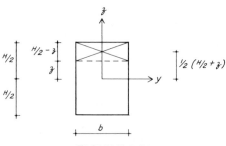

FIGURE 1.31.

where Z is the arm of the resisting moment of a cross section. The product bZ of Z with the width of the section b, measured on the centroidal axis, is called the shear area of a section, and it defines a section's shear strength.

When the shape of a cross section is rectangular, the area $\bar{A}$ of the ends of the notch has the expression (Fig. 1.31)

$$\bar{A} = b \left(\frac{H}{2} - z \right),$$

and it increases linearly with the depth of the notch as the distance z from its base to the centroid decreases. The area moment $Q_{\bar{A}}$ has the expression (Fig. 1.31)

$$Q_{\bar{A}} = \frac{1}{2} \left(\frac{H}{2} + z \right) \bar{A} = \frac{b}{2} \left(\frac{H^2}{4} - z^2 \right),$$

which increases parabolically with the depth of the notch.

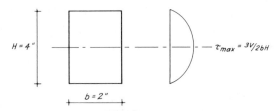

FIGURE 1.32.

The arm Z of the resisting moment is given for the rectangular section by the formula

$$Z = \frac{bH^3/12}{(bH/2)\,(H/4)} = \frac{2H}{3}$$

Thus the vertical shear stress on a rectangular cross section increases parabolically from zero at the extreme fibers to its greatest value

$$\frac{V}{b(2H/3)} = \frac{3V}{2bH}$$

at the centroid (Fig. 1.32).

Example

A shear force $V = 150$ k is applied to the cross section shown in Fig. 1.33.

The calculations of the cross-sectional properties are shown below in tabular form. The symbols used are as follows:

A_i = a partial area of the section (flange or web),

z_{iT} = depth of the centroid of a partial area measured from the section's top fibers,

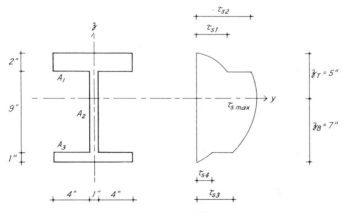

FIGURE 1.33.

I_i = moment of inertia of a partial area about its own centroidal axis,

z_i = z coordinate of the centroid of a partial area,

z_T = z coordinate of the top fibers,

I = moment of inertia of the section,

A_{2U} = area of upper part of web (above the y axis),

z_{2U} = z coordinate of the centroid of A_{2U},

A_{2L} = area of lower part of web

z_{2L} = z coordinate of the centroid of A_{2L}.

i	A_i (in.^{2})	z_{iT} (in.)	$A_i z_{iT}$ (in.^{3})	I_i (in.^{4})	z_i (in.)	$A_i z_i^2$ (in.^{4})	$Q_i = A_i z_i$ (in.^{3})
1	18	1	18	6.00	+4	288.0	72
2	9	6.5	58.5	60.75	-1.5	20.25	
3	9	11.5	103.5	0.75	-6.5	380.25	-58.5
Σ	36		180.0	66.50		688.5	

$$z_T = \frac{\Sigma A_i z_{iT}}{\Sigma A_i} = \frac{180}{36} = 5 \text{ in.}$$

$$I = \Sigma I_i + \Sigma A_i z_i^2 = 66.5 + 688.5 = 755 \text{ in.}^4,$$

$$A_{2U} = 1(3) = 3 \text{ in.}^2,$$

$$A_{2L} = A_2 - A_{2U} = 9 - 3 = 6 \text{ in.}^2,$$

$$Q_{max} = A_{2U} z_{2U} + A_1 z_1 = 3(1.5) + 72 = 76.5 \text{ in.}^3,$$

$$Q_{max} = A_{2L} z_{2L} + A_3 z_3 = 6(-3) - 58.5 = -76.5 \text{ in.}^3,$$

$$Z = \frac{I}{Q_{max}} = \frac{755}{76.5} = 9.87 \text{ in.}$$

The arm of the resisting couple has a value close to the distance between the centers of the flanges (here 10.5 in.). The shear stresses are

$$\tau_{s1} = \frac{V}{I}\frac{Q_1}{b_1} = \frac{150}{755}\left(\frac{72}{9}\right) = 1.6 \text{ k/in.}^2,$$

where

$b_1 = 9$ in. is the width of the top flange,

$$\tau_{s2} = \frac{V}{I}\frac{Q_1}{b_2} = \frac{150}{755}\left(\frac{72}{1}\right) = 14.4 \text{ k/in.}^2,$$

$b_2 = 1$ in. is the width of the web.

In the transition from the top flange to the web, the width b of the cross section is the only parameter that changes. Indeed, moving an infinitesimal distance into the web does not change the value of the area $\bar{A}$ (here the area of the top flange) and that of the area moment $Q_{\bar{A}}$.

$$\tau_s^{\max} = \frac{V}{I}\frac{Q_{\max}}{b_2} = \frac{150}{755}\frac{(76.5)}{1} = 15.2 \text{ k/in.}^2.$$

Repeating the same operations but starting from the bottom flange of the section, one obtains

$$\tau_{s4} = \frac{V}{I}\frac{Q_4}{b_4} = \frac{150}{755}\left(\frac{58.5}{9}\right) = 1.3 \text{ k/in.}^2$$

$$\tau_{s3} = \frac{V}{I}\frac{Q_4}{b_2} = \frac{150}{755}\left(\frac{58.5}{1}\right) = 9\tau_4 = 11.7 \text{ k/in.}^2.$$

The distribution of shear stresses on cross sections of flexural members made of reinforced masonry or reinforced concrete shows constant values of τ_s outside of the compression zone (shaded in Fig. 1.34). These structural materials in fact lack tensile strength, which is provided by reinforced steel rods. Therefore the cross section considered is that made only by the compressive area and the reinforcing steel area. Bending stresses are not transferred through the tension area of concrete or masonry because the flexural member is con-

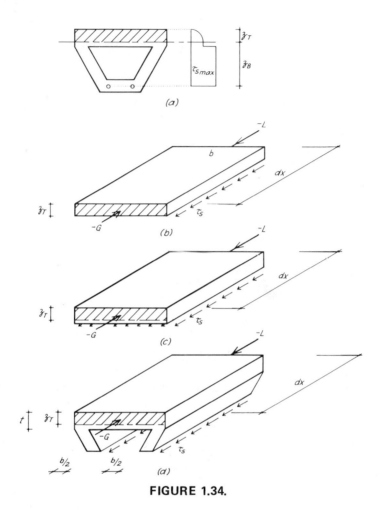

FIGURE 1.34.

siderably split by hairline cracks, and as a result there are air gaps in the tension zones.

Whether the infinitesimal notch used in the derivation of the shear stress formula cuts down to the neutral axis or below the neutral axis, the values of the unbalanced resultants L and G remain the same (Fig. 1.34b and c). In fact the areas below the neutral axis are stress free. Equilibrium is therefore provided by the same shear stress τ_s multiplied with the area $b(dx)$ of the bottom face of the notch. Of course if the area $b(dx)$ is reduced by a diminished value of b

(Fig. 1.34d), then τ_s must increase to neutralize the same imbalance $G - L$ (Fig. 1.34a and d). The diagram of τ_s steps back to its baseline at the level of the reinforcing steel rods, which are considered the bottom fibers of the flexural member.

In the preceding discussion of shear stresses the cross section has been assumed to have constant shape and measurements along the x axis. Flexural members, however, may have variable depth, width, or both, along their geometric axis, in which case I varies with x. The increment $d\sigma_b$ of the bending stress along the x axis no longer has the expression

$$d\sigma_b = z\frac{V}{I}\,dx,$$

and it is obtained rather as

$$d\sigma_b = \frac{d}{dx}\left(\frac{M}{I}\,z\right)dx = \frac{z}{I}\frac{dM}{dx}\,dx + zM\frac{d}{dx}\left(\frac{1}{I}\right)dx.$$

The first term of this new expression replaced in the equation of equilibrium of the notch along x yields the shear stress already discussed. The second term in the new expression of $d\sigma_b$ produces a corrective shear stress.

The derivation of the corrective stress is beyond the scope of this book. It is, however, possible to recognize the existence of the corrective shear stress by observing that the extreme fiber stresses must be colinear with the fibers of structural material (Fig. 1.35). In fact the extreme fibers would be peeled out if a stress component at right angle to the fibers existed.

Thus the extreme fiber stress on a tapered face of a flexural member has a bending stress component at right angle to the cross section

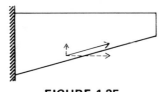

FIGURE 1.35.

and a shear stress component on the plane of the cross section (Fig. 1.35). This shear stress component proves the existence of a corrective term in τ_s, a term that does not vanish at the extreme fibers.

1.6. SHEAR STRESSES IN FLANGES

When the infinitesimal parallepiped used in the derivation of the formula of τ_s (Fig. 1.30) is notched from one of the flanges of a flanged flexural member (Fig. 1.36), one readily sees that its equilibrium in the x direction is maintained by shear stresses τ_f distributed on the area $t\,dx$ of the side of the parallelepiped previously attached to the beam (Fig. 1.36). Again, the resultant of these shear stresses neutralizes the difference $G - L$ between the resultants of the bending stresses on the ends of the element. With the notations of Fig. 1.36, the condition of the equilibrium is stated by

$$\tau_f t\,dx = G - L.$$

The identical algebraic operations performed in the derivation of the formula of the shear stress in the web give in this case

$$\tau_f t\,dx = \frac{V}{I}\,dx\,Q_{\bar{A}},$$

from which

$$\tau_f = \frac{VQ_{\bar{A}}}{It},$$

where t is the thickness of the notched flange and $Q_{\bar{A}}$ is the moment of the area $t\Delta y$ of the end of the notch about the centroidal axis of the section. By increasing the depth Δy of the notch in the flange, the area $\bar{A}$ given by the product $t\Delta y$ increases linearly. The area moment $Q_{\bar{A}}$ also increases linearly since the distance from the centerline of the flange to the centroidal axis of the section is constant. The shear stresses in the flanges have therefore a linear distribution (V, I, and t are constants). Their resultant on an outstanding leg of the top

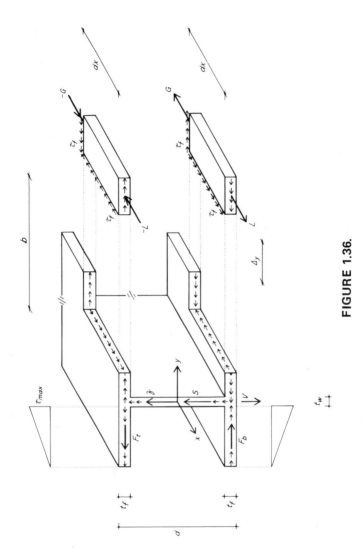

FIGURE 1.36.

or bottom flange is obtained by the product of the average stress with the area of the flange leg.

Figure 1.36 shows the directions and the signs of the shear stresses induced by the shear force V and also those of their resultants. In sum, these are the features of Fig. 1.36:

V is oriented like the negative z semiaxis.

τ_s, the vertical shear stresses in the web, and S, their resultant, are therefore oriented like the positive z semiaxis.

τ_f, the shear stress on the area $t\,dx$ of the infinitesimal parallelepiped, has the sign justified by those of the forces L and G in the tension or compression flange.

τ_f, the shear stress on the matching area $t\,dx$ of the beam, has the sign justified by the principle of action and reaction.

τ_f, the shear stress around the corners of the matching area $t\,dx$ of the beam, concurs or diverges with the stress on the area $t\,dx$.

F_t and F_b, the resultants of the shear stresses τ_f on the left legs of the flanges, have signs opposite to their counterparts on the right legs of the flanges for symmetry.

Example

The shear force V on the cross section in Fig. 1.36 and the geometries of the section have the following values:

$$V = 120 \text{ k,}$$

$$b = 9 \text{ in. (width of the flanges),}$$

$$t_f = 2 \text{ in. (thickness of flanges),}$$

$$t_w = 1 \text{ in. (thickness of web),}$$

$$d = 12 \text{ in. (depth of the section).}$$

Therefore the cross section has these properties:

Moment of inertia about the centroidal axis

$$I = \frac{b}{12} d^3 - \frac{(b - t_w)}{12} (d - 2t_f)^3 = \frac{9}{12} (12)^3 - \frac{8}{12} (8)^3 = 955 \text{ in.}^4$$

Area $\bar{A}$ of the outstanding leg of a flange

$$\bar{A} = t\Delta_y^{\max} = 2(4) = 8 \text{ in.}^2$$

Area moment $Q_{\bar{A}}$ about the centroidal axis

$$Q_{\bar{A}} = \bar{A} \left(\frac{d}{2} - \frac{t}{2} \right) = 8(6 - 1) = 40 \text{ in.}^3$$

Largest shear stress in the flange

$$\tau_f = \frac{VQ_{\bar{A}}}{It} = \frac{120(40)}{955(2)} = 2.5 \text{ k/in.}^2$$

Force resultant of the shear stresses in the outstanding leg of a flange

$$F = \frac{1}{2}\tau_f \bar{A} = 1.25(8) = 10 \text{ k.}$$

1.7.   THE CENTER OF SHEAR

The resultants of the shear stresses on the flanges of a cross section are not mutually in equilibrium if the section lacks symmetry about the centerline of the web. For example, the section of the channel shown in Fig. 1.37 is subject to an induced twisting moment which is the moment of the couple of forces F_t and F_b produced by the shear stresses τ_f in the top and bottom flanges. The cross section therefore tends to twist with a clockwise rotation. The induced torsion stress must be taken into account, along with the shear stresses, in the investigation of the beam. If the applied shear force V is shifted to the left, the counterclockwise moment of the couple of forces V and S reduces the effect of the clockwise moment.

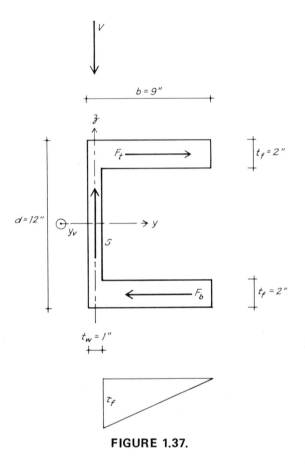

FIGURE 1.37.

The center of shear of the channel is defined as the point where V crosses the y axis under the condition that the moment of the couple V, S neutralizes that of the couple F_t, F_b. Using the notation y_v for the coordinate of the center of shear, the equation of equilibrium of the twisting moments under this condition is

$$\sum M_x = 0 = y_v V - F_t \left(\frac{d}{2} - \frac{t_f}{2} \right) - F_b \left(\frac{d}{2} - \frac{t_f}{2} \right).$$

Using the simpler notation F for the two equal forces F_t and F_b, one obtains

$$y_v = \frac{F}{V}(d - t_f).$$

Example

The shear force on the cross section of Fig. 1.37 and the geometries of the section have the values

$$V = 120 \text{ k},$$

$$b = 9 \text{ in.}$$

$$d = 12 \text{ in.}$$

$$t_f = 2 \text{ in.}$$

$$t_w = 1 \text{ in.}$$

The cross-sectional properties are as follows:

Moment of inertia about the y axis

$$I = \frac{b}{12}(d)^3 - \frac{(b - t_w)}{12}(d - 2t_f)^3 = \frac{9}{12}(12)^3 - \frac{8}{12}(8)^3 = 955 \text{ in.}^4$$

Area of the outstanding leg of the flanges

$$\bar{A} = t_f(b - t_w) = 2(9 - 1) = 16 \text{ in.}^2$$

Moment of $\bar{A}$ about the y axis

$$Q_{\bar{A}} = t_f(b - t_w)(d - t_f)\frac{1}{2} = 16(12 - 2)0.5 = 80 \text{ in.}^3$$

The largest shear stress in the flanges is

$$\tau_f = \frac{VQ_{\bar{A}}}{It_f} = \frac{120(80)}{955(2)} = 5 \text{ k/in.}^2$$

The value of the resultants F_t, F_b is

$$F_t = F_b = \frac{1}{2}\tau_f t_f(b - t_w) = 2.5(2)8 = 40 \text{ k.}$$

The coordinate of the center of shear is

$$y_v = \frac{F}{V}(d - t_f) = \frac{40}{120}(12 - 2) = 3.33 \text{ in.}$$

1.8.   TORSIONAL STRESSES

The stresses induced by a twisting moment on the typical cross section of a structural bar are also frictional stresses. As it is the case for shear stresses, torsional stresses develop simultaneously and with identical magnitude on a cross section and at a right angle to the section along the fibers of structural material. The action of the torsional stresses can be observed in the deformation of an orthogonal grid drawn on the surface of a cylindrical bar (Fig. 1.38). As each section rotates with respect to the next, a straight line on the grid turns into a helix. The diagonals of a cylindrical rectangle on the grid become one longer, one shorter, indicating that the torsional stresses are resolved into tension and compression at 45° to the cross sections. In fact the twisting of a soaked sponge shows the effect of the compression at 45° to the cross-section by the extrusion

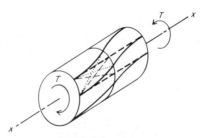

FIGURE 1.38.

of water, the twisting of a bar of chalk (a material weak in tension) shows the effect of the diagonal tension by the splitting of the bar along a corkscrewlike surface.

In the derivation of the formulas of the axial, bending and shear stresses, it is not necessary to specify the shape of the cross section. These formulas are generally valid regardless of the geometries of the cross-sectional outline. Moreover they reflect rather simple stress distributions such as the uniform distribution of the axial stresses and the y-independent distributions of the bending and shear stresses, both of which have constant values on cords parallel to the neutral axis and vary only with the z coordinate.

In the case of torsional stresses the neutral axis of bending loses any relevance with respect to the stress distribution on the cross section. The distribution of torsional stresses depends rather on the form of the outline of the cross section in a way that is best visualized by resorting to the hydrodynamic analogy. This is the analogy that exists between the pattern of torsional stresses on a cross section and that of the flow of liquid particles in a container, with an outline same as that of the section, when it spins with uniform speed around the x axis (the line containing the centroids of all cross sections).

More specifically, the torsional stresses have the same direction and sign as the velocities of the liquid particles. The magnitude of the stresses is proportional to that of the velocity of the particles. The hydrodynamic analogy helps us realize which cross-sectional outlines improve the uniformity of the stress distribution by eliminating zones of idle material and zones of stress concentration. For example, the stress pattern on the cross section of Fig. 1.39a (similar to the liquid flow pattern in an identically shaped container) shows a concentration of stresses near the flange-web connection. As the idle material in the low outer corners of the flange is moved closer to the flange-web connection, as shown in Fig. 1.39b, the distribution of torsional stresses becomes smoother. This is one important reason why flanges appear fluted in the cross sections of I beams, channels, angles, and other structural components produced by the steel industry.

Another useful analogy to be made for the study of the torsional stress pattern on cross sections of various shapes is the "soap bubble"

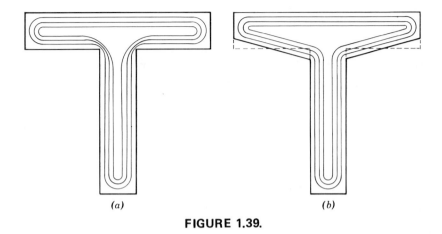

(a)   (b)

FIGURE 1.39.

analogy. A film of soapy water blown by uniform air pressure out of a hole with the same outline as the section under consideration has contour lines that resemble the stress pattern on the section. Moreover the direction sign and magnitude of the stress at a given point of the section is related to the slope of the plane tangent to the soap bubble directly above that point. The steeper the surface of the bubble, the greater the slope of its tangent plane; the denser the contour lines of the surface, the greater the local torsional stress. This analogy, which is not as readily visualized as that of liquid flow, is not going to be used in the specific cases that follow.

1.8.1. Torsional Stresses on Round Sections

Structural bars with round cross sections are ideally suited to carry twisting moments. Indeed, in a cylindrical vase spinning around its axis, the particles of a liquid infill will move with uniform velocity around a given circular orbit. The lack of convex or concave corners eliminates idle zones of structural material as well as zones of stress concentration. If the round section is hollow, as in the case of pipes, the structural material is used even more efficiently by eliminating the zone where the velocity of the liquid particles, and thus the magnitude of the torsional stresses, is negligible.

The derivation of the stress formula proceeds with analoguous reasoning, as in the derivation of bending stresses, and so the formula of τ_t resembles formally that of σ_b. One starts by considering an infinitesimal area dA on a cross section at the typical radial coordinate r from the center (Fig. 1.40). The local stress τ_t produces the elemental force $\tau_t\,dA$. The product of this infinitesimal force with its radial arm r is an infinitesimal twisting moment. The formula of τ_t is obtained from the equilibrium equation of the applied and resisting twisting moments:

$$\Sigma M_x = 0 = T - \int_A r\tau_t\,dA.$$

One realizes by observing the twisted deck of playcards in Fig. 1.2 that the displacements, and therefore the strains at various points along a card's edge, increase linearly with the radial coordinate measured from the centroid of a card, the only point that does not displace. Thus in the stress range defined by proportionality between stresses and strains, the twisting stresses increase linearly from zero at the centroid of the section to a maximum value at the edge (Fig. 1.40). Labeling τ_{t1} the twisting stress at a unit radial coordinate, one obtains the linear relation between τ_t and r from proportionality of the sides of similar triangles (Fig. 1.40):

$$\frac{\tau_t}{\tau_{t1}} = \frac{r}{1},$$

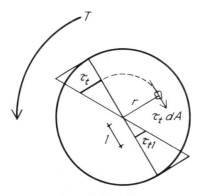

FIGURE 1.40.

from which

$$\tau_t = r\tau_{t1}.$$

Replacing this linear function of r in the equilibrium equation gives

$$T = \int_A r(r\tau_{t1})\, dA = \tau_{t1} \int_A r^2 (dA).$$

τ_{t1}, the constant of proportionality between τ_t and r, is let out of the integral sign. $r^2\, dA$ is the polar moment of inertia dI_p of the elemental area dA.

The equilibrium equation is then written in the form

$$T = \tau_{t1} \int_A dI_p = \tau_{t1}I_p,$$

from which

$$\tau_{t1} = \frac{T}{I_p};$$

thus

$$\tau_t = \frac{T}{I_p}\, r.$$

Example

The cross section of a pipe column carries a twisting moment, as shown by Fig. 1.41. The polar moment of inertia of the section is

$$I_p = \frac{\pi}{2}(R_0^4 - R_i^4) = \frac{\pi}{2}(4^4 - 3^4) = 275 \text{ in.}^4$$

The torsional stress at the outer boundary is

$$\tau_{t0} = \frac{T}{I_p} R_0 = \frac{550}{275}(4) = 8 \text{ k/in.}^2.$$

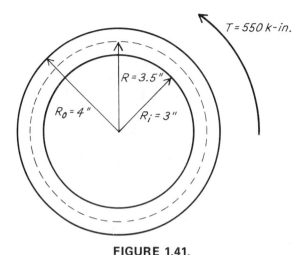

FIGURE 1.41.

The torsional stress at the inner boundary is

$$\tau_{ti} = \frac{T}{I_p} R_i = \frac{550}{275} (3) = 6 \text{ k/in.}^2.$$

1.8.2. Torsional Stresses on the Section of a Thin-Walled Shaft

The structural core of a high-rise building is often made of shear walls of modest thickness with respect to the length of their sides. These walls occasionally form elevator or utility shafts, which means their horizontal cross section is a band closed on itself. When the centers of the building volume and mass are off the center of the core shaft, horizontal loads, such as wind loads with a resultant on the center of volume or earthquake forces with a resultant on the center of mass, produce twisting moments on the core shaft. The frictional stresses induced by the twisting moment must be compounded with those produced by the shear forces in order to ascertain the safety of the structure.

An adequate torsional stress formula for this or any other case of torsion on a thin-walled shaft is derived with the aid of the hydrodynamic analogy (Fig. 1.42). The flow of liquid, which is the volume of liquid passing in a second through any section of the double wall,

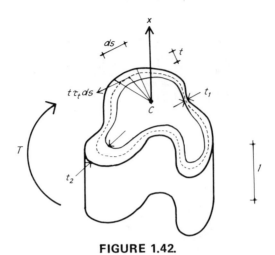

FIGURE 1.42.

must be a constant. If indeed the flow were not constant between any two sections 1 and 2, then the liquid in the container would overflow or diminish in the tract 1–2. This contradicts the experimental observation of the spinning of a filled container with constant speed.

Thus the liquid particles move faster through narrow sections like section 1 and slowly through wider sections like section 2 in order to keep the flow constant. According to the hydrodynamic analogy, the distribution of torsional stresses on the cross section of the thin-walled shaft is similar to that of the liquid particles' velocity in the container. Thus the stresses are greater where the wall is thinner, and vice versa.

The product

$$t(1)\tau_t$$

must be constant just like the flow

$$t(1)v$$

through a section of the walls with thickness t and unit depth along x (v is the velocity of the liquid). Physical intuition confirms that the torsional stress is greater where the structural material is scarce, and vice versa.

The stress τ_t on the elemental area $t\,ds$ of the shaft's cross section (Fig. 1.42) produces the infinitesimal force $\tau_t t\,ds$. The product of this force with its arm r about the centroid C is the elemental twisting moment $r\tau_t t\,ds$. The formula of τ_t is obtained from the equation of equilibrium of the twisting moments around the x axis:

$$\Sigma M_x = 0 = T - \int_A r\tau_t t\,ds.$$

Letting the constant $t\tau_t$ outside of the integral sign, one obtains

$$T = t\tau_t \int_A r\,ds = 2t\tau_t \int_A d\bar{\bar{A}} = 2t\tau_t\bar{\bar{A}}$$

where the notation $d\bar{\bar{A}}$ is used for the area of the infinitesimal triangle with base ds and altitude r.

The product $r\,ds$ equals twice the area $d\bar{\bar{A}}$. The integral $\bar{\bar{A}}$ is the sum of all the infinitesimal triangles $d\bar{\bar{A}}$, and it is thus the area bordered by the dotted centerline of the wall.

Solving the equilibrium equation for τ_t gives its formula

$$\tau_t = \frac{T}{2t\bar{\bar{A}}}.$$

Example

The cross section of a pipe with average radius 3.5 in. and thickness 1 in. carries a twisting moment 550 in.-k (Fig. 1.41).

The area $\bar{\bar{A}}$ encircled by the dotted centerline of the wall is

$$\bar{\bar{A}} = \pi R^2 = \pi(3.5)^2 = 38.5 \text{ in.}^2$$

The torsional stress is constant along the centerline of the wall because the wall thickness is constant. Its value is

$$\tau_t = \frac{T}{2t\bar{\bar{A}}} = \frac{550}{2(1)38.5} = 7.143 \text{ k/in.}^2.$$

The torsional stresses on the outer and inner circles calculated with the formula of round sections are

$$\tau_{t0} = 8 \text{ k/in.}^2; \quad \tau_{ti} = 6 \text{ k/in.}^2.$$

Their average of 7 k/in.^{2} practically coincides with the stress calculated with the formula of thin-walled shafts, despite the considerable thickness of this wall.

1.8.3. Torsional Stresses on Cross Sections Formed by One or Several Rectangles

The flow pattern of the liquid particles in a vase with rectangular section that spins around its vertical axis with uniform speed is shown by Fig. 1.43a. The velocity of the particles must be greater across the smaller median than across the larger median for the flow to be constant. The velocity vanishes in the corners of the rectangular section and on its centroid. According to the hydrodynamic analogy, the stresses produced by a twisting moment on a rectangular cross section vanish in the corners and at the centroid, from where they increase with a growth rate greater on the smaller median. The maximum value of τ_t is attained at the intersection of the smaller median with the section's outline (Fig. 1.43b).

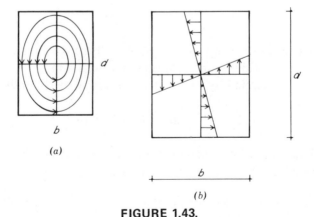

(a)

(b)

FIGURE 1.43.

An approximate expression of this largest stress is

$$\tau_t = \frac{T}{b^2 d^2} (1.8b + 3d),$$

where b and d are the dimensions of the smaller and larger median, respectively.

Example

The twisting moment on the cross section of a square timber column and the size of the section are

$$T = 5 \text{ k-in.}$$

$$b = d = 6 \text{ in.}$$

The largest torsional stress is thus

$$\tau_t = \frac{5}{(6)^4} (1.8 + 3)6 = 0.11 \text{ k/in.}^2$$

In the case of a very elongated rectangular cross section ($d \gg b$), the term $1.8b$ in the formula of τ_t is negligible by comparison with the other term $3d$ in the parenthesis. The torsional stress is then given approximately by the formula

$$\tau_t = \frac{3T}{b^2 d}.$$

The formula remains approximately valid when the long rectangle is folded to form angles, channels, and other shapes (Fig. 1.44), and it even gives a good approximation for sections, such as those of T and I beams.

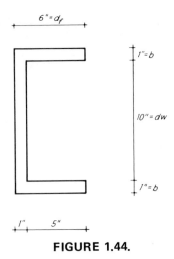

FIGURE 1.44.

Example

The cross section of the channel shown by Fig. 1.44 is subject to a twisting moment $T = 60$ k-in. The total length of the rectangular parts is

$$d = d_w + 2d_f = 10 + 2(6) = 22 \text{ in.}$$

The torsional stress is

$$\tau_t = \frac{3T}{b^2 d} = \frac{3(60)}{22(1)^2} = 8.2 \text{ k/in.}^2$$

When the partial areas of a section have different widths (Fig. 1.45) the largest stress occurs on the outline of the widest rectangle. The latter formula of τ_t is modified as

$$\tau_t = \frac{3T}{\Sigma d_i b_i^3} b_{\max}$$

where b_i and d_i are, respectively, the thickness and length of the ith rectangular partial area.

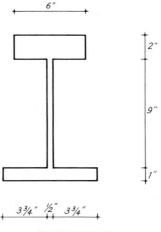

FIGURE 1.45.

Example: The twisting moment on the cross section of Fig. 1.45 and the dimensions of the section are

$$T = 120 \text{ k-in. (twisting moment)},$$

$$b_t = 2 \text{ in. (thickness of top flange)},$$

$$b_w = 0.5 \text{ in. (thickness of web)},$$

$$b_b = 1 \text{ in. (thickness of bottom flange)},$$

$$d_t = 6 \text{ in. (length of top flange)},$$

$$d_w = 9 \text{ in. (length of web)},$$

$$d_b = 8 \text{ in. (length of bottom flange)}.$$

The largest torsional stress is

$$\tau_t = \frac{3Tb_t}{d_t b_t^3 + d_w b_w^3 + d_b b_b^3} = \frac{3(120)2}{6(2)^3 + 9(0.5)^3 + 8(1)^3} = 12.6 \text{ k/in.}^2$$

FIGURE 1.46.   (Courtesy of Portland Cement Association.)

1.9.   DIAGONAL STRESSES

The observation of beams tested to failure reveals that stresses other
than those on the planes of the cross sections or at right angle to the
cross sections are at work in the structural material and are responsi-
ble for its failure. For instance, the side elevation of a collapsed pre-
stressed concrete beam (Fig. 1.46) shows cracks which are produced
by tensile stresses at right angle to the cross section only in the
neighborhood of the shear-free zone (midspan). Away from the middle of the span, the cracks are produced by diagonal stresses that
seemingly prevail on both the frictional and orthogonal stresses.

The same fact is confirmed by the wrinkling pattern of the thin
webs of steel beams when they are tested to failure. In this case

the collapse of the beam web is produced by compressive diagonal stresses, as opposed to the tensile stresses that split the concrete beams. The patterns of failure of the concrete and steel beams show that the diagonal stresses in the two cases are approximately orthogonal to each other.

The importance of diagonal stresses as triggers of the failure of the structural materials makes it necessary to establish with a physical and mathematical analysis their relation to the familiar frictional and orthogonal stresses. Indeed, a thorough procedure of structural design or investigation requires considerably more than a check on the compliance of frictional and orthogonal stresses with specified limitations. One of these further requirements is the evaluation of the diagonal stresses.

An infinitesimal prism of a structural material is shown on Fig. 1.47*a*, with one face on the same plane *yz* as the typical cross section. This face—henceforth called the vertical face—has an infinitesimal side *dz* and a side with unit length. Another face of the prism is at right angle to the typical cross section. This face also has an infinitesimal side *dx* and a side with unit length. The inclined face of the prism forms an unspecified angle θ with the plane *yz* of the cross section.

On the vertical face of the prism, the orthogonal stress σ, and the frictional stress τ produce, respectively, the forces $\sigma(1)\,dy$, $\tau(1)\,dy$. The orthogonal stress σ may be any combination of bending and axial stresses. The orthogonal stress τ may be any combination of shear and torsional stress. On the horizontal face of the prism, the frictional stress τ produces the force $\tau(1)\,dx$.

The equilibrium of the infinitesimal prism requires that orthogonal and frictional stresses should also develop on the inclined face of the prism. The signs of all the forces on the vertical and horizontal faces are indeed shown so that their components at right angle to the inclined face are opposite to a positive (tensile) orthogonal force on that face. Accordingly, the force $\sigma(1)\,dz$ is also a tensile one, and the forces $\tau(1)\,dz$, $\tau(1)\,dx$ concur rather than diverge.

The orthogonal stress on the inclined face of the prism σ_θ is obtained from an equation of equilibrium in the direction orthogonal to the inclined face:

$$\sigma_\theta(1)\ \frac{dz}{\cos\theta} = \sigma(1)\ dz\ \cos\theta + \tau(1)\ dz\ \sin\theta + \tau(1)\ dx\ \cos\theta.$$

Multiplication of both sides of the equation by $\cos\theta/dz$ gives

$$\sigma_\theta = \sigma\ \cos^2\theta + \tau\ \sin\theta\ \cos\theta + \tau\left(\frac{dx}{dz}\right)\cos^2\theta.$$

One realizes from Fig. 1.47 that

$$\frac{dx}{dz} = \tan\theta = \frac{\sin\theta}{\cos\theta}.$$

Substituting in the equilibrium equation yields

$$\sigma_\theta = \sigma\ \cos^2\theta + 2\tau\ \sin\theta\ \cos\theta = \sigma\ \cos^2\theta + \tau\ \sin 2\theta,$$

which shows the relation of σ_θ with the angle θ, the frictional stress τ, and the orthogonal stress σ.

There is a value of the unspecified angle θ corresponding to the largest of all local positive (tensile) values of σ_θ. There is also a value of the unspecified angle θ corresponding to the largest local negative (compressive) value of σ_θ. These two values of the angle θ are found by equating to zero the derivative of σ_θ with respect to θ:

$$\frac{\partial\sigma_\theta}{\partial\theta} = -2\sigma\ \cos\theta\ \sin\theta + 2\tau\ \cos 2\theta = 0.$$

The derivative

$$\frac{\partial\sigma_\theta}{\partial\theta} = \lim_{\Delta\theta\to 0}\frac{\Delta\sigma_\theta}{\Delta\theta}$$

is in fact the limit that the slope of a cord (of the plot of σ_θ versus θ) approaches when the intervals $\Delta\sigma_\theta$ and $\Delta\theta$ are very small (Fig. 1.48). Of course this slope vanishes (horizontal tangent) as σ_θ approaches its maximum and minimum values.

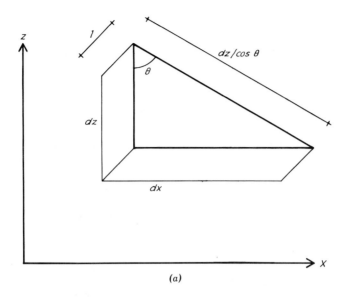

(a)

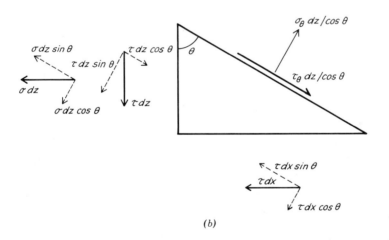

(b)

FIGURE 1.47.

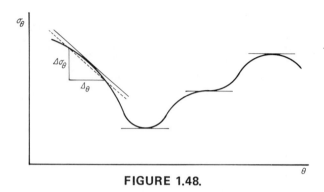

FIGURE 1.48.

Multiplying the equation by −1, and adding to both sides $2\tau \cos 2\theta$, gives

$$2\sigma \cos \theta \sin \theta = 2\tau \cos 2\theta$$

or

$$\sigma \sin 2\theta = 2\tau \cos 2\theta,$$

from which

$$\frac{\sin 2\theta}{\cos 2\theta} = \tan 2\theta = \frac{2\tau}{\sigma}.$$

Thus when the unspecified angle θ takes the value given by this expression, the orthogonal stress σ_θ on the inclined face of the prism

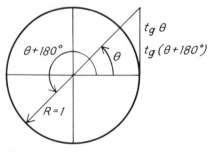

FIGURE 1.49.

is greatest. Two angles $180°$ apart have the same trigonometric tangent (Fig. 1.49). Thus $2\tau/\sigma$ is the trigonometric tangent of the angle 2θ and of the angle $(2\theta + 180°)$ as well. Accordingly, for given values of σ, τ, and $2\tau/\sigma$, σ_θ takes its extremal values on two planes, one inclined on the cross section with the angle

$$\theta = \frac{1}{2} \arctan \frac{2\tau}{\sigma},$$

the other on a plane spaced

$$\frac{2\theta + 180°}{2} = \theta + 90°$$

from the latter. These planes are henceforth called principal planes or diagonal planes.

Example

A bending moment $M = 2460$ in.-k produces on the cross section in Fig. 1.33 bending stresses which at the connection web-top flange have the value

$$\sigma_b = \frac{M}{I} z = \frac{2400}{755} (3) = 9.5 \text{ k/in.}^2$$

At the same z coordinate the shear stress is

$$\tau_{S2} = 14.4 \text{ k/in.}^2$$

If other stresses are lacking, then σ and τ coincide with σ_b and τ_{S2}, respectively. The planes on which the diagonal stress σ_θ attains its greatest positive and negative values are inclined on the cross section, one with the angle (Fig. 1.50)

$$\theta = \frac{1}{2} \arctan \frac{2(14.4)}{9.5} = 35.9°,$$

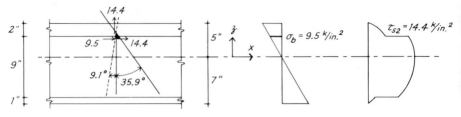

FIGURE 1.50.

the other with the angle

$$\theta + 90° = 125.9°.$$

The evaluation of the greatest positive and negative diagonal stresses requires the substitution of the unspecified angle θ with the angles

$$\frac{1}{2} \arctan \frac{2\tau}{\sigma} \quad \text{and} \quad 90° + \frac{1}{2} \arctan \frac{2\tau}{\sigma}$$

in the general expression of σ_θ.
With the use of the trigonometric formula

$$\cos \theta = \sqrt{\frac{1 + \cos 2\theta}{2}},$$

the expression of σ_θ becomes

$$\sigma_\theta = \frac{\sigma}{2} (1 + \cos 2\theta) + \tau \sin 2\theta.$$

With the use of the trigonometric formulas

$$\cos 2\theta = \pm \frac{1}{\sqrt{1 + \tan^2 2\theta}}; \quad \sin 2\theta = \pm \frac{\tan 2\theta}{\sqrt{1 + \tan^2 2\theta}},$$

the expression of σ_θ takes the form

$$\sigma_\theta = \frac{\sigma}{2} \pm \frac{\sigma}{2} \frac{1}{\sqrt{1 + \tan^2 2\theta}} \pm \tau \frac{\tan 2\theta}{\sqrt{1 + \tan^2 2\theta}}.$$

Replacing $\tan 2\theta$ with $2\tau/\sigma$ gives

$$\sigma_\theta^{\max,\min} = \frac{\sigma}{2} \pm \frac{\sigma}{2} \frac{1}{\sqrt{(\sigma^2/\sigma^2) + (4\tau^2/\sigma^2)}} \pm \tau \frac{2\tau/\sigma}{\sqrt{(\sigma^2/\sigma^2) + (4\tau^2/\sigma^2)}}.$$

Multiplying the second term on the right side of the equation by σ/σ, the third term by $2/2$, and factoring out $\pm 1/2\sqrt{\sigma^2 + 4\tau^2}$, gives

$$\sigma_\theta^{\max,\min} = \frac{\sigma}{2} \pm \frac{1}{2}\sqrt{\sigma^2 + 4\tau^2},$$

which is the expression of the diagonal stresses as functions of the frictional and orthogonal stresses at a given point in the structural material.

Example

The diagonal stresses at the web-top flange connection on the cross section of Figs. 1.33 and 1.50 are

$$\sigma_\theta^{\max,\min} = \frac{-9.5}{2} \pm \frac{1}{2}\sqrt{9.5^2 + 4(14.4)^2} = \frac{-9.5}{2} \pm \frac{30.3}{2},$$

from which

$$\sigma_\theta^{\max} = -19.9 \quad \text{(compression)},$$

$$\sigma_\theta^{\min} = 10.4 \quad \text{(tension)}.$$

The approach followed in the derivation of the formula that links σ_θ with the frictional stress τ, the orthogonal stress σ, and the angle θ is again followed for the derivation of the frictional stress τ_θ on the inclined face of the elemental prism of structural material.

With the notations of Fig. 1.47b, the equation of equilibrium in the direction of τ_θ is

$$\tau_\theta \frac{dz}{\cos \theta} + \tau \, dz \cos \theta = \sigma \, dz \sin \theta + \tau \, dx \sin \theta.$$

Multiplication of the equation by $\cos \theta / dz$ gives

$$\tau_\theta = \sigma \sin \theta \cos \theta + \tau \frac{dx}{dz} \sin \theta \cos \theta - \tau \cos^2 \theta.$$

Substituting dx/dz with $\sin \theta / \cos \theta$ and $\sin \theta \cos \theta$ with $\frac{1}{2} \sin 2\theta$, and factoring out τ, one obtains

$$\tau_\theta = \frac{\sigma}{2} \sin 2\theta - \tau (\cos^2 \theta - \sin^2 \theta).$$

Since $\cos^2 \theta - \sin^2 \theta = \cos 2\theta$, the final formula of τ_θ is

$$\tau_\theta = \frac{\sigma}{2} \sin 2\theta - \tau \cos 2\theta.$$

The expression of τ_θ suggests that the diagonal planes on which σ_θ attains its greatest positive and negative values lack frictional stress. Indeed, equating τ_θ to zero, one obtains

$$\frac{\sin 2\theta}{\cos 2\theta} = \tan 2\theta = \frac{2\tau}{\sigma},$$

which gives the same angles of the principal planes.

τ_θ attains its greatest values on planes at $45°$ to the diagonal planes. To prove it, one needs to equate to zero the derivative of τ_θ with respect to θ and solve for θ. The equation is

$$\frac{\partial \tau_\theta}{\partial \theta} = \sigma \cos 2\theta + 2\tau \sin 2\theta = 0,$$

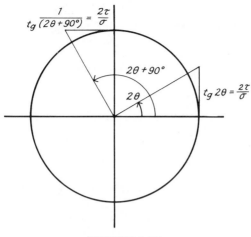

FIGURE 1.51.

from which

$$\frac{\sin 2\theta}{\cos 2\theta} = \tan 2\theta = - \frac{\sigma}{2\tau}$$

Comparing this formula with the one that gives the inclination of the principal planes on the cross section,

$$\tan 2\theta = \frac{2\tau}{\sigma},$$

one sees that the angle 2θ has in the two different cases trigonometric tangents with opposite sign and inverse value. Thus the angles 2θ calculated for $\sigma_\theta^{\max,\min}$ and $\tau_\theta^{\max,\min}$ are 90° apart (Fig. 1.51), and the angles θ are 45° apart.

In the expression of τ_θ, replacing the unspecified angle θ with the values given by

$$\tan 2\theta = \frac{-\sigma}{2\tau},$$

one obtains the values of $\tau_\theta^{max,min}$. The algebraic operations (here omitted) are similar to those performed for $\sigma_\theta^{max,min}$. They yield

$$\tau_\theta^{max,min} = \pm \frac{1}{2} \sqrt{\sigma^2 + 4\tau^2}.$$

These are the second terms in the formula of the diagonal stresses.

Example

The data of the examples for the diagonal planes and stresses,

$$\sigma = -9.5 \text{ k/in.}^2,$$

$$\tau = 14.4 \text{ k/in.}^2,$$

are used again for the greatest frictional stresses at the web-top flange connection of the *I* beam in Figs. 1.33 and 1.50:

$$\tau_\theta^{max,min} = \pm \frac{1}{2} \sqrt{9.5^2 + 4(14.4)^2} = \pm 15.2 \text{ k/in.}^2.$$

These stresses develop on planes which form with the cross section the angles (Fig. 1.50).

$$\frac{1}{2} \arctan \left(\frac{-9.5}{2(4.4)} \right) = 9.1°$$

and

$$90° + 9.1° = 99.1°.$$

1.9.1.   The Circle of Mohr

The diagonal stresses, the inclination of the diagonal planes, and the largest frictional stresses at a given point in the structural material can be obtained by a graphical method using Cartesian coordinates with the horizontal axis labeled σ, and the vertical axis labeled τ (Fig. 1.52). The τ axis also represents the trace of the plane of a typical cross section on the sheet. The orthogonal and frictional stresses (σ, τ) at a point in the structural material are drawn on the horizontal and vertical axes by starting from the origin and using the same scale for both types of stresses (points [σ, 0] and [0, τ]). The frictional stress is also drawn in scale at the horizontal coordinate σ with a sign opposite to that used for τ on the vertical axis (point [σ, -τ]). The coordinate points [0, τ] and [σ, -τ] are joined by a rectilinear segment which is used as the diameter of a circle. The center of the circle called the Mohr circle, is where the diameter crosses with the σ axis (point [$\sigma/2$, 0]).

The Mohr circle can now be drawn. It crosses the positive semiaxis of the orthogonal stresses at a coordinate given by $\sigma/2$ plus the horizontal radius R of the circle. Using the Phythagorean theorem,

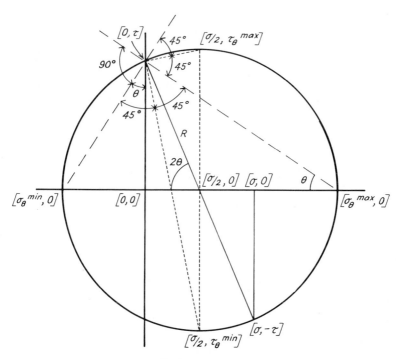

FIGURE 1.52.

$$\frac{\sigma}{2} + R = \frac{\sigma}{2} + \sqrt{\left(\frac{\sigma}{2}\right)^2 + \tau^2} = \frac{\sigma}{2} + \frac{1}{2}\sqrt{\sigma^2 + 4\tau^2}.$$

This coordinate thus measures σ_θ^{max}. The Mohr circle crosses the negative σ semiaxis at a coordinate given by

$$-R + \frac{\sigma}{2} = \frac{\sigma}{2} - \frac{1}{2}\sqrt{\sigma^2 + 4\tau^2}$$

This coordinate thus coincides with σ_θ^{min}.

The radius of the Mohr circle gives in scale the largest frictional stresses $\tau_\theta^{max, min}$. In Fig. 1.52 the slope of the radius R on the σ axis is

$$\frac{\tau}{\sigma/2} = \frac{2\tau}{\sigma} = \tan 2\theta.$$

The angle θ of a diagonal plane with the cross section (Fig. 1.52) is then the same as that between the σ axis and the segment that joins the coordinate points $[0, \tau]$ and $[\sigma_\theta^{max}, 0]$. In fact this angle is one-half of that 2θ limited by the radius R and the σ axis. Note that both angles are defined by the arc $[\sigma_\theta^{min}, 0]$, $[0, \tau]$, but in addition the former is defined by the diameter $[\sigma_\theta^{min}, 0]$, $[\sigma_\theta^{max}, 0]$, and the latter by the radius $[\sigma_\theta^{min}, 0]$, $[\sigma/2, 0]$ of the Mohr circle.

The trace of the other diagonal plane on the drawing is shown in Fig. 1.52 at a right angle to the former. The right angles between the diagonal planes are bisected by dotted lines which are the traces on the sheet of the planes with largest frictional stresses.

Example (Fig. 1.53)

The data of the preceding numerical examples

$$\sigma = -9.5 \text{ k/in.}^2,$$

$$\tau = 14.4 \text{ k/in.}^2,$$

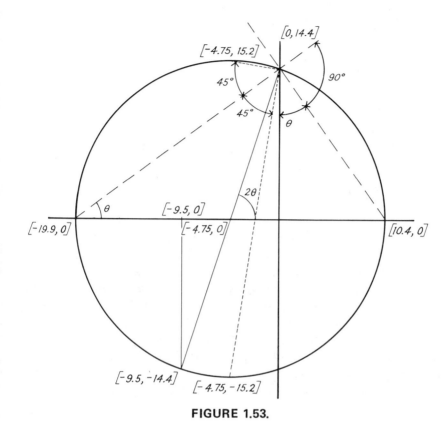

FIGURE 1.53.

are here used to seek graphically the results previously found numerically. The stress scale used is 10 k/in.[2] per in.

1.10.   THE BUCKLING STRESS OF COMPRESSION BARS

A majority of structural failures are caused by a sudden, conspicuous bending of compression elements essential to the stability of the whole structure. It is very important to understand the reasons for this bending of bars that, originally in pure compression, should shorten rather than bend, and hence to derive an expression for the critical axial stress under which this effect occurs.

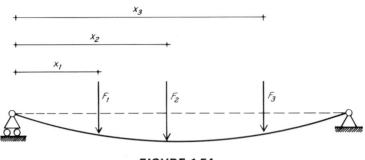

FIGURE 1.54.

The typical deflection of a bar subject to shear forces (and therefore to bending moments) occurs without any bending moment increase due to the deflection itself. Indeed, within the range of moderate deformations the coordinates of the loads and of the constraints, measured on the axis of the bar, remain unchanged during deformation (Fig. 1.54). Thus shear forces and bending moments remain unchanged. As the deformation due to these internal forces materializes, the structural material responds, with internal stresses gradually increasing with the deformation. The internal moment M_i produced on the typical cross section by the internal stresses increases as well, and at the instant it reaches a value equal to the local bending moment M, the deformation stops increasing because equilibrium of the external and internal moments exists ($M_i = M$).

To have a clear understanding of the instability of compression bars, it is essential to recognize the difference between the internal moment M_i and the external moment M. The bending or external moment M on a cross section is calculated with the external forces (loads and reactions) of a structural element, and it has a fixed value if these forces and their distances from the section are not changed.

The internal moment M_i is calculated with the internal forces produced by the internal stresses. M_i is less than M from the beginning of the deformation until its completion. M_i equals M when the deformation is complete. The largest potential value of M_i is called the resisting moment M_R of the cross section and should not be exceeded by the bending moment M.

Say that a bar subject to axial forces deflects. As this occurs, a lever arm materializes between the typical cross section and some of the loads or reactions (Fig. 1.55), and therefore a bending moment (wP in the case of Fig. 1.55) and a moment due to the internal stresses also materialize. These two moments are mutually independent because the internal moment only depends on the value of the potential deflection w which is not dependent on P. The bending moment wP obviously depends on w and P.

Three cases are thus possible:

The bending moment wP is less than the internal moment because P is small.

The bending moment is equal to the internal moment.

The bending moment wP is greater than the internal moment because P is large.

In the first case, since the internal moment is greater than the bending moment, the bar returns to its original geometric shape (the straight line in Fig. 1.55). The axially loaded bar is thus said to be in a state of *stable equilibrium*. In the third case, when the bending moment wP is greater, it increases the value of the deflection w. Thus wP becomes ever greater until the bar collapses. This is the case of *unstable equilibrium*.

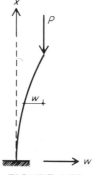

FIGURE 1.55.

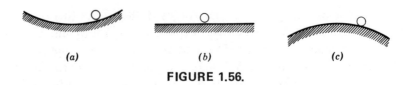

(a)   (b)   (c)

FIGURE 1.56.

In the second case the deflection w produces a bending moment wP and an internal moment M_i equal to each other. A typical cross section is thus in equilibrium, and the deflection w does not increase or decrease. Under the intermediate value of P called *critical load*, for which the notation P_{cr} is often used, the bar becomes as ductile as clay, which means it does not have the ability to return to its original configuration when a deforming action ends nor moves onto a new configuration except if it is displaced by a new external action. This state is one of *indifferent equilibrium.*

These three types of behavior of a structural bar are comparable to that of a marble (Figs. 1.56a, b, c) displaced in a bowl (case 1), on a flat surface (case 2), or on a spherical cap (case 3). In the first case the bar and the marble tend to return to the original position of rest. In the third case the bar and the marble abandon indefinitely their position of rest. In the intermediate case the bar and the marble are at rest in any position.

The meaning of the notation "critical load" given the intermediate value of P ought to be self-evident: the critical load marks the dividing line between a condition of structural safety and one of structural failure. Theoretically, under the critical load a bar does not collapse, but the slightest increase in P will produce instability. Of course, a bar that lacks the ability to keep its original shape, that is, the one with which it has been designed, is unacceptable as a component of a structural frame.

In reality a structural bar is never subject to pure axial forces, for it is impossible to fabricate a perfectly straight bar and to center its loads perfectly on its axis. There will be some deviation of loads from the bar's axis, and thus the accompanying bending moments. In other words a real bar is more prone to bending under axial forces (buckling) than an ideal bar. Even for an axially loaded ideal bar, however, the potential for lateral deformation under the load P_{cr} is as great as the potential for motion of a perfectly smooth marble at rest on a perfectly smooth plane (Fig. 1.56b). The critical load of a compression bar must therefore be carefully evaluated to ascertain that it exceeds a specified number of times the axial load actually placed on the bar.

The formula for the evaluation of the critical load is derived in the appendix to this chapter. It has the form

$$P_{cr} = EI \frac{\pi^2}{(kL)^2},$$

where

E = the stress/strain ratio of the structural material (Young's modulus). It measures the toughness of a structural material.

I = the moment of inertia from the formula of the bending stress σ_b. It measures the bending resistance of a cross section.

L = the length of a compression bar.

k = a coefficient that reflects the influence of the constraints on the rigidity of a compression bar.

π = the constant 3.14.

The buckling load formula verifies the intuitive conclusion that a compression bar made of a stronger material (large stress/strain ratio E) and stronger in bending (large I) will buckle under a greater P_{cr} load, whereas a bar whose length L is greater compared to the size of the cross section will buckle under a small P_{cr} load. However, greater restraints at the bar ends will reduce this buckling liability. Indeed, as the table in the appendix and Fig. 1.57 show, values of the coefficient k are smaller (larger P_{cr}) for bars with greater degree of restraint.

Because a compression bar curves on buckling on the plane where the bar is weakest, the least moment of inertia I_{min} must be used in the formula of P_{cr}. Using the definition of the radius of gyration, the critical load formula is then

$$P_{cr} = EI_{min} \frac{\pi^2}{(kL)^2} = EA\rho_{min}^2 \frac{\pi^2}{(kL)^2}.$$

Dividing the numerator and denominator by ρ_{min}^2 gives

$$P_{cr} = EA \, \frac{\pi^2}{(kL/\rho_{min})^2}.$$

The ratio kL/ρ_{min} is called the slenderness ratio of a bar, and it measures a bar's buckling liability. Indeed, a large slenderness ratio reduces P_{cr} quadratically, and it is produced by a great length, by a modest degree of restraint (large k), or by a small value of ρ_{min} (the property that measures the combined axial and bending resistance of a cross section).

Dividing P_{cr} by the cross-sectional area A gives the critical stress under which a compression bar buckles:

$$\sigma_{cr} = \frac{P_{cr}}{A} = E \, \frac{\pi^2}{(kL/\rho_{min})^2}.$$

For a given structural material, E, this stress only depends on the slenderness ratio. Thus various construction manuals provide tables and charts, where for given values of the slenderness ratio kL/ρ_{min} one finds the value of the safe axial stress which is a specified fraction of the buckling stress. In the case of very short compression bars (small kL/ρ_{min}), σ_{cr} may exceed the crushing stress of a structural material. The compression strength rather than the critical load thus rules the design of the bar.

The constraint conditions of the compression bars of structural frames are never identical to the theoretical conditions shown by Fig. 1.57. It is important that sharp engineering judgment guide architects and engineers in identifying the coefficient k that most closely approximates real conditions. Several sample cases are discussed here to help in the identification task:

The case of Fig. 1.57a applies to the compression bars of trusses for which the bending moments of the terminal sections are negligible. It also applies to timber columns that are not moment connected at their ends.

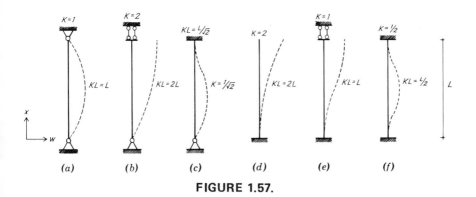

FIGURE 1.57.

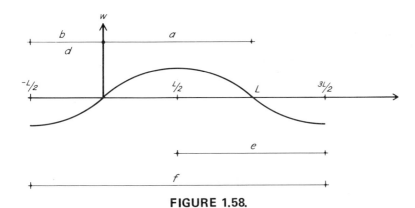

FIGURE 1.58.

The case of Fig. 1.57*d* applies, for example, to the columns of portal frames fixed on their footings, with top sections free to rotate and displace. This occurs when the beams are hinge connected to the columns, and otherwise when the beams are flexible. Figure 1.59 shows the deformation of the portals in these two cases. The case of Fig. 1.57*e* applies when the beam of the portal is very rigid or is replaced by a deep truss. Such framing elements, unlike the beam of Fig. 1.59*b*, keep a rectilinear axis and restrain the rotation of the column top (Fig. 1.60). The case of Fig. 1.57*b* applies if the columns of a rigid beam portal are hinged on their footings (Fig. 1.61).

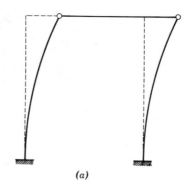

(a)

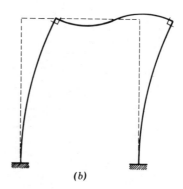

(b)

FIGURE 1.59.

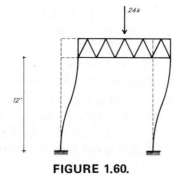

12'

FIGURE 1.60.

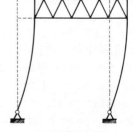

FIGURE 1.61.

The cases of Fig. 1.57c and f apply, for example, to the columns of high-rise buildings whose rigid structural cores minimize lateral displacements. The shear or moment connections of the column ends and the rigidity of the horizontal framing members determine the choice of case c or f for the calculation of the column critical load (Fig. 1.62).

Example

The timber frame of Fig. 1.60 has columns with a 4″ × 6″ cross section. The E modulus of the wood is 1800 k/in.² The critical load is calculated as follows:

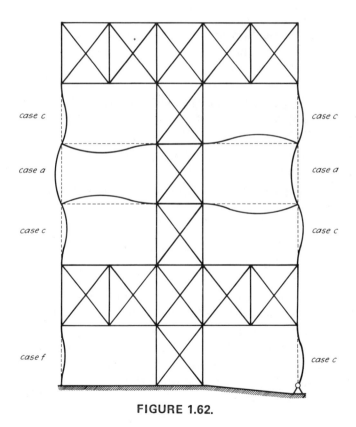

FIGURE 1.62.

$$A = (4) \, 6 = 24 \text{ in.}^2,$$

$$\rho_{min} = \frac{4}{\sqrt{12}} = 1.155 \text{ in.},$$

$$L = 144 \text{ in.},$$

$$K = 1,$$

$$P_{cr} = EA \, \frac{\pi^2}{(kL/\rho_{min})^2} = \frac{1800(24) \, \pi^2}{(144/1.155)^2} = 27.43 \text{ k},$$

$$P = 12 \text{ k.}$$

Since the column buckles under a load greater than twice the actual load P, the column can be considered safe.

APPENDIX: DERIVATION OF THE BUCKLING LOAD FORMULA

The relation between the deflection w of the typical section of a structural bar and the moment M_i produced by the internal stresses on the section with the deflection w is derived in Chapter 3. This relation is

$$M_i = EI \, \frac{d^2w}{dx^2},$$

where E is the stress/strain ratio of a structural material (Young's modulus) and I the cross-sectional moment of intertia about the neutral axis of pure bending.

The internal moment M_i equals the bending moment wP on the typical section of a bar subject to axial load P with a deflection w (Fig. 1.55) when P has the critical value P_{cr}:

$$M_i = wP_{cr}.$$

With the expression of M_i given earlier, this equilibrium equation becomes

$$EI \frac{d^2 w}{dx^2} - w P_{cr} = 0,$$

which is a second-order ordinary differential equation with the deflection w as an unknown parameter.

The buckled shape of a bar, thus the relation between the deflection w and the typical coordinate x, is influenced by the constraints of the bar ends (the boundary conditions of the bar). Under any constraint conditions the solution $w(x)$ of the differential equation must be compatible with those boundary conditions. The various possible constraint conditions of a compression bar are shown by Figs. 1.57a, b, c, d, e, and f, which also show the buckled shapes of the bar, compatible in each case with the boundary conditions.

The solutions of the differential equation for the various cases are the following:

Cases of Fig. 1.57a and e

The buckled shape of the bar resembles that of a half wave (Fig. 1.58) with deflections w and internal moments $EI(d^2 w/dx^2)$ that in case a vanish at both ends $x = 0$ and $x = L$.

The sine wave deflection

$$w(x) = C \sin \frac{\pi x}{L},$$

with the unspecified constant

$$C = w_{max},$$

is suitable solution of the differential equation since it vanishes with its second derivative:

$$\frac{d^2 w}{dx^2} = - \frac{C \pi^2}{L^2} \sin \pi \frac{x}{L} = \frac{M_i}{EI}$$

at $x = 0$ and $x = L$ ($\sin 0 = \sin \pi = 0$). Replacing $C \sin (\pi x/L)$ in the equilibrium equation gives

$$C \left(- \frac{\pi^2}{L^2} EI + P_{cr} \right) \sin \frac{\pi x}{L} = 0,$$

which is satisfied at every x coordinate and with any value of the constant C if

$$P_{cr} - \frac{\pi^2}{L^2} EI = 0.$$

Thus

$$P_{cr} = EI \frac{\pi^2}{L^2}$$

is the critical load under which a compression bar restrained at both ends from lateral displacement, but not from rotation, is in equilibrium with any deflection:

$$w_{max} = C.$$

The critical load has the same expression in case e since the buckled shape of the compression bar is again that of a half wave (Fig. 1.58).

Cases of Fig. 1.57b and d

The buckled shape of the bar resembles the curve of one-fourth of a wave (Fig. 1.58), with deflections w and rotations dw/dx vanishing in case d at $x = 0$ (fixed end) and with moment $EI (d^2 w/dx^2)$ vanishing in case d at $x = L$ (free end).

A suitable wave deflection is

$$w(x) = C \left(\cos \frac{\pi x}{2L} - 1 \right),$$

which vanishes with its first derivative

$$\frac{dw}{dx} = -C \frac{\pi}{2L} \sin \frac{\pi x}{2L} = \phi(x)$$

at $x = 0$ ($\cos 0 = 1$, $\sin 0 = 0$) and which has a second derivative

$$\frac{d^2 w}{dx^2} = -C \frac{\pi^2}{4L^2} \cos \frac{\pi x}{2L} = \frac{M_i}{EI}$$

vanishing at $x = L$. C is an unspecified constant ($C = w_{max}$).

It is convenient in this case to differentiate twice the equilibrium equation, which of course does not change the equation's validity or its physical meaning. The double differentiation gives

$$EI \frac{d^4 w(x)}{dx^4} + P \frac{d^2 w(x)}{dx^2} = 0.$$

Replacing the second and fourth derivative of $w(x)$ in the equation gives

$$EIC \left(\frac{\pi}{2L}\right)^4 \cos \frac{\pi x}{2L} - PC \left(\frac{\pi}{2L}\right)^2 \cos \frac{\pi x}{2L} = 0,$$

from which

$$C \left(\frac{\pi}{2L}\right)^2 \left(EI \frac{\pi^2}{(2L)^2} - P\right) \cos \frac{\pi x}{2L} = 0.$$

This equilibrium condition is satisfied by

$$P_{cr} = EI \frac{\pi^2}{(2L)^2}.$$

The critical load of case b is the same in case d. Indeed, the buckled shape of the compression bar is identical in the two cases.

Case of Fig. 1.57f

The buckled shape of the bar is a complete wave with deflections w and rotations dw/dx vanishing at both ends. A suitable expression for the deflection w is

$$w(x) = C \left(\cos \frac{\pi x}{L/2} - 1 \right),$$

since it vanishes with its derivative

$$\frac{dw}{dx} = - \frac{C\pi}{L/2} \sin \frac{\pi x}{L/2} = \phi(x)$$

at the coordinates $x = 0$ and $x = L$ ($\cos 0 = 1$, $\sin 2\pi = 0$). The unspecified constant C coincides with w_{max}.

After double differentiation, the equation of equilibrium between the internal and external moments is

$$EI \frac{d^4 w}{dx^4} + P_{cr} \frac{d^2 w}{dx^2} = 0.$$

Substitution of $w(x)$ in this equation yields

$$EIC \frac{\pi^4}{(L/2)^4} \cos \frac{\pi x}{L/2} - P_{cr} C \frac{\pi^2}{(L/2)^2} \cos \frac{\pi x}{L/2} = 0,$$

from which

$$C \frac{\pi^2}{(L/2)^2} \left[EI \frac{\pi^2}{(L/2)^2} - P_{cr} \right] \cos \frac{\pi x}{L/2} = 0.$$

This equilibrium equation is satisfied at any coordinate x with any value of the constant C by

$$P_{cr} = EI \; \frac{\pi^2}{(L/2)^2} \; .$$

Case of 1.57c

A procedure analogous to those thus far followed yields in this case

$$P_{cr} = EI \; \frac{\pi^2}{(L/\sqrt{2})^2}.$$

In conclusion, in every case the critical load formula has the product $EI\pi^2$ in the numerator and in the denominator the square of a length that an inspection of Fig. 1.57 and 1.58 shows to be that of a half wave on the buckled curve of the bar. For example, in Figs. 1.57a and c the length of the half wave coincides with the length L of the bar, and L^2 appears in the denominator of the buckling load formula. In Figs. 1.57b and d one-fourth the length of a wave coincides with the bar length. Thus the length of a half wave coincides with $2L$, twice the bar length, and $(2L)^2$ appears in the denominator of the expression of P_{cr}. In Fig. 1.57f the length of the half wave coincides with $L/2$, one-half the bar length, and $(L/2)^2$ appears in the formula of P_{cr}, and so on.

It is therefore apparent that the *effective length* of a bar with respect to buckling is not the actual bar length but rather the half-wave length of the buckling curve which depends on the constraints of the bar ends. It is therefore possible to give P_{cr} the general formula

$$P_{cr} = EI \; \frac{\pi^2}{(kL)^2}$$

by using the notation kL for the effective length. The values coefficient k takes in these various cases are summarized as follows:

Fig. 1.57 Case	a	b	c	d	e	f
k	1	2	$1/\sqrt{2}$	2	1	$1/2$

Since the relation

$$M_i = EI \, \frac{d^2 w}{dx^2}$$

is obtained (Chapter 3) under conditions of proportionality between stresses and strains (Hook's law, $\sigma = E\epsilon$), the formula of P_{cr} (Euler's formula) given here is not valid in a stress range exceeding the range of proportionality.

PROBLEMS

1.1.1. The steel used for the cable in Fig. 1.63 allows a working stress of 100 k/in.^{2} Evaluate the diameter of a round bar suitable for this cable structure.

Solution. The results of Steps 2 and 3 for this problem (R_{max}, P_{max}) are shown in Fig. 1.63.

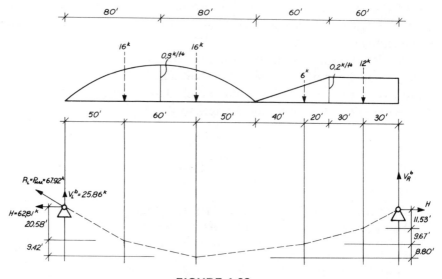

FIGURE 1.63.

Steps 4, 5 (Cross-Sectional Properties, Stresses)

$$A = \frac{\pi}{4} d^2 = \frac{P_{max}}{\sigma_a} = \frac{67.92}{100} = 0.68 \text{ in.}^2$$

A round bar with $\frac{7}{8}''$ diameter has an area

$$\frac{\pi}{4} (0.875)^2 = 0.6 \text{ in.}^2 < 0.68 \text{ in.}^2$$

A round bar with $1''$ diameter has an area

$$\frac{\pi}{4} (1)^2 = 0.785 \text{ in.}^2$$

The latter bar must be chosen if the stress of 100 k/in.^{2} is not to be exceeded.

1.1.2. The truss in Fig. 1.64 is being prefabricated in a steel manufacturing shop from steel pipes. The properties of the available pipes are shown in the following table. Choose suitable pipes for the tension bars of the truss using an allowable stress of 20 k/in.^{2} Choose the suitable pipes for a first trial in the design of the compression bars using an allowable stress of 10 k/in.^{2} (the final design of the compression bars is shown in Problems 1.10.1 and 1.10.2.

Available Pipes

Outside diameter (in.)	2.375	1.66	0.84	0.54
Thickness (in.)	0.154	0.14	0.109	0.088
Area (in.^{2})	1.075	0.669	0.25	0.125
Standard weight (lbs/ft)	3.65	2.27	0.85	0.42

Solution. The reactions and the axial forces of this truss are shown in Fig. 1.64.

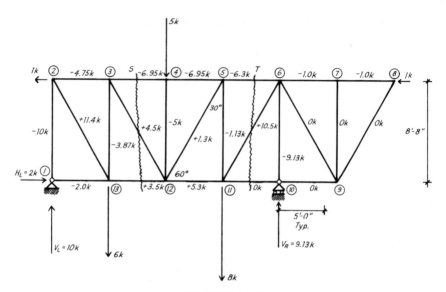

FIGURE 1.64.

Steps 4, 5 (Properties, Stresses)

The required cross-sectional areas of the tension bars are the ratios of the axial forces P with the allowable stress 20 k/in.[2]

The first trial areas of the compression bars are the ratios of the negative axial forces P with the negative stress of 10 k/in.[2]

The chosen pipes are indicated by their outside diameter:

Bar	P/σ_a	Pipe	Bar	P/σ_a	Pipe	Bar	P/σ_a	Pipe
1–2	1	2.375	9–10	0	0.54	12–4	0.5	1.66
2–3	0.475	1.66	10–11	0	0.54	12–5	0.065	0.54
3–4	0.695	1.66	11–12	0.265	0.84	11–5	0.113	0.54
4–5	0.695	1.66	12–13	0.175	0.84	11–6	0.525	1.66
5–6	0.63	1.66	13–1	0.2	0.84	10–6	0.913	2.375
6–7	0.1	0.54	13–2	0.57	1.66	9–6	0	0.54
7–8	0.1	0.54	13–3	0.387	1.66	9–7	0	0.54
8–9	0	0.54	12–3	0.225	0.84			

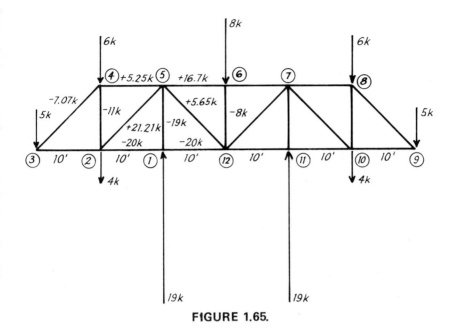

FIGURE 1.65.

The cross-sectional area of the pipe chosen for the bars 3–4 and 4–5 is 3.75% smaller than the required area 0.695 in.^{2} However, 3–4 and 4–5 are compression bars, and this is only a first trial for the bar size.

1.1.3. Repeat the tasks of Problem 1.1.2 for the truss in Fig. 1.65. Use the same allowable stresses of Problem 1.1.2 and the following steel pipes:

Outside diameter (in.)	3.5	2.375	1.66	1.05
Thickness (in.)	0.216	0.154	0.14	0.113
Area (in.^{2})	2.228	1.075	0.669	0.333
Standard weight (lbs/ft)	7.58	3.65	2.27	1.13

1.1.4. A cable carries the loads in Fig. 1.63 over the span of 280 ft. The sags of the cable measured from the left and right anchors are $S_l = 30$ ft and $S_r = 3$ ft. The largest reactions are*

$$V_l = 37.8 \text{ k},$$

$$H = 123.9 \text{ k}.$$

Evaluate the diameter of a steel bar to be used for this cable with a working stress of 100 k/in.[2] The available bar diameters vary with $\frac{1}{8}''$ increments.

1.1.5. Perform the tasks in Problem 1.1.2 for the half truss in Figs. 1.66a and b. Use the steel pipes listed in the table of the Steel Construction Manual published by the American Institute of Steel Construction. In the Maxwell diagram in Fig. 1.66b tensile axial forces are dotted.

1.1.6. Perform the tasks in Problem 1.1.5 for the truss of Fig. 1.67.

1.1.7. Perform the tasks in Problem 1.1.5 for the truss in Fig. 1.68.

1.1.8. Perform the tasks in Problem 1.1.5 for the truss in Figs. 1.69a and b.

1.2.1. The beam in Fig. 1.70 is made with a steel pipe with outside diameter $D_0 = 12.75$ in. and inside diameter $D_i = 12$ in. Find the bending stresses due to the cantilever moments.

---

*See G. de Campoli, *Statics of Structural Components* (New York: Wiley, 1983), Problem 6.12.

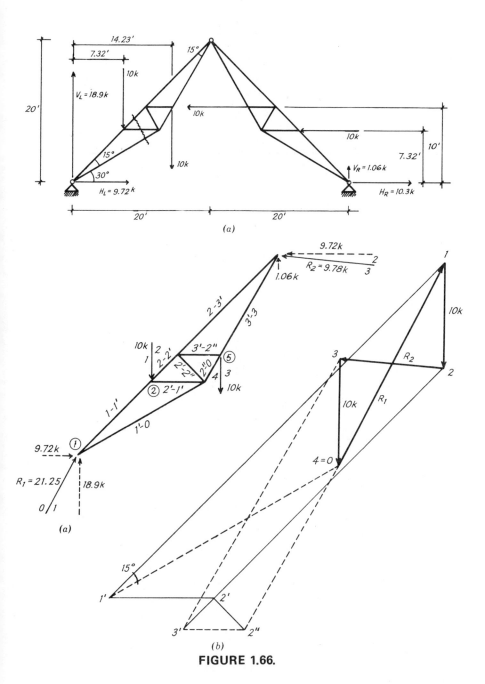

FIGURE 1.66.

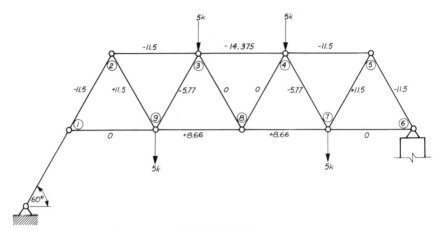

FIGURE 1.67.

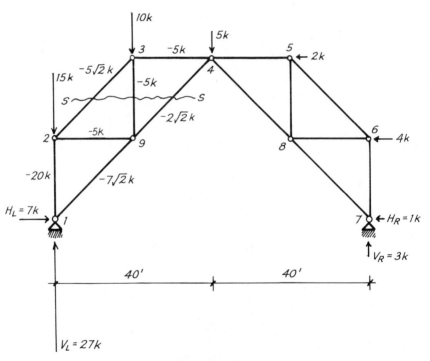

FIGURE 1.68.

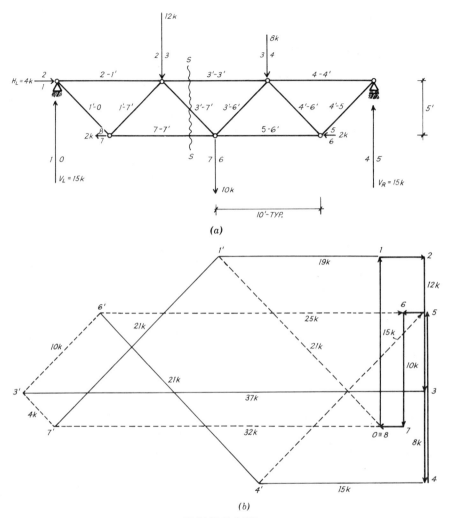

(a)

(b)

FIGURE 1.69.

Solution. The results of Step 2 (reactions) and Step 3 (internal forces) are shown in Fig. 1.70.

Step 4 (Properties)

$$I = \frac{\pi}{64} (D_0^4 - D_i^4) = \frac{\pi}{64} (12.75^4 - 12^4) = 279.3 \text{ in.}^4$$

Step 5 (Stresses)

For the left overhang

$$\sigma_b = \frac{M}{I} \frac{D_0}{2} = \frac{15(12)6.375}{279.3} = 4.1 \text{ k/in.}^2$$

For the right overhang

$$\sigma_b = \frac{27(12)6.375}{279.3} = 7.4 \text{ k/in.}^2$$

1.2.2. Using the bending moment diagram in Fig. 1.70, design a rectangular timber beam following these specifications:

Allowable bending stress = 1 k/in.^{2}

Depth/width ratio = $\dfrac{d}{b}$ = 2.

Solution.

Steps 4 and 5 (Properties and Stresses)

The rectangular section modulus is

$$S = \frac{I}{d/2} = \frac{bd^3/12}{d/2} = \frac{b}{6} d^2$$

replacing b with $d/2$, $S = d^3/12$.
The required section modulus is

$$S = \frac{M}{\sigma_b} = \frac{27(12)}{1} = 324 \text{ in.}^3 = \frac{d^3}{12},$$

from which

$$d = \sqrt[3]{12(324)} = 15.79 \text{ in.}   \text{ (use 16 in.).}$$

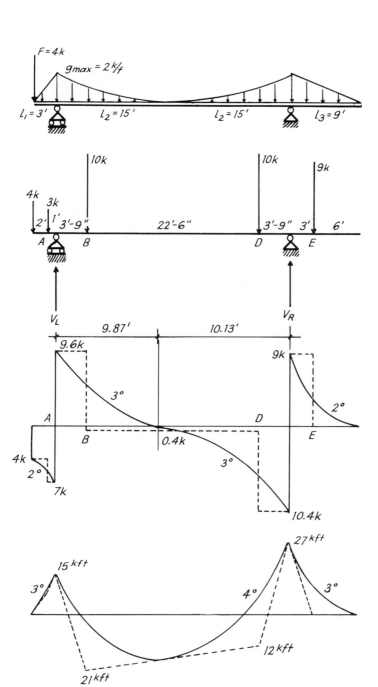

FIGURE 1.70.

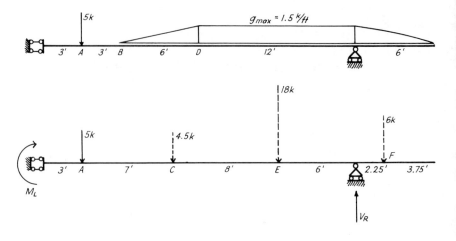

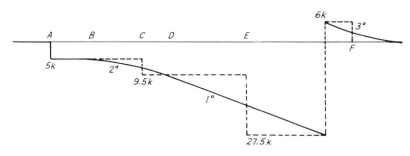

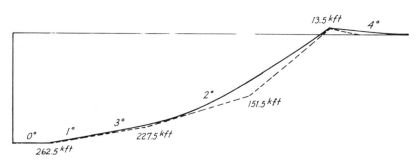

FIGURE 1.71.

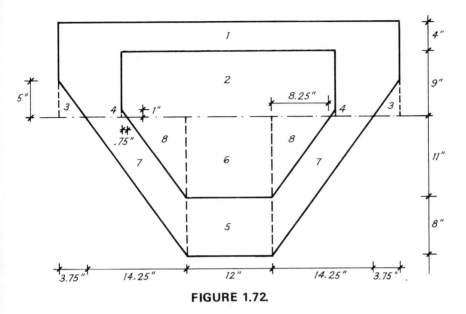

FIGURE 1.72.

1.2.3. The beam in Fig. 1.71 has the cross section shown in Fig. 1.72. Find the extreme fiber bending stresses at the left end of the beam.

Solution. The results of Step 2 (reactions) and Step 3 (internal forces) are shown in Fig. 1.71.

Step 4 (Cross-Sectional Properties)*

$$z_{top} = 13 \text{ in.}; \quad z_{bot} = 19 \text{ in.}; \quad Z = 22.9 \text{ in.}; \quad A = 612 \text{ in.}^2$$

$$\dot{I}_y = 64{,}356 \text{ in.}^4; \quad I_z = 118{,}206 \text{ in.}^4; \quad I_p = 182{,}562 \text{ in.}^4$$

$$\rho_z = 10.25 \text{ in.}; \quad \rho_y = 13.9 \text{ in.}$$

*See G. de Campoli, *Statics of Structural Components* (New York: Wiley, 1983), Problems 9.5, 9.6, 9.7, 9.12, 9.14.

Step 5 (Stresses)

$$\sigma_b^{top} = \frac{M_y}{I_y} z_{top} = \frac{262.5(12)\,13}{64,356} = 0.636 \text{ k/in.}^2.$$

$$\sigma_b^{bot} = \frac{M_y}{I_y} z_{bot} = \frac{262.5(12)\,19}{64,356} = 0.93 \text{ k/in.}^2.$$

1.2.4. Find the compressive resultant C and the equal tensile resultant T on the left end of the beam in Figs. 1.71 and 1.72.

Solution. The lever arm of the resisting moment is (Problem 1.2.3)

$$Z = 22.9 \text{ in.}$$

Thus

$$C = T = \frac{M}{Z} = \frac{262.5(12)}{22.9} = 135.5 \text{ k.}$$

1.2.5. The cantilever beam in Fig. 1.73 has the cross section shown in Fig. 1.74. Calculate the extreme fiber bending stresses at the fixed end.

Solution. The distributed loads are replaced with their resultants (Step 1), which have the following values and coordinates:

Linear load resultant

$$2(3)\,\frac{1}{2} = 3 \text{ k at } x = 8 \text{ ft.}$$

Uniform load resultant

$$2(3) = 6 \text{ k at } x = 10.5 \text{ ft.}$$

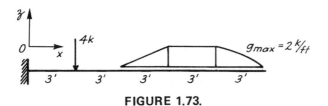

FIGURE 1.73.

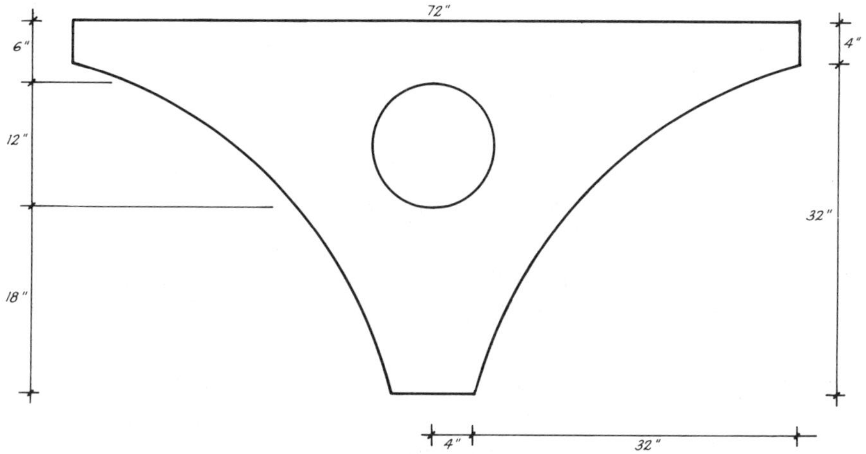

FIGURE 1.74.

Parabolic load resultant

$$2(3)\frac{2}{3} = 4 \text{ k at } x = 13.125 \text{ ft.}$$

Steps 2 and 3 (Reactions and Internal Forces)

The fixed end moment is the largest bending moment on the beam. Its value is calculated with the forces and lever arms just listed:

$$M_{\max} = 4(3) + 3(8) + 6(10.5) + 4(13.125) = 151.5 \text{ k-ft.}$$

Step 4 (Properties)*

$$z_{top} = 10.6 \text{ in.}; \quad z_{bot} = 25.4 \text{ in.}; \quad A = 870.5 \text{ in.}^2$$

$$I_y = 80,195 \text{ in.}^4; \quad I_z = 195,118 \text{ in.}^4; \quad I_p = 275,313 \text{ in.}^4$$

$$\rho_z = 9.6 \text{ in.}; \quad \rho_y = 14.97 \text{ in.}$$

Step 5 (Stresses)

$$\sigma_b^{top} = \frac{M_y}{I_y} z_{top} = \frac{151.5(12)10.6}{80,195} = 0.24 \text{ k/in.}^2.$$

$$\sigma_b^{bot} = \frac{M_y}{I_y} z_{bot} = \frac{151.5(12)25.4}{80,195} = 0.576 \text{ k/in.}^2.$$

In visualizing the beam deformation, we readily see that σ_b^{top} is positive (tension) and σ_b^{bot} negative (compression).

1.2.6. The beam of Fig. 1.75 has the cross section shown in Fig. 1.76. Find the extreme fiber bending stress on the section 6 ft from the beam's right end.

Solution. The results of Steps 2 and 3 (reactions and internal forces) are shown in Figs. 1.75d and e.

Step 4 (Cross-Sectional Properties)†

$$I_y = 2(69.8) = 139.6 \text{ in.}^4; \quad Z = 2(3.23) = 6.46 \text{ in.}$$

Step 5 (Stresses)

$$\sigma_b^{top} = \sigma_b^{bot} = \frac{M_y}{I_y} z = \frac{36(12)4}{139.6} = 12.4 \text{ k/in.}^2.$$

*See G. de Campoli, *Statics of Structural Components* (New York: Wiley, 1983), Problems 9.9, 9.11, 9.13, 9.15.

† See G. de Campoli, *Statics of Structural Components* (New York: Wiley, 1983), Problem 9.17.

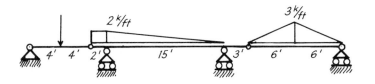

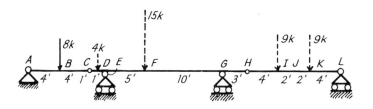

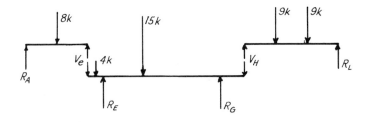

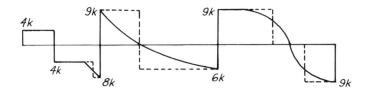

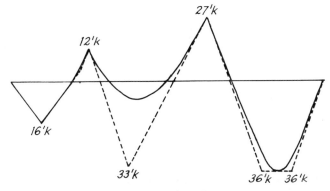

FIGURE 1.75.

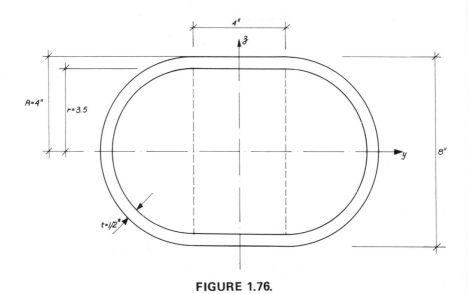

FIGURE 1.76.

1.2.7. For the beam in Figs. 1.75 and 1.76 find the value of compressive resultant C (and tensile resultant T) on the cross section 6 ft from the beam's right end.

Solution.

$$C = T = \frac{M_y}{Z} = \frac{36(12)}{6.46} = 66.9 \text{ k.}$$

1.2.8. Find the depth of an adequate cross-section for the timber beam in Fig. 1.75. Follow these specifications:

$$\sigma_b = 1.5 \text{ k/in.}^2,$$

$$\frac{\text{depth}}{\text{width}} = \frac{d}{b} = 2.$$

1.2.9. For the beam of Problem 1.2.8, find the compressive resultant C on the cross section 6 ft from the beam's right end.

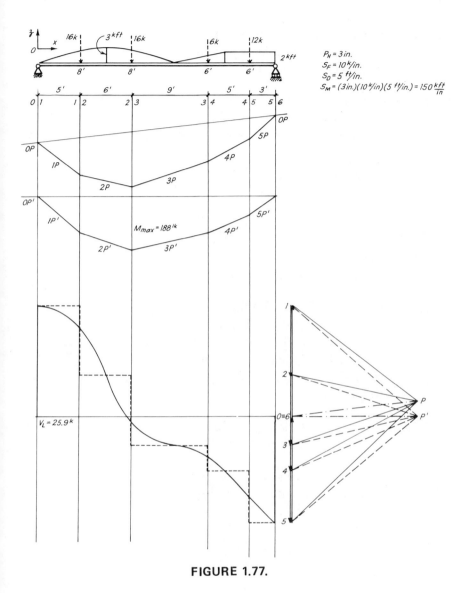

FIGURE 1.77.

1.2.10. The beam in Fig. 1.77 has an I-shaped cross section with $1'' \times 9''$ flanges and $\frac{1}{2}'' \times 16''$ web. Find the extreme fiber bending stress on the section at $x = 11$ ft. Reactions and internal forces (Steps 2 and 3) are found graphically and shown in Fig. 1.77.

1.2.11. For the beam in Problem 1.2.10, find the arm Z of the resisting moment and the compressive resultant C on the cross section at $x = 11$ ft.

1.2.12. Evaluate the reactions (Step 2) and the bending moments (Step 3) on the beam in Fig. 1.78. Then find the depth of its rectangular cross section (Steps 4 and 5) following these specifications:

$$b = 6 \text{ in.,}$$

$$\sigma_b = 1.85 \text{ k/in}^2.$$

1.2.13. Find the compressive resultant C on the right end section of the beam in Problem 1.2.12.

1.2.14. Fig. 1.78 shows the span and loads of a steel truss with an 18″ depth between the centroids of the chords. The bottom chord of the truss is made with a $\frac{5}{8}$″ thick plate. Use the bending moment diagram from Problem 1.2.12 and an allowable tension of 20 k/in.[2] to find the width of the bottom chord.

1.2.15. Repeat the tasks of Problems 1.2.12 and 1.2.13 for the symmetric beam of Fig. 1.79.

1.2.16. Repeat the tasks of Problem 1.2.14 for a symmetric truss with the spans and loads in Fig. 1.79.

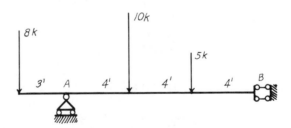

FIGURE 1.78.

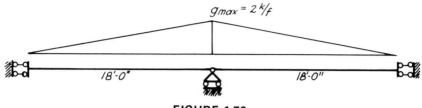

FIGURE 1.79.

1.3.1. Horizontal earthquake load produces a 10 k-ft bending moment on the left support of the beam in Problem 1.2.1 Draw the diagram of combined bending stresses due to gravity and earthquake loads on the cross section of the left support.

Solution (Fig. 1.80). In this case due to polar symmetry, $I_z = I_y = I$. Thus the extreme earthquake stresses are

$$\sigma_b^e = \frac{M^e}{I_z} R_0 = \frac{10(12)6.375}{279.3} = 2.74 \text{ k/in.}^2.$$

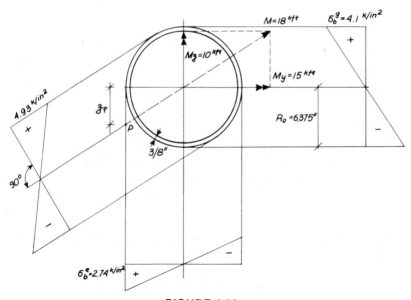

FIGURE 1.80.

The neutral axis coincides with the line of action of the resultant moment vector. This is confirmed by the value of the coordinate z_p of a stress-free point on the vertical tangent. This coordinate is given by

$$\left(\frac{\sigma_b^g}{R_0}\right) z_p = \sigma_b^e,$$

where σ_b^g is the extreme gravity stress in Problem 1.2.1. Solving, we obtain

$$z_p = \left(\frac{\sigma_b^e}{\sigma_b^g}\right) R_0 = \left(\frac{2.74}{4.10}\right) 6.375 = 4.25 \text{ in.}$$

Also

$$z_p = \frac{M_z}{M_y} R_0 = \frac{10}{15}(6.375) = 4.25 \text{ in.}$$

The baseline of the combined diagram is at $90°$ to the neutral axis, and the extreme combined stresses are

$$\sigma_b = \frac{M}{I} R_0 = \frac{18(12)6.375}{279.3} = 4.93 \text{ k/in.}^2.$$

1.3.2. Perform the task in Problem 1.3.1 on the cross section at the right support, with an earthquake moment $M_e = M_z = 18$ k-ft.

1.3.3. Horizontal earthquake load produces a 10 k-ft bending moment on the left support of the beam in Problem 1.2.2. Draw the diagram of combined bending stresses due to gravity and earthquake load on the cross section at the left support.

Solution (Fig. 1.81). The extreme bending stresses due to gravity are

$$\sigma_b^g = \frac{6M_y}{bd^2} = \frac{6(15)12}{7.5(16)^2} = 0.56 \text{ k/in.}^2.$$

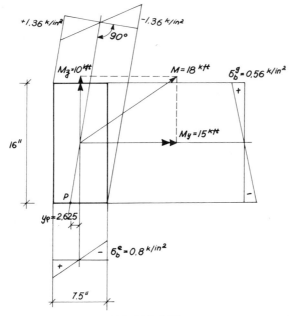

FIGURE 1.81.

The extreme bending stresses due to earthquake are

$$\sigma_b^e = \frac{6M_z}{db^2} = \frac{6(10)12}{16(7.5)^2} = 0.8 \text{ k/in.}^2.$$

The coordinate y_P of a point P on the neutral axis at the left bottom side is given by

$$\left(\frac{\sigma_b^e}{b/2}\right) y_P = \sigma_b^g,$$

from which

$$y_P = \left(\frac{\sigma_b^g}{\sigma_b^e}\right)\frac{b}{2} = \left(\frac{0.56}{0.8}\right) 3.75 = 2.625 \text{ in.}$$

The neutral axis is thus defined by this point and the centroid. The baseline of the combined diagram is at $90°$ to the neutral axis. The extreme fiber stresses are as follows:

Upper left corner

$$\sigma_b = \sigma_b^g + \sigma_b^e = 0.56 + 0.8 = +1.36 \text{ k/in.}^2.$$

Lower right corner

$$\sigma_b = -1.36 \text{ k/in.}^2.$$

Upper right corner

$$\sigma_b = +0.56 - 0.8 = -0.24 \text{ k/in.}^2.$$

Lower left corner

$$\sigma_b = -0.56 + 0.8 = +0.24 \text{ k/in.}^2.$$

1.3.4. Perform the task in Problem 1.3.3 on the cross section at the right support with an earthquake moment $M_e = M_z = 13$ k-ft.

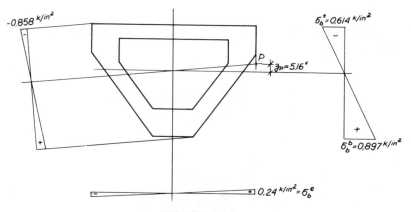

FIGURE 1.82.

1.3.5. Horizontal earthquake load produces a 100 k-ft bending moment at the left end of the beam in Problem 1.2.3. Draw the diagram of combined bending stresses due to gravity and earthquake loads on the left end section.

Solution (Fig. 1.82). The extreme bending stresses due to earthquake are

$$\sigma_b^e = \frac{M_z}{I_z} \, y_{max} = \frac{100(12)24}{118.206} = 0.244 \text{ k/in.}^2.$$

The coordinate z_P of a point P on the neutral axis at the upper right outline is given by

$$\left(\frac{\sigma_b^t}{z_t}\right) z_P = \sigma_b^e,$$

from which

$$z_P = \left(\frac{\sigma_b^e}{\sigma_b^t}\right) z_t = \frac{0.244}{0.614} \, 13 = 5.16 \text{ in.}$$

Point P and the centroid define the neutral axis. The baseline of the combined diagram is at $90°$ to the neutral axis. The extreme fiber stress in compression is

$$-\sigma_b^t - \sigma_b^e = -0.614 - 0.244 = -0.858 \text{ k/in.}^2,$$

The extreme tensile stress can be scaled on the diagram.

1.3.6. Horizontal wind load produces a bending moment

$$M_z = 75 \text{ k-ft}$$

on the fixed end of the beam in Problem 1.2.5. Assume wind stresses to be tensile on the left side of the cross section. Draw the diagram of combined gravity and wind bending stresses on the fixed end section.

1.3.7. A horizontal earthquake load produces a 50 k-ft bending moment on the section 6 ft from the right end of the beam in Problem 1.2.6. Calculate the cross-sectional properties I_z, Q_z, I_p (Step 4). Find the extreme bending stresses σ_b^e due to earthquake, and draw the diagram of combined gravity and earthquake bending stresses (Step 5).

1.3.8. A horizontal wind load produces a bending moment

$$M_z = 50 \text{ k-ft}$$

on the section of the beam in Problem 1.2.10 at $x = 11$ ft. Calculate I_z and the extreme bending stress due to wind

$$\sigma_b^w = \frac{M_z}{I_z}\, y_{\max}.$$

Draw the diagram of combined bending stresses due to gravity and wind on the beam section at $x = 11$ ft.

1.4.1. Replace the roller of the beam in Problem 1.3.1 with a hinge, and let the ambient temperature rise by

$$\Delta T = 40°\text{F}.$$

Calculate the thermal axial force P and the axial stress σ_a. Draw the combined diagram of axial (thermal) and bending (gravity and earthquake) stresses on the cross section on the left support.

Solution (Fig. 1.83). The temperature rise should elongate the span by the amount

$$\Delta l = \alpha l \Delta T.$$

The horizontal reactions P of the hinges neutralize this elongation with an equal shrinkage:

$$\Delta l = \frac{Pl}{EA}.$$

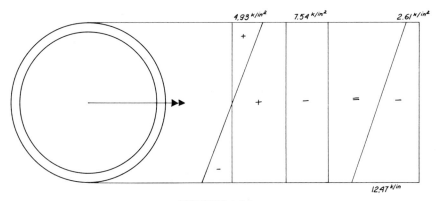

FIGURE 1.83.

Thus

$$\frac{Pl}{EA} = \alpha l \Delta T,$$

from which

$$P = \alpha EA \, \Delta T \quad \text{and} \quad \frac{P}{A} = \alpha E \Delta T,$$

where

$\alpha = 65(10)^7 \ (1/°\text{F})$ is the steel's coefficient of thermal expansion,

$E = 29{,}000 \ \text{k/in.}^2$ is the Young modulus for steel,

$A = \pi(6.375^2 - 6^2) = 14.6 \ \text{in.}^2$ is the cross-sectional area.

The numerical values are

$$P = 110 \ \text{k} \quad \text{and} \quad \sigma_a = \frac{P}{A} = 7.54 \ \text{k/in.}^2.$$

The combined bending stresses are shown in Fig. 1.80. Their algebraic sum with the preceding axial stress produces the diagram in Fig. 1.83 from which we realize that the section is fully in compression.

1.4.2.   Find the combined thermal, gravity, and earthquake stresses on the cross section at the right support of the beam in Problems 1.3.2 and 1.4.1.

1.4.3.   Replace the roller of the beam in Problem 1.3.3 with a hinge, and let the ambient temperature fall by

$$\Delta T = 60°\text{F}.$$

Calculate the thermal axial force P and axial stress σ_a. Draw the combined diagram of axial and bending stresses on the cross section of the left support.

Solution (Fig. 1.84).   The temperature fall should shrink the span by the amount

$$\Delta l = \alpha l \Delta T.$$

The horizontal reactions P of the hinges neutralize this shrinkage with an equal extension

$$\Delta l = \frac{Pl}{EA}.$$

Equating the preceding expressions of Δl, we obtain

$$P = \alpha E A \Delta T \quad \text{and} \quad \frac{P}{A} = \sigma_a = \alpha E \Delta T,$$

where

$\alpha = 25/(10)^7$ $(1/°\text{F})$ is the coefficient of thermal expansion of this timber beam,

$E = 1800$ k/in.^{2} is Young's modulus,

$A = bd = 7.5(16) = 120$ in.^{2} is the cross-sectional area.

The numerical values are

$$P = 32.4 \text{ k} \quad \text{and} \quad \sigma_a = \frac{P}{A} = 0.27 \text{ k/in.}^2.$$

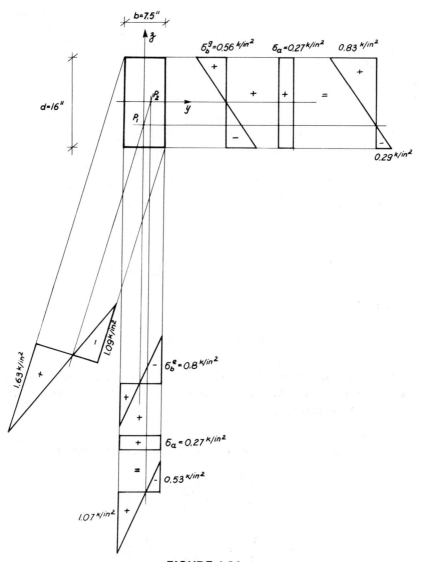

FIGURE 1.84.

121

The bending stresses due to gravity and earthquake loads shown in Fig. 1.81 are reproduced in Fig. 1.84. Temporarily disregarding earthquake stresses, we combine thermal and gravity stresses and obtain the neutral axis of this combination. Its point P_1 on the z axis actually belongs to the neutral axis of the three-stress combination, for the earthquake stresses also vanish at P_1. Next we temporarily disregard gravity stresses and combine earthquake with axial stresses, obtaining the neutral axis of this combination. Its point P_2 on the y axis actually belongs to the neutral axis of the three-stress combination, for gravity stresses also vanish at P_2. Thus the true neutral axis is defined by P_1 and P_2. The baseline of the three-stress combination is at $90°$ to the neutral axis. The extreme stresses are as follows:

Lower right corner

$$-\sigma_b^g - \sigma_b^e + \sigma_a = -0.56 - 0.8 + 0.27 = -1.09 \text{ k/in.}^2,$$

Upper left corner

$$\sigma_b^g + \sigma_b^e + \sigma_a = 0.56 + 0.8 + 0.27 = +1.63 \text{ k/in.}^2.$$

1.4.4.   Obtain anew the neutral axis in Problem 1.4.3 with the graphic method that uses the eccentricities e_y and e_z and the gyrators ρ_y and ρ_z.

Solution (Fig. 1.85).   The values of the eccentricities are

$$e_z = \frac{M_y}{P} = \frac{15(12)}{32.4} = 5.6 \text{ in.},$$

$$e_y = \frac{M_z}{P} = \frac{10(12)}{32.4} = 3.7 \text{ in.}$$

The radii of gyration are

$$\rho_z = \frac{d}{\sqrt{12}} = \frac{16}{\sqrt{12}} = 4.6 \text{ in.},$$

$$p_y = \frac{b}{\sqrt{12}} = \frac{7.5}{\sqrt{12}} = 2.2 \text{ in.}$$

The gyrator ρ_z is flipped onto the y axis. Its tip is connected by a straight line to the center of pressure, C_1. A segment at 90° to this line drawn from the tip of ρ_z crosses the z axis at P_1.

Analogously, ρ_y is flipped onto the z axis. Its tip is connected by a straight line to the center of pressure, C_2. A segment at 90° to this line drawn from the tip of ρ_y crosses the y axis at P_2. The graphic results may be checked with the Euclidean theorem. From the triangle with base $C_1 P_1$ and altitude ρ_z, we obtain

$$CP_1 = \frac{\rho_z^2}{e_z} = \frac{4.6^2}{5.6} = 3.78 \text{ in.}$$

From the triangle with base $C_2 P_2$ and altitude ρ_y, we obtain

$$CP_2 = \frac{\rho_y^2}{e_y} = \frac{2.2^2}{3.7} = 1.31 \text{ in.}$$

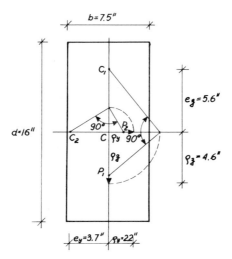

FIGURE 1.85.

The neutral axis is colinear with segment P_1P_2.

1.4.5.   Find the combined thermal, gravity, and earthquake stresses on the cross section at the right supports of the beam in Problems 1.3.4 and 1.4.3.

1.4.6.   Obtain anew the neutral axis in Problem 1.4.5 with the graphic method in Problem 1.4.4.

1.4.7.   Assume that the beam in Problem 1.3.5 is pretensioned. The uniform value of the axial prestress on the left end section is

$$\sigma_a = -1.0 \text{ k/in.}^2$$

Draw the neutral axis and a diagram of the combined gravity and pretensioning stresses. Draw the neutral axis and a diagram of the combined earthquake and pretensioning stresses. Draw the neutral axis and a diagram of the three-stress combination.

1.4.8.   Perform the last task in Problem 1.4.7 with the graphic method that uses eccentricities e_y, e_z and gyrators ρ_y and ρ_z.

Solution (Fig. 1.86).   The cross-sectional properties are given in Problem 1.2.3:

$A = 612$ in.^{2}

$z_{top} = 13$ in.

$z_{bot} = 19$ in.

$I_y = 64{,}356$ in.^{4}

$I_z = 118{,}206$ in.^{4}

$\rho_z = 10.25$ in.

$\rho_y = 13.9$ in.

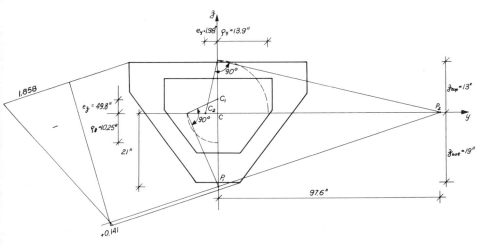

FIGURE 1.86.

Thus

$$P = \sigma_a A = (1)\,612 = 612 \text{ k},$$

$$e_z = \frac{M_y}{P} = \frac{262.5(12)}{612} = 4.98 \text{ in.}$$

$$e_y = \frac{M_z}{P} = \frac{100(12)}{612} = 1.98 \text{ in.}$$

The gyrator ρ_z is flipped onto the y axis. Its tip is connected by a straight line to the center of pressure, C_1. A segment at 90° to this line drawn from the tip of ρ_z crosses the z axis at P_1.

Analogously, ρ_y is flipped onto the z axis. Its tip is connected by a straight line to the center of the pressure, C_2. A segment at 90° to this line, drawn from the tip of ρ_y, crosses the y axis at P_2. The neutral axis is colinear with segment $P_1 P_2$. The graphic results may be checked with the Euclidean theorem: from the triangle with base $C_1 P_1$ and altitude ρ_z, we obtain

$$CP_1 = \frac{\rho_z^2}{e_z} = \frac{10.25^2}{4.98} = 21.1 \text{ in.}$$

From the triangle with base $C_2 P_2$ and altitude ρ_y, we obtain

$$CP_2 = \frac{\rho_y^2}{e_y} = \frac{13.9^2}{1.98} = 97.6 \text{ in.}$$

1.4.9.   The arch in Fig. 1.87* has the cross section in Fig. 1.74 whose properties are given in Problem 1.2.5. A horizontal earthquake load produces a bending moment

$$M_e = 500 \text{ k-ft}$$

on the arch's left end section. Draw the neutral axis and the diagram of the combined stresses due to M_L, R_L, and M_e.

Solution (Fig. 1.88).

$$\sigma_a = \frac{R_L}{A} = \frac{269}{870.5} = -0.31 \text{ k/in.}^2,$$

$$\sigma_b^{\text{bot}} = \frac{M_L}{I_y} z_{\text{bot}} = \frac{12(985)\, 25.4}{80,195} = -3.74 \text{ k/in.}^2,$$

$$\sigma_b^{\text{top}} = \frac{M_L}{I_y} z_{\text{top}} = \frac{12(985)\, 10.6}{80,195} = +1.56 \text{ k/in.}^2,$$

$$\sigma_b^l = \frac{M_e}{I_z} y_{\text{max}} = \frac{12(500)\, 36}{195,118} = +1.11 \text{ k/in.}^2,$$

$$\sigma_b^r = -1.11 \text{ k/in.}^2.$$

Temporarily disregarding earthquake bending, we obtain the neutral axis of the gravity stress combination (Fig. 1.88). Its intersection point P_1 with the z axis belongs to the final neutral axis, for earth-

---

*See G. de Campoli, *Statics of Structural Components* (New York: Wiley, 1983), Fig. 8.10, *passim.*

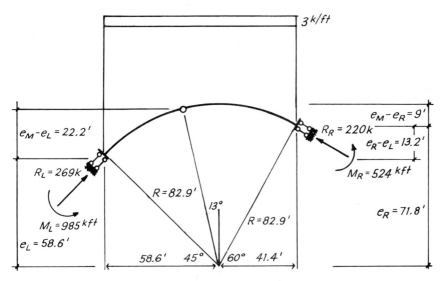

FIGURE 1.87.

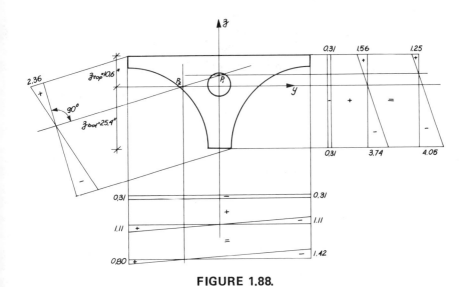

FIGURE 1.88.

quake bending also vanishes at this point. Temporarily disregarding gravity bending (but not gravity axial force), we obtain the neutral axis of combined earthquake bending and gravity axial stress. Its intersection point P_2 with the y axis belongs to the final neutral axis, for gravity bending also vanishes at this point. The final neutral axis is thus defined by P_1 and P_2. The baseline of the total stress combination is at $90°$ to $P_1 P_2$. The largest tensile stress is

$$\sigma_a + \sigma_b^{top} + \sigma_b^l = -0.31 + 1.56 + 1.11 = 2.36 \text{ k/in.}^2.$$

The largest compressive stress can be scaled on the diagram.

1.4.10. Check the neutral axis $P_1 P_2$ in Fig. 1.88 with the graphic method that uses eccentricities e_y, e_z and gyrators ρ_y and ρ_z. In addition, verify the graphic results with the Euclidean theorem (see Problems 1.4.4 and 1.4.8).

1.4.11. Perform the tasks in Problem 1.4.9 for the cross section at the right end of the arch. Assume the same value of the earthquake moment M_e. Note that the moment M_R in Fig. 1.87 produces tension at the bottom and compression at the top of the cross section in Fig. 1.74.

1.4.12. Check the neutral axis in the solution of Problem 1.4.11 with the graphic method that uses eccentricities e_y, e_z and gyrators ρ_y and ρ_z. In addition, verify the graphic results with the Euclidean theorem (see Problems 1.4.4 and 1.4.8).

1.4.13. Beams framing into a column, with the hollow cross section in Fig. 1.76, transfer an axial force

$$P = 25 \text{ k}$$

and bending moments

$$M_y = 36 \text{ k-ft,}$$

$$M_z = 50 \text{ k-ft.}$$

Find the following cross-sectional properties:

$$A, \quad I_y, \quad I_z, \quad \rho_y, \quad \rho_z.$$

Draw separate diagrams of axial stresses and bending stresses due to M_y and M_z. Draw the neutral axis and the diagram of combined stresses with both procedures practiced in the preceding problems.

1.4.14. A steel column has an I-shaped cross section with $1'' \times 9''$ flanges and $2'' \times 16''$ web. Beams framing into this column transfer an axial force

$$P = 50 \text{ k},$$

a bending moment around the web center line

$$M_z = 50 \text{ k-ft},$$

and a bending moment

$$M_y = 188 \text{ k-ft}.$$

Perform the tasks in Problem 1.4.13 for this column.

1.4.15. For the cross section in Fig. 1.72, find the following dimensions of the Kern region:

k_T outline coordinate on the upper z axis.
k_B outline coordinate on the lower z axis.
k_y outline coordinates on the y axis.

Solution (Figs. 1.89 and 1.90). The properties of the cross section are given in Problem 1.2.3. We use the Euclidean theorem to verify the graphic solution in Fig. 1.89:

$$k_B = \frac{\rho_z^2}{z_{\text{top}}} = \frac{(10.25)^2}{13} = 8.08 \text{ in.}$$

Analogously, we obtain

$$k_T = \frac{\rho_z^2}{z_{bot}} = \frac{(10.25)^2}{19} = 5.53 \text{ in.}$$

Verification of the graphic solution in Fig. 1.90 gives

$$k_y = \frac{\rho_y^2}{y_{max}} = \frac{(13.9)^2}{24} = 8.05 \text{ in.}$$

1.4.16. Perform graphically and numerically the tasks in Problem 1.4.15 for the cross section in Fig. 1.74. Use the properties in Problem 1.2.5.

1.4.17. Perform graphically and numerically the tasks in Problem 1.4.15 for the cross section in Fig. 1.76. Relevant cross-sectional properties must first be calculated unless available from the solution of Problem 1.4.11.

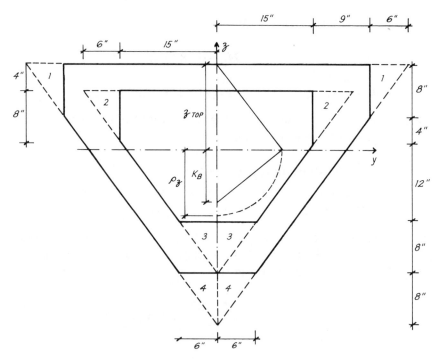

FIGURE 1.89.

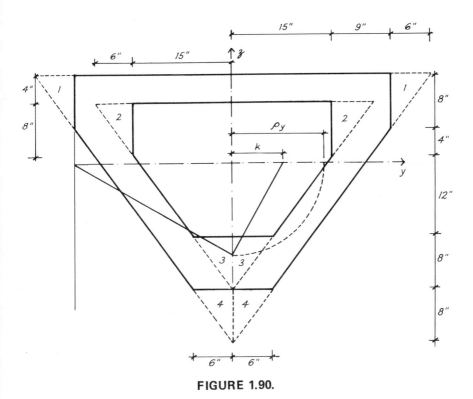

FIGURE 1.90.

1.4.18. Perform graphically and numerically the tasks in Problem 1.4.15 for the cross section in Problem 1.4.12.

1.4.19. Find the points of the Kern region's outline on the z axis of the cross section in Fig. 1.91.

Solution.

$$A = 2tB + \pi(R_0^2 - R_i^2) = 2(10) + \pi(5^2 - 4.5^2) = 34.9 \text{ in.}^2 \quad \text{(area)}.$$

$$I_y = \frac{B}{12}(H)^3 - \frac{B}{12}(H - 2t)^3 + \frac{\pi}{4}(R_0^4 - R_i^4) = \frac{10}{12}(12^3 - 10^3)$$

$$+ \frac{\pi}{4}(5^4 + 4.5^4) = 755 \text{ in.}^4 \quad \text{(moment of inertia)}.$$

$$\rho_z = \sqrt{\frac{I_y}{A}} = \sqrt{\frac{775}{34.9}} = 4.7 \text{ in.} \quad \text{(gyrator).}$$

$$k_z = \frac{p_z^2}{z_{\text{bot}}} = \frac{4.7^2}{6} = 3.68 \text{ in.} \quad \text{(answer).}$$

The graphic solution is shown in Fig. 1.91.

1.4.20. Find the points of the Kern region's outline on the y axis of the cross section in Fig. 1.91.

Solution.

Area (from Problem 1.4.19)

$$A = 34.9 \text{ in.}^2$$

Moment of inertia of a half large circle about its own diameter

$$I_0 = \frac{\pi}{8} R_0^4 = 245 \text{ in.}^4$$

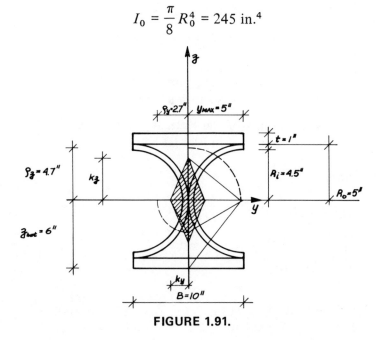

FIGURE 1.91.

Moment of inertia of a half large circle about its own centroidal axiz z_c

$$I_{0c} = I_0 - \frac{\pi}{2} R_0^2 \left(\frac{4R_0}{3\pi}\right)^2 = 245 - 177 = 68 \text{ in.}^4$$

Moment of inertia of a half large circle about the cross section's centroidal axis z

$$I_{0z} = I_{0c} + \frac{\pi}{2} R_0^2 (0.5756R_0)^2 = 68 + 325 = 393 \text{ in.}^4$$

Analogous properties for a small half circle

$$I_i = \frac{\pi}{8} R_i^4 = \frac{\pi}{8} (4.5)^4 = 161 \text{ in.}^4$$

$$I_{ic} = I_i - \frac{\pi}{2} R_i^2 \left(\frac{4R_i}{3\pi}\right)^2 = 45 \text{ in.},$$

$$I_{iz} = I_{ic} + \frac{\pi}{2} R_i^2 \left(R_0 - \frac{4R_i}{3\pi}\right)^2 = 349 \text{ in.}^4$$

Moment of inertia of half pipe about the z axis

$$I_{pz} = I_{0z} - I_{iz} = 44 \text{ in.}^4$$

Moment of inertia of complete section about the z axis

$$I_z = 2I_{pz} + 2 \frac{t}{12} (B)^3 = 2(44) + \frac{2}{12} (10)^3 = 255 \text{ in.}^4$$

Radius of gyration on the y axis

$$\rho_y = \sqrt{\frac{I_z}{A}} = \sqrt{\frac{255}{34.9}} = 2.7 \text{ in.}$$

Answer to the problem

$$k_y = \frac{\rho_y^2}{y_{max}} = \frac{2.7^2}{5} = 1.46 \text{ in.}$$

The graphic solution is shown in Fig. 1.91.

1.4.21. A bridge is supported on massive unreinforced concrete piers with the typical cross section shown in Fig. 1.92. The deck of the bridge transfers to the top of each 60-ft tall pier an axial force,

$$P_{top} = 500 \text{ k},$$

and a horizontal force in the z direction,

$$H = 12.5 \text{ k},$$

due to the breaking forces of vehicles that cross the bridge. Calculate the stresses on the base of a typical pier.

Solution. The area, moment of inertia, gyrator, and intermediate eccentricity of the cross section are as follows:

$$A = \pi(40)^2 + 40(80) = 8226 \text{ in.}^2, \text{ or } 57 \text{ ft}^2.$$

$$I_y = \frac{40}{12}(80)^3 + \frac{\pi}{4}(40)^4 = 3,717,286 \text{ in.}^4, \text{ or } 180 \text{ ft}^4.$$

$$\rho_z = \sqrt{\frac{I_y}{A}} = \sqrt{\frac{180}{57}} = 1.78 \text{ ft.}$$

$$k_z = \frac{\rho_z^2}{z_{max}} = \frac{(1.78)^2}{3.33} = 0.95 \text{ ft.}$$

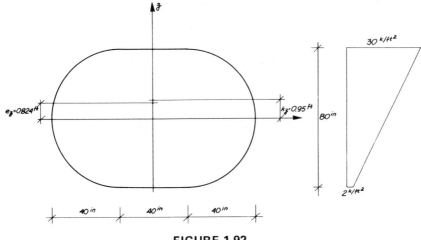

FIGURE 1.92.

The pier's self-weight, G_p, is calculated with the data

$$\gamma_c = 0.12 \text{ k/ft}^3, \quad \text{density of concrete,}$$

$$h = 60 \text{ ft}, \quad \text{height of pier.}$$

Thus

$$G_p = Ah\gamma_c = 57(60)\,0.12 = 410.4 \text{ k.}$$

The axial force P on the base is

$$P = P_{\text{top}} + G_p = 500 + 410.4 = 910.4 \text{ k}$$

The moment on the base is

$$M_y = hH = 60(12.5) = 750 \text{ k-ft.}$$

The eccentricity of P on the base is

$$e_z = \frac{M_y}{P} = \frac{750}{910.4} = 0.824 \text{ ft} < k_z.$$

Since the center of pressure is in the Kern region ($e_z < k_z$), the base section is not partialized. The extreme stresses are thus

$$\sigma = \frac{P}{A} \pm \frac{M_y}{I_y}\, z_{max} = \frac{910.4}{57} \pm \left(\frac{750}{180}\right)3.33 = 16 \pm 14 = \begin{array}{l} 30\ \text{k/ft}^2 \\ 2\ \text{k/ft}^2 \end{array}.$$

1.4.22. Determine the diagram of pressure on the foundation ground exerted by the footings of the symmetric frame in Fig. 1.93.

Solution.

Load discharged by the beam on each column

$$P_{top} = g\,\frac{l}{2} = \frac{2}{2}\,(20) = 20\ \text{k.}$$

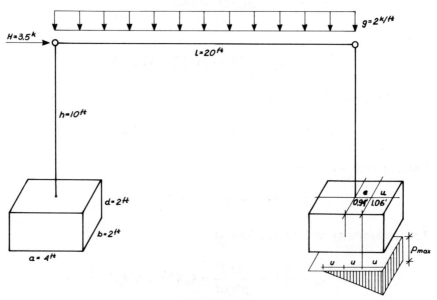

FIGURE 1.93.

Weight of a footing (use a concrete density $\gamma_c = 0.15$ k/ft³)

$$G_f = abd\gamma_c = 4(2)\,2(0.15) = 2.4 \text{ k.}$$

Axial force on the foundation

$$P = P_{\text{top}} + G_f = 20 + 2.4 = 22.4 \text{ k.}$$

Bending moment on the foundation:

$$M = \frac{H}{2}(h + d) = \frac{3.5}{2}(10 + 2) = 21 \text{ k-ft.}$$

Eccentricity of the axial force

$$e = \frac{M}{P} = \frac{21}{224} = 0.94 \text{ ft.}$$

Outline coordinate of Kern region

$$k = \frac{a}{6} = \frac{4}{6} = 0.67 \text{ ft} < e$$

The footing-ground contact area is partialized for $e > k$; thus

$$p_{\max} = \frac{2P}{3bu}.$$

Distance between center of pressure and compression edge

$$u = \frac{a}{2} - e = 2 - 0.94 = 1.06 \text{ ft.}$$

Thus

$$p_{\max} = \frac{2(22.4)}{3(2)\,1.06} = 7 \text{ k/ft}^2.$$

1.4.23. Perform the task in Problem 1.4.22 after doubling the gravity load on the beam.

1.4.24. Determine the diagrams of pressure on the foundation ground exerted by the footings of the frame in Fig. 1.94a.

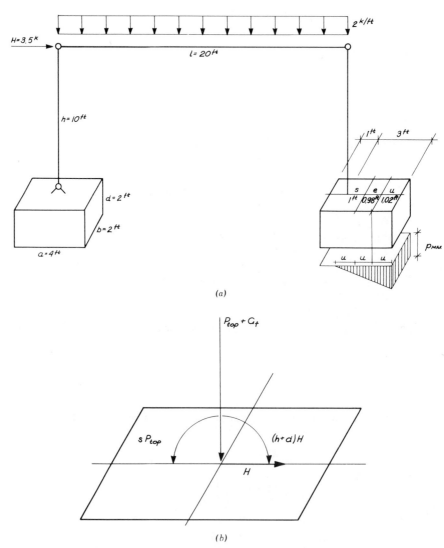

FIGURE 1.94.

Solution. The left column does not absorb any horizontal load. Thus the axial force P (calculated in Problem 1.4.20) produces a uniform pressure under the left footing

$$p = \frac{P}{ab} = \frac{22.4}{8} = 2.8 \text{ k/ft}^2.$$

The load P_{top} discharged by the beam on the right column is eccentric on the base of the footing. This is usually done to improve the stability of a footing threatened by a large overturning moment. P_{top}, however, can be shifted onto the center of the base area, provided the shift moment is considered. In this case the shift distance is 1 ft, and the shift moment is

$$sP_{top} = 1(20) = 20 \text{ k-ft counterclockwise.}$$

The moment of H on the base is

$$(d + h) H = 12(3.5) = 42 \text{ k-ft clockwise.}$$

Figure 1.94b shows all the forces and moments on the base of the footing. The total axial force is

$$P = P_{top} + G_f = 20 + 2.4 = 22.4 \text{ k.}$$

The total moment is

$$M = sP_{top} - (h + d) H = 20 - 42 = -22 \text{ k-ft clockwise.}$$

The eccentricity of P is

$$e = \frac{M}{P} = \frac{22}{22.4} = 0.982 \text{ ft.}$$

The outline coordinate of the Kern region is

$$\frac{a}{6} = \frac{4}{6} = 0.67 < e.$$

Thus the largest pressure on the foundation is

$$p_{max} = \frac{2P}{3b[(a/2) - e]} = \frac{2(22.4)}{(3)\,2(2 - 0.982)} = 7.335 \text{ k/ft}^2.$$

We note that due to the eccentricity of the column on the footing, the preceding value of p_{max} is not much greater than that in Fig. 1.93, while the overturning moment is twice as large.

The sliding stability of the footing must also be checked. This is done by checking that the resisting force (product of P with the frictional coefficient) exceeds the value of H.

1.4.25. Repeat the task in Problem 1.4.24 with a horizontal force $H = 3$ k and an eccentricity of the column $s = 1.25$ ft.

1.4.26. For the frame in Fig. 1.95, design two equal footings with sides a, b, d such that the contact with the foundation ground is over the entire base of a footing. Use concrete density $\gamma_c = 0.15$ k/ft^3. Do not exceed a pressure of 10 k/ft^2.

1.4.27. Reduce the size of the footings in the solution of Problem 1.4.26 by allowing partialization of the contact area; the same specifications apply.

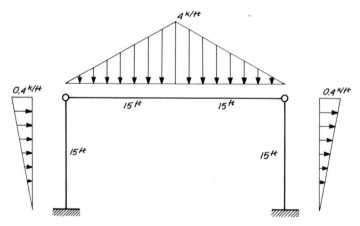

FIGURE 1.95.

1.4.28. Using the footings from the solution of Problem 1.4.26, reduce the largest pressure by 20% by placing the columns eccentrically on the footings.

1.5.1. Find the lever arm Z of the resisting moment and the largest shear stress τ_s^{max} on the section of the beam in Problem 1.2.1.

Solution.

Step 4: The moment Q_{max} of the compression (or tension) zone of the cross section about the centroidal axis is

$$Q_{max} = \frac{\pi}{8} D_0^2 \left(\frac{4D_0}{6\pi}\right) - \frac{\pi}{8} D_i^2 \left(\frac{4D_i}{6\pi}\right) = \frac{1}{12} (D_0^3 - D_i^3)$$

$$= \frac{1}{12} (12.75^3 - 12^3) = 28.7 \text{ in.}^3$$

Thus

$$Z = \frac{I}{Q_{max}} = \frac{279.3}{28.7} = 9.73 \text{ in.}$$

The width b of the steel measured on the centroidal axis is

$$b = D_0 - D_i = 0.75 \text{ in.}$$

Step 5: Since the largest shear force on the beam is $V = 10.4$ k (Fig. 1.70) then

$$\tau_s^{max} = \frac{V}{bZ} = \frac{10.4}{0.75(9.73)} = 1.4 \text{ k/in.}^2.$$

1.5.2. Find the largest shear stress on the beam in Problem 1.2.2.

Solution. Rounding the required beam depth of 15.79 in. to 16 in., the measurements of the cross section are

$$b = 7.5 \text{ in}, \quad d = 16 \text{ in}.$$

Step 4: The cross-sectional area is

$$A = bd = 7.5(16) = 120 \text{ in.}^2$$

Step 5: The largest shear force is $V = 10.4$ k (Fig. 1.70). Thus

$$\tau_s^{max} = \frac{3V}{2A} = \frac{3(10.4)}{2(120)} = 0.13 \text{ k/in.}^2.$$

1.5.3. Find the shear stresses on the cross section in Problem 1.2.3 at the coordinates $z = 9$ in., $z = 5$ in., $z = 0$ in., $z = -11$ in.

Solution.

Step 4: The area above the coordinate $z = 9$ in. is $48(4) = 192$ in.^{2}

Its moment about the y axis is $192(11) = 2112$ in.^{3}
The width of concrete at $z = 9$ in. is 18 in.
The area above the coordinate $z = 5$ in. is $48(8) - 30(4) = 264$ in.^{2}
Its moment about the y axis is $384(9) - 120(7) = 2616$ in.^{3}
The width of concrete at $z = 5$ in. is 18 in.
The area below the coordinate $z = -11$ in. is $12(8) + 6(8) = 144$ in.^{2}
Its moment about the y axis is $-96(15) - 48(13.67) = -2096$ in.^{3}
The width of concrete at $z = -11$ in. is 12 in.
From Problem 1.2.3, $Z = 22.9$ in., $I_y = 64{,}536$ in.^{4}

Step 5: From Fig. 1.71, $V = 27.5$k.

The shear stress at $z = 9$ in. is

$$\tau_{s9} = \frac{27.5(2112)}{64{,}536(18)} = 0.05 \text{ k/in.}^2$$

The shear stress at $z = 5$ in. is

$$\tau_{s5} = \frac{27.5(2616)}{64{,}536(18)} = 0.062 \text{ k/in.}^2.$$

The shear stress on the y axis

$$\tau_s^{max} = \frac{27.5}{22.9(12)} = 0.1 \text{ k/in.}^2.$$

The shear stress at $z = -11$ in. is

$$\tau_{s11} = \frac{27.5(2096)}{64{,}536(12)} = 0.074 \text{ k/in.}^2.$$

1.5.4. Use the largest shear force on the beam in Problem 1.2.6 and find τ_s^{max} on its cross section.

1.5.5. Perform the task in Problem 1.5.4 for the beam in Problem 1.2.8.

1.5.6. Show with a complete diagram the distribution of shear stress τ_s on the left end section of the beam in Problem 1.2.10.

1.5.7. Use the largest shear force and the cross section of the beam in Problem 1.2.12 to find the largest shear stress τ_s^{max} on the beam.

1.5.8. Find the shear force at the fixed end of the beam in Problem 1.2.5. From a scale drawing of its cross section (Fig. 1.74) measure the width b of structural material at $z = 0$ in., $z = 4.6$ in., $z = 6.6$ in., $z = -7.4$ in. Find the values of the shear stresses at the preceding coordinates.

1.5.9. Find the shear stress at $z = 0$ on the cross section in Problem 1.4.19 using a shear force $V = 100$ k.

Solution. The moment of the compression or tension zone about y is

$$Q_{max} = tB \left(\frac{H}{2} - \frac{t}{2}\right) + \frac{\pi}{2} R_0^2 \left(\frac{4R_0}{3\pi}\right) - \frac{\pi}{2} R_i^2 \left(\frac{4R_i^2}{3\pi}\right)$$

$$= 1(10)5.5 + \frac{2}{3}(5^3 - 4.5^3) = 77.6 \text{ in.}^3$$

The lever arm of the resisting moment is

$$Z = \frac{I_y}{Q_{max}} = \frac{775}{77.6} = 10 \text{ in.}$$

Thus

$$\tau_{s0} = \frac{V}{bZ} = \frac{100}{1(10)} = 10 \text{ k/in.}^2.$$

1.6.1. Find the maximum horizontal shear stress in the flanges of the beam in Problem 1.2.10.

Solution. The beam's cross section has two axes of symmetry; thus the shear stresses are equal in all four outstanding flange legs. The thickness of one such leg is 1 in., the length Δy_{max} is 4.25 in., the area $\bar{A}$ is 4.25 in.^{2}, its distance $z_{\bar{A}}$ to the y axis (centroidal) is 8.5 in., and its moment $Q_{\bar{A}}$ is 36.125 in.^{3} Thus the largest flange stress at the connection with the web is

$$\tau_{max}^h = \frac{V_{max} Q_{\bar{A}}}{I_y t} = \frac{25.86(36.125)}{1473(1)} = 0.63 \text{ k/in.}^2,$$

where I_y is the cross section's moment of inertia about the horizontal centroidal axis given by

$$I_y = \frac{9}{12}(18)^3 - \frac{8.5}{12}(16)^3 = 1473 \text{ in.}^4$$

The shear stress in the flange decreases linearly and vanishes at the tip.

1.6.2. Find the maximum shear stress in the flanges of the cross section in Problem 1.4.20 due to a shear force V_y = 100 k. Assume that contact between the half pipes occurs at a point.

Solution. The moment of one-fourth of the cross section about the z axis is

$$Q_{z\bar{A}} = t\,\frac{B}{2}\,\frac{B}{4} + \frac{\pi}{4}R_0^2(0.5756R_0) - \frac{\pi}{4}R_i^2(0.5 + 0.5756R_i) = 19.85 \text{ in.}^3$$

Due to the assumption of single point contact between pipes at the centroid, the thickness of material cut by the upper (or lower) z semiaxis is the same as the flange thickness t. Thus

$$\tau_s = \frac{VQ_{z\bar{A}}}{I_z t} = \frac{100(19.85)}{255(1)} = 7.78 \text{ k/in.}^2.$$

1.6.3. Find the maximum horizontal shear stress in the flanges of the cross section in Fig. 1.96 due to a vertical shear force V = 100 k.

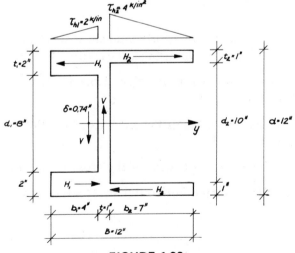

FIGURE 1.96.

Solution. The moment of inertia about the y axis is

$$I_y = \frac{B}{12} d^3 - \frac{b_1}{12} d_1^3 - \frac{b_2}{12} d_2^3 = (12)^3 - \frac{4}{12}(8)^3 - \frac{7}{12}(10)^3 = 974 \text{ in.}^4$$

The moment $Q_{\bar{A}1}$ of the left leg of a flange about the y axis is

$$Q_{\bar{A}1} = t_1 b_1 \left(\frac{d_1}{2} + \frac{t_1}{2} \right) = 2(4)5 = 40 \text{ in.}^3$$

The analogous moment of the right leg is

$$Q_{\bar{A}2} = \frac{t_2 b_2}{2} (d_2 + t_2) = 7(5.5) = 38.5 \text{ in.}^3$$

Thus the maximum stresses in the diagrams of Fig. 1.96 are

$$\tau_{h1} = \frac{V Q_{\bar{A}1}}{I_y t_1} = \frac{100(40)}{974(2)} = 2.05 \text{ k/in.}^2,$$

$$\tau_{h2} = \frac{V Q_{\bar{A}2}}{I_y t_2} = \frac{100(38.5)}{974} = 3.95 \text{ k/in.}^2.$$

1.6.4. Find the maximum horizontal shear stress in a flange of the beam in Fig. 1.97a, using a shear force $V = 100$ k.

1.6.5. Perform the task in Problem 1.6.4 for the cross section in Fig. 1.97b.

1.6.6. Perform the tasks in Problem 1.6.3 for the cross section in Fig. 1.97c.

1.7.1. Find the center of shear of the cross section in Fig. 1.96.

Solution. The average horizontal shear stress in the thin leg of a flange is

$$\frac{1}{2} \tau_{h2} = 2 \text{ k/in.}^2.$$

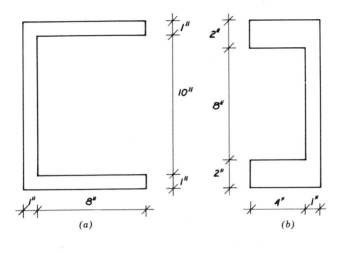

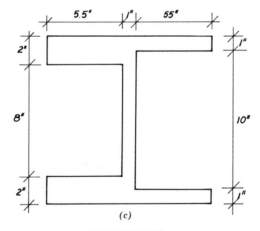

FIGURE 1.97.

Thus the horizontal force on this flange is

$$H_2 = \frac{1}{2} \tau_{h2} t_2 b_2 = 2(1)7 = 14 \text{ k}.$$

The moment of the couple of forces H_2 is

$$T_2 = H_2(d_2 + t_2) = 14(11) = 154 \text{ k-in.} \quad \text{(clockwise)}.$$

Analogously, we obtain for the thick flanges

$$H_1 = \frac{1}{2} \tau_{h1} t_1 b_1 = 1(2)4 = 8 \text{ k,}$$

$$T_1 = H_1 (d_1 + t_1) = 8(10) = 80 \text{ k-in.} \quad \text{(counterclockwise).}$$

The resultant moment is

$$T = T_2 - T_1 = 154 - 80 = 74 \text{ k-in.} \quad \text{(clockwise).}$$

To neutralize this twisting moment, the 100 k shear force must have a line of action on the left of the 100 k resultant of shear stresses in the web, at a distance δ such that the moment $V\delta$ of this couple be the same as T. Thus from

$$V\delta = T,$$

we obtain

$$\delta = \frac{T}{V} = \frac{74}{100} = 0.74.$$

δ does not depend on the shear V that appears both in the denominator and in the numerator through τ_{h1} and τ_{h2}.

1.7.2. Find the center of shear for the cross section in Problem 1.6.4.

1.7.3. Find the center of shear for the cross section in Problem 1.6.5.

1.7.4. Find the center of shear for the cross section in Problem 1.6.6.

1.7.5. Find the center of shear for the cross section in Fig. 1.98.

Solution. The resultants of the shear stresses in the two equal legs have horizontal components that neutralize each other. The vertical components are equal and colinear. Their sum equals the ap-

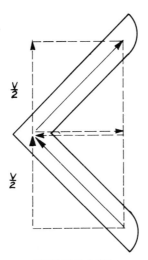

FIGURE 1.98.

plied shear V. To avoid twisting moment on the section, the applied shear must have their same line of action. Thus the center of shear is at the intersection of the leg's center lines.

1.8.1. The cross section in Fig. 1.72 is not exactly round. Regardless, find the torsional stresses in the flanges due to a moment $T = 100$ k-ft, with the formula for round sections. These stresses are later compared with those given by other formulas (see discussion in Problem 1.8.4).

Solution. From Problem 1.2.3, we obtain

$$I_p = 182{,}562 \text{ in.}^4$$

Thus

$$\tau_t^{top} = \frac{T}{I_p} z_{top} = \frac{100(12)13}{182{,}562} = 0.085 \text{ k/in.}^2,$$

$$\tau_t^{bot} = \frac{100(12)19}{182{,}562} = 0.125 \text{ k/in.}^2.$$

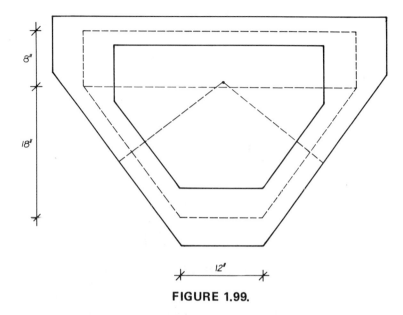

FIGURE 1.99.

1.8.2. The cross section in Fig. 1.72 is not exactly thin walled. Regardless, perform the task in Problem 1.8.1 with the formula for thin-walled shafts (see discussion in Problem 1.8.4).

Solution. The area within the center line of the wall is (Fig. 1.99)

$$\bar{A} = 39(8) + 0.5(39 + 12)18 = 744 \text{ in.}^2$$

Thus

$$\tau_t^{\text{top}} = \frac{T}{2\bar{A}t_{\text{top}}} = \frac{100(12)}{2(4)744} = 0.202 \text{ k/in.}^2,$$

$$\tau_t^{\text{bot}} = \frac{100(12)}{2(8)744} = 0.101 \text{ k/in.}^2.$$

1.8.3. Perform the task in Problem 1.8.1 for the side walls of the cross section.

Solution.   The distance of the centroid from the outline of the side walls, measured at 90° to the walls, is 16.2 in. (verify it on a scale drawing). Thus

$$\tau_t = \frac{100(12)16.2}{182,522} = 0.106 \text{ k/in.}^2.$$

1.8.4.   Perform the task in Problem 1.8.2 for the side walls of the cross section.

Solution.   The thickness of the side walls is 4.8 in. (verify it on a scale drawing). Thus

$$\tau_t = \frac{100(12)}{2(4.8)744} = 0.168 \text{ k/in.}^2.$$

We now turn to a discussion of the results of Problems 1.8.1 through 1.8.4. The use of two different formulas yields the results summarized in the following table:

Place	Top Flange	Bottom Flange	Side Walls
rT/I_p	0.085	0.125	0.106
$T/2t\bar{A}$	0.202	0.101	0.168
Average	0.144	0.113	0.137

The formula for thin-walled shafts yields larger stress values on most of the cross section. Since the wall that concerns us is not thin, using the area within the wall centerline for $\bar{A}$ leaves out a considerable area, actually most of the centrifugal zones which increase the value of I_p and therefore reduce rT/I_p. The reason for the reversal in the magnitude of the flange stresses between first and second row in the table is the high position of the centroid. This reduces the radial distance r and the stress of the top fibers and increases the radial distance and the stress of the bottom fibers. In round sections these values are of course the same. In the formula of thin-walled shafts (second row) the radial distance of the fibers is not influential. The wall thickness becomes influential instead. Its small value in the top flange produces large stress locally. Its large value in the bottom flange produces small stress locally. In the author's opinion, the values in the third line of the table represent a realistic and reliable appraisal of the torsional stresses.

1.8.5.   Using the formula for thin-walled shafts, find the torsional stresses due to a 30 k-ft torque on the section in Fig. 1.91.

Solution.   The area within the centerline of the wall is

$$\bar{A} = B(d - t) - \pi \left(\frac{R_0 + R_i}{2} \right)^2 = 10(11) - \pi(1.75)^2 = 39 \text{ in.}^2$$

Thus in the pipe's wall the stress is

$$\frac{30(12)}{2(0.5)39} = 9.23 \text{ k/in.}^2.$$

In the flanges the stress is

$$\frac{30(12)}{2(1)39} = 4.62 \text{ k/in.}^2.$$

1.8.6.   Using the formula for thin-walled shafts, find the torsional stress due to a 60 k-ft torque on the section in Fig. 1.76.

1.8.7.   Find the maximum torsional stress due to 15 k-ft torque on the cross section in Fig. 1.97c.

Solution.   The section is made of the following rectangles:

Left flange legs

$$b = 2 \text{ in.,} \quad d = 5.5 \text{ in.}$$

Right flange legs

$$b = 1 \text{ in.,} \quad d = 5.5 \text{ in.}$$

Web

$$b = 1 \text{ in.}, \quad d = 12 \text{ in.}$$

Thus,

$$\sum_{i=1}^{5} d_i b_i^3 = 5.5(2)^3 2 + 5.5(1)^3 2 + 12(1)^3 = 111 \text{ in.}^4,$$

with which

$$\tau_t^{\max} = \frac{3 T b_{\max}}{\sum d_i b_i^3} = \frac{3(15)12(2)}{111} = 9.73 \text{ k/in.}^2.$$

1.8.8. Perform the task in Problem 1.8.7 for the cross section in Fig. 1.96.

1.8.9. Perform the task in Problem 1.8.7 for the cross section in Fig. 1.97a.

1.8.10. Perform the task in Problem 1.8.7 for the cross section in Fig. 1.97b.

1.9.1. Find the diagonal stresses and their inclination on the left end cross section of the beam in Problems 1.2.3 and 1.5.3 at the coordinate $z = 9$ in.

Solution.

$$\sigma_{b9} = \frac{262.5(12)9}{64,356} = -0.425 \text{ k/in.}^2,$$

$$\tau_{s9} = 0.05 \text{ k/in.}^2.$$

Thus

$$\tau_{\max, \min} = \pm \frac{1}{2} \sqrt{\sigma_{b9}^2 + 4\tau_{s9}^2}$$

$$= \pm \frac{1}{2} \sqrt{(0.425)^2 + 4(0.05)^2} = \pm 0.218 \text{ k/in.}^2$$

$$\sigma_{max} = -\frac{0.425}{2} - 0.218 = -0.43 \text{ k/in.}^2,$$

$$\sigma_{min} = -0.425 + 0.218 = +0.006 \text{ k/in.}^2.$$

The inclinations of the planes on which σ attains its extremal values are given by

$$\theta = \frac{1}{2} \arctan \frac{2\tau_{s9}}{\sigma_{b9}} = \frac{1}{2} \arctan 0.2353 = 6.62°$$

and

$$\theta + 90° = 96.62°.$$

The planes on which τ is extremal bisect the principal planes.

1.9.2. Perform the tasks in Problem 1.9.1 at the coordinate $z = 5$ in.

1.9.3. Perform the tasks in Problem 1.9.1 at the coordinate $z = -11$ in.

1.9.4. Perform the tasks in Problem 1.9.1 for the beam in Problems 1.2.10 and 1.5.6 at the coordinate $z = 8$ in.

1.9.5. Obtain the results in Problem 1.9.1 with a Mohr circle.

1.9.6. Obtain the results in Problem 1.9.2 with a Mohr circle.

1.9.7. Obtain analogous results as in Problem 1.9.1 at $z = 0$ with a Mohr circle.

Solution. The reason for 45° cracks in concrete beams near failure can be seen in Fig. 1.100. The Mohr circle shows that in zones free of bending but not of shear, that is, at the centroid of sections near the beam ends, the tensile diagonal stress acts at 45°.

1.9.8. Obtain the results in Problem 1.9.3 with a Mohr circle.

1.10.1. Check the preliminary design of the truss in Problem 1.1.2 by accepting (a) or rejecting (r) the pipes used for the compression bars. The safe stress is 0.5 of critical stress.

Solution. The answers are in the last column of the following table:

Bar	P (k)	l (in.)	$2R_0$ (in.)	A (in.^{2})	ρ (in.)	kl/ρ	$0.5E\pi^2/(kl/\rho)^2$ (k/in.^{2})	P/A (k/in.^{2})	a/r
1-2	10	104	2.375	1.075	0.787	132	8.2	9.3	r
2-3	4.75	60	1.66	0.669	0.54	111	11.6	7.1	a
3-4	6.95	60	1.66	0.669	0.54	111	11.6	10.4	a
4-5	6.95	60	1.66	0.669	0.54	111	11.6	10.4	a
5-6	6.3	60	1.66	0.669	0.54	111	11.6	9.4	a
6-7	1.0	60	0.54	0.125	0.164	366	1.1	8.0	r
7-8	1.0	60	0.54	0.125	0.164	366	1.1	8.0	r
13-1	2.0	60	0.84	0.25	0.261	230	2.7	8.0	r
13-3	3.87	104	1.66	0.669	0.54	193	3.8	5.8	r
12-4	5.0	104	1.66	0.669	0.54	193	3.8	7.5	r
11-5	1.13	104	0.54	0.125	0.164	634	0.4	9.0	r
10-6	9.13	104	2.375	1.075	0.787	132	8.2	8.5	r

1.10.2 Redesign the bars rejected in Problem 1.10.1.

Solution. The task is performed with the aid of the following table:

Bar	P (k)	l (in.)	$2R_0$ (in.)	A (in.²)	ρ (in.)	kl/ρ	$0.5E\pi^2/(kl/\rho)^2$ (k/in.²)	P/A (k/in.²)
1-2	10	104	2.875	1.7	0.947	109.8	11.9	5.9
6-7	1.0	60	1.05	0.333	0.334	179.6	4.4	3
7-8	1.0	60	1.05	0.333	0.334	179.6	4.4	3
13-1	2.0	60	1.315	0.494	0.421	142.5	7.0	4
13-3	3.87	104	1.900	0.799	0.623	166.9	5.1	4.8
12-4	5.0	104	2.375	1.07	0.787	132	8.2	4.7
11-5	1.13	104	1.315	0.494	0.421	247	2.4	2.3
10-6	9.13	104	2.875	1.7	0.947	109.8	11.9	5.4

1.10.3. Perform the tasks in Problem 1.10.1 for the truss in Problem 1.1.3.

1.10.4. Perform the tasks in Problem 1.10.2 for the truss in Problen 1.1.3. Obtain cross-sectional properties from the handbook of Steel Construction of the American Institute of

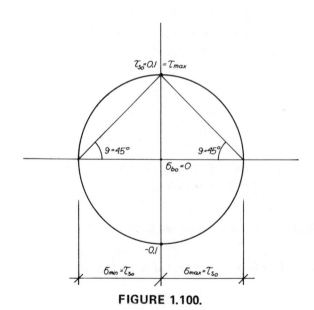

FIGURE 1.100.

Steel Construction, or use the best approximation among the pipe properties in Problem 1.1.3.

1.10.5. The roof of a museum rests on niched walls made of 30 ft high precast elements with the cross section shown in Fig. 1.74. The roof does not provide any restraint for an element's top section and discharges on it an axial force

$$P = 2000 \text{ k}.$$

The wall elements are fixed in the foundation. Neglecting an element's self-weight, find the buckling safety coefficient P_{cr}/P, with the cross-sectional properties in Problem 1.2.5 and a Young's modulus $E = 3000$ k/in.^{2}

Solution.

$$P_{cr} = \frac{EA^2}{(kh/\rho_z)^2} = \frac{3000(870.5)\pi^2}{(2 \times 360/9.6)^2} = 4582 \text{ k}$$

Thus

$$\frac{P_{cr}}{P} = \frac{4582}{2000} = 2.3.$$

1.10.6. Assume that structural cores around vertical circulation shafts restrain the roof in Problem 1.10.5 from displacing horizontally. The roof in turn so restrains the wall elements. Find the new safety coefficient P_{cr}/P.

1.10.7. The left column of the portal in Fig. 1.94a is made of a $5\frac{1}{2}'' \times 7\frac{1}{2}''$ timber. Using a Young's modulus $E = 1800$ k/in.^{2}, find the buckling safety coefficient P_{cr}/P.

Solution. The least gyrator is $5.5/\sqrt{12} = 1.59$ in.; thus

$$P_{cr} = \frac{EA\pi^2}{(kh/\rho_{min})^2} = \frac{1800(41.25)\pi^2}{(120/1.59)^2} = 128 \text{ k},$$

$$\frac{P_{cr}}{P} = \frac{128}{20} = 6.4.$$

1.10.8. Disregard the 3.5 k horizontal earthquake load on the frame in Fig. 1.94a. Use a $5\frac{1}{2}'' \times 7\frac{1}{2}''$ timber for the right column and a Young's modulus $E = 1800$ k/in.^{2} Find the buckling safety coefficient P_{cr}/P of the right column.

1.10.9. Disregard the horizontal wind load on the frame in Fig. 1.93. Using the cross section in Fig. 1.76 (whose properties are given in Problem 1.2.6) for the steel columns, find the buckling safety coefficient P_{cr}/P.

Solution.

$$P_{cr} = \frac{EI_{min}\pi^2}{(kh)^2} = \frac{29000(139.6)\pi^2}{(2 \times 180)^2} = 308 \text{ k,}$$

$$\frac{P_{cr}}{P} = \frac{308}{30} = 10.2.$$

1.10.10. Assume that diagonal bracing restrains the horizontal displacement of the top sections of the columns in Problem 1.10.9. Find the new safety coefficient P_{cr}/P.

1.10.11. The roof of an exhibition hall rests on 40 ft tall columns with the cross section in Fig. 1.72. The columns are fixed in the foundation. The roof does not restrain the top section of the columns and discharges on each of them an axial load $P = 1000$ k. Find the buckling safety coefficient P_{cr}/P with the properties in Problem 1.2.3 and $E = 3000$ k/in.^{2}

Solution.

$$P_{cr} = \frac{EA\pi^2}{(kh/\rho_z)^2} = \frac{3000(612)\pi^2}{[2(480/10.25]^2} = 2066 \text{ k,}$$

$$\frac{P_{cr}}{P} = \frac{2066}{1000} = 2.07.$$

1.10.12. Assume that the roof beams of the hall in Problem 1.10.11 are much more rigid than the columns and are continuous with them, so that the top sections of the columns cannot rotate. Assume also that structural cores around vertical circulation shafts prevent horizontal displacement of the roof, so the top sections of the columns cannot displace. Find the buckling safety coefficient of the columns in this case.

TWO

STRESS–STRAIN
RELATIONS

Stresses at 90° to the typical cross section of structural elements, such as the axial stress σ_a and the bending stress σ_b, produce shrinkage or elongation of the longitudinal fibers of structural materials. The shortening or extension of a fiber segment, initially with unit length, is called the longitudinal fiber strain ϵ. Thus, if the original length L of a bar, pulled at both ends by axial forces P, increases in the amount ΔL, the strain of the longitudinal fibers is

$$\epsilon = \frac{\Delta L}{L}.$$

The relation of the strains to the stresses is obtained with laboratory tests on specimens of structural materials. The size and form of the specimens, as well as the type of test, vary with the materials. In every case the testing apparatus provides a graph of the function $\sigma = \sigma(\epsilon)$, that is, a curve on which for a given value of the stress σ one can find the corresponding value of the strain ϵ and vice versa.

In the case of steel a bar with known cross section A and initial length L is pulled in the testing machine with increasing axial forces P. The values of P and of the stress P/A are known at any given time through the pressure in the hydraulic mechanism of the testing machine. As the stress gradually increases and the bar extends, a marker traces a continuous curve on mesh paper wrapped around a rotating

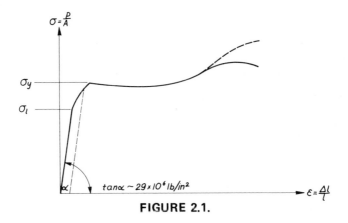

FIGURE 2.1.

drum (Fig. 2.1). In compression tests steel behaves the same as in tension tests. Thus the curve $\sigma = \sigma(\epsilon)$ has the same shape, if buckling does not occur, in the first quadrant of its Cartesian frame (positive σ and ϵ) and in the third quadrant (negative σ and ϵ). Both curves start at the origin ($\epsilon = 0$ when $\sigma = 0$) with a straight segment very close to the σ axis. The slope of this segment is called Young's modulus E of the material

$$E = \frac{\sigma}{\epsilon}.$$

A tough structural material such as steel has a high Young modulus ($E_s = 29,000$ k/in.^{2}) because the strain ϵ is small under large stress σ. A soft material such as wood has low Young modulus (i.e. $E_w = 1800$ k/in.^{2}) because the deformation is considerable even under stresses comparatively lower. The linear part of the steel stress-strain plot is followed by a curve along which the strains grow more than linearly as the stress increases. At this stage of the test the specimen shows elastic-plastic behavior. Indeed, if the hydraulic pressure in the machine and the pull P on the bar are lowered before the stress reaches the linear limit σ_L, the strains diminish, following the straight segment through the origin, and vanish completely if P vanishes (elastic behavior). If the elastic limit σ_L is exceeded, lowering the pressure produces a reduction in the strains according to a linear law (dotted line of Fig. 2.1). This time, however, the straight path of the stress-strain values starts with the largest stress and strain attained in the bar, descends with slope E, and ends away from the origin on the ϵ axis. This indicates that part of the deformation has vanished with the stress (elastic part) while another part is permanent (plastic). Along the curved portion of the stress-strain plot, the slope of the curve $d\sigma/d\epsilon$ diminishes as the stress increases, that is, the material becomes gradually softer and equal increments of stress produce larger and larger increments of strain. Continuing to increase the stress finally produces an abrupt change in the slope of the curve (a cuspid). At this point the slope $d\sigma/d\epsilon$ becomes zero, that is, the material becomes completely soft and the strain increases without any increment $d\sigma$. The stress that produces this behavior is called the yield stress, or the strength of the structural material. The stress-strain curve of steel and other ductile materials shows an extended horizontal tract corresponding to the yield stress, that is, the deformation of a ductile structure must be much larger than that at its first yielding before disintegration occurs.

Ductility is thus a desirable quality of structural materials. Indeed, when the stress reaches the yield value in some fibers of a structural element or in some element of a frame, its ductility prevents collapse. Under additional loads the stress flow avoids the yield zone (where the material has been weakened and cannot offer resistance) and finds new channels within the structure in transferring the loads to the constraints. This is impossible of course if every element and every connection of the structure is essential to its stability because there are no alternate routes of transfer. Moreover in the case of great deformations due to exceptional loads, such as earthquake forces, a ductile structure needs to be less strong to remain coherent than a structure unable to deform plastically. Indeed a material that lacks horizontal tract on the stress-strain curve (brittle material) needs the stress capacity σ^* in Fig. 2.2 to tolerate the large strain ϵ^* while remaining coherent.

The last part of the stress-strain curve of Fig. 2.1 shows that the stress increases just before the breaking of the material. The increase is moderate, and it is not caused by an increased load capacity of the test bar, rather by a reduction of the cross-sectional area that becomes conspicuous near the breaking of the bar. Thus the stress P/A increases for the reduction of A.

The thinning that accompanies the stretching of structural materials, most conspicuous in a rubber band, is called the Poisson effect.

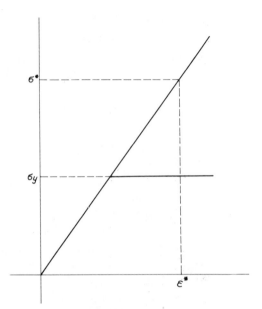

FIGURE 2.2.

The transversal strain is evidently not caused by transversal stresses that are lacking on the lateral surface of a stretched rubber band and therefore across its exiguous thickness. Moreover the transversal strain has opposite sign and is much smaller than the longitudinal strain. The ratio between transversal and longitudinal strains is called the Poisson ratio ν:

$$\nu = \frac{\epsilon_t}{\epsilon_l}.$$

The Poisson ratio of steel equals approximately 0.3, that is, the transversal thinning that accompanies the longitudinal extension or the transversal thickening that accompanies the longitudinal contraction is only 30% of the longitudinal deformation.

The stress-strain curve of concrete is obtained with a compression test on a 12 in. high cylindrical specimen 6 in. in diameter. Concrete is a structural material almost ten times stronger in compression than in tension. Thus its limited tensile strength is often completely dismissed, and only the behavior in compression is investigated. Indeed,

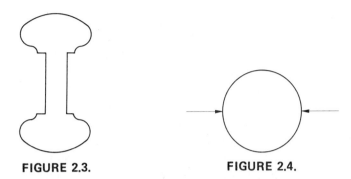

FIGURE 2.3.   FIGURE 2.4.

the transfer of tensile stresses in concrete flexural members is entrusted to reinforcing steel rods.

In cases where the tensile strength of concrete is important, for
example, in waterproof structures, it can be appraised with the help
of tests on specimens of cement mortar (sand and cement paste)
shaped as in Fig. 2.3. This shape permits an easy grasp in the test
machine. However, a complete stress-strain curve, extending in the
tension quadrant of the σ, ϵ Cartesian frame as well as in the compression quadrant, requires testing of identical concrete specimens
in both tension and compression. The traction test is then performed
indirectly by splitting a 12 in. long cylindrical specimen 6 in. in diameter with diametrally opposed compressive forces (Fig. 2.4).
Under these conditions the specimen fails by spalling off concrete
in a direction at 90° to the forces.

The compression branch of the σ, ϵ curve is different from the
tension branch (Fig. 2.5) since concrete behaves like a softer material (lesser slopes $d\sigma/d\epsilon$) and a weaker one (lower strength) under
traction than it does under compression. The curve in Fig. 2.5 lacks
a horizontal (plastic) tract, and the initial rectilinear tract is very
short. Its slope, Young's modulus of concrete E_c, is considerably less
than the steel modulus E_s (E_c = 3000 to 4000 k/in.^{2}) but larger than
the modulus of wood E_w. Thus the compressive strain of concrete
increases proportionally to the stress only for moderate stress values,
and then concrete starts behaving like a softening material (decreasing slope $d\sigma/d\epsilon$) and crashes rather suddenly as the stress reaches its
yield value. Concrete, however, makes an excellent structural material
if reinforced by steel rods for the transfer of tensile stresses, and by
steel cages that delay its disintegration under compression by con-

straining it in an armor of stronger material. The convenient features of concrete are its shapability before hardening and its compressive strength. On the one hand, the value of concrete's strength (approximately one-eighth of steel's strength) requires heftier structural elements. On the other hand, bulkier structures are less prone to buckle. Moreover concrete is a less deformable material because its strain σ_c/E_c under working stresses is approximately one-half of the steel strain σ_s/E_s under working stresses. Concrete is also considerably stronger than natural structural materials like wood and stone, and some man-made materials such as brick. The Poisson coefficient of concrete has approximately the value 0.1.

While axial and bending stresses produce strains ϵ in the longitudinal fibers, and transversal strains $\nu\epsilon$ at 90° to the fibers, that preserve the 90° angle between the typical cross section and the fibers of material, shear and torsional stresses alter the 90° angle. This is readily seen by holding a pack of playing cards between the palms of one's hands with fingertips up and then moving the hands vertically, one up and one down. The side elevation of the pack, initially rectangular, deforms into a rhombus (Fig. 7.7). Thus the top and bottom lines of the elevation, initially at 90° to a typical card, form, after deformation, acute or obtuse angles with the cards. The change in the 90° angle is called angular strain. Deforming a stack of playing cards by twisting it, as in Fig. 1.2, also changes the 90° angle between a corner line of the pack and a typical card. Indeed, a corner line of the pack turns into a helix whose slope on the vertical axis of the stack is the angular strain.

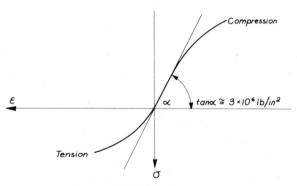

FIGURE 2.5.

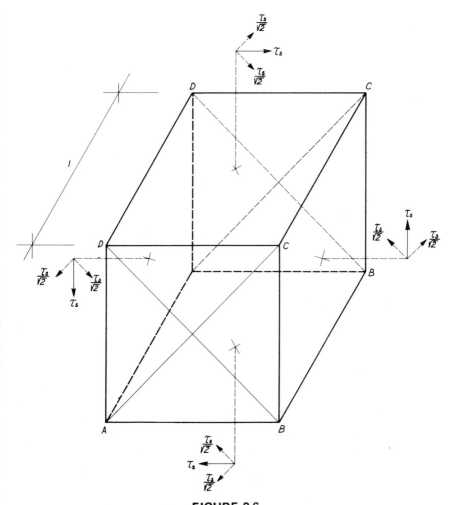

FIGURE 2.6.

The relation between shear stresses and the angular strains they produce is found by the following reasoning. The shear stresses τ_s on four sides of the cube of structural material in Fig. 2.6 produce forces $1(1)\tau_s$. The 45° components of these forces have the value $\tau_s/\sqrt{2}$. The area of the diagonal planes of the cube measures $1\sqrt{2}$, and thus the compressive forces $\tau_s/\sqrt{2}$ produce the stress

$$\frac{2(\tau_s/\sqrt{2})}{\sqrt{2}} = \tau_s$$

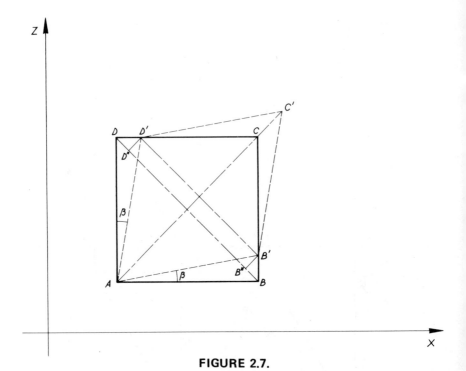

FIGURE 2.7.

on the diagonal plane $AACC$ and the compressive strain $-\tau_s/E$ at 90°
to that plane, that is, in the direction of the diagonal BD.

The compressive stress τ_s also produces a transversal strain $+\nu(\tau_s/E)$
in the direction of the diagonal AC. The tensile forces $\tau_s/\sqrt{2}$ similarly produce a stress τ_s on the diagonal plane $BBDD$ and a tensile
strain $+\tau_s/E$ at 90° to that plane, that is, in the direction of the diagonal AC. The tensile stress τ_s also produces a transversal strain
$-\nu(\tau_s/E)$ in the direction of the diagonal BD.

Thus the total strain in the direction of the diagonal AC is

$$\epsilon_{AC} = +\frac{\tau_s}{E} + \nu\,\frac{\tau_s}{E} = +\frac{\tau_s}{E}\,(1+\nu),$$

which makes the diagonal AC extend to the new length AC'

$$AC' = AC + \epsilon_{AC}\sqrt{2} = \sqrt{2} + \frac{\tau_s}{E}\,(1+\nu)\sqrt{2} \quad \text{(Fig. 2.7)}.$$

Similarly, the total strain in the direction of the diagonal BD is

$$\epsilon_{BD} = -\frac{\tau_s}{E} - \nu\,\frac{\tau_s}{E} = -\frac{\tau_s}{E}(1 + \nu),$$

and it makes this diagonal shrink to a new length $B'D'$

$$B'D' = BD + \epsilon_{BD}\sqrt{2} = \sqrt{2} - \frac{\tau_s}{E}(1 + \nu)\sqrt{2}.$$

Figure 2.7 shows how the expansion and contraction of the diagonals changes the square section $ABCD$ of the cube into a rhombus $AB'C'D'$. The angle $\pi/2$ between the sides AB and AD diminishes to the acute angle $(\pi/2) - 2\beta$.

The change 2β is the angular strain γ, and due to its extremely small value, it can be identified with $2 \tan \beta$.

$$\gamma = 2 \tan \beta = 2\,\frac{BB'}{AB} = \frac{2}{AB}\,\frac{\epsilon_{BD}\sqrt{2}}{2}\,\sqrt{2}.$$

Since $AB = 1$ and $\epsilon_{BD} = (\tau_s/E)(1 + \nu)$, then

$$\gamma = 2\,\frac{\tau_s}{E}(1 + \nu).$$

Using the notation

$$G = \frac{E}{2(1 + \nu)},$$

the angular strain is given by

$$\gamma = \frac{\tau}{G}.$$

The ratio G between the frictional stresses and strains is called the Lamé modulus, or frictional modulus.

THREE

DEFORMATIONS
OF STRUCTURES

The strains of the longitudinal fibers of structural materials cause a typical cross section of a framing element to move. When the strains of all the longitudinal fibers have the same sign and magnitude, such as those produced by axial stresses, the typical cross section translates in the direction of the fibers (Fig. 3.1a). When the sign and the magnitude or simply the magnitude, of the strain vary according to the coordinate of a fiber's intersection with the yz plane of the cross section, the motion of the typical section is a rotation with or without translation. Such is the case when the strains are produced by bending stresses or by combined bending and axial stresses. In the former case the typical cross section rotates around the centroidal axis y; in the latter case it rotates around the neutral axis n. This is equivalent to a rotation around y and a translation in the direction of the x axis (Fig. 3.1b and c).

The rotation of the cross sections produces bending deformation of structural elements (Fig. 3.6). This is the most important of the deformations because it is the most conspicuous. Axial deformation under working conditions is of lesser importance and magnitude in comparison with bending deformation. A high-rise building, for instance, can bend under the action of gale winds with a 2 ft displacement of its top. The contraction of the same building under the effect of the design gravity load is probably only a couple of inches. In other words the bending deformation can be 12 times greater than the axial deformation, although wind loads are not as great as gravity loads.

Angular strains or the extensional strains of ideal fibers at 45° to the longitudinal fibers usually cause miniscule displacements and rotations of the cross sections. Thus they are not discussed here.

171

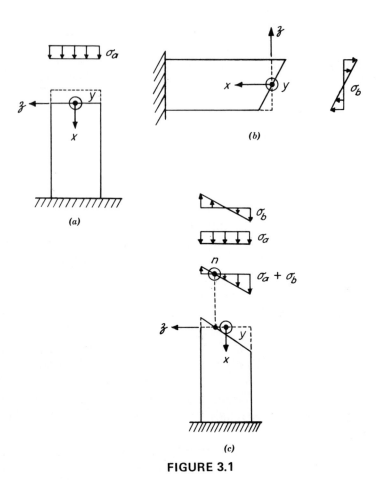

FIGURE 3.1

3.1. AXIAL DEFORMATION

The axial strain ϵ at the x coordinate on the axis of a framing bar changes the initial length dx of the local element of the axis in the amount ϵdx. Compounding all the elemental increments ϵdx along the axis of the bar gives the total change in the bar length. Thus, using the notation L for the initial length of the bar, its change ΔL is given by

$$\Delta L = \int_0^L \epsilon \, dx.$$

The axial strain ϵ is given by

$$\epsilon = \frac{\sigma_a}{E} = \frac{P}{AE}$$

Replacing it in ΔL gives

$$\Delta L = \int_0^L \frac{P}{AE} \, dx$$

In general, the axial force P, the cross-sectional area A, and Young's modulus E can vary with the coordinate x on the axis of the framing bar. Consequently the general expression of ΔL is

$$\Delta L = \int_0^L \frac{P(x)}{A(x)\,E(x)} \, dx.$$

However, E seldom varies within the same structure, A varies usually in steps, and P varies most frequently. A simple example is that of a transfer beam that delivers the wind load against the curtain wall of a high-rise building to the central core, such as beam AB on the floor plan in Fig. 3.2. In this case the axial force P is constant along the x

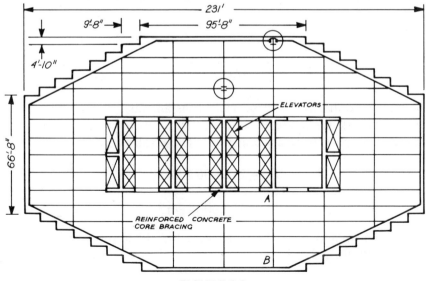

FIGURE 3.2

axis of the beam. If A and E are also constants, the shortening of the beam is

$$\Delta L = \frac{P}{AE} \int_0^L dx = \frac{PL}{EA}.$$

Assuming

$$\text{Young's modulus } E = 29,000 \text{ k/in.}^2. \quad \text{(steel),}$$

$$\text{Axial stress } \frac{P}{A} = 4.5 \text{ k/in.}^2,$$

$$\text{Initial length } L = 48'\text{-}4'' = 580 \text{ in.,}$$

then

$$\Delta L = \frac{4.5\,(580)}{29,000} = 0.09 \text{ in.}$$

In the case of the obelisk in Fig. 3.3, P/AE is not a constant. The contraction is calculated by integration in Problem 3.1.8. The integral, however, is also given by the area under the diagram of the integrand:

$$\frac{P(x)}{A(x)\,E(x)}.$$

Young's modulus in this case has a constant value in the upper 40 ft of the obelisk (lightweight concrete) and a different constant value in the lower part (ordinary concrete). These values are

$$E_1 = 216,000 \text{ k/in.}^2,$$

$$E_2 = 432,000 \text{ k/in.}^2.$$

In the lightweight zone the axial force has the approximate expression (see Problem 3.1.8):

$$P(x) = 0.02x^2 + 0.9x + 10.$$

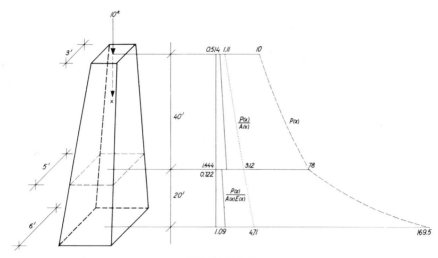

FIGURE 3.3

In the lower zone the axial force is given by

$$P(x) = 0.04125x^2 + 0.45x - 6.$$

The cross-sectional area has the approximate expression

$$A(x) = 0.45x + 9.$$

Thus the diagram of $P(x)/A(x)E(x)$ has the two linear parts shown qualitatively in Fig. 3.3. The area under this diagram that is the contraction of the obelisk is calculated in the following table; the values of $P(x)$ and $A(x)$ in it are obtained from the preceding expressions.

x (ft)	$P(x)$ (k)	$A(x)$ (ft^2)	$P(x)/A(x)$ (k/ft^2)	$\dfrac{100{,}000P(x)}{A(x)E(x)}$	$\displaystyle\int \dfrac{P}{AE}\,dx$
0	10	9	1.11	0.514	0
40	78	25	3.12	1.444	0.000392
40[a]	78	25	3.12	0.722	0.000392
60	169.5	36	4.71	1.090	0.000573

[a]$E = 432{,}000$ k/ft^2.

3.2.   BENDING DEFORMATION

The longitudinal strains ϵ produced by bending stresses have opposite signs on opposite sides of the centroidal axis of a cross section. Their magnitude decreases linearly from the extreme fibers in compression to the centroidal axis, from where it increases as far as the extreme fibers in tension. The diagrams of bending strains on the ends of an element of a flexural member are shown in Fig. 3.4; in the figure the dotted lines indicate the undeformed element, and solid lines the element's shape after deformation. Using the notations ϵ_T and ϵ_B for the strains of the top and bottom fibers, respectively, the extension of the top fibers is given by

$$AA' + BB' = \epsilon_T \, dx,$$

and the contraction of the bottom fibers by

$$CC' + DD' = \epsilon_B \, dx.$$

Replacing the strains with the ratios of the bending stresses with Young's modulus gives

$$AA' + BB' = \frac{\sigma_b^T}{E} \, dx,$$

$$CC' + DD' = \frac{\sigma_b^B}{E} \, dx,$$

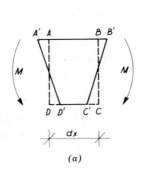

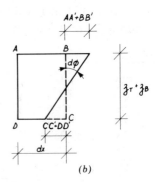

(a)

(b)

FIGURE 3.4

in which we substitute the expression of the bending stresses to obtain

$$AA' + BB' = \frac{M}{I} z_T \frac{dx}{E},$$

$$CC' + DD' = \frac{M}{I} z_B \frac{dx}{E}.$$

It is evident from Fig. 3.4 that the extension and contraction of the longitudinal fibers produce the rotation of the ends of the element. These rotations are consolidated in Fig. 3.4b where $d\phi$ is the angle between the terminal sections after the bending deformation. Since this angle is infinitesimal, it can be interchanged with its tangent, given by

$$\tan d\phi = \frac{AA' + BB' + CC' + DD'}{z_T + z_B} = \frac{\epsilon_T \, dx + \epsilon_B \, dx}{z_T + z_B}$$

$$= \frac{(\sigma_b^T + \sigma_b^B) \, dx}{(z_T + z_B) \, E} = \frac{(z_T + z_B) \, M \, dx}{(z_T + z_B) \, IE}.$$

Thus the expression of the elemental bending rotation is

$$d\phi \simeq \tan d\phi = \frac{M}{EI} \, dx.$$

Integration of this expression gives the rotation

$$\phi = C_1 + \int \frac{M}{EI} \, dx,$$

where C_1 is the rigid rotation a flexural member may receive at its boundary, and the integral is the change in the angle between the terminal sections of the member. Every symbol in the integrand M/EI can vary along the axis of the flexural member x. Thus the integrand should be written in general as $M(x)/E(x)I(x)$. Young's modulus, however, seldom varies within the same structure. The moment

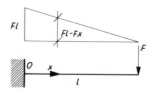

FIGURE 3.5

of inertia varies occasionally, and the bending moment is usually the only variable. The evaluation of the rotation ϕ by integration is shown in several of the problems. The integral is also given by the area under the diagram of M/EI, just as the axial deformation is given by the area under the diagram of P/AE.

For example, the cantilever beam of Fig. 3.5 with constant moment of inertia I and Young's modulus E has the bending moment

$$M(x) = FL - Fx$$

at a typical coordinate x. Thus the rotation is

$$\phi(x) = C_1 + \frac{1}{EI} \int (FL - Fx)\, dx$$

where the rotation C_1 of the fixed boundary is zero and the integral is the area under the moment diagram from the origin to the coordinate x. For $x = L$, this area is given by $\frac{1}{2}(FL)L$, and the rotation of the free end is

$$\phi(L) = \frac{FL^2}{2EI}.$$

From the fixed end to the typical coordinate x, the trapezoidal area is $x(FL + FL - Fx)/2$, and the rotation is

$$\phi(x) = \frac{x}{2EI}(2FL - Fx) = \frac{FL^2}{2EI}\left(2\frac{x}{L} - \frac{x^2}{L^2}\right).$$

With the values

$$E = 1800 \text{ k/in.}^2,$$

$$I = \frac{2}{12}(4)^3 \cong 11 \text{ in.}^4,$$

$$L = 48 \text{ in.,}$$

$$F = 0.2 \text{ k,}$$

the rotation of the tip of this 2″ × 4″ timber is

$$\phi(L) = \frac{0.2(48)^2}{2(1800)\,11} = 0.0116 \text{ rad} = 0.6667°.$$

Figures 3.6a and b show schematically a flexural member made of two infinitesimal elements in progressive stages of deformation. It is evident that the rotation ϕ between the ends of the left element produces the vertical displacement dw of the tip of the cantilever. Moreover the rotation ϕ and the deflection dw are linked by the relation

$$\phi(x) = \frac{dw(x)}{dx},$$

which by integration gives

$$w(x) = C_2 + \int \phi(x)\, dx.$$

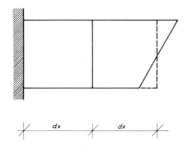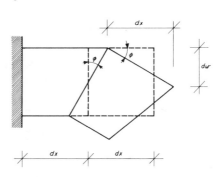

FIGURE 3.6

The integration constant C_2 is the vertical displacement, if any, at the coordinate 0, usually a boundary of the flexural element. The integral is the deflection at the coordinate x of the typical cross section with respect to the coordinate zero.

Calculations of deflections by integration are performed and proposed in several of the probelms. However, the value of the integral is also given by the area under the curve $\phi(x)$. For example, the deflections of the cantilever beam in Fig. 3.5 are given by the areas under the parabolic diagram of the rotations $\phi(x)$ in Fig. 3.7. The deflection of the tip at $x = L$ is then

$$w(L) = \frac{2}{3} \left(\frac{FL^2}{2EI}\right) L = \frac{FL^3}{3EI}.$$

3.2.1. The Method of the Conjugate Beam

Rotations and deflections produced by bending stresses can be obtained with the same facility as shear forces and bending moments. Indeed, the interdependence of loads g, shear forces V, and bending moments M, stated by the formulas

$$g = -\frac{dV}{dx},$$

$$V = \frac{dM}{dx},$$

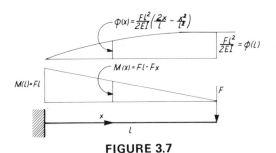

FIGURE 3.7

is the same as that of M/EI, ϕ, and w, stated by

$$\frac{M}{EI} = \frac{d\phi}{dx},$$

$$\phi = \frac{dw}{dx}.$$

This similarity becomes even more evident with the use of the notations

$$g^* = \frac{M}{EI}, \quad V^* = \phi, \quad M^* = w,$$

which allow us to write

$$g^* = \frac{dV^*}{dx},$$

$$V^* = \frac{dM^*}{dx}.$$

Thus, if we regard the diagram of M/EI as a load distribution g^*, the rotations ϕ and the deflections w can be obtained as shear forces V^* and bending moments M^*.

Incidentally, the ratio $M(x)/E(x)I(x)$ is the curvature or the inverse of the radius of the curved beam axis at the coordinate x. This can be realized with the aid of Fig. 3.8 and by writing

$$dx = \frac{EI}{M} d\phi = R d\phi.$$

Indeed, an elemental arc ds of the curve of the beam axis, interchangeable with an elemental segment dx of its tangent, is given by the product of the elemental angle $d\phi$ with the local radius of the curve $R(x)$.

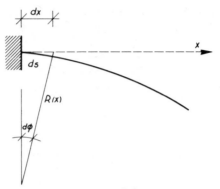

FIGURE 3.8

Thus

$$R(x) = \frac{EI}{M},$$

from which

$$\frac{1}{R(x)} = \frac{M}{EI}.$$

We now attempt the evaluation of the rotations and deflections of the cantilever beam in Fig. 3.7, much as we would evaluate shear forces V^* and bending moments M^* due to the load g^*, that is, M/EI. In this attempt we obtain for the coordinate $x = 0$ the shear

$$V^* = \frac{1}{EI}\,(FL)\,\frac{L}{2} \neq 0.$$

Similarly, we obtain at $x = 0$ the moment

$$M^* = \frac{FL^2}{2EI}\,\frac{L}{3} \neq 0.$$

These results conradict not only those obtained by different approaches but also the physical evidence that requires vanishing rotation and deflection at the fixed end of the beam.

If, however, the same load g^* is placed on a reversed cantilever, that is, one free at $x = 0$ (its left end), and fixed at $x = L$ (its right end), then

$$V^*(0) = \phi(0) = 0,$$

$$M^*(0) = w(0) = 0,$$

$$V^*(L) = \phi(L) = \frac{FL^2}{2EI},$$

$$M^*(L) = w(L) = \frac{FL^3}{3EI}.$$

These results agree with the physical evidence and with the results of other methods.

It is therefore apparent that the load M/EI needs to be placed on a beam so constrained that its boundary shear forces and bending moments behave like the boundary deflections and rotations of the original beam. The new beam is called a conjugate beam.

For each type of external and internal constraint of the real beam, Table 3.1 summarizes the behavior of the shear force V, the bending moment M, the rotation ϕ, and the deflection w—that is, the shear V^* and the moment M^* of the conjugate beam. In the last column the table gives the conjugate constraint that is the constraint of the conjugate beam replacing that of the real beam.

At a fixed end (first row) the shear V and the moment M do not vanish; the rotation ϕ vanishes (on the conjugate beam $V^* = 0$), and the deflection w vanishes (on the conjugate beam $M^* = 0$). If V^* and M^* vanish, the conjugate beam must lack vertical support and clamping; thus it is completely free at that end.

At an internal hinge (second row), V does not vanish, M vanishes, ϕ has two different values on the left and right side of the hinge, and w does not vanish. The constraint of the conjugate beam that pro-

TABLE 3.1.

Real Beam			Conjugate Beam		
Constraint	V	M	V^*	M^*	Constraint
	$\neq 0$	$\neq 0$	$= 0$	$= 0$	Free end
	$\neq 0$	$= 0$	$\neq 0$ and discontinuous (step)	$\neq 0$ (cuspid)	
	$= 0$	$\neq 0$	$\neq 0$ continuous	$\neq 0$ and discontinuous (step)	
	$\neq 0$	$= 0$	$\neq 0$	$= 0$	Same

					Same
	= 0	≠ 0	= 0	≠ 0	
	≠ 0 and discontinuous (step)	≠ 0 (cuspid)	≠ 0	= 0	
	≠ 0 continuous	≠ 0 discontinuous (step)	= 0	≠ 0	
Free end	= 0	= 0	≠ 0	≠ 0	

185

duces a step of the shear V^* by providing a vertical reaction is a roller. Of course on a roller the moment M^* is not zero.

At an internal slide (third row), V is zero, but M is not; ϕ is the same on the left and right side of the slide; w is different on the left and right side of the slide. The constraint of the conjugate beam that does not change the shear V^* but produces a step of the moment M^* by providing a reactive moment is an intermediate external slide.

At a terminal roller, V is not zero, M is zero, ϕ is not zero, w is zero. The constraint of the conjugate beam that provides a reaction V^* but no moment M^* is again a roller. Thus a terminal roller of the real beam remains in the conjugate beam.

At a terminal slide (fifth row), V is zero, M is not zero, ϕ is zero, w is not zero. The constraint of the conjugate beam that provides a reactive moment M^* but no vertical reaction V^* is again an external slide. Thus a terminal slide of the real beam remains in the conjugate beam.

At an intermediate roller (sixth row), V is different on the left and right side of the roller; M is not zero; ϕ is not zero, but w is. The constraint of the conjugate beam that transfers the shear V^* but makes the moment M^* vanish is an internal hinge.

At an intermediate external slide (seventh row), V is the same on the left and right side, M is different on the left and right side, ϕ is zero, w is not. The constraint of the conjugate beam that makes the shear V^* vanish but transfers the moment M^* is an internal slide.

At a free end (eighth row), V is zero, M is zero, ϕ is not, w is not. The constraint of the conjugate beam that provides a reaction V^* and a reactive moment M^* is a fixed end.

It is clear from the preceding discussion that only the top four rows of the table are essential, for the others are obtained by reading the top four rows from right to left with real beams in place of conjugate ones, and vice versa. Thus, if the real beam has any of the constraints shown in the last column, the corresponding constraint of the conjugate beam is found on the same line in the first column.

In the example in Fig. 3.9 the conjugate beam $A'B'C'D'$ is drawn by replacing the constraints of the real beam $ABCD$ according to the preceding table. The diagram of bending moments produced on the real beam by its loads (the three 10 k forces) is placed as a load dis-

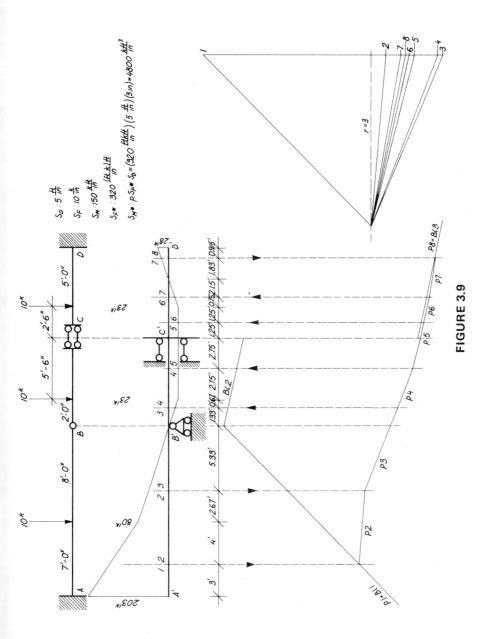

$S_D = 5 \frac{ft}{in}$

$S_F = 10 \frac{k}{in}$

$S_M = 150 \frac{k \cdot ft}{in}$

$S_L = 320 \frac{ft \cdot k \cdot ft}{in}$

$S_{H^*} = P \cdot S_F = S_D = \left(320 \frac{ft \cdot k \cdot ft}{in}\right)\left(5 \frac{ft}{in}\right)(3 in) = 4800 \frac{k \cdot ft^3}{in}$

FIGURE 3.9

187

tribution g^* on the conjugate beam. The partial resultants of the loads g^* are calculated as follows:

$$F^*_{1-2} = \frac{7}{2} (80 + 203) = 990.5 \text{ k-ft}^2,$$

$$F^*_{2-3} = \frac{8}{2} (80) = 320 \text{ k-ft}^2,$$

$$F^*_{3-4} = -\frac{2}{2} (23) = -23 \text{ k-ft}^2,$$

$$F^*_{4-5} = -5.5(23) = -126.5 \text{ k-ft}^2,$$

$$F^*_{5-6} = -2.5(23) = -57.5 \text{ k-ft}^2,$$

$$F^*_{6-7} = \frac{-2.256}{2} (23) = -25.93 \text{ k-ft}^2,$$

$$F^*_{7-8} = \frac{-2.745}{2} (28) = 38.43 \text{ k-ft}^2.$$

An equation of vertical equilibrium gives the reaction of the roller

$$R^*_{B'} = 1116 \text{ k-ft}^2.$$

The values of the moments M^* are calculated as follows:

$$M^*_{2-3} = 990.5(6.67) = 6606.6 \text{ k-ft}^3,$$

$$M^*_{B'} = 990.5(12) + 320(5.33) = 13,592.7 \text{ k-ft}^3,$$

$$M^*_{3-4} = 990.5(13.33) + 320(6.67) - 1116(1.33) = 13,853.5 \text{ k-ft}^3,$$

$$M^*_{4-5} = 990.5(16.75) + 320(10.08) - 1116(4.75) - 23(3.42)$$

$$= 14,436.8 \text{ k-ft}^3,$$

$$M^*_{C'L} = 990.5(19.5) + 320(12.83) - 1161(7.5) - 23(6.17) - 126.5(2.75)$$

$$= 14,223.1 \text{ k-ft}^3,$$

$M^*_{C'R} = 38.43(6.585) - 25.93(3.252) - 57.5(1.25) = 96.86$ k-ft^3.

(The subscripts L and R denote left and right sides of point C'.)

$$M^*_{5-6} = 38.43(5.332) - 25.93(2) = 153 \text{ k-ft}^3,$$

$$M^*_{6-7} = 38.43(3.33) = 128 \text{ k-ft}^3.$$

The preceding moments M^* give the beam deflections after division by EI. If, for example,

$$E = 29,000 \text{ k/in.}^2 \quad \text{(steel)},$$

$$I = 1200 \text{ in.}^4,$$

then the largest deflection is

$$\frac{M^*_{C'L}}{EI} = \frac{14,223.1(12)^3}{29,000(1200)} = 0.706 \text{ in.}$$

The difference

$$M^*_{C'} = M^*_{C'L} - M^*_{C'R} = 14,223.1 - 96.86 = 14,126.2 \text{ k-ft}^3,$$

that is, the reactive moment of the constraint at C', after division by EI, gives the discontinuity of deflection at the internal slide.

3.2.2. Deflections by Graphics

Diagrams of bending moments are obtained graphically as string polygons of the loading forces. We have observed in the preceding discussion that the bent configuration of a beam is the same as the diagram of the moments M^* on the conjugate beam under a load distribution g^*, that is, M/EI. Consequently this moment diagram can be obtained not only by plotting values calculated numerically but also by the string polygon technique. Of course the baseline of each span is drawn according to the constraint conditions of the conjugate beam.
    In Fig. 3.9 the diagram of distributed loads g^* is first replaced by

the resultants F^*_{1-2}, F^*_{2-3}, F^*_{3-4}, F^*_{4-5}, F^*_{5-6}, F^*_{6-7}, F^*_{7-8}. Their values have already been calculated in Section 3.2.1. Next, the force polygon 1, 2, 3, 4, 5, 6, 7, 8 is drawn. These forces are projected from a pole P, 3 in. away from the forces. The string polygon $P1$, $P2$, $P3$, $P4$, $P5$, $P6$, $P7$, $P8$ is then drawn. The baseline for the left end overhanging span $A'B'$ is the side $P1$ of the string polygon. Indeed, this is the only baseline that makes the moments M^* vanish from the tip A' of the overhang to first force F^*_{1-2}. Similarly, the baseline for the right end overhang $C'D'$ is the side $P8$ of the string polygon. The baseline for the intermediate span $B'C'$ concurs with baseline $P1$ and is parallel to baseline $P8$. Such a baseline indeed makes the moment $M^*_{B'R}$ on the right side of roller B' equal to the moment $M^*_{B'L}$ on the left side of B'. It also makes the slope of side $P5$ of the moment diagram the same on the left and right side of slide C' as required by the lack of concentrated force R^* at C'. Such a force would change the shear V^* at C', that is, the slope of the moment M^*.

The scale of the moments is obtained by multiplication of the following factors:

p = 3 in., the polar distance.

S_{F^*} = 320 k-ft²/in., the scale of the loads F^*.

S_D = 5 ft/in., the scale of the drawing.

Thus

$$S_{M^*} = pS_D S_{F^*} = (3 \text{ in.})(320 \text{ k-ft/in.}^2)(5 \text{ ft/in.}) = 4800 \text{ k-ft}^3/\text{in.}$$

For example, the moment $M^*_{C'L}$ is obtained by multiplying the 3.17 in. segment (defined by $P5$ and $BL2$) at C with S_{M^*}. Then

$$M^*_{C'L} = (3.17 \text{ in.})(4800 \text{ k-ft}^3/\text{in.}) = 15,216 \text{ k-ft}^3.$$

This moment was evaluated numerically in Section 3.2.1. The numerical value of 14,223.1 k-ft³ is 6.5% smaller than the result obtained by graphics. A large-scale drawing usually reduces the error.

In Fig. 3.10 the moment diagram is also shown with a unique hori-

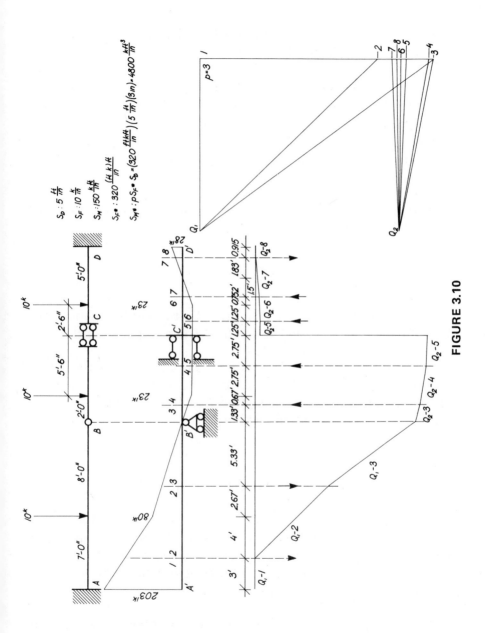

FIGURE 3.10

191

zontal baseline which is obtained by using the following poles:

Pole Q_1 for span $A'B'$ on line $Q_1 1$ that divides the equilibrant 3–1 of the span's load into the left end shear $V_A^* = 0$ and the right shear $V_{B'L}^* = 3$–1.

Pole Q_2 for span $B'C'$ on line $Q_2 8$ that divides the equilibrant 5–3 of the span's load into the left end shear $V_{B'R}^* = 8$–3 and the right end shear $V_{C'L}^* = 5$–8.

Pole $Q_3 = Q_2$ for span $C'D'$ on the line $Q_2 8$ that divides the equilibrant 8–5 of the span's load into the left end shear $V_{C'R}^* = 8$–5 and the right end shear $V_{D'}^* = 0$.

The reaction of the roller at B' is the algebraic sum of the shear forces $V_{B'R}^* = 8$–3 and $V_{B'L}^* = 3$–1; thus

$$R_B^* = V_{B'L}^* + V_{B'R} = 8\text{--}1.$$

The reaction of the slide at C' is given by the algebraic sum of the shear forces $V_{C'L}^* = 5$–8 and $V_{C'R}^* = 8$–5. This sum is zero since a slide does not provide vertical support.

The moments M^* of the conjugate beam $A'B'C'D'$ give the deflections of the real beam $ABCD$ after division by EI. The reaction $R_{B'}^*$ gives the relative rotation of section B of part AB with respect to section B of part BC, after division by EI. The relative rotation is zero at slide C.

3.3.   THE PRINCIPLE OF VIRTUAL WORKS

When a structure subject to a set of forces in equilibrium is given a deformation that is arbitrary but very small (as deformations of architectural structures usually are) and compatible with the constraints and geometric integrity of the structure, the work performed by the equilibrated forces vanishes.

The set of equilibrated forces could be that of loads and reactions of a structure, or that of the external forces and the internal forces

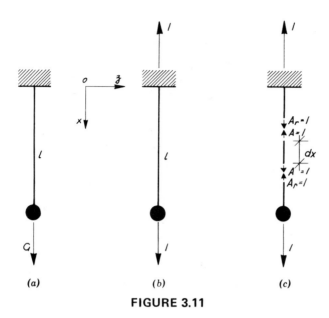

FIGURE 3.11

with which the structural material responds to their action, or that of the internal forces produced by distortions (thermal variations, creep, shrinkage, foundation settlements) in statically indeterminate structures and the reactions with which the constraints respond to the distortions, or any arbitrarily chosen equilibrated set. (See examples and problems in this chapter and Chapter 4.) Similarly, the small coherent deformation can be arbitrary.

We consider for demonstration the vertical hanger in Fig. 3.11a, to which a weight G is connected. Each element dx of the hanger extends by the amount $G\,dx/EA$, and the lower end of the hanger moves down by Gl/EA. When an equilibrated set of forces (Fig. 3.11b) made of a unit gravity load at the lower end of the hanger, the reaction of the fixed end, and the internal response axial forces are all affixed to the structure, their work for the coherent deformation due to G is

$$1\left(\frac{Gl}{EA}\right) - 1(0) - \int_{0}^{l} (1)\,\frac{G}{EA}\,dx,$$

where the first term is the work of the unit gravity load, the second term is the work of the fixed end reaction, and the third term is the work of the internal response axial forces. The total of the preceding sum is indeed zero, as claimed by the principle of virtual works.

The third term in the summation has a negative sign because, the work done during the extension of the element dx by the *response* axial forces $A_r = 1$ (equal and opposite to the axial forces $A = 1$ *equivalent* to the unit load) is negative (Fig. 3.11c). If the equilibrated set of forces were chosen with reversed sign, the work of the response axial forces would be positive and that of the unit external forces would be negative; thus the opposite signs of the first and third term in the equation would still be correct. Choosing the external and internal forces associated with G as the equilibrated force system and as coherent deformation that due to the unit load of the hanger's low end, the equations of the virtual work would be identical. Choosing the equilibrated force system and coherent deformation both associated with load G, the virtual work is

$$G\left(\frac{Gl}{EA}\right) - G(0) - \int_0^l G\,\frac{G}{EA}\,ds,$$

which amounts to zero. Finally, choosing both the equilibrated force system and the coherent deformation as those associated with the unit gravity load, the virtual work is

$$1\left(\frac{1l}{EA}\right) - 1(0) - \int_0^l 1\,\frac{1}{EA}\,ds = 0.$$

The purpose of the preceding simple example is of course to explain and justify the statement of the principle of virtual work; it is assumed that reactions and deformations are known by other means. However, the equation of virtual work can be used to find reactions or deformations of structures as well.

The advantage of this investigative approach is its unrestricted validity and applicability. It can be used to evaluate deformations or reactions of statically determinate as well as indeterminate structures, both planar and tridimensional. Structures can be subject to any combination of loads and distortions and be supported on rigid or deformable constraints. Of course inelastic deformations of constraints do not depend on the values of the reactions; thus, in design phase, they must be predicted for use with the principle of virtual work. In investigating existing structures, the actually measured inelastic deformations are entered in the equation of virtual work.

This principle is also applicable when nonlinear stress-strain dependence and large deformations that alter the relative positions of the external forces impair the validity of the principle of superposition and Hook's law (see last example in this section). The only requirements are that the forces doing virtual work be equilibrated and that the deformations for which work is done be coherent and small in comparison with the size of the structures.

In a first example, in which we find the tip deflection of a cantilever beam subject to uniform gravity load g (Fig. 3.12a), the set of equilibrated forces is made of the external forces in Fig. 3.12b and the internal response forces associated with them. These are the constant shear force $V_1(x) = 1$ and the linear bending moments $M_1(x) = 1x$. We choose as coherent deformation that produced by the uniform gravity load. Neglecting the shear deformation, and thus the work of the shear forces, the virtual work is done by the external forces of Fig. 3.12b and by the internal moments $M_1(x) = 1x$. With the notation $w(0)$ for the tip deflection due to load g, the former work is $1w(0)$. Indeed, other external forces (unit reaction and reactive moment $1l$) do not work, for the fixed end does not move. The internal response moments $M_{1r}(x)$ do work, since the moments $M(x)$ due to g produce the rotation $d\phi$ of the ends of an element dx of beam (Fig. 3.12c):

$$d\phi = \frac{M}{EI}\, dx.$$

According to the principle of virtual work,

$$1w(0) - \int_0^l M_{1r}\, \frac{M}{EI}\, dx = 0.$$

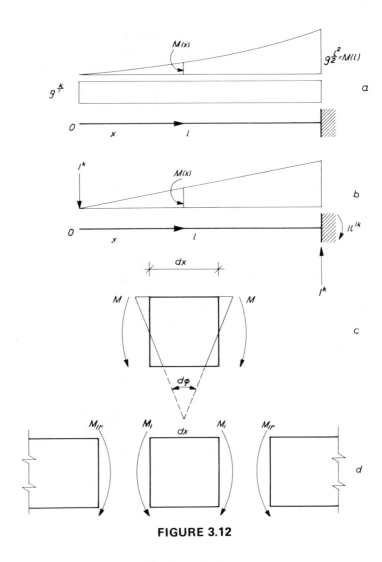

FIGURE 3.12

We note the negative sign of the second term and the subscript r in M_{1r}. In fact, the internal moments M_1 on the element dx (Fig. 3.12d) are *equivalent* to the unit tip load, whereas the moments part of the equilibrated set of external and internal forces are the *response* moments M_{1r} whose work for the rotation $d\phi$ in Fig. 3.12c is negative. Thus we need a minus sign before the integral. If the set of equilibrated forces were chosen with reversed sign (upward tip load), the integral

$$\int_0^l M_{1r} \frac{M}{EI} \, dx$$

would be positive, and the work of the tip load negative. Thus the opposite signs of the two works are correct in any case. We replace in the equations of virtual work the expressions of M_{1r} and M:

$$M_{1r} = 1x, \quad M = g \frac{x^2}{2},$$

and obtain (with EI constant)

$$w(0) = \frac{g}{2EI} \int_0^l x^3 \, dx = \frac{g}{8EI} \, l^4.$$

It appears from the preceding example that the set of equilibrated forces and coherent deformations must be chosen judiciously, with the task at hand in mind. In the preceding case we are seeking the tip deflection due to the load g, thus the chosen system of equilibrated forces is such that only the deflection $w(0)$ appears in the equation of virtual work. Other deformations that would clutter the picture are left out due to the lack of forces doing work for deflections other than $w(0)$.

In a second example, we seek the vertical displacement of joint 8 of the truss in Fig. 1.67. For this purpose we use as system of equilibrated forces a unit gravity load at joint 8, the reactions of the constraints due to this load, and the axial forces induced by this load in the bars of the truss. The link that constrains the truss at its left end is considered deformable and is treated like a bar of the truss. We use the actual deformation of the truss as the system of coherent and small virtual deformations.

The work of the virtual external forces is $1 \cdot w_8$. Actually, the right end reactions do not work, for joint 6 does not move, and the work of the link's reaction for the deformation of this constraint is included in the work of the axial forces (see demonstration of the principle in the case of a vertical hanger). This work is

$$-\sum_{1}^{16} P_1 \frac{Pl}{EA},$$

where the symbols indicate virtual axial force P_1, real axial force P, length l, Young's modulus E, and cross-sectional area A of the 16 bars (this number includes the link). We assume for simplicity that all the bars, link included, have the same length, area, and Young's modulus. The real axial forces P are shown in Fig. 1.67. The virtual axial forces P_1 are shown in Fig. 4.15b, with reversed signs. The axial force in the link is

$$(10^2 + 5.77^2)^{1/2} = 11.5 \text{ k.}$$

The sum of the virtual work is equated to zero:

$$1w_8 - \frac{l}{EA} \sum_{1}^{16} P_1 P = 0.$$

Table 3.2 lists the axial forces P_1 and P, and their product for each bar. At the end of the last row we find the summation

$$\sum_{1}^{16} P_1 P = 80.19$$

in the expression of w_8.

With the values

$$l = 10 \text{ ft} = 120 \text{ in.,}$$

TABLE 3.2

Bar Link	1-2	2-3	3-4	4-5	5-6	6-7	7-8	8-9	9-1	2-9	3-9	3-8	4-8	4-7	5-6
P_1	-0.58	-0.58	-1.16	-0.58	-0.58	0	+0.58	+0.58	0	+0.58	-0.58	+0.58	+0.58	-0.58	+0.58
P	-11.5	-11.5	-14.4	-11.5	-11.5	0	+8.7	+8.7	0	+11.5	-5.8	0	0	-5.8	+11.5
P_1P	6.67	6.67	16.7	6.67	6.67	0	5.0	5.0	0	6.67	3.4	0	0	3.4	6.67

$\Sigma P_1 P = 80.19$

$$A = 1.2 \text{ in.}^2,$$

$$E = 29,000 \text{ k/in.}^2,$$

the deflection of joint 8 is

$$w_8 = \frac{120(80.19)}{29,000(1.2)} = 0.28 \text{ in.}$$

In the next chapter we are going to consider the application of the principle of virtual work in the evaluation of statically indeterminate reactions. The knowledge of those reactions allows the further application of the principle for the evaluation of deformations of statically indeterminate structures.

We resort to the statically indeterminate truss in Fig. 4.15*a* to demonstrate this. Seeking, for example, the deflections of joints 7 and 9, we use as a set of equilibrated forces (Fig. 3.13) two 1 k gravity loads at joints 7 and 9 of the principal structure, the reactions and the axial forces induced by these loads in the constraints and in the bars of the principal structure. Note that in evaluating true deformations, the only requirement on the virtual force set is that it be in equilibrium without necessarily resembling the set of real loads, reactions, and internal forces of the structure. Similarly, in evalu-

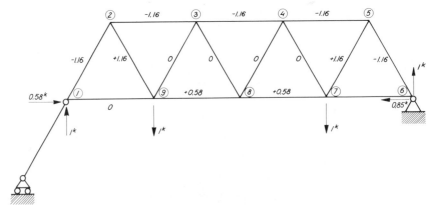

FIGURE 3.13

ating true reactions, the only requirement on the virtual deformations is that they be coherent and small in comparison with the size of the structure.

The work done by the virtual forces for the real deformations of the statically indeterminate truss is

$$1w_7 + 1w_9 + \sum R_1 \delta - \sum P_1 \Delta l = 0,$$

where

w_7 and w_9 = the components of the real displacements δ_7 and δ_9 of joints 7 and 9, in the direction of the virtual gravity loads,

R_1 = the reactions of the constraints of the principal structure due to the unit virtual loads,

δ = the real displacements of the points of application of the preceding reactions measured in their direction,

P_1 = the virtual axial forces in the principal structure,

Δl = the real extensions of the bars of the statically indeterminate truss.

Since the real constraints of joints 6 and 8 do not permit displacements in the direction of the local virtual reaction, and the work of the link's reaction is included among those of the internal forces, the summation $\sum R_1 \delta$ vanishes. Due to symmetry the equation of virtual work thus becomes

$$2w_7 = 2w_9 = \sum P_1 \Delta l = \frac{l}{EA} \sum P_1 P,$$

where P are the real axial forces of the truss found in Chapter 4. Table 3.3 lists the values of P_1, P, and $P_1 P$ for each bar. The values P_1 in the table and in Fig. 4.15b are obtained by Ritter sections or by a Maxwell diagram.

TABLE 3.3

Bar Link	1-2	2-3	3-4	4-5	5-6	6-7	7-8	8-9	9-1	2-9	3-9	3-8	4-8	4-7	5-7
P	-3.64	-3.64	+1.33	-3.64	-3.64	0	+0.80	+0.80	0	+3.64	+2.09	-7.86	-7.86	+2.09	+3.64
P_1	-1.16	-1.16	-1.16	-1.16	-1.16	0	+0.58	+0.58	0	+1.16	0	0	0	0	+1.16
P_1P	4.22	4.22	-1.54	4.22	4.22	0	0.46	0.46	0	4.22	0	0	0	0	4.22
$\Sigma P_1P = 28.92$															

With the values from Table 3.3, we can obtain

$$2w_7 = \frac{120(28.92)}{1.2(29,000)} = 0.1 \text{ in.}$$

In a last example in this section we plan to show the application of the principle of virtual work in a case where the actual stresses in the material exceed the elastic limit and the actual deformations are sufficiently large to alter the mutual positions of the external forces. The preceding conditions impair the validity of the principle of superposition and Hook's law, but not that of the principle of virtual work. We consider a timber column ($E = 2000$ k/in.^{2}) 100 in. high with a 6″ × 6″ cross section. The column is subject to a 1 k wind load H at its top and to a 15 k gravity load P. Expecting a non-negligible displacement δ of the top section (Fig. 3.14), we include in the reactive moment M of the fixed end that $P\delta$ of the couple of vertical forces P. Thus the total reactive moment is

$$M = hH + P\delta.$$

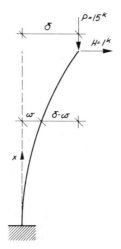

FIGURE 3.14

In evaluating the displacement δ by the principle of virtual work, we use as a set of equilibrated forces the loads and reactions in Fig. 3.14 and the internal bending moments produced by them. We neglect the internal shear and axial forces, both to simplify the problem and because their deformations, hence their work, are small in comparison with those of the bending moments.

We use as a set of coherent deformations, those associated with a deflection diagram

$$w(x) = \delta \left(1 - \cos \frac{\pi x}{2l} \right)$$

where δ is the unknown real deflection of the top of the column. The preceding expression vanishes with its derivative

$$\frac{dw}{dx} = \delta \frac{\pi}{2l} \sin \frac{\pi x}{2l}$$

at $x = 0$, as required by the local constraint (fixed end). At $x = l$, the preceding expression produces the real displacement δ and makes the internal moment

$$EI \frac{d^2 w}{dx^2} = EI\delta \left(\frac{\pi}{2l} \right)^2 \cos \frac{\pi x}{2l}$$

vanish, as required by the absence of an equal and opposite moment of the external forces. The chosen deflection diagram is compatible with the loads, constraints, and geometries of the real structure, and thus is realistic. This permits equating the internal moment $EI(d^2 w/dx^2)$, associated with the deflection w, to the moment of the external forces.

The work done by the set of equilibrated forces (neglecting axial and shear deformations) is

$$H\delta - \int_0^l M \frac{M}{EI} \, dx = 0.$$

The moment M at the coordinate x is given by

$$M(x) = P(\delta - w) + H(l - x).$$

From the equation

$$EI \frac{d^2w}{dx^2} = P(\delta - w) + H(l - x)$$

we obtain expanding

$$EI \frac{d^2w}{dx^2} + Pw = P\delta + H(l - x).$$

Substituting w and its second derivate gives

$$EI\left(\frac{\pi}{2l}\right)^2 \delta \cos \frac{\pi x}{2l} + P\delta - P\delta \cos \frac{\pi x}{2l} = P\delta + H(l - x).$$

Simplifying and consolidating we obtain

$$\delta \cos \frac{\pi x}{2l} \left[EI\left(\frac{\pi}{2l}\right)^2 - P\right] = H(l - x)$$

from which

$$\delta - w = \delta \cos \frac{\pi x}{2l} = \frac{H(l - x)}{EI(\pi/2l)^2 - P}.$$

Thus the moments are

$$M = H(l - x)\left[1 + \frac{P}{EI(\pi/2l)^2 - P}\right]$$

and the virtual work equation becomes

$$EIH\delta = \int_0^l M^2 \, dx = H^2\left[1 + \frac{P}{EI(\pi/2l)^2 - P}\right]^2 \int_0^l (l - x)^2 \, dx.$$

Integrating gives

$$\frac{EI\delta}{H\left[1 + \dfrac{P}{EI(\pi/2l)^2 - P}\right]^2} = \frac{l^3}{3}$$

from which

$$\delta = \frac{Hl^3}{3EI}\left[1 + \frac{P}{EI(\pi/2l)^2 - P}\right]^2.$$

When P vanishes δ equals the deflection $Hl^3/3EI$ of a cantilever column loaded at its top by a transversal force H. When P equals the critical load of a cantilever column $EI\pi^2/(2l)^2$ the deflection is infinitely large.

In our case with the values

$$E = 2000 \text{ k/in.}^2$$

$$I = (6)^4/12 = 108 \text{ in.}^4$$

$$P = 15 \text{ k}$$

$$H = 1 \text{ k}$$

$$l = 100 \text{ in.}$$

we obtain

$$\delta = \frac{100^3}{3(108)2000}\left[1 + \frac{15}{108(\pi/200)^2 2000 - 15}\right]^2 = 2.15 \text{ in.}$$

Lacking P the deflection would be

$$\frac{100^3}{3(108)2000} = 1.54 \text{ in.}$$

With a load P equal to P_{cr}

$$P_{cr} = EI \frac{\pi^2}{(2l)^2} = \frac{2000(108)\pi^2}{200^2} = 53.3 \text{ k}$$

the deflection would grow out of finite bounds. The actual deflection is only 2.15% of the column length, thus sufficiently small to comply with the requirements for the validity of the principle of virtual works. The bending moment at the base of the column is

$$P\delta + Hl = 15(2.15) + 1(100) = 132.25 \text{ in./k.}$$

Thus the deformation alters sufficiently the original mutual positions of the external forces to produce a non-negligible increase of bending. The extreme fiber stresses on the base section of the column are

$$\frac{P}{A} \pm \frac{lH}{I} z \pm \frac{P\delta}{I} z = \frac{15}{36} \pm \frac{100(1)}{108} \pm \frac{15(2.15)^3}{108} = \begin{matrix} 4.1 \\ -3.3 \end{matrix} \text{ k/in.}^2$$

of which the last term

$$\frac{P\delta}{I} z = 0.9 \text{ k/in.}^2$$

is a non-negligible share.

The principle of superposition would neglect this share and it is not valid in this case, more so because the values of the stress are very close to the strength of any good timber and therefore out of linear range. However the principle of virtual work allows accurate evaluation of stresses and deformations which proves its greater field of validity.

PROBLEMS

3.1.1. Evaluate the shrinkage produced by the horizontal reactions P to neutralize the thermal dilatation of the beam in Problem 1.4.1.

Solution.

$$\Delta l = \frac{Pl}{EA} = \frac{110(360)}{29,000(14.6)} = 0.094 \text{ in.}$$

3.1.2. Evaluate the extension produced by the horizontal reactions P to neutralize the thermal shrinkage of the beam in Problem 1.4.3.

3.1.3. The beam in Figs. 1.71 and 1.72 is pretensioned from the cantilever tip to its left end with a uniform compression of 1 k/in.^{2} Evaluate the shrinkage of the beam with the properties in Problem 1.2.3 and $E = 4000$ k/in.^{2}

3.1.4. Evaluate the shrinkage of the column in Problem 1.4.13 with a height of 12 ft and $E = 29,000$ k/in.^{2} Neglect self-weight of the column.

3.1.5. Evaluate the shrinkage of the column in Problem 1.4.14 with a height of 15 ft and $E = 29,000$ k/in.^{2} Neglect self-weight of the column.

3.1.6. List the shrinkages of the bars of the truss in Problem 1.10.2.

3.1.7. Evaluate the shrinkage of the column in Problem 1.10.7. Neglect the self-weight.

3.1.8. Calculate the shrinkage of the obelisk in Fig. 3.3.

Solution. The cross section of the obelisk which supports a 10 k heavy statue varies from 9 ft^2 at the top to 36 ft^2 at the base. At a typical coordinate x the cross section is

$$A(x) = 0.0025x^2 + 0.3x + 9.$$

We replace this with the approximate but simpler formula

$$A(x) = 0.45x + 9.$$

In order to lower the center of mass, and improve the stability, the top 40 ft of the obelisk is made of lightweight concrete weighing

0.1 k/ft³. The lower part is made of normal concrete weighing 0.15 k/ft³. Thus the self-weight of the obelisk is 0.9 k/ft at $x = 0$ ft, 2.5 k/ft at $x = 40$ ft in lightweight zone, and 3.75 k/ft at $x = 40$ ft in normal concrete zone. At $x = 60$ ft, the self-weight is 5.4 k/ft.

In lightweight zone the axial force varies with the law

$$P(x) = 10 + 0.1 \left(\frac{x^3}{1200} + 0.15x^2 + 9x \right).$$

Thus at $x = 40$ the axial force is

$$P = 10 + 65.3 = 75.3 \text{ k}.$$

Replacing the expression of $P(x)$ with its simpler approximation

$$P(x) = 0.02x^2 + 0.9x + 10$$

we obtain at $x = 40$ ft, $P = 78$ k.

In the zone of normal concrete the variation law of P is

$$P(x) = 10 + 0.15 \left(\frac{x^3}{1200} + 0.15x^2 + 9x \right) - \frac{65.3}{3}$$

we replace this with the simpler approximation

$$P(x) = 0.04125x^2 + 0.45x - 6$$

Young's modulus of the lightweight concrete is $E_1 = 1500$ k/in.², or 216,000 k/ft²; that of the normal concrete is $E_2 = 3000$ k/in.², or 432,000 k/ft². Thus the contraction of the obelisk in lightweight zone from the top to the typical section with coordinate x is

$$\frac{1}{E_1} \int_0^x \frac{P(\xi)}{A(\xi)} \, d\xi = \frac{1}{E_1} \int_0^x \frac{(0.02\xi^2 + 0.9\xi + 10) \, d\xi}{0.45\xi + 9}.$$

Expanding gives

$$\frac{0.02}{E_1} \int_0^x \frac{\xi^2 \, d\xi}{0.45\xi + 9} + \frac{0.9}{E_1} \int_0^x \frac{\xi \, d\xi}{0.45\xi + 9} + \frac{10}{E_1} \int_0^x \frac{d\xi}{0.45\xi + 9}.$$

Integrating gives (e.g., Pierce-Foster, "A Short Table of Integrals")

$$\frac{0.02}{E_1} \frac{1}{(0.45)^3} \left[\frac{1}{2} (9 + 0.45x)^2 - 2(9)(9 + 0.45x) \right.$$

$$\left. + 9^2 \log (9 + 0.45x) \right] - \frac{0.02}{E_1} \frac{1}{(0.45)^3} \left(\frac{9^2}{2} - 2(9)9 + 9^2 \log 9 \right)$$

$$+ \frac{0.9}{E_1} \frac{1}{(0.45)^2} [9 + 0.45x - 9 \log (9 + 0.45x)]$$

$$- \frac{0.9}{E_1} \frac{1}{(0.45)^2} (9 - 9 \log 9) + \frac{10}{E_1} \frac{1}{0.45} \log (9 + 0.45x)$$

$$- \frac{10}{E_1} \frac{1}{0.45} \log 9.$$

At $x = 40$ ft, the preceding expression gives

$$\frac{1}{E_1} (31.926 - 12.395 - 11.834 + 47.889 + 73.240 - 48.827)$$

$$= \frac{80}{216,000} = 0.00037 \text{ ft} = 0.0044 \text{ in.}$$

The value 0.000392 in the table in Section 3.1 is 5.6% larger.

The contraction of the obelisk from the top to the typical coordinate x in the zone of normal concrete is

$$\frac{1}{E_1} \int_0^{40} \frac{P(\xi)}{A(\xi)} \, d\xi + \frac{1}{E_2} \int_{40}^x \frac{P(\xi)}{A(\xi)} \, d\xi.$$

The first term of this sum has the value 0.00037 ft. Replacing in the second term the expressions of $P(\xi)$ and $A(\xi)$ gives

$$0.00037 + \frac{1}{E_2} \int_{40}^{x} \frac{(0.04125\xi^2 + 0.45\xi - 6)}{0.45\xi + 9} \, d\xi.$$

This integral is calculated like the preceding one.

3.1.9. Calculate the shrinkage of the column in Problem 1.10.5.

Solution. The axial force $P(x)$ increases linearly with the law

$$P(x) = 2000 + 0.15(6.045)x,$$

where 0.15 k/ft^3 is the density of concrete and 6.045 ft^2 is the area of the column's cross section. Thus

$$P(0) = 2000 \text{ k},$$

$$P(30) = 2000 + 0.907(30) = 2027.2 \text{ k}.$$

The total shrinkage is

$$\Delta L = \frac{1}{EA} \int_{0}^{30} P(x) \, dx$$

$$= \frac{2000(30)}{432,000(6.045)} + \frac{0.907}{432,000(6.045)} \int_{0}^{30} x \, dx$$

$$= \frac{1}{432,000(6.045)} \left(60,000 + (0.907) \frac{30^2}{2} \right)$$

$$= 0.023132 \text{ ft} = 0.2776 \text{ in.}$$

3.1.10. Perform the task in Problem 3.1.9 for the column in Problem 1.10.11.

3.2.1. Draw the diagrams of rotations and deflections for the beam in Problem 1.2.5. Approximate the load diagram g with concentrated forces F and the load diagram g^* with point loads F^*.

Solution. The diagrams of loads g^* (bending moments), shear forces V^* (rotations), and moments M^* (deflections) on the conjugate beam are shown in Fig. 3.15. The rotation at the tip of the cantilever is

$$\phi_{max} = \frac{V_{max}^*}{EI} = \frac{789.3(12)^2}{3000(80,195)} = \frac{0.47}{10^3} \text{ rad} = 0.027°.$$

The deflection of the free end is

$$w_{max} = \frac{M_{max}^*}{EI} = \frac{8900(12)^3}{3000(80,195)} = 0.064 \text{ in.}$$

3.2.2. Perform the tasks in Problem 3.2.1 for the beam in Problem 1.2.10.

3.2.3. Perform the tasks in Problem 3.2.1 for the beam in Problem 1.2.3. The diagrams of g^*, V^*, and M^* on the conjugate beam are shown in Fig. 3.16. We note from the diagram M^* that the rotation on the roller produces uplift of the overhang. True rotations and deflections are obtained by division of V^* and M^* with E (3000 k/in.^{2}) and I_y (64,356 in.^{4}).

3.2.4. Perform the tasks in Problem 3.2.3 for the beam in Problem 1.2.12.

3.2.5. Find rotation and deflection of the top section of the columns in Fig. 1.95 by integration.

Solution. (Fig. 3.17).

Equation of wind load

$$v(x) = 0.4 - \frac{0.4}{15} x.$$

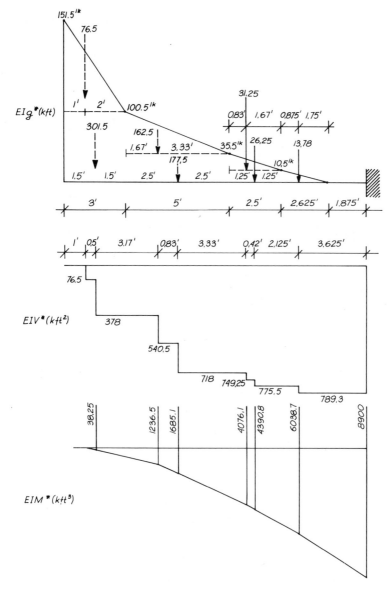

FIGURE 3.15

213

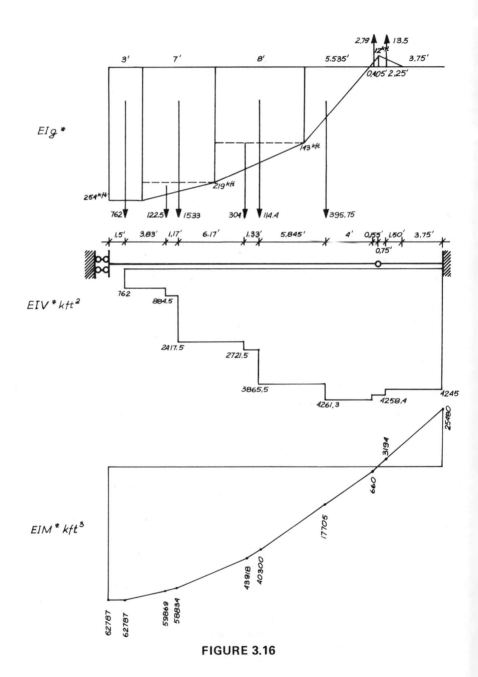

FIGURE 3.16

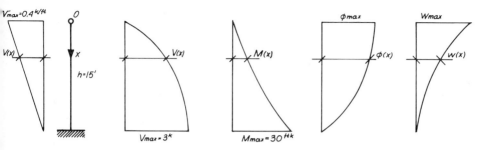

FIGURE 3.17

Equation of shear

$$V(x) = 0.4x - \frac{0.4}{15}(x)\frac{x}{2}.$$

Equation of moment

$$M(x) = 0.4(x)\frac{x}{2} - \frac{0.4}{15}(x)\frac{x}{2}\left(\frac{x}{3}\right) = \frac{x^2}{5} - \frac{x^3}{225}.$$

Equation of rotation

$$EI\phi(x) = \int_0^x M(\xi)\,d\xi + C_1 = \frac{1}{5}\int_0^x \xi^2\,d\xi - \frac{1}{225}\int_0^x \xi^3\,d\xi + C_1$$

$$= \frac{x^3}{15} - \frac{x^4}{900} + C_1.$$

Boundary conditions on $\phi(x)$: at $x = L$, $\phi(L) = 0$. Thus

$$EI\phi(L) = 0 = \frac{L^3}{15} - \frac{L^4}{900} + C_1,$$

from which

$$EI\phi(x) = \frac{1}{15}(x^3 - L^3) - \frac{1}{900}(x^4 - L^4).$$

At $x = 0$,

$$EI\phi_{max} = -\frac{180^3}{15} + \frac{180^4}{900} = -388{,}800 + 1{,}166{,}400 = 777{,}600 \text{ k-in.}^2$$

Equation of deflection

$$EIw(x) = C_2 + \int_0^x \phi(\xi)\, d\xi$$

$$= C_2 + \frac{1}{15} \int_0^x \xi^3\, d\xi - \frac{L^3}{15} \int_0^x d\xi$$

$$- \frac{1}{900} \int_0^x \xi^4\, d\xi + \frac{L^4}{900} \int_0^x d\xi,$$

$$EIw(x) = C_2 + \frac{1}{60} x^4 - \frac{L^3 x}{15} - \frac{x^5}{4500} + \frac{L^4 x}{900}.$$

Boundary condition on $w(x)$: at $x = L$, $w(L) = 0$. Thus

$$EIw(L) = 0 = C_2 + \frac{L^4}{60} - \frac{L^4}{15} - \frac{L^5}{4500} + \frac{L^5}{900},$$

from which

$$C_2 = +\frac{L^4}{20} - \frac{L^5}{1125}$$

and

$$4500\, EIw(x) = -x^5 + 75x^4 + (5L^4 - 300L^3)x - 4L^5 + 225L^4.$$

At $x = 0$,

$$EIw_{max} = \frac{4(180)^5 - 225(180)^4}{4500} = 115{,}473{,}600 \text{ k-in.}^3$$

Division by EI gives the values of ϕ_{max} and w_{max}.

3.2.6. through 3.2.11.   Using the method of the conjugate beam, verify the rotation and deflection formulas in the Manual of Steel Construction of the American Institute of Steel Construction, Section 2, Beams, Diagrams and Formulas, Cases Nos. 8, 11, 14, 17, 23, and 26.

3.2.12. Using the method of the conjugate beam, draw diagrams of rotations and deflections for the beam in Fig. 3.18. The solution is given in the same figure through the various

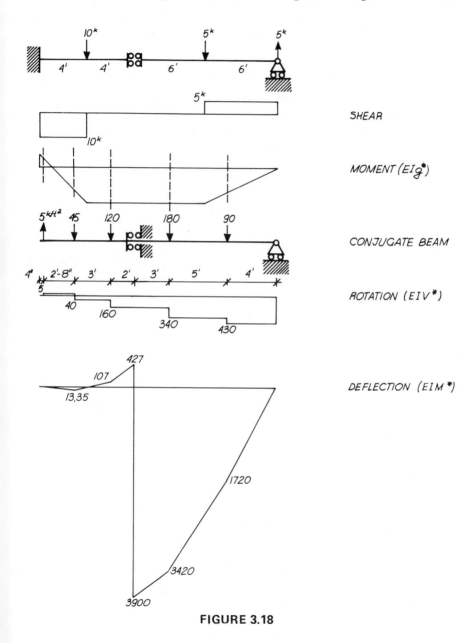

SHEAR

MOMENT (EI_g^*)

CONJUGATE BEAM

ROTATION (EIV^*)

DEFLECTION (EIM^*)

FIGURE 3.18

steps of the shear diagram, moment diagram (EIg^*), EIV^* diagram (ϕEI), and EIM^* diagram (wEI).

3.2.13. Find the deflection w_a at the coordinate a of the beam in Problem 3.2.7 (Case 11) with the principle of virtual work. Use the following data: $l = 30$ ft, $a = 5$ ft, $b = 14$ ft, $P_1 = 12$ k, $P_2 = 6$ k.

Solution. We choose a unit gravity load at $x = a$, the reactions of the constraints to this load, and the bending moments produced by these external forces, as a system of equilibrated virtual forces (shear forces are neglected). We choose the real deformations as a system of small coherent deformations. The equation of virtual work is thus

$$1w_a = \frac{1}{EI} \int_0^l M_1 M \, dx$$

for the real deflections at $x = 0$ and $x = l$ vanish, and the local virtual external forces do not work.

The virtual moments $M_1(x)$ have the following expressions:

$$M_1(x) = \frac{5}{6} x \quad (\text{for } 0 \leqslant x \leqslant 5),$$

$$M_1(x) = \frac{5}{6}(x) - 1(x - 5) = 5 - \frac{x}{6} \quad (\text{for } 5 \leqslant x \leqslant 30).$$

The real reactions are

$$R_L = 13 \text{ k}, \quad R_R = 5 \text{ k}.$$

The real moments $M(x)$ have the following expressions:

$$M(x) = 13x \quad (\text{for } 0 \leqslant x \leqslant 5),$$

$$M(x) = 13x - 12(x - 5) = 60 + x \quad (\text{for } 5 \leqslant x \leqslant 15),$$

$$M(x) = 13x - 12(x - 5) - 6(x - 15) = 150 - 5x \quad \text{(for } 15 \leqslant x \leqslant 30\text{)}.$$

Thus the virtual work equation becomes

$$EIw_a = \int_0^5 \frac{5x}{6}(13x)\,dx + \int_5^{15}\left(5 - \frac{x}{6}\right)(60 + x)\,dx$$

$$+ \int_{15}^{30}\left(5 - \frac{x}{6}\right)(150 - 5x)\,dx.$$

Expanding, we obtain

$$EIw_a = \frac{65}{6}\int_0^5 x^2\,dx + 300\int_5^{15} dx - 5\int_5^{15} x\,dx$$

$$- \frac{1}{6}\int_5^{15} x^2\,dx + 750\int_{15}^{30} dx - 50\int_{15}^{30} x\,dx + \frac{5}{6}\int_{15}^{30} x^2\,dx.$$

Integrating gives

$$EIw_a = 451.4 + 3000 - 500 - 180.6 + 11{,}250 - 16{,}875 + 6562.5$$

$$= 3708 \text{ k-ft}^3.$$

This is the answer to Problem 3.2.7 if the same data are used.

3.2.14 through 3.2.18. Verify the answers to Problems 3.2.6 and 3.2.8 through 3.2.11 with the principle of virtual work.

FOUR

REACTIONS OF REDUNDANT CONSTRAINTS

A monolithic framing bar has three degrees of freedom on its x, z Cartesian plane (Fig. 4.1a). Of course, if there are no constraints the bar can move rigidly (without changing shape or length) in the x and z directions, and it can rotate. If a set of constraints leaves the bar some of its degrees of freedom, the bar is unstable. If the number of constraints is sufficient to block all three degrees of freedom, the bar is stable. If the number of constraints exceeds those strictly necessary to block the three degrees of freedom, the bar is overconstrained, and some of its constraints are redundant.

Unstable structures seldom serve any purpose and are irrelevant to us. For example, a door is a structure that, lacking constraints, could move on the floor plane in the direction of the wall in which it is framed or at 90° to it. The door of course could also swing (Fig. 4.1a). When the door is hinged to the wall (Fig. 4.1b), its double constraint blocks the freedom of translation in two directions but does not provide stability since the door is still free to swing. Evidently the free and open door is not a useful structure since it does not provide privacy nor thermal and acoustical insulation. If, however, a third constraint is provided by a lock, the door becomes a stable, useful structure (Fig. 4.1c). Additionally constraining the door by glueing one of its sides to the frame makes the door overconstrained, and the additional connection is redundant (Fig. 4.1d).

Stable structures are also called statically determinate because the reactions of their constraints are evaluated by solving equations of

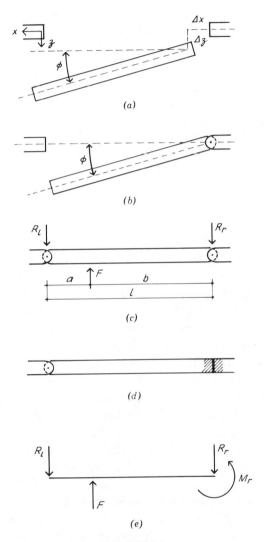

FIGURE 4.1

statics (equilibrium). If, for example, someone pounding on the door of Fig. 4.1c applies a force F to it, the reactions R_l and R_r of the constraints are determined by the two equations of statics

$$\sum M = 0,$$

$$\sum F_z = 0.$$

Pivoting the moments of the first equation around the door's left end we obtain

$$\sum M = 0 = aF - lR_r$$

from which

$$R_r = \frac{a}{l} F.$$

Then the second equation gives

$$R_l = F - R_r = F \left(1 - \frac{a}{l} \right) = F \left(\frac{l - a}{l} \right) = \frac{b}{l} F.$$

The reactions of overconstrained structures cannot be determined by statics. Indeed, the free body in Fig. 4.1e of the door in Fig. 4.1d shows two reactions and a reactive moment, and their total of three exceeds by one the number of equilibrium equations (in this case, two for lack of any forces along x). Other equations in addition to those of statics are therefore needed to evaluate reactive forces and moments. The task of setting and solving these equations is an important step in structural analysis since most architectural structures are manifold overconstrained.

4.1.   STATICALLY INDETERMINATE REACTIONS BY THE METHOD OF FORCES

In the method of forces, equations of *compatibility* state that the specified loads and the reactive forces or moments of the redundant constraints produce, in combination, structural deformations compatible with the redundant constraints. We use the example of the door in Figs. 4.1d and e to illustrate this method. The door's hori-

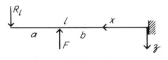

FIGURE 4.2

zontal section is shown in Fig. 4.2, with statically determinate constraints and with the redundant constraint of the left end replaced
by an unknown load R_l that is its reaction. Such a statically determinate structure, subject to some specified and some unknown loads,
is called *the principal structure*.

Force F produces a rotation at $x = b$,

$$\phi(b) = \frac{Fb^2}{2EI},$$

and a deflection,

$$w(b) = \frac{Fb^3}{3EI}.$$

Thus at the left end force F produces a deflection

$$w_1(l) = \frac{Fb^3}{3EI} + \left(\frac{Fb^2}{2EI}\right) a = \frac{Fb^2}{6EI}(2b + 3a) = \frac{Fb^2}{6EI}(2l + a).$$

At the same end, the unknown reaction R_l produces a deflection

$$w_2(l) = -\frac{R_l l^3}{3EI}.$$

Since at the left end the door lock does not allow any deflection, the
compatibility equation must state in this case that

$$w_1(l) + w_2(l) = 0,$$

that is,

$$\frac{Fb^2}{6EI}(a + 2l) - \frac{R_l l^3}{3EI} = 0.$$

Multiplying the equation by $3EI/l^3$ and solving for R_l we obtain

$$R_l = \frac{Fb^2}{2l^3}(a + 2l).$$

With the values

$$l = 3 \text{ ft,}$$

$$a = 1 \text{ ft,}$$

$$b = 2 \text{ ft,}$$

$$F = 30 \text{ lb.}$$

The redundant constraint reaction is

$$R_l = 15.6 \text{ lb.}$$

With the known value of R_l, the remaining reactions R_r and M_r are evaluated by statics. Thus

$$R_r = F - R_l = 30 - 15.6 = 14.4 \text{ k,}$$

$$M_r = lR_l - bF = 3(15.6) - 2(30) = -13.2 \text{ ft-lb.}$$

Of course any one of the reactive forces and moments in Fig. 4.1e can be considered redundant and the others statically determinate.

For example, the principal structure could be the one shown in Fig. 4.3a where M_r is the redundant reaction. In this case the known load F produces at $x = 0$ the right end rotation $\phi_1(0)$, which can be obtained as right end shear $V_1^*(0)$ on the conjugate beam in Fig. 4.3b:

$$\phi_1(0) = \frac{a}{2l}\left(\frac{Fab}{lEI}\right)\left(\frac{2a}{3}\right) + \left(\frac{b}{2l}\right)\frac{Fab}{lEI}\left(a + \frac{b}{3}\right).$$

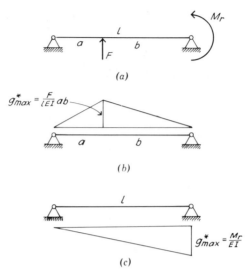

FIGURE 4.3

Replacing b with $l - a$ gives

$$\phi_1(0) = \frac{Fab}{6EI}(a + l).$$

The moment M_r at the right end of the beam in Fig. 4.3a produces the rotation $\phi_2(0)$, which can be obtained as a right end shear, $V_2^*(0)$ on the conjugate beam in Fig. 4.3c:

$$\phi_2(0) = \frac{M_r l}{3EI}.$$

Since the original structure is fixed at the end $x = 0$ and does not rotate, the compatibility equation states symbolically

$$\phi_1(0) + \phi_2(0) = 0$$

Explicitly,

$$\frac{ab}{6l}\frac{F}{EI}(a + l) - \frac{M_r l}{3EI} = 0.$$

Multiplying the equation by $3EI/l$ and solving for M_r gives

$$M_r = \frac{abF}{2l^2}(a + l).$$

With the preceding values of $a, b, l,$ and $F,$

$$M_r = \frac{2(30)}{2(3)^2}(1 + 3) = 13.3 \text{ ft-lb},$$

a result identical to that found by statics with a known value of R_l. Knowing M_r from the compatibility equation, we can find R_l and R_r by statics (Fig. 4.3a):

$$R_l = \frac{bF}{l} - \frac{M_r}{l} = \frac{2}{3}(30) - \frac{13.3}{3} = 15.6 \text{ lb},$$

$$R_r = \frac{aF}{l} + \frac{M_r}{l} = 14.4 \text{ lb}.$$

In still another choice of the redundant reaction, we could select R_r, and the principal structure would then be the one in Fig. 4.4a. In this case the compatibility equation sets the sum of the deflections, produced by F and R_r at the right end, equal to zero. As a matter of fact the original structure is fixed at $x = 0$ and will not deflect. The right end deflection due to F can be obtained as the moment $M_1^*(0)$ on the conjugate beam in Fig. 4.4b:

$$w_1(0) = M_1^*(0) = b\left(\frac{aF}{EI}\right)\left(\frac{b}{2}\right) + \frac{a}{2}\left(b + \frac{a}{3}\right)\frac{aF}{EI} - l\left(\frac{abF}{EI} + \frac{a^2F}{2EI}\right)$$

Replacing b with $l - a$ and simplifying, we obtain

$$w(0) = M_1^*(0) = \frac{-Fa}{EI}(3l^2 - a^2).$$

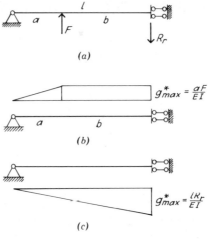

FIGURE 4.4

The right end deflection due to R_r can be obtained as the moment $M_2^*(0)$ on the conjugate beam in Fig. 4.4c:

$$w_2(0) = M_2^*(0) = \frac{R_r l^2}{2EI}\left(l - \frac{l}{3}\right) = \frac{R_r l^3}{3EI}$$

The compatibility equation is

$$w_1(0) + w_2(0) = 0,$$

and with the use of the preceding expression it becomes

$$-\frac{Fa}{EI}(3l^2 - a^2) + \frac{R_r l^3}{3EI} = 0.$$

Multiplying by $3EI/l^3$ and solving for R_r gives

$$R_r = \frac{aF}{2l^3}(3l^2 - a^2) = \frac{30}{2(3)^3}(27 - 1) = 14.4 \text{ lb.}$$

With this value of R_r, which confirms the previous results, we can proceed to find R_r and M_r by statics. In Table 4.1 all the preceding operations and results are compiled in a convenient summary.

TABLE 4.1.

Original structure			
Principal structure			
Compatibility equation	$w_1(l) + w_2(l) = 0$	$\phi_1(0) + \phi_2(0) = 0$	$w_1(0) + w_2(0) = 0$
ϕ_1 or w_1	$w_1(l) = \dfrac{Fb^2}{6EI}(a+2l)$	$\phi_1(0) = \dfrac{Fab}{6EIl}(a+l)$	$w_1(0) = -\dfrac{Fa}{6EI}(3l^2 - a^2)$
ϕ_2 or w_2	$w_2(l) = -\dfrac{R_l l^3}{3EI}$	$\phi_2(0) = -\dfrac{M_r l}{3EI}$	$w_2(0) = \dfrac{R_r l^3}{3EI}$
Solution	$R_l = \dfrac{Fb^2}{2l^3}(a+2l)$	$M_r = \dfrac{Fab}{2l^2}(a+l)$	$R_r = \dfrac{Fa}{2l^3}(3l^2 - a^2)$

TABLE 4.2.

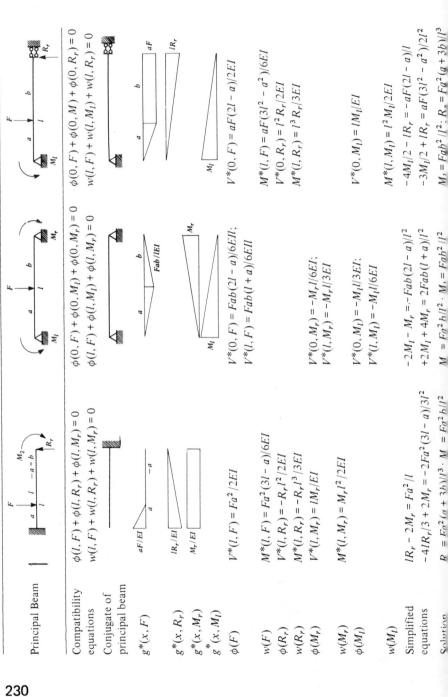

	Principal Beam		
Compatibility equations	$\phi(l,F) + \phi(l,R_r) + \phi(l,M_r) = 0$ $w(l,F) + w(l,R_r) + w(l,M_r) = 0$	$\phi(0,F) + \phi(0,M_l) + \phi(0,M_r) = 0$ $\phi(l,F) + \phi(l,M_l) + \phi(l,M_r) = 0$	$\phi(0,F) + \phi(0,M) + \phi(0,R_r) = 0$ $w(l,F) + w(l,M_l) + w(l,R_r) = 0$
Conjugate of principal beam			
$g^*(x,F)$			
$g^*(x,R_r)$			
$g^*(x,M_r)$			
$g^*(x,M_l)$			
$\phi(F)$	$V^*(l,F) = Fa^2/2EI$	$V^*(0,F) = Fab(2l-a)/6EIl;$ $V^*(l,F) = Fab(l+a)/6EIl$	$V^*(0,F) = aF(2l-a)/2EI$
$w(F)$	$M^*(l,F) = Fa^2(3l-a)/6EI$		$M^*(l,F) = aF(3l^2-a^2)/6EI$
$\phi(R_r)$	$V^*(l,R_r) = -R_r l^2/2EI$		$V^*(0,R_r) = l^2 R_r/2EI$
$w(R_r)$	$M^*(l,R_r) = -R_r l^3/3EI$		$M^*(l,R_r) = l^3 R_r/3EI$
$\phi(M_r)$	$V^*(l,M_r) = lM_r/EI$	$V^*(0,M_r) = -M_r l/6EI;$ $V^*(l,M_r) = -M_r l/3EI$	
$w(M_r)$	$M^*(l,M_r) = M_r l^2/2EI$		
$\phi(M_l)$		$V^*(0,M_l) = -M_l l/3EI;$ $V^*(l,M_l) = -M_l l/6EI$	$V^*(0,M_l) = lM_l/EI$
$w(M_l)$			$M^*(l,M_l) = l^2 M_l/2EI$
Simplified equations	$lR_r - 2M_r = Fa^2/l$ $-4lR_r/3 + 2M_r = -2Fa^2(3l-a)/3l^2$	$-2M_l - M_r = -Fab(2l-a)/l^2$ $+2M_l + 4M_r = 2Fab(l+a)/l^2$	$-4M_l/2 - lR_r = -aF(2l-a)/l$ $-3M_l/2 + lR_r = aF(3l^2-a^2)/2l^2$
Solution	$R_r = Fa^2(a+3b)/l^3;$ $M = Fa^2 b/l^2$	$M = Fa^2 b/l^2;$ $M_r = Fab^2/l^2$	$M_l = Fab^2/l^2;$ $R_r = Fa^2(a+3b)/l^3$

When several constraints are redundant, their reactions are found by solving simultaneously a number of compatibility equations equal to the number of redundant constraints. We resort to the case of a beam fixed at both ends (Fig. 4.14) to show the typical approach.

The optional principal structures are shown in Table 4.2. The principal structure with unknown loads R_l and M_l and that with unknown loads R_l and M_r are not shown because they would duplicate two of the principal structures already appearing in the table. The table also lists all the steps to the solutions. For greater clarity the typical steps are discussed in detail for the principal structure with M_l and R_r unknown reactions.

The compatibility equations state in the table that the known load F and the unknown reactions M_l and R_r produce rotations with a sum vanishing at $x = 0$ and deflections with a sum vanishing at $x = l$. That is, the rotation $\phi(0, F)$ is neutralized by the rotations $\phi(0, M_l)$ and $\phi(0, R_r)$ produced by the unknown reactions; the deflection $w(l, F)$ is similarly nuetralized by the deflections $w(l, M_l)$ and $w(l, R_r)$ produced by the unknown reactions.

The rotations and deflections in the compatibility equations are evaluated as shear forces V^* and bending moments M^* on the conjugate of the principal beam due to the loads g^* which are the moment distributions produced by F, M_l, and R_r on the principal beam. The preceding rotations and deflections replace their symbols in the compatibility equations; these are shown after simplification. Then the equations are solved for M_l and R_r.

Obviously, the evaluation of reactions for structures with a large number of redundant constraints requires solving large systems of simultaneous equations, a task insurmountable a few decades ago but routinely performed on the computer.

4.2. STATICALLY INDETERMINATE REACTIONS BY THE METHOD OF DEFORMATIONS

The method of deformations uses equations of *equilibrium* of the joints of statically indeterminate structures in order to obtain the unknown interactions among the framing bars that converge at the joints. Such interactions are the axial and shear forces and the bending and twisting moments that each bar end receives from a joint (i.e., from the other bars converging at the joint). If the internal forces are known at one end of a bar, the same internal forces can be evaluated all along the bar and at its opposite end by simple summation with the known bar loads.

There are two differences between these equations of equilibrium and those used for evaluating statically determinate reactions. First, the equations of statics are written for an entire bar whereas the equations of equilibrium for the evaluation of statically indeterminate interactions are written for one cross section of a bar. Second, the reactions of the external constraints appear directly as forces or moments in the equations of statics, whereas the interactions at an internal connection of a statically indeterminate structure appear in the equations of equilibrium of a joint through the unknown rotations and deflections of the joint common to all the bars that converge there. A few simple examples are used to clarify the method.

Example.

Three timber piles are randomly gathered in a mill yard and are used for the foundation of a column. The piles are driven into the ground to different depths l_1, l_2, and l_3. The top sections of the piles are joined by a single pile cap (Fig. 4.5a). The piles are made of different woods with Young's moduli E_1, E_2, and E_3 and have unequal cross sections A_1, A_2, and A_3. In order to investigate the safety of each pile, it is necessary to obtain the share of the column load P carried by each pile. The foundation is a statically indeterminate structure,

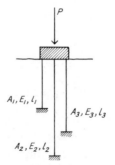

FIGURE 4.5

since the only equation of vertical equilibrium cannot yield the three reactions of the piles: We know, however, that the top sections of all piles have the same vertical displacement, that is, the displacement of the pile cap. Therefore, labeling P_1, P_2, and P_3 the axial forces delivered by the joint (the pile cap) to the piles and Δ the vertical displacement of the pile cap, we state

$$\frac{P_1 l_1}{A_1 E_1} = \Delta \quad \text{or} \quad P_1 = A_1 E_1 \frac{\Delta}{l_1},$$

$$\frac{P_2 l_2}{A_2 E_2} = \Delta \quad \text{or} \quad P_2 = A_2 E_2 \frac{\Delta}{l_2},$$

$$\frac{P_3 l_3}{A_3 E_3} = \Delta \quad \text{or} \quad P_3 = A_3 E_3 \frac{\Delta}{l_3}.$$

Using the method of deformations, we now write the equation of vertical equilibrium of the internal connection among the piles (the pile cap):

$$P_1 + P_2 + P_3 - P = 0.$$

Substituting the axial forces in the piles with the preceding expressions, we obtain

$$A_1 E_1 \frac{\Delta}{l_1} + A_2 E_2 \frac{\Delta}{l_2} + A_3 E_3 \frac{\Delta}{l_3} = P,$$

from which

$$\Delta = \frac{P}{(A_1 E_1 / l_1) + (A_2 E_2 / l_2) + (A_3 E_3 / l_3)}.$$

Knowing Δ, the axial forces atop each pile are readily evaluated, and the ground reaction R_i on the pile i is obtained by summing the axial force P_i withe the self-weight W_i of the pile:

$$R_i = P_i + W_i.$$

Assuming, for instance, the geometric and material properties listed in columns 2 through 5 of Table 4.3 and the load P shown at the bottom of column 10, the top axial forces and the bottom reactions for each pile have the values in columns 10 and 11.

The table shows that it is really not necessary to calculate the vertical displacement Δ. Here Δ is given by

$$\Delta = \frac{P}{\Sigma P_{i1}} = \frac{100}{59{,}212} = 0.0017 \text{ ft} = 0.02 \text{ in.}$$

A ratio $P_{i1} = A_i E_i / l_i$ coincides with the pile-top axial force P_i when $\Delta = 1$. It is called the axial stiffness of a pile and has the unit of k/ft because it represents the axial force required to produce a unit contraction at the top of the pile. The ratios $P_{i1} / \Sigma P_{i1}$ are called, for rather evident reasons, the piles' relative stiffnesses.

Example.

We now assume that the same pile cap in Fig. 4.5 receives from the column, hinged on the pile cap, a shear force S as well as the axial force P, and we plan to determine the shares of S carried by each of the three piles (Fig. 4.6). We consider the piles fixed in the bedrock at depths l_1, l_2, and l_3, respectively, and we consider as negligible the horizontal resistance of the topsoil. The problem is twice statically indeterminate since the equation of horizontal equilibrium of the joint (pile cap),

$$S_1 + S_2 + S_3 = S,$$

cannot yield the three unknown shares S_1, S_2, and S_3. Following the method of deformations, we write the expressions of S_1, S_2, and S_3 as functions of the horizontal deflection δ common to the top sections of all three piles. Since

$$\delta = \frac{S_1 l_1^3}{3 E_1 I_1} = \frac{S_2 l_2^3}{3 E_2 I_2} = \frac{S_3 l_3^3}{3 E_3 I_3},$$

TABLE 4.3.

Pile i	Radius R_i (in.)	$A_i = R_i^2 \pi$ (in.²)	Density γ_i (k/ft³)	Length l_i (ft)	$W_i = \dfrac{A_i l_i \gamma_i}{144}$ (k)	E_i (k/in.²)	$P_{i1} = \dfrac{A_i E_i}{l_i}$ (k/ft)	$\dfrac{P_{i1}}{\Sigma P_{i1}}$	$P_i = \dfrac{P_{i1} P}{\Sigma P_{i1}}$ (k)	$R_i = P_i + W_i$ (k)
1	7.5	176.7	0.04	10	0.491	1500	26,505	0.44763	44.763	45.254
2	9	254.5	0.05	20	1.767	1800	22,905	0.38683	38.683	40.450
3	6	113.1	0.03	15	0.353	1300	9,802	0.16554	16.554	16.907
							$\Sigma\, 59,212$	$\Sigma = 1$	$\Sigma = 100 = P$	

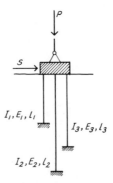

FIGURE 4.6

then

$$S_1 = \frac{3E_1 I_1 \delta}{l_1^3}$$

$$S_2 = \frac{3E_2 I_2 \delta}{l_2^3}$$

$$S_3 = \frac{3E_3 I_3 \delta}{l_3^3}.$$

The equation of horizontal equilibrium of the pile cap can now be written in the form

$$S = \delta \left(\frac{3E_1 I_1}{l_1^3} + \frac{3E_2 I_2}{l_2^3} + \frac{3E_3 I_3}{l_2^3} \right) = \delta \sum_{i=1}^{3} \frac{3E_i I_i}{l_i^3},$$

from which

$$\delta = \frac{S}{(3E_1 I_1/l_1^3) + (3E_2 I_2/l_2^3) + (3E_3 I_3/l_3^3)}.$$

The known value of δ allows us to evaluate the three shares S_1, S_2, and S_3 of S.

Using the same data from the preceding example and $S = 100$ k, Table 4.4 on page 240 shows the operations and results of the method in this case. It is not necessary to calculate the horizontal displacement δ of the joint. Its value, however, is given by

$$\delta = \frac{100}{109.98} = 0.909 \text{ ft.}$$

[*Note* that in the preceding and following discussion the pile cap (connection of piles' top sections) is considered a pointlike joint.]

The ratio S_{i1} is the shear stiffness of a bar fixed at one end and free to rotate and displace at the other—that is, the force needed to produce a unit transversal displacement. The ratios $S_{i1}/\Sigma S_{i1}$ are the relative stiffnesses.

Example

It is now assumed that the piles in Fig. 4.5 receive from the column, slide connected to the pile cap, a moment M as well as the axial force P (Fig. 4.7). The piles are fixed in the bedrock and the topsoil offers negligible lateral support. We want to determine the shares of

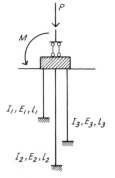

FIGURE 4.7

M carried by each of the three piles. The problem is twice statically indeterminate because only one equation of equilibrium is available:

$$M_1 + M_2 + M_3 = M,$$

which is insufficient to obtain moments in the three piles. The method of deformations specifies writing the expressions of the moments in function of the common rotation of the top sections of the piles (i.e., the rotation of the pile cap):

$$\phi = \frac{M_1 l_1}{E_1 I_1} = \frac{M_2 l_2}{E_2 I_2} = \frac{M_3 l_3}{E_3 I_3}.$$

Thus

$$M_1 = \frac{E_1 I_1}{l_1}\,\phi,$$

$$M_2 = \frac{E_2 I_2}{l_2}\,\phi,$$

$$M_3 = \frac{E_3 I_3}{l_3}\,\phi.$$

The equation of moment equilibrium is then written in the form

$$M = \phi\left(\frac{E_1 I_1}{l_1} + \frac{E_2 I_2}{l_2} + \frac{E_3 I_3}{l_3}\right) = \phi \sum_{i=1}^{3} \frac{E_i I_i}{l_i}.$$

Thus

$$\phi = \frac{M}{\displaystyle\sum_{i=1}^{3}(E_i I_i / l_i)}.$$

The newly found value of ϕ allows us to evaluate the unknown moments in each pile.

With the same data from the previous two examples and $M = 100$ k-ft, the operations and the results of the method of deformations in this case are shown in Table 4.5.

The rotation ϕ of the pile cap is not needed to obtain the moments M_i. Its value, however, is given by

$$\phi = \frac{100}{6421.8} = 0.0155 \text{ rad} = 0.88°$$

The typical ratio M_{i1} is the bending stiffness of a bar fixed at one end and free to rotate and displace at the other, that is, the moment needed to produce a 1 rad rotation at the free end of the bar. The ratios $M_{i1}/\Sigma M_{i1}$ are the relative bending stiffnesses of the piles.

The axial, shear, bending, and twisting stiffness of a framing bar depend on the bar's material and geometric properties and on the constraints of the bar ends.

In other words, different forces and moments are needed to produce unit deformations of bars differently constrained and with different geometries and E moduli.

Example

The column erected on the foundation in Fig. 4.5 is assumed fixed on the pile cap. Thus it can simultaneously transfer to it a shear force S and a bending moment M as well as the vertical force P (Fig. 4.8). We need to determine the shares of S and M carried by each pile in order to investigate the safety of the structure. The two equations of equilibrium of the pile cap

$$S = S_1 + S_2 + S_3,$$

$$M = M_1 + M_2 + M_3,$$

are insufficient to determine the six unknown forces and moments. If, however, we express them all as functions of the rotation ϕ and horizontal displacement δ of the pile cap, the two equations can be

TABLE 4.4.

Pile i	Radius R_i (in.)	$I_i = \dfrac{\pi}{4}R_i^4$ (in.^{4})	Length l_i (ft)	E_i (k/ft^2)	$S_{i1} = \dfrac{3E_iI_i}{144l_i^3}$ (k/ft)	$\dfrac{S_{i1}}{\Sigma S_{i1}}$	$S_i = \dfrac{SS_{i1}}{\Sigma S_{i1}}$ (k)
1	7.5	2485	10	1500	77.656	0.706	70.6
2	9	5153	20	1800	24.155	0.220	22.0
3	6	1018	15	1300	8.169	0.074	7.4
					$\Sigma = 109.98$	$\Sigma = 1$	$\Sigma = 100$

TABLE 4.5.

Pile i	Radius R_i (in.)	$I_i = \dfrac{\pi}{4}R_i^4$ (in.^{4})	Length l_i (ft)	E_i (k/in.^{2})	$M_{i1} = \dfrac{E_iI_i}{144l_i}$ (k-ft)	$\dfrac{M_{i1}}{\Sigma M_{i1}}$	$M_i = \dfrac{MM_{i1}}{\Sigma M_{i1}}$ (k-ft)
1	7.5	2485	10	1500	2588.5	0.4025	40.25
2	9	5153	20	1800	3220.6	0.5015	50.15
3	6	1018	15	1300	612.7	0.096	9.6
					$\Sigma 6421.8$	$\Sigma = 1$	$\Sigma = 100$

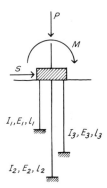

FIGURE 4.8

used to determine ϕ and δ, which are then fed back in the expressions of the forces S_i and moments M_i to find their values. Assuming equal signs for the deflections due to S and M and for the rotations as well, then the rotation of a pile's top section is

$$\phi = \frac{M_i l_i}{E_i I_i} + \frac{S_i l_i^2}{2 E_i I_i},$$

and the deflection is

$$\delta = \frac{M_i l_i^2}{2 E_i I_i} + \frac{S_i l_i^3}{3 E_i I_i}.$$

We multiply δ with $-2/l_i$ to obtain

$$-\frac{2\delta}{l_i} = -\frac{M_i l_i}{E_i I_i} - \frac{2}{3} \frac{S_i l_i^2}{E_i I_i}.$$

Adding this with ϕ gives

$$\phi - \frac{2\delta}{l_i} = \frac{3}{6} \frac{S_i l_i^2}{E_i I_i} - \frac{4}{6} \frac{S_i l_i^2}{E_i I_i} = -\frac{S_i l_i^2}{6 E_i I_i},$$

from which

$$S_i = \frac{6E_iI_i}{l_i^2}\left(\frac{2\delta}{l_i} - \phi\right) = \frac{12E_iI_i}{l_i^3}\,\delta - \frac{6E_iI_i}{l_i^3}\,\phi.$$

Here we note that the preceding expression of S_i with $\phi = 0$ and $\delta = 1$ (sliding pile top) becomes

$$S_{i1} = \frac{12E_iI_i}{l_i^3},$$

which is therefore the shear stiffness of a bar fixed at one end and sliding at the opposite end. If we multiply δ by $-3/2l_i$ and add with ϕ, we obtain

$$\phi - \frac{3\delta}{2l_i} = \frac{4}{4}\frac{M_il_i}{E_iI_i} - \frac{3}{4}\frac{M_il_i}{E_iI_i} = \frac{M_il_i}{4E_iI_i},$$

from which

$$M_i = 4\,\frac{E_iI_i}{l_i}\left(\phi - \frac{3\delta}{2l_i}\right) = -6\,\frac{E_iI_i}{l_i^2}\,\delta + 4\,\frac{E_iI_i}{l_i}\,\phi.$$

Here we note that the preceding expression of M_i with $\delta = 0$ and $\phi = 1$ (hinged pile top) becomes

$$M_{i1} = \frac{4E_iI_i}{l_i},$$

which gives the bending stiffness of a bar fixed at one end and hinged at the other.

The two equations of equilibrium with the preceding expressions of S_i and M_i become

$$S = \sum_{i=1}^{3} S_i = -6\phi\sum_{i=1}^{3}\frac{E_iI_i}{l_i^2} + 12\delta\sum_{i=1}^{3}\frac{E_iI_i}{l_i^3},$$

$$M = \sum_{i=1}^{3} M_i = 4\phi \sum_{i=1}^{3} \frac{E_i I_i}{l_i} - 6\delta \sum_{i=1}^{3} \frac{E_i I_i}{l_i^2}.$$

The summations which are the coefficients of the equations can be conveniently organized in a table. With the same data as in all of the preceding examples, we compile the following table.

Pile i	I_i (in.^{4})	E_i (k/in.^{2})	l_i (ft)	$E_i I_i/144 l_i$ (k-ft)	$E_i I_i/144 l_i^2$ (k)	$E_i I_i/144 l_i^3$ (k/ft)
1	2485	1500	10	2588.5	258.9	25.9
2	5153	1800	20	3220.6	161.0	8.1
3	1018	1300	15	612.7	40.8	2.7
				$\Sigma = 6421.8$	$\Sigma = 460.7$	$\Sigma = 36.7$

With the coefficients (summations) from the preceding table, with $S = 50$ k and $M = 100$ k-ft, the equations are

$$50 = -6(460.7)\phi + 12(36.7)\delta,$$

$$100 = 4(6421.8)\phi - 6(460.7)\delta,$$

and after performing the multiplications, we obtain

$$50 = -2764.2\phi + 440.4\delta,$$

$$100 = 25{,}687.2\phi - 2764.2\delta.$$

Multiplication of the second equation by 2764.2/25,687.2 and addition with the first equation give

$$50 + 10.76 = \delta(440.4 - 297.4),$$

from which

$$\delta = \frac{60.76}{143} = 0.425 \text{ ft.}$$

Substituting δ in the first equilibrium equation gives

$$50 = -2764.2\phi + 187.1,$$

from which

$$\phi = \frac{137.1}{2764.2} = 0.0496 \text{ rad} = 2.84°.$$

Finally, δ and ϕ are replaced in the expressions of S_i and M_i to find the shear forces and bending moments at the top of the three piles. In this case we obtain

$$S_1 = 12E_1I_1 \frac{\delta}{l_1^3} - 6E_1I_1 \frac{\phi}{l_1^2}$$

$$= 12(25.9)0.425 - 6(258.9)0.0496 = 55 \text{ k},$$

$$S_2 = 12E_2I_2 \frac{\delta}{l_2^3} - 6E_2I_2 \frac{\phi}{l_2^2}$$

$$= 12(8.1)0.425 - 6(161)0.0496 = -6.6 \text{ k},$$

$$S_3 = 12E_3I_3 \frac{\delta}{l_3^3} - 6E_3I_3 \frac{\phi}{l_3^2}$$

$$= 12(2.7)0.425 - 6(40.8)0.0496 = 1.6 \text{ k},$$

$$S = S_1 + S_2 + S_3$$

$$= 55 - 6.6 + 1.6 = 50 \text{ k}.$$

$$M_1 = -6E_1I_1 \frac{\delta}{l_1^2} + 4E_1I_1 \frac{\phi}{l_1}$$

$$= -6(258.9)0.425 + 4(2588.5)0.0496 = -146.6 \text{ k-ft},$$

$$M_2 = -6E_2I_2 \frac{\delta}{l_2^2} + 4E_2I_2 \frac{\phi}{l_2}$$

$$= -6(161)0.425 + 4(3220.6)0.0496 = 228.4 \text{ k-ft},$$

$$M_3 = -6E_3I_3 \frac{\delta}{l_3^2} + 4E_3I_3 \frac{\phi}{l_3}$$

$$= -6(40.8)0.425 + 4(612.7)0.0496 = 17.5 \text{ k-ft},$$

$$M = M_1 + M_2 + M_3$$

$$= -146.6 + 228.4 + 17.5 = 99.3 \text{ k-ft}.$$

Since ΣM_i should be 100 k-ft, there is a negligible error of 0.7%.

The advantage of the method of deformations over the method of forces should be evident from the preceding examples. In the first example the three axial forces in the piles are obtained by solving one equation of equilibrium. Three equations of compatibility would be needed with the method of forces. Moreover the calculations for the coefficients of the unknown forces or moments in the compatibility equations are usually more laborious, as shown by a comparison between the preceding table and that compiled for a beam fixed at both ends in Section 4.1. In the second and third examples the total number of unknown parameters is six (three axial forces and three shear forces in the second example; three axial forces and three bending moments in the third). These are obtained by solving the one equation of equilibrium for the axial forces (as in the first example) and one equation of equilibrium for the shear forces or moments. Six equations of compatibility are to be solved using the method of forces. In the fourth example the total number of unknown parameters is 9, and they are found with only three equilibrium equations. Thus the convenience of the method of deformations increases with the number of unknown interactions. On the other hand, students who are not comfortable with abstract reasoning occasionally find the method of forces more palatable: the statically indeterminate reactions appear explicitly in the compatibility equations. This also explains the reasons for the notation "method of forces." The notation "method of deformation" is due to the use of the deformations ϕ, δ, and Δ as unknown parameters in the equations of equilibrium.

4.3.   THE METHODS OF RELAXATION

Architectural structures are usually statically indeterminate, with a great number of redundant constraints. The simultaneous solution of a large number of equations for the evaluation of statically indeterminate reactions was an impossible task before the computer became available. Structural engineers had to resort to other techniques to perform that task. The method of Hardy-Cross was the first to provide a way of reducing the number of equations needed for the evaluation of redundant reactions. Later methods refined the Hardy-Cross approach to eliminate altogether the difficulty associated with large systems of equations. All of these methods were clever but still required crafty, lengthy, and tedious operations when applied to large multistoried frames. Today such large computations are done on the computer. The manual methods are used merely in the analysis of small structures or parts of larger structures.

However, the historic importance of the relaxation methods and their effectiveness in prompting an awareness of the flow of internal forces in structures according to the relative stiffness of the frame elements suggest that we review at least the first and most important method, the Hardy Cross method. For this purpose, we first define the stiffness of a framing element that is the force or moment applied at the end of an otherwise unloaded bar and that produces a unit motion of the bar's end. This concept has already been introduced in Section 4.2, where we have observed the following:

The axial force that applied at a bar's end produces a unit displacement of that end along the beam axis (axial stiffness) is

$$\frac{AE}{l} \cdot$$

The shear force that applied at the free end of a cantilever bar produces a unit transversal displacement of that end (shear stiffness of the cantilever) is

$$\frac{3EI}{l^3} \cdot$$

The bending moment that applied to the free end of a cantilever bar produces locally a unit rotation (bending stiffness of the cantilever) is

$$\frac{EI}{l} \cdot$$

The bending moment that applied to the hinged end of a bar fixed at the other end produces locally a unit rotation (bending stiffness of the bar) is

$$\frac{4EI}{l} \cdot$$

The shear force that applied to the sliding end of a bar fixed at the other end produces locally a unit transversal displacement (shear stiffness of the bar) is

$$\frac{12EI}{l^3} \cdot$$

The shear and bending stiffnesses in all the other possible cases are obtained with a systematic procedure and are organized in Table 4.6. The first row in the table summarizes the preceding results.

248

TABLE 4.6.

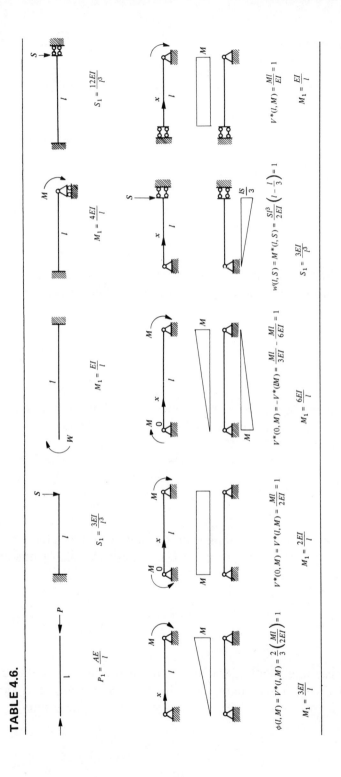

The table is self-explanatory: in each case the deflection or rotation of the loaded end is obtained as the moment M^* or shear V^* on the conjugate beam loaded by the moment diagram g^*. Equating the deformation ϕ or w to 1, we obtain the stiffness of the bar. Both symmetric and antisymmetric bars are included.

Another structural property used in the Hardy-Cross method is the transfer coefficient of a framing element. This is the fraction of the bending moment applied to one end that is transferred to the opposite end. The moment diagram in the first column of the table clearly shows that the transfer coefficient is 0 in the case of a simply supported beam. The moment diagram in the last column of the table shows that the transfer coefficient is −1 in that case: the left end slide reacts with a moment equal and opposite to M. The value of the transfer coefficient on a cantilever is also −1. The transfer coefficient for the moment applied to the hinged end of a bar fixed at the other end is 0.5 (see Problem 4.1.14).

We are now ready to work with the Hardy-Cross method, and we first apply it to a case in which the joints of the structure do not displace. The frame in Fig. 4.9a, is symmetric and symmetrically loaded, and it therefore cannot move to the right or to the left (unsymmetric motions). The joints of the structure are initially prevented from rotating by constraints applied to them as shown in Fig. 4.9b. Under these conditions the moments produced by the loads at the ends of loaded bars are fixed end moments. For instance, on the beam of the frame in Fig. 4.9a, the fixed end moments are

$$M_f = \frac{5(24)}{8} = 15 \text{ k-ft.}$$

These moments are shown in Fig. 4.9b with the graphic notation of an arc of circle, centered on the joint and with an arrowhead on the side of the bar's tensile fibers. This graphic notation is consistently used in the following discussion.

The auxiliary constraints used to block the rotation of the joints (the slides in Fig. 4.9b) do not exist in reality, and they must be removed to obtain the true bending moments in the bars of the frame.

We remove them by applying to each joint of the frame, where we initially placed an auxiliary constraint, a moment equal and opposite to the reactive moment exerted on the joint by the auxiliary constraint. This is the same as saying that the joint and all the bar ends converging at the joint are given back the possibility of rotating. The moment applied to a joint (equal and opposite to the reactive moment of the auxiliary constraint) is *distributed* among the bars converging at the joint according to their relative bending stiffness. This explains why the relaxation methods (relaxation of the initial auxiliary constraints) are also called distribution methods. The reason for a distribution according to relative stiffness is rather evident: in a tug-of-war game a stronger teammate at one end of the rope absorbs a greater share of the pull of the opposite team.

We start practicing this procedure by applying to joint A of the frame a moment +15 k-ft equal and opposite to the –15 k-ft moment with which the slide at A prevents the joint from rotating.

In the relaxation methods clockwise moments are positive, whereas counterclockwise moments are negative.

The +15 k-ft moment applied to joint A must now be distributed between bar AB and bar AD. Since the auxiliary constraint at B has not been removed yet, and since section D is fixed, beam AB and column AD are similarly constrained with end A free again to rotate and the opposite ends fixed. The bending stiffnesses are therefore (see preceding table)

$$\frac{4E_bI_b}{l} \quad \text{and} \quad \frac{4E_cI_c}{h}.$$

The total stiffness of joint A is the sum of the preceding stiffness, and the relative stiffness of the beam is

$$\frac{4E_bI_b/l}{(4E_bI_b/l) + (4E_cI_c/h)} = \frac{1}{1 + (lE_cI_c/hE_bI_b)}.$$

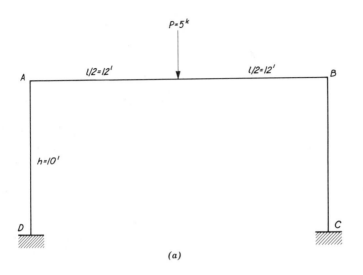

(a)

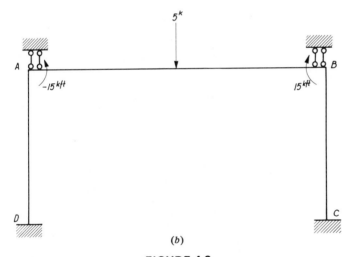

(b)

FIGURE 4.9

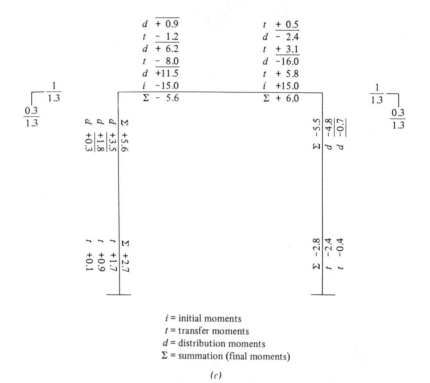

i = initial moments
t = transfer moments
d = distribution moments
Σ = summation (final moments)

(c)

FIGURE 4.9. (*Continued*)

Using, for instance,

$$\frac{I_b}{I_c} = 4, \qquad \frac{E_b}{E_c} = 2,$$

the relative stiffness of the beam is

$$\frac{1}{1 + (24/10)(1/2)(1/4)} = \frac{1}{1.3}.$$

The relative stiffness of the column is then 0.3/1.3, for the sum of the relative stiffnesses at a joint must be 1. The relative stiffnesses are also called distribution coefficients and are shown next to each joint in the distribution chart (Fig. 4.9c). The distribution coefficients at B are the same as at A due to symmetry.

The beam share of the +15 k-ft moment at A is thus

$$\frac{1}{1.3}(15) = 11.5.$$

The column share of the 15 k-ft moment at A is

$$\frac{0.3}{1.3}(15) = 3.5.$$

These moments are written in their places on the distribution chart, and a line is drawn past them to indicate that at this stage the sum of all moments at joint A is equal to 0 (the joint has been equilibrated).

The moments distributed to the beam and the column at A send to the opposite ends B of the beam and D of the column some fraction of their values, according to the transfer coefficients. For a bar free to rotate at one end (A) and fixed at the opposite end (B or D), the transfer is 0.5. Thus at end B of the beam we write a moment

$$0.5(11.5) = 5.8$$

on the distribution chart. Similarly, at end D of the column we write the moment 1.7.

We again place the slide at A to block further rotations and remove the slide at B which is keeping joint B from rotating by reacting with a total moment of +20.8 k-ft. We do so by applying a −20.8 k-ft moment to joint B. This moment is distributed between beam BA and column BC. The beam share is

$$\frac{1}{1.3}(-20.8) = -16,$$

half of which is transferred to end A of bar BA. The column share is

$$\frac{0.3}{1.3}(-20.8) = -4.8,$$

half of which is transferred to end C of bar BC.

All these moments are written on the distribution chart, and a line indicating equilibrium of joint B is drawn past the moments -16 (beam) and -4.8 (column). The transfer moment -8 was determined by assuming that joint A is clamped by the slide, which in reality does not exist. We therefore remove once again the slide at A by applying a $+8$ k-ft moment to joint A which is a moment equal and opposite to the reaction of the slide. This moment is distributed to beam and column, as before. The two shares are written on the distribution chart and a new line indicates that joint A is again in equilibrium. We also write on the distribution chart the transfer moments from A to B and from A to D.

Again we place the slide at A and remove the slide at B which reacts with the moment $+3.1$ k-ft. The slide at B is removed by applying a moment -3.1. The beam and column shares of the -3.1 k-ft moment are written on the distribution chart, as are the transfer moments -1.2 (joint A) and -0.4 (joint C). A moment $+1.2$ is now distributed at A. Since the $+0.5$ k-ft moment transferred from A to B is negligible (1/30 of the initial fixed end moment at B), we can say that the slide at B is not reacting and therefore does not need to be removed to give joint B its real freedom. The process of gradually neutralizing the influence of the auxiliary clamps (slides) which in reality do not exist is thus completed.

The final moment at each bar end is the algebraic sum of the initial fixed end moment, with the shares given that end each time when the clamp at the joint is removed and the true freedom of the joint is reestablished. After all the bar end moments are summed (see the distribution chart), we see that each joint is in equilibrium.

For instance, joint A exerts a moment -5.6 on the beam and a moment $+5.6$ on the column. Their sum is 0 (equilibrium). Similarly, joint B exerts a moment $+6.0$ on the beam and a moment -5.5 on the column. Their sum is small and not equal to zero only because we did not proceed very far in the refinement of the solution and neglected to distribute the $+0.5$ k-ft moment. Thus we take the frame from an initial state in which the joints lack equilibrium (see the fixed end moments) to a final state of equilibrium through a series of stages, in each of which the deformation of the frame preserves the original mutual positions of the bars. Indeed, when a joint rotates, all the bar ends at the joint rotate equally, as assured by the

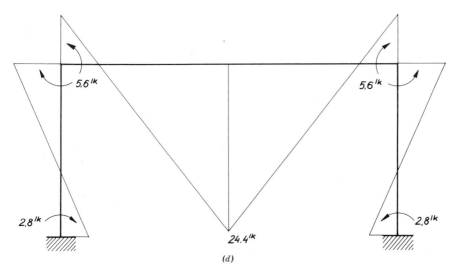

(d)

FIGURE 4.9. (*Continued*)

distribution of moments in conformity with relative stiffnesses. Since this final state of the frame is at once equilibrated and geometrically coherent, it is the true state of the frame under the given loads.

The final moment diagram is drawn in Fig. 4.9d with the moments consistently shown on the side of the tensile fibers. In this particular frame, consideration of symmetry would permit the distribution process to be performed in one operation. In fact, if both clamps at joints *A* and *B* are removed at once, we apply simultaneously a mo-

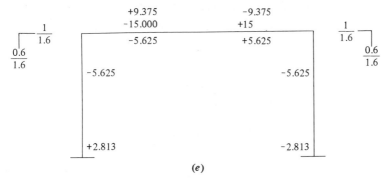

(e)

FIGURE 4.9. (*Continued*)

ment +15 at joint A and a moment -15 at joint B. Then the beam stiffness is $2E_bI_b/l$ (see second column in stiffness table) and the beam relative stiffness (distribution coefficient) is

$$\frac{2E_bI_b/l}{(2E_bI_b/l)+(4E_cI_c/h)} = \frac{1}{1+(2l/h)(E_cI_c/E_bI_b)}$$

$$= \frac{1}{1+[(2)24/10](1/2)(1/4)} = \frac{1}{1.6}.$$

The column stiffness is $0.6/1.6$ (Fig. 4.9e). Thus the column share of 15 k-ft is

$$\frac{0.6}{1.6}(15) = 5.625.$$

The beam share of 15 k-ft is 9.375, which, when algebraically summed with -15, gives -5.625 (see Fig. 4.9e). These are the final moments, for there is no transfer in the case of a beam hinged at both ends and the joints are both in equilibrium.

In a second application of the Hardy-Cross method we consider the more general case of a nonsymmetric frame (Fig. 4.10a), in which therefore the joints displace as well as rotate. In the beginning we apply to joint A (or B) the roller shown in Fig. 4.10b so that the joints cannot displace. As long as the roller is in place, the procedure is identical to that of the preceding case, which is as follows:

Clamps are applied to joints A and B to prevent their rotation.

The fixed end moments are calculated and written on the distribution chart (Fig. 4.10c). They are in this case

$$M_f^A = \frac{Pab^2}{l^2} = \frac{5(8)^2 16}{(24)^2}$$

$$= -8.889 \text{ k-ft} \quad \text{(counterclockwise)},$$

$$M_f^B = \frac{Pa^2b}{l^2} = \frac{5(16)^2 8}{(24)^2}$$

$$= +17.778 \text{ k-ft} \quad (\text{clockwise}).$$

The distribution coefficients are calculated and written near the joints on the distribution chart. Here they are already available from the first example.

The distribution procedure is carried to the desired approximation.

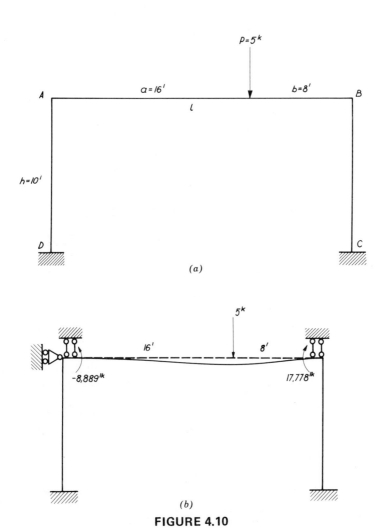

(a)

(b)

FIGURE 4.10

The algebraic sums of all the bars' end moments are written on the distribution chart.

The moment diagram is drawn (Fig. 4.10d).

The shear forces in the columns (slopes of the moment diagrams) are calculated. They are in this case

$$S_{AD} = \frac{(4.251 + 2.124)}{10} = 0.6375 \text{ k,}$$

$$S_{BC} = \frac{(-5.739 - 2.87)}{10} = -0.861 \text{ k.}$$

t	-0.026	d	$-\ 0.052$
d	$+0.137$	t	$+\ 0.068$
t	-0.178	d	$-\ 0.357$
d	$+0.928$	t	$+\ 0.464$
t	-1.206	d	$-\ 2.412$
d	$+6.272$	t	$+\ 3.136$
t	-8.153	d	-16.305
d	$+6.838$	t	$+\ 3.419$
i	-8.889	i	$+17.778$
Σ	-4.251	Σ	$+\ 5.739$

1/1.3
0.3/1.3

1/1.3
0.3/1.3

d +0.041
d +0.278
d +1.881
d +2.051
Σ +4.251

Σ -5.739
d -4.892
d -0.724
d -0.107
d -0.016

t +0.02
t +0.139
t +0.940
t +1.025
Σ +2.124

Σ -2.870
t -2.446
t -0.362
t -0.053
t -0.008

i = initial moments
t = transfer moments
d = distribution moments
Σ = summation (final moments)

(c)

FIGURE 4.10. (*Continued*)

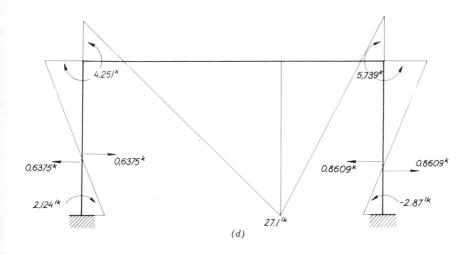

(d)

(e)

FIGURE 4.10. (*Continued*)

The algebraic sum of the shear forces discharged by the columns on the roof beam as axial loads are calculated. Here the sum is

$$S_{AD} + S_{BC} = 0.6375 - 0.861 = -0.2235 \text{ k}.$$

This force is neutralized by a +0.2235 k reaction of the roller placed at A, so the beam does not displace horizontally (Fig. 4.10e). In the symmetric frame S_{AD} and S_{BC} were of course equal and opposite. As far as this point the application of the Hardy-Cross method to the unsymmetric frame has proceeded the same as in the case of a frame without joint displacement. The roller at A, however, does not exist in reality, and it must be removed in order to obtain the true moments in the frame. The removal of the roller is equivalent to applying a -0.2235 k force to the beam, that is, a force equal and opposite to the reaction of the roller. To see the effect of the removal of the roller, we do the following:

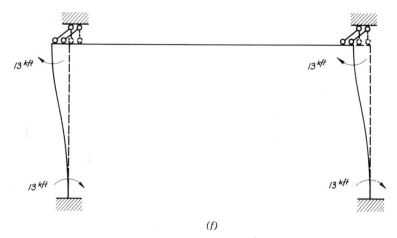

(f)

FIGURE 4.10.   *(Continued)*

We apply slides to joints A and B to prevent their rotation and give beam AB a horizontal displacement (Fig. 4.10f). Sliding end moments are thus generated in the columns while the beam remains undeformed and moment free. One always uses a horizontal displacement that produces convenient sliding-end moments of the columns (i.e., an integer number not too large nor too small) here 13 k-ft. Observing the column deformation due to the horizontal displacement of the beam, we recognize that the sliding end moments are the same at the top and bottom of every prismatic column (constant cross section). This is also evident if we recall that the shear force producing the sliding motion Δ (see stiffness table) is

$$S_1\Delta = \frac{12\Delta EI}{h^3},$$

and due to antisymmetry the moment at both ends is

$$\frac{h}{2}\,S_1\Delta = \frac{6EI}{h^2}\,\Delta.$$

The beam is now immobilized by the application of a roller, and the sliding-end moments of the columns are distributed as usual (see distribution chart in Fig. 4.10g). The moment's sum at each bar end is calculated, the moment diagram is drawn (Fig. 4.10h), and the columns' shear forces are obtained. Here they are

$$S_{AB} = S_{BC} = \frac{(10.83 + 11.92)}{10} = 2.275 \text{ k.}$$

Their sum, 4.55 k, is equal and opposite to the thrust needed to displace the beam by the amount Δ.

If a -4.55 k thrust produces in the frame a beam displacement Δ and the moments shown in Fig. 4.10h, then applying to the beam a

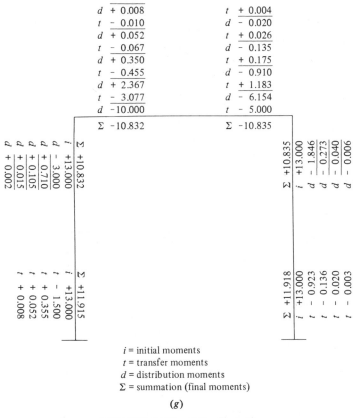

i = initial moments
t = transfer moments
d = distribution moments
Σ = summation (final moments)

(g)

FIGURE 4.10. (*Continued*)

−0.2235 k thrust (equivalent to removing the roller initially placed at A) will produce bending moments in the frame proportional to those in Fig. 4.10h through the proportionality ratio −0.2235/−4.55. These moments are shown in the diagram in Fig. 4.10i. The final moments on the frame with displaceable joints are obtained by the superposition of those in Fig. 4.10d with those in Fig. 4.10i, which

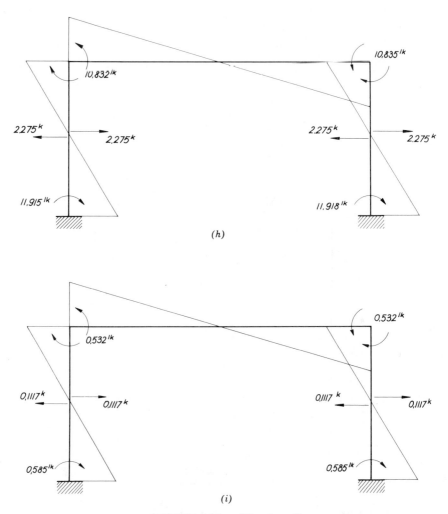

FIGURE 4.10. (*Continued*)

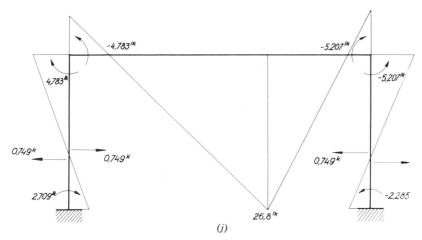

(j)

FIGURE 4.10. *(Continued)*

account for the displacement of the frame. The diagram of final moments is shown in Fig. 4.10j.

We are going to consider next a frame with more than one displaceable story. The application of the Hardy Cross method requires in these cases the solution of as many simultaneous equations as there are displaceable floors, a task that before the computer age was prohibitive for high-rise buildings.

We begin the application of the Hardy Cross method in this case by applying rollers at joints A and D of the frame in Fig. 4.11a, thus preventing the horizontal displacement of the beams. We also apply clamps to all joints (Fig. 4.11b) to prevent them from rotating.

With these constraints in place, the loads produce fixed end moments on the bars of the frame. Since AB is the only loaded bar, in our case the fixed end moments at ends A and B, respectively, are

$$M_f^A = \frac{Pab^2}{l^2} = \frac{50(8)^2 16}{(24)^2} = -88.89 \text{ k-ft} \quad \text{(counterclockwise)},$$

$$M_f^B = \frac{Pa^2 b}{l^2} = \frac{5(16)^2 8}{(24)^2} = \frac{50(16)^2 8}{(24)^2} = +177.78 \text{ k} \quad \text{(clockwise)}.$$

Using the same Young's moduli E_b, E_c and moments of inertia I_b,

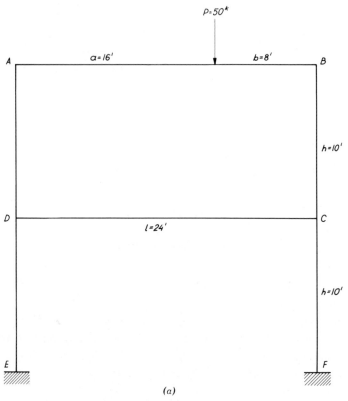

(a)

FIGURE 4.11

I_c of the preceding frame's beam and columns, also for this frame's beams and columns, we obtain the following distribution coefficients:

$$D_{AB} = D_{BA} = \frac{1}{1.3},$$

$$D_{AD} = D_{BC} = \frac{0.3}{1.3},$$

as in the preceding case. Moreover

$$D_{DC} = \frac{4E_bI_b/l}{(4E_bI_b/l) + (4E_cI_c/h) + (4E_cI_c/h)}$$

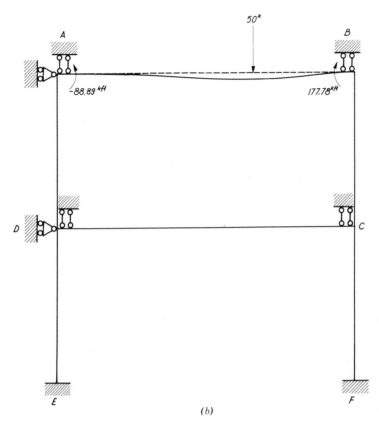

FIGURE 4.11. *(Continued)*

$$= \frac{1}{1 + 2[(24/10)(1/2)(1/4)]} = \frac{1}{1.6},$$

$$D_{DA} = D_{DE} = \frac{0.3}{1.6}.$$

Indeed, the sum $D_{DC} + D_{DA} + D_{DE}$ must be equal to 1. Similarly,

$$D_{CD} = \frac{1}{1.6},$$

$$D_{CB} = D_{CF} = \frac{0.3}{1.6}.$$

$\frac{1}{1.3}$ | $\frac{0.3}{1.3}$

$\frac{1}{1.6}$ | $\frac{0.3}{1.6}$ | $\frac{0.3}{1.6}$

```
t + 0.11        d + 0.23
d - 0.3         t - 0.15
t + 0.53        d + 1.06
d - 1.48        t + 0.74        d +0.23        t +0.11
t + 0.89        d + 1.79        d +1.06        t +0.53
d - 7.91        t - 3.95        d +1.79        i +0.89
t   2.29        t + 4.59        p +4.59        i +2.29
d -48.92        i -24.46        Σ +7.67        Σ +3.82
Σ  54.9         Σ -21.63
```

```
d - 1.00                                  d +15.29
t + 1.07                                  t - 5.59
d - 4.93                                  d + 5.96
t + 5.52                                  t - 3.93
d - 26.38                                 d + 3.54
t +32.00            Σ + 55.2              t - 1.07
d -163.05                                 d - 0.76
t + 34.19                                 t - 0.22
i +177.78                                 Σ +14.52
```

```
t - 0.5                                   t + 7.64
d + 2.14                                  d -11.18
t - 2.46                                  t + 2.98
d +11.05                                  d - 7.86
t -13.19           Σ - 40.5              t + 1.77
d +63.99                                  d - 2.14
t -81.52                                  d + 0.38
d +68.38                                  d - 0.44
i -88.84                                  Σ - 8.85
```

```
Σ +40.5        Σ +15.35               Σ -6.48      Σ -3.2
d +20.51   t +10.25                   d -3.35   t -1.67
t - 1.67   d - 3.35                   d -2.36   t -1.18
d +19.20   t + 9.60                   d -0.64   t -0.32
t - 1.18   d - 2.36                   d -0.13
d + 3.32   t + 1.66
t - 0.32   d - 0.64
d + 0.64   t + 0.32
           d - 0.13
```

$\frac{1}{1.3}$ | $\frac{0.3}{1.3}$

$\frac{1}{1.6}$ | $\frac{0.3}{1.6}$ | $\frac{0.3}{1.6}$

i = initial moments
t = transfer moments
d = distribution moments
Σ = summation (final moments)

(c)

FIGURE 4.11. (Continued)

All the preceding distribution coefficients are shown near the joints on the distribution chart in Fig. 4.11c.

The fixed end moments are now distributed throughout the frame. The algebraic sums of all the moments at each bar end are entered on the distribution chart. The diagram of the moments on the frame is drawn (Fig. 4.11d).

The shear forces in the columns (slopes of the moment diagrams on the columns) are calculated. In this case they are (Fig. 4.11d, e):

$$S_{AD} = \frac{(40.5 + 15.4)}{10} = 5.59 \text{ k,}$$

$$S_{BC} = \frac{(-54.9 - 21.6)}{10} = -7.65 \text{ k,}$$

$$S_{DE} = \frac{(-6.5 - 3.2)}{10} = -0.97 \text{ k,}$$

$$S_{CF} = \frac{(7.7 + 3.8)}{10} = 1.15 \text{ k.}$$

The algebraic sums of the shear forces, discharged as axial loads by the columns on each beam, are calculated. In this case they are (Fig. 4.11e)

$$S_{AD} + S_{BC} = 5.59 - 7.65 = -2.06 \text{ k} \quad \text{(on beam } AB\text{)}$$

$$S_{DA} + S_{CB} + S_{DE} + S_{CF} = -5.59 + 7.65 - 0.97 + 1.15$$

$$= +2.24 \text{ k} \quad \text{(on beam } DC\text{).}$$

These forces are neutralized by equal and opposite reactions in the rollers initially placed at joints A and B, respectively, to prevent the beams from displacing horizontally. These rollers, however, do not exist in reality and must be removed to obtain the true moments in the frame. We are going to remove them one at a time following the same approach used in the preceding case of the frame with one

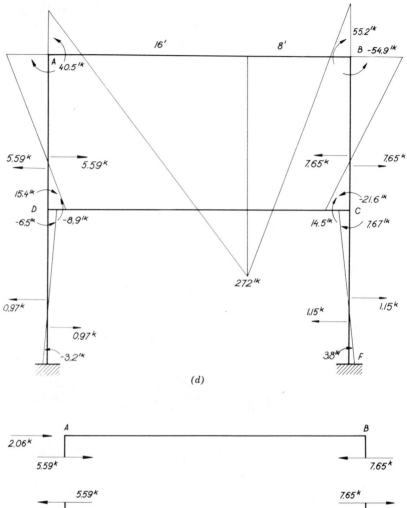

16'   8'

55.2^{lk}

B -54.9^{lk}

A 40.5^{lk}

5.59^k 5.59^k 7.65^k 7.65^k

15.4^{lk} -21.6^{lk}

D   -8.9^{lk} C

-6.5^{lk} 14.5^{lk} 7.67^{lk}

272^{lk}

0.97^k 1.15^k 1.15^k

0.97^k

-3.2^{lk} 3.8^{lk} F

(d)

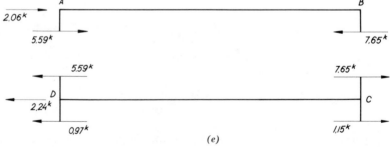

A   B

2.06^k

5.59^k 7.65^k

5.59^k 7.65^k

D   C

2.24^k

0.97^k 1.15^k

(e)

FIGURE 4.11.   (*Continued*)

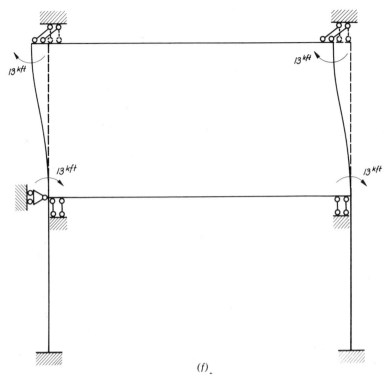

(f)

FIGURE 4.11.   (*Continued*)

beam. For this purpose we first apply the slides in Fig. 4.11*f* to the ends of beams *AB* and *DC*. We remove the roller at *A*, and we give beam *AB* a horizontal displacement such that the sliding end moments in Figs. 4.11*f* are produced. These moments

$$\frac{h}{2} S_1 \Delta = \frac{6EI}{h^2} \Delta$$

are as arbitrary as Δ. We have chosen a convenient value 13 k-ft.

After the displacement Δ of beam *AB*, a roller is again placed at joint *A* to prevent further displacement of *AB*, and the sliding end moments in the columns are distributed throughout the frame as shown in Fig. 4.11*g*. A moment diagram is drawn with the sum totals

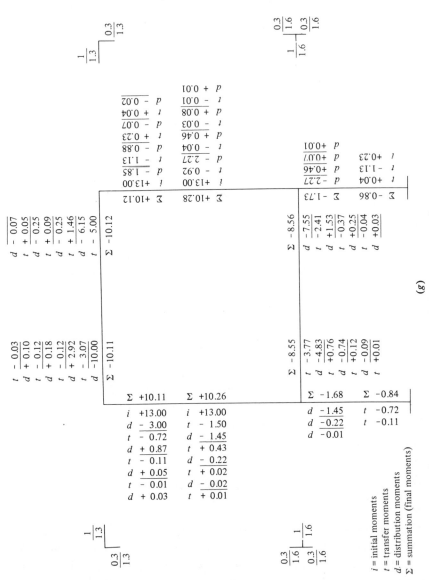

FIGURE 4.11. (Continued)

i = initial moments
t = transfer moments
d = distribution moments
Σ = summation (final moments)

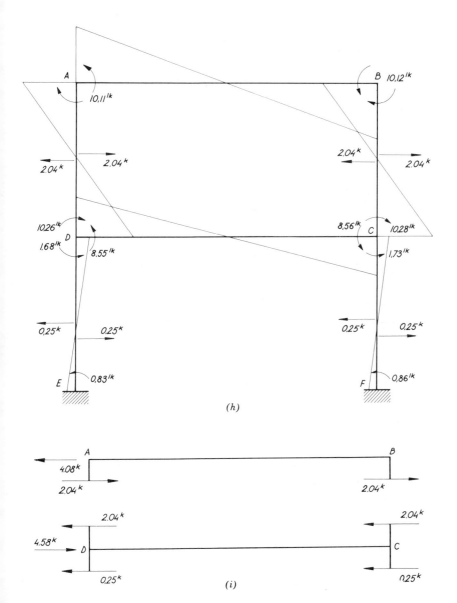

FIGURE 4.11. (Continued)

271

of all the moments of each bar end (Fig. 4.11h) and the columns'
shear forces are calculated. They are

$$S_{AD} = S_{BC} = \frac{(10.11 + 10.26)}{10} = 2.04 \text{ k},$$

$$S_{DE} = S_{CF} = \frac{(1.7 + 0.8)}{10} = 0.25 \text{ k}.$$

These shear forces are discharged as axial loads by the columns on
the beams. The sum of the axial loads on beam AB (Fig. 4.11i) is

$$S_{AD} + S_{BC} = +2.04 + 2.04 = +4.08 \text{ k}.$$

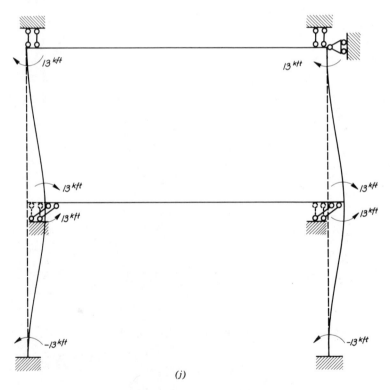

(j)

FIGURE 4.11.   (*Continued*)

The analogous sum on beam DC is

$$S_{DA} + S_{CB} + S_{DE} + S_{CF} = -2.04 - 2.04 - 0.25 - 0.25 = -4.58 \text{ k.}$$

Physically, the sum 4.08 k with reversed sign is the pull to be applied to beam AB in order to produce its displacement Δ and 13 k-ft sliding end moments in the columns; the sum -4.58 k with reversed sign is the reaction of the roller at D to the preceding pull.

We set aside these results for a while and return to the undeformed frame with all joints fixed by the use of rollers at A and D and slides at A, B, C, and D. We remove the roller at D and push beam DC horizontally with a displacement Δ' chosen in this case equal to $-\Delta$ (Fig. 4.11j). Thus this arbitrary displacement produces 13 k-ft moments in the columns, as before. This time of course sliding end moments $6EI\Delta/h^2$ are also produced in the columns of the first floor.

Through the same series of steps followed after the removal of the roller at A (Figs. 4.11k, l, and m), we obtain the sum of the axial loads discharged by the columns on the beams. For beam AB this sum is

$$S'_{AD} + S'_{BC} = 2.29 + 2.29 = 4.58 \text{ k.}$$

For beam DC the sum is

$$S'_{DA} + S'_{CB} + S'_{DE} + S'_{CF} = -2.29 - 2.29 - 2.58 - 2.58 = -9.74 \text{ k.}$$

Physically, the sum -9.74 with reversed sign is the push to be applied to beam DC to produce in the four columns the sliding end moments of Fig. 4.11j. The sum 4.58 k with reversed sign is the reaction of the roller at A to the preceding push.

We must now recall that the rollers placed at A and D before distributing the fixed end moments due to gravity loads react with forces equal to 2.06 k and -2.24 k, respectively. Removal of the roller at A is equivalent to applying a -2.06 k horizontal force at joint A to neutralize the reaction of the local roller. Similarly, removing the roller at D is equivalent to applying a $+2.24$ k horizontal force at joint D to neutralize the local roller. The simultaneous removal of

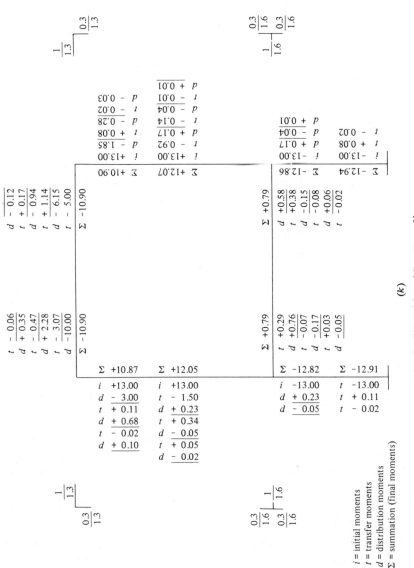

(k)

FIGURE 4.11. (Continued)

i = initial moments
t = transfer moments
d = distribution moments
Σ = summation (final moments)

274

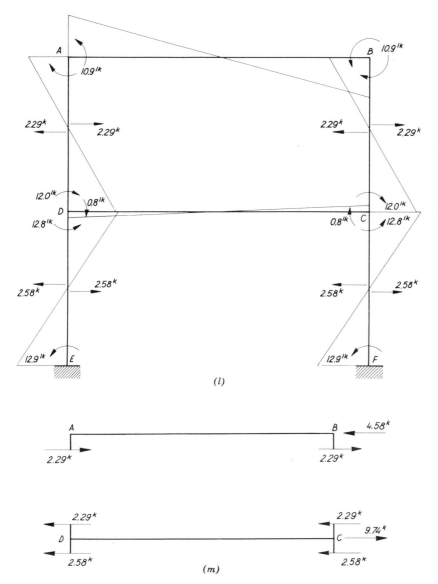

(l)

(m)

FIGURE 4.11. (*Continued*)

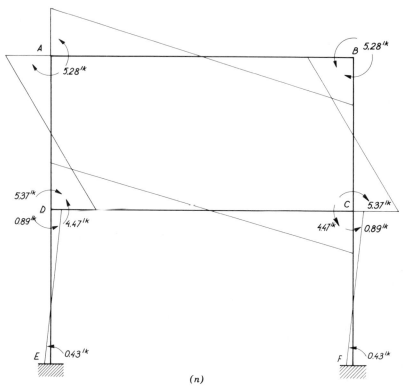

(n)

FIGURE 4.11. (*Continued*)

the rollers at A and D (i.e., the simultaneous application of horizontal forces -2.06 k at A and 2.24 k at D) will produce bending moments in all bars of the frame. The moment at each bar's end is given by the sum of a moment proportional (through a coefficient α_1) to that produced by a -4.08 k pull on joint A and a $+4.58$ k reaction of the roller at D with a moment proportional (through a coefficient α_2) to that produced by a $+9.74$ k push on joint D and a -4.58 k reaction of the roller at A. The coefficients α_1 and α_2 are obtained by solving the system of two simultaneous equations:

$$-2.06 = -4.08\alpha_1 - 4.58\alpha_2,$$

$$+2.24 = +4.58\alpha_1 + 9.74\alpha_2.$$

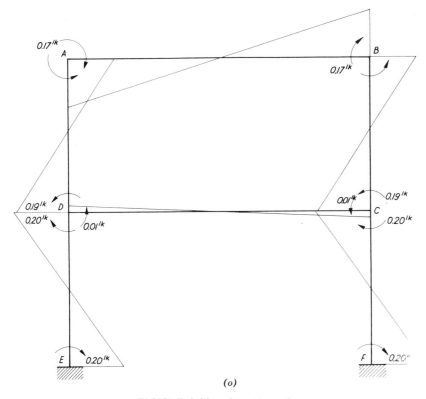

(o)

FIGURE 4.11.   (*Continued*)

If indeed multiplication by α_1 of the −4.08 pull at A (and of the +4.58 reaction of the roller at D), multiplication by α_2 of the +9.74 k push at D (and of the −4.58 k reaction of the roller at A), and summations at joints A and D of these products give the values of the forces −2.06 k and +2.24 k, then multiplication by α_1 of the moments produced by pull −4.08 at A, multiplication by α_2 of the moments produced by push +9.74 at D, and summation of these products give the same moments produced by simultaneously applying forces −2.06 and +2.24 at joints A and D, respectively.

The solution of the preceding system of equations is

$$\alpha_1 = 0.5227, \quad \alpha_2 = -0.0158.$$

Thus we multiply the bar end moments in Fig. 4.11h by α_1 to obtain the true moments due to the displacement of beam AB (Fig. 4.11n). We then multiply the bar end moments in Fig. 4.11l by α_2 to obtain the true moments due to the displacement of beam DC (Fig. 4.11o). To obtain the final moments on the frame, we sum the moments in Fig. 4.11d, produced by the loads on the frame with rollers at A and D, with the true moments produced by the displacement of beams AB (Fig. 4.11n) and DC (Fig. 4.11o).

The final and complete moment diagram is shown in Fig. 4.11p. The final and complete shear diagram is shown in Fig. 4.11q. The final and complete diagram of axial forces is shown in Fig. 4.11r. The Figs. 4.11p and q show the equilibrium in rotation of each

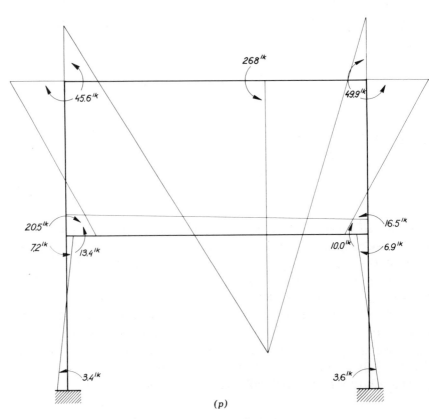

(p)

FIGURE 4.11.   (*Continued*)

joint ($\Sigma M = 0$ at each joint) and the equilibrium in translation of each beam ($\Sigma F_x = 0$ on each beam axis x), thus satisfying two necessary tests of a correct procedure.

The application of the Hardy-Cross method to this sixfold indeterminate two-story frame reduces the number of equations required with the method of forces (six) to only two. For a much larger (and many more times statically indeterminate) two-story frame, the number of equations would remain the same (two). However, a twenty-story frame would require solving a system of twenty simultaneous equations, a major task if done by hand. Moreover the lengthy and elaborate steps preceding the solution of the equations greatly reduce the practical advantages of the method. Many refinements of

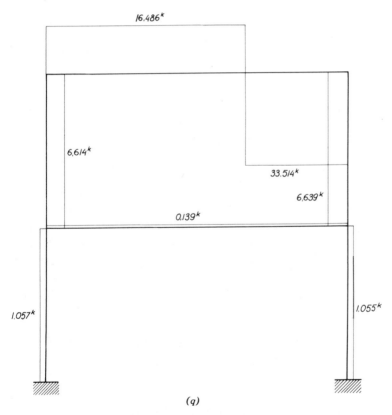

(q)

FIGURE 4.11. (Continued)

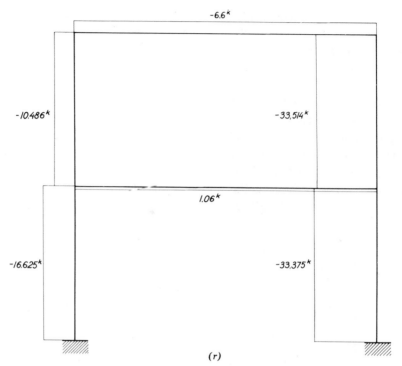

FIGURE 4.11. (*Continued*)

the Hardy-Cross method by other authors have eliminated altogether the need for writing and solving systems of equations. Their intricacy, however, is much greater and could lead to errors without great care and concentration. The tests of a correct solution ($\Sigma\, M = 0$ at each joint, $\Sigma\, F_x = 0$ on each beam axis x) are always therefore the very important last steps in the application of any distribution (relaxation) method.

4.4. STATICALLY INDETERMINATE REACTIONS BY THE PRINCIPLE OF VIRTUAL WORK

The principle of virtual work, introduced in Chapter 3 with its application to the evaluation of structural deformations, is used in evaluating reactions of constraints as well. In the case of statically determinate reactions the statement and solution of equations of equilibrium is a more physically intuitive approach than resorting to the equation of virtual work. Therefore the virtual work approach is seldom if ever used. However, in the evaluation of statically indeterminate reactions there are cases where this approach has practical advantages, in addition to that of greater generality. We are going to discuss briefly an application in the case of statically determinate reactions and then consider, to a greater extent, cases of application in the research of indeterminate reactions.

When a structure is statically determinate, evaluating the reactions by the principle of virtual work requires discarding one of the constraints, replacing it with its unknown reaction, and giving the structure a small virtual motion that is compatible with its remaining constraints and geometric integrity. Since the removal of a constraint of a stable structure makes it unstable, the virtual motion is rigid, that is, without change in shape or volume (Fig. 4.12b). Internal forces therefore do not materialize, and the system of equilibrated forces doing work for the virtual motion includes only loads and the unknown reaction. In the example we are going to discuss, these are the gravity loads G_1 and G_2 and the reaction V_r.

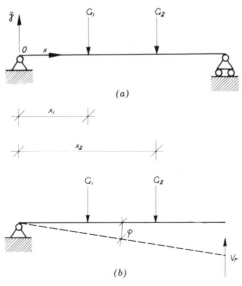

FIGURE 4.12

Thus giving the beam in Fig. 4.12a the small, rigid virtual rotation ϕ produces the work

$$G_1 x_1 \phi + G_2 x_2 \phi - V_r l \phi.$$

Equating this work to zero gives

$$V_r = \frac{(G_1 x_1 + G_2 x_2)}{l},$$

the same solution of an equation of moment equilibrium with pivot point at the origin of the Cartesian frame x, z.

In evaluating statically indeterminate reactions by the principle of virtual work, the redundant constraints are discarded and replaced by their unknown reactive forces or moments. The indeterminate structure is replaced in this manner by its statically determinate principal structure. The deformation of this structure (same as that of the real structure) is used as the coherent deformation. Virtual unit loads, with the same line of action as that of the unknown loads of the principal structure, are used in conjunction with their reactions and internal forces as a set of equilibrated forces doing work for the real deformation.

For example, the beam in Fig. 4.13a is replaced by a principal structure in Fig. 4.13b. The known load F produces a deflection $w_1(0)$ at $x = 0$ and mutual rotation of the ends of each beam element dx from $x = a$ to $x = l$:

$$d\phi_1 = F(x - a) \frac{dx}{EI},$$

where $F(x - a)$ are the bending moments due to F (Fig. 4.13c). We neglect shear deformations. The unknown load R_l (redundant reaction) produces a deflection $w_2(0)$ at $x = 0$ and mutual rotation of the ends of each beam element dx

$$d\phi_2 = x R_l \left[\frac{dx}{EI} \right].$$

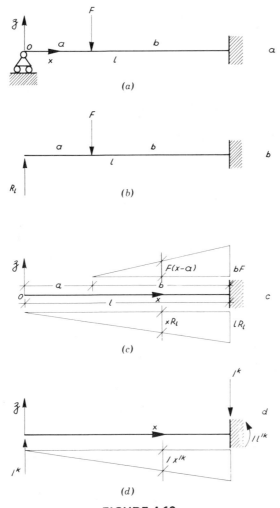

FIGURE 4.13

The preceding deformations are used as coherent deformations in the virtual work equation. We use as a set of equilibrated forces a unit load with the same line of action as R_l, the reaction and reactive moment at $x = l$ due to this load, and the associated internal forces, that is, bending moments (Fig. 4.13d). With the signs of all forces and moments in Figs. 4.13a, b, c, and d, the virtual work is thus

$$1(-w_1 + w_2) + \int_0^l 1 \cdot x \, (d\phi_1) - \int_0^l 1 \cdot x \, (d\phi_2).$$

The 1 k reactive force and $1l$ k-ft reactive moment in the set of equilibrated forces do not work, for the fixed end does not move. The first term of the virtual work also vanishes because the total deflection at the roller is

$$w_1(0) - w_2(0) = 0$$

Replacing the expressions of $d\phi_1$, and $d\phi_2$ in the virtual work and equating it to zero gives

$$\int_a^l 1x \left(\frac{F(x-a)}{EI} \right) dx - \int_0^l 1x \left(\frac{xR_1}{EI} \right) dx = 0,$$

from which

$$F \int_a^l x^2 \, dx - aF \int_a^l x \, dx - R_1 \int_0^l x^2 \, dx = 0.$$

Integrating gives

$$\frac{F}{3} (l^3 - a^3) - \frac{aF}{2} (l^2 - a^2) - R_1 \frac{l^3}{3} = 0,$$

from which

$$\frac{F}{6} (2l^3 - 2a^3 - 3al^2 + 3a^3) = R_1 \frac{l^3}{3}.$$

The preceding equation can be written in the form

$$\frac{Fb^2}{6} (2l + a) = R_1 \frac{l^3}{3}.$$

This can be verified by replacing b with $l - a$. Solving for R_l gives

$$R_l = \frac{Fb^2}{2l^3}\,(a + 2l),$$

a result already found in this chapter by the method of forces.

The preceding example leads one to believe that the virtual work approach is more laborious than other methods for the evaluation of indeterminate reactions. However, in cases more complex than that just discussed, it proves to be very effective, as we will show in the evaluation of redundant reactions and axial forces in trusses.

In a second case study of indeterminate reactions, we consider the beam in Fig. 4.14a. Its principal structure and the moment diagrams produced on it by the known load and unknown reactions are shown in Figs. 4.14b and c. The relevant deformations produced by load F are

$$w_1(0), \quad \phi_1(0),$$

and between $x = a$ and $x = l$,

$$d\phi_1(x) = F(x - a)\,\frac{dx}{EI}.$$

The relevant deformations produced by R_l are

$$w_2(0), \quad \Phi_2(0),$$

$$d\Phi_2(x) = xR_l\,\frac{dx}{EI}.$$

Analogously, M_l produces

$$w_3(0), \quad \phi_3(0),$$

$$d\phi_3(x) = M_l\,\frac{dx}{EI}.$$

Using as a set of equilibrated virtual forces the unit load in Fig. 4.14d with the same line of action of R_l, its reactions and internal moments, the equation of virtual work with the signs of all forces and moments in Figs. 4.14a, b, c, and d is

$$1(-w_1 + w_2 - w_3) + \int_a^l 1x(d\phi_1) - \int_0^l 1x(d\phi_2) + \int_0^l 1x(d\phi_3) = 0.$$

Next using the set of equilibrated forces made by the unit moment at $x = 0$ (Fig. 4.14e) and the reactions and internal moments produced by it, we obtain the second equation required to evaluate R_l and M_l:

$$1(\phi_1 - \phi_2 + \phi_3) - \int_a^l 1(d\phi_1) + \int_0^l 1(d\phi_2) - \int_0^l 1(d\phi_3) = 0.$$

In the two preceding equations we have neglected shear deformation and work. The total deflection of the fixed end at $x = 0$ is

$$w_1(0) - w_2(0) + w_3(0) = 0.$$

The total rotation of the same end is

$$\phi_1(0) - \phi_2(0) + \phi_3(0) = 0.$$

Replacing the expressions of rotations and deflections, the equations become therefore

$$F \int_a^l x^2 \, dx - aF \int_a^l x \, dx - R_l \int_0^l x^2 \, dx + M_l \int_0^l x \, dx = 0,$$

$$-F \int_a^l x \, dx + aF \int_a^l dx + R_l \int_0^l x \, dx - M_l \int_0^l dx = 0.$$

Integrating gives

$$\frac{F(l^3 - a^3)}{3} - \frac{aF}{2}(l^2 - a^2) = R_l \frac{l^3}{3} - M_l \frac{l^2}{2},$$

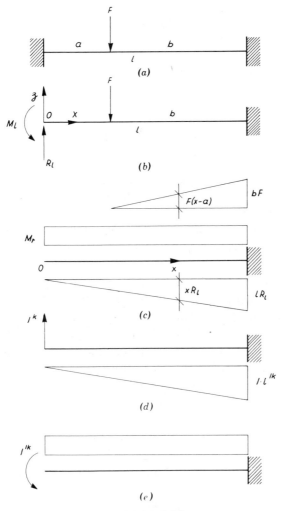

FIGURE 4.14

$$-\frac{F}{2}(l^2 - a^2) + aF(l - a) = -R_l\frac{l^2}{2} + M_l l.$$

The left side of the first equation is $Fb^2(2l + a)/6$. This can be verified by replacing b with $l - a$. Thus the first equation becomes after multiplication by $2/l^2$

$$\frac{Fb^2}{3l^2}(2l+a) = \frac{2l}{3}R_l - M_l$$

Replacing in the second equation $(l-a)^2$ with b^2, and then dividing by l gives

$$\frac{Fb^2}{2l} = \frac{l}{2}R_l - M_l.$$

This system of two simultaneous equations in the unknown reactions R_l and M_l, and its solutions, have been found earlier in this chapter by the method of forces.

In the next example, we apply the principle of virtual work to a structure free of bending moments and subject rather to axial internal forces.

The truss in Fig. 4.15a varies from that in Fig. 1.67a by intermediate vertical support at joint 8. The former truss therefore has one redundant constraint whose reaction we plan to evaluate. We use as a system of equilibrated forces a unit upright (positive) vertical force at joint 8, and the associated reactions and internal forces of the principal structure, that is, the truss without a roller at joint 8 (Fig. 4.15b). Due to symmetry the vertical reactions have a value -0.5 k, and the horizontal reactions are

$$0.5 \tan 30° = 0.29 \text{ k.}$$

The reaction at the link is therefore

$$(0.5^2 + 0.29^2)^{1/2} = 0.58 \text{ k.}$$

These reactions, as well as the internal forces (obtained with Ritter sections or a Maxwell diagram) are shown in Fig. 4.15b, where negative axial forces are compressive and positive forces tensile. We use as a system of small coherent deformations those of the real structure. They are obtained by superposition of the deformations of the principal structure due to the 5 k gravity loads with those due to the unknown reaction. The latter ones constitute the products of the de-

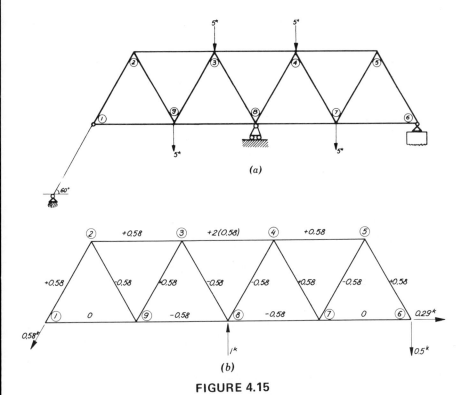

FIGURE 4.15

formations produced by the unit reaction in Fig. 4.15*b* and the un-known magnitude R of the reaction. Thus

$$\delta = \delta_g + R\delta_1,$$

$$\Delta l = \frac{(P_g + RP_1)\,l}{EA},$$

where

δ = the real displacements of the joints of the statically indeter-minate structure,

δ_g = the displacements of the joints of the principal structure due to the 5 k gravity loads,

δ_1 = the analogous displacements due to the 1 k virtual load at joint 8,

R = the magnitude of the statically indeterminate reaction,

Δl = the real extension of the bars of the statically indeterminate structure,

P_g = the axial forces of the bars of the principal structure due to the 5 k gravity loads,

P_1 = the axial forces of the bars of the principal structure due to the 1 k virtual load at joint 8.

With the additional notation R_v for the virtual reactions of the principal structure due to the unit virtual load, the equation of virtual work in our case is

$$1\delta_8 + \sum R_v \delta - \sum P_1 \Delta l = 0.$$

The real displacements δ of the points of application of the virtual load (joint 8) and right end reaction (joint 6) are zero, since joints 8 and 6 do not move. The link has been considered a deformable constraint, but the work of its virtual reaction is included among those of the virtual axial forces in the bars. Indeed, we have no reason to treat the link differently from all other bars of the truss. Thus the first two terms of the virtual work vanish, and we obtain

$$\sum \frac{P_1(P_g + RP_1)l}{EA} = 0,$$

which, by expanding, gives

$$\sum \frac{P_1 P_g l}{EA} = -R \sum P_1^2 \frac{l}{EA}.$$

Thus

$$R = \frac{- \sum P_1 P_g l/EA}{\sum P_1^2 l/EA}.$$

For each bar of the principal structure Columns 1 to 10 of Table 4.7 give the following:

l = length,

A = area,

l/EA = inverse of axial stiffness,

P_g = axial force due to 5 k gravity loads,

P_1 = axial force due to 1 k virtual load at joint 8,

$P_g l/EA$ = extension due to P_g,

$P_g P_1 l/EA$ = work done by P_1 for the preceding extension,

$P_1 l/EA$ = extension due to P_1,

$P_1^2 l/EA$ = work done by P_1 for the preceding extension.

With the summations at the bottom of columns 8 and 10, we obtain

$$R = \frac{-(-267.2)}{19.7} = 13.56 \text{ k.}$$

The real axial forces P in the bars of the statically indeterminate truss are now obtained by superposing the values P_g in column 5 of the preceding table to the products 13.56 P_1 of the axial forces P_1 in column 6 with the magnitude 13.56 of the redundant reaction R. Column 11 shows the results of the superposition.

As another example of statically indeterminate truss, both externally and internally, we consider the structure in Fig. 4.16a and its principal structure in Fig. 4.16b, in which the left end horizontal constraint and bar 5-11 have been removed and replaced by indeterminate forces H_l and P_{5-11}. In order to evaluate these forces, we write two equations of virtual work. In the first equation the set of virtual equilibrated forces is made of a horizontal force at joint 1 and of the associated reactions and internal forces of the principal structure (Fig. 4.16c). The coherent deformation for which the preceding forces do work is that of the real truss. In the second equation the set of virtual equilibrated forces is made of unit thrusts of bar 5-11 on joints 5 and 11, and of the internal forces of the principal truss due to these unit forces. The constraints of the

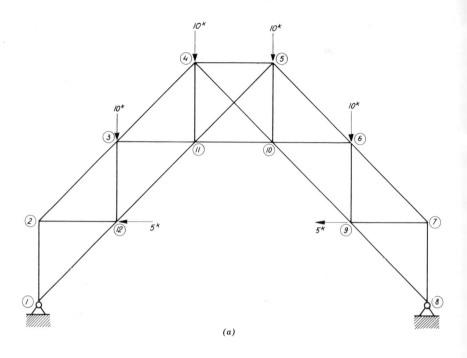

(a)

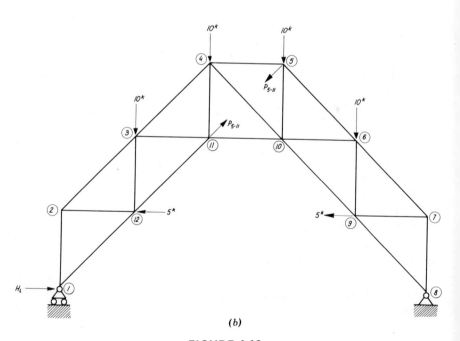

(b)

FIGURE 4.16

TABLE 4.7.

1 Bar	2 l (in.)	3 A (in.^{2})	4 $10^3 l/EA$ (in./k)	5 P_g (k)	6 P_1 (k)	7 $10^3 P_g l/EA$ (in.)	8 $10^3 P_g P_1 l/EA$ (k-in.)	9 $10^3 P_1 l/EA$ (in.)	10 $10^3 P_1^2 l/EA$ (k-in.)	11 P (k)
Link	120	1.2	3.448	−11.5	+0.58	−39.7	−23	+2	+1.16	−3.64
1–2	120	1.2	3.448	−11.5	+0.58	−39.7	−23	+2	+1.16	−3.64
2–3	120	1.2	3.448	−11.5	+0.58	−39.7	−23	+2	+1.16	−3.64
3–4	120	1.2	3.448	−14.4	+1.16	−49.7	−57.6	+4	+4.64	+1.33
4–5	120	1.2	3.448	−11.5	+0.58	−39.7	−23	+2	+1.16	−3.64
5–6	120	1.2	3.448	−11.5	+0.58	−39.7	−23	+2	+1.16	−3.64
6–7	120	1.2	3.448	0	0	0	0	0	0	0
7–8	120	1.2	3.448	+8.66	−0.58	+29.9	−17.3	−2	+1.16	+0.80
8–9	120	1.2	3.448	+8.66	−0.58	+29.9	−17.3	−2	+1.16	+0.80
9–1	120	1.2	3.448	0	0	0	0	0	0	0
2–9	120	1.2	3.448	+11.5	−0.58	+39.7	−23	−2	+1.16	+3.64
3–9	120	1.2	3.448	−5.77	+0.58	−19.9	−11.5	+2	+1.16	+2.09
3–8	120	1.2	3.448	0	−0.58	0	0	−2	+1.16	−7.86
4–8	120	1.2	3.448	0	−0.58	0	0	−2	+1.16	−7.86
4–7	120	1.2	3.448	−5.77	+0.58	−19.9	−11.5	+2	+1.16	+2.09
5–7	120	1.2	3.448	+11.5	−0.58	+39.7	−23	−2	+1.16	+3.64
							$\Sigma -267.2$		$\Sigma +19.7$	

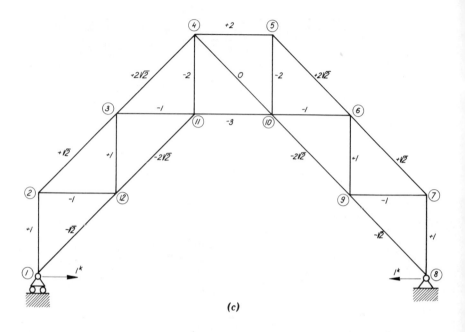

(c)

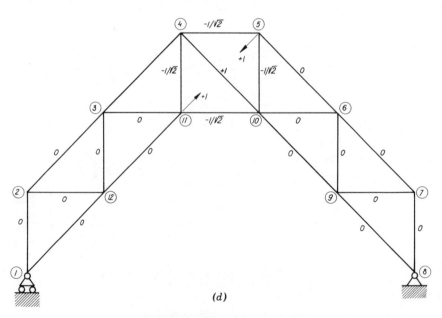

(d)

FIGURE 4.16. (*Continued*)

294

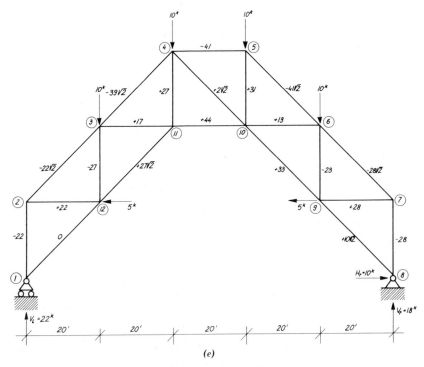

(e)

FIGURE 4.16.   (*Continued*)

principal structure do not react to the pair of unit thrusts: they are equal, opposite, and colinear. Thus only in a few bars in the neighborhood of joints 5 and 11 are the internal forces other than zero (Fig. 4.16d). The virtual work in the second equation is done by this second set of virtual equilibrated forces for the deformation of the real truss. The two equations then are

$$- \sum P_1 \frac{Pl}{EA} = 0,$$

$$-(1)\, \Delta l_{5-11} - \sum P_2 \frac{Pl}{EA} = 0,$$

where the summations extend over the bars of the principal structure in Fig. 4.16b.

The first of the preceding equations lacks the work of the external forces because joints 1 and 8 of the real structure do not move. Thus the 1 k load at joint 1 and the 1 k reaction at joint 8 in Fig. 4.16c do not work. The first term of the second equation can also be written as

$$-(1\delta_5 + 1\delta_{11}),$$

where δ_5 and δ_{11} are the real displacements of joints 5 and 11 in the direction of the bar 5–11. If we factor out the unit force, then the preceding work is

$$-1(\delta_5 + \delta_{11}) = -(1)\Delta l_{5-11},$$

for the sum of δ_5 and δ_{11} is the shrinkage or extension of bar 5–11. This work is negative, as well as the work of the internal forces. The explanation is that if the axial force in bar 5–11 is tensile as it has been assumed, joints 5 and 11 move farther apart, and the unit virtual loads do negative work. If bar 5–11 were rather in compression (reversed unit virtual loads), joints 5 and 11 would move closer to one another, and again the unit virtual loads would do negative work. More synthetically, we can say that work $1\Delta l_{5-11}$ is in reality internal work and has therefore the same sign as that of the internal works.

In the equations of virtual work P_1 and P_2 are the internal forces of the trusses in Figs. 5.16c and d, Pl/EA are the extensions of the bars in Fig. 4.16b which are the same as the extensions of the bars of the real truss in Fig. 4.16a. Calling P_0 the axial forces produced by the known loads in the principal structure (Fig. 4.16e), the real axial forces P are given by

$$P = P_0 + P_1 H_l + P_2 P_{5-11}.$$

Thus the two equations of virtual work become

$$\sum P_1 P_0 \frac{l}{EA} + H_l \sum P_1^2 \frac{l}{EA} + P_{5-11} \sum P_1 P_2 \frac{l}{EA} = 0,$$

$$P_{5-11} \left(\frac{l}{EA}\right)_{5-11} + \sum P_2 P_0 \frac{l}{EA} + H_l \sum P_2 P_1 \frac{l}{EA} +$$

$$+ P_{5-11} \sum P_2^2 \, \frac{l}{EA} = 0,$$

in which H_l and P_{5-11} are unitless numbers that give the magnitudes of the indeterminate forces.

All the bars of the truss are assumed made of the same material; thus multiplication of both sides of the equations by E eliminates it. In a first design trial all cross-sectional areas may be considered equal; this eliminates A from the equations. Then the coefficients of the equations are obtained from Table 4.8 (similar to that of the preceding example). They are the summations at the bottoms of columns 6, 7, 8, 9, and 10.

With the numerical values of the coefficients obtained in the table, the equations become

$$1712 H_l + 70.7 P_{5-11} = 29{,}434,$$

$$70.7 H_l + (68.3 + 28.2) P_{5-11} = 782.7.$$

Multiplication of the first equation by $-70.7/1712$ and summation with the second equation give

$$- \frac{70.7}{1712} \, (70.7) \, P_{5-11} + 96.5 P_{5-11} = - \frac{70.7}{1712} \, (29{,}434) + 782.7,$$

from which

$$P_{5-11} = -4.6.$$

This negative solution indicates that the axial force in bar 5–11 has a sign opposite to that assumed. Replacing the preceding value in the first equation gives

$$H_l = \frac{29434 + 327}{1712} = 17.4.$$

The real axial force in each bar is obtained by the summation

$$P = P_0 + 17.4 P_1 - 4.6 P_2.$$

TABLE 4.8.

1 Bar	2 l (ft)	3 P_0 (k)	4 P_1 (k)	5 P_2 (k)	6 P_0P_1l (ft-k²)	7 P_1^2l (ft-k²)	8 P_1P_2l (ft-k²)	9 P_0P_2l (ft-k²)	10 P_2^2l (ft-k²)	11 P (k)
1-2	20	−22	+1	0	−440	20	0	0	0	−4.60
2-3	$20\sqrt{2}$	$-22\sqrt{2}$	$+\sqrt{2}$	0	−1244.5	56.6	0	0	0	−6.50
3-4	$20\sqrt{2}$	$-39\sqrt{2}$	$+2\sqrt{2}$	0	−4412.3	226.3	0	0	0	−5.94
4-5	20	−41	+2	$-1/\sqrt{2}$	−1640	80.0	−28.3	+579.8	+10	−2.95
5-6	$20\sqrt{2}$	$-41\sqrt{2}$	$+2\sqrt{2}$	0	−4638.6	226.3	0	0	0	−8.77
6-7	$20\sqrt{2}$	$-28\sqrt{2}$	$+\sqrt{2}$	0	−1583.9	56.6	0	0	0	−14.99
7-8	20	−28	+1	0	−560	20	0	0	0	−10.60
8-9	$20\sqrt{2}$	$+10\sqrt{2}$	$-\sqrt{2}$	0	−565.7	56.6	0	0	0	−10.47
9-10	$20\sqrt{2}$	$+33\sqrt{2}$	$-2\sqrt{2}$	0	−3733.5	226.3	0	0	0	−2.54
10-11	20	+44	−3	$-1/\sqrt{2}$	−2640	180	+42.4	−622.3	+10	−4.95
11-12	$20\sqrt{2}$	$+27\sqrt{2}$	$-2\sqrt{2}$	0	−3054.7	226.3	0	0	0	−11.03
12-1	$20\sqrt{2}$	0	$-\sqrt{2}$	0	0	56.6	0	0	0	−24.61
2-12	20	+22	−1	0	−440	20	0	0	0	+4.60
3-12	20	−27	+1	0	−540	20	0	0	0	−9.60
3-11	20	+17	−1	0	−340	20	0	0	0	−0.40
4-11	20	+27	−2	$-1/\sqrt{2}$	−1080	80	+28.3	−381.8	+10	−4.55
4-10	$20\sqrt{2}$	$+2\sqrt{2}$	0	+1	0	0	0	+80.0	28.3	−1.77
5-10	20	+31	−2	$-1/\sqrt{2}$	−1240	80	+28.3	−438.4	10.0	−0.55
6-10	20	+13	−1	0	−260	20	0	0	0	−4.40
6-9	20	−23	+1	0	−460	20	0	0	0	−5.60
7-9	20	+28	−1	0	−560	20	0	0	0	+10.60
Σ					−29,434	+1712	+70.7	−782.7	68.3	

298

These internal forces are shown in column 11 of the preceding table. The required cross-sectional areas A can be now obtained from the axial forces. Then the routine is repeated with the aid of a table similar to the preceding one, in which the new ratios l/A replace the values in column 2. Trials must continue until the cross-sectional areas selected in a given trial are adequate for the axial forces in column 11 of the table associated with that trial.

In the preceding examples, we have not considered the virtual work of internal forces on the plane of a cross section that is shear forces and twisting moments, because this work is either lacking or negligible. Applications of the principle of virtual work in evaluating indeterminate external or internal forces due to distortions or lack of fit are shown in some of the problems.

PROBLEMS

4.1.1. Find the moment on the intermediate support of the continuous beam in Fig. 4.17a. Use an equation of compatibility and a principal beam with a moment release (hinge) on that support.

Solution. Figure 4.17b shows the principal beam; Fig. 4.17c shows its conjugate, loaded by the moment diagrams (load EIg^*), from which we obtain the rotations V^* of the two spans at the intermediate support:

$$EIV_1^* = \frac{1}{2} \left(\frac{2}{3}\right) \frac{gl_1^3}{8} - \frac{2}{3} \left(\frac{1}{2}\right) l_1 M,$$

$$EIV_2^* = -\frac{1}{2} \left(\frac{2}{3}\right) \frac{gl_2^3}{8} + \frac{2}{3} \left(\frac{1}{2}\right) l_2 M,$$

where counterclockwise rotations have positive sign. Since the real beam is continuous on the intermediate support, the local moment M common to both spans must correct the counterclockwise rotation $gl_1^3/24$ and the clockwise rotation $gl_2^3/24$, so that $V_1^* = V_2^*$. Thus

$$\frac{gl_1^3}{24} - \frac{l_1 M}{3} = -\frac{gl_2^3}{24} + \frac{l_2 M}{3}.$$

Consolidating gives

$$M(l_2 + l_1) = \frac{g}{8} (l_2^3 + l_1^3),$$

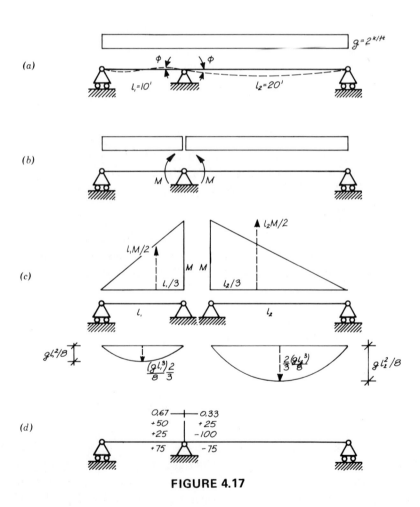

FIGURE 4.17

from which

$$M = \frac{g}{8}\left(\frac{l_2^3 + l_1^3}{l_2 + l_1}\right) = \frac{2}{8}\left(\frac{8000 + 1000}{20 + 10}\right) = 75 \text{ k-ft.}$$

4.1.2. Perform the task in Problem 4.1.1 for the continuous beam in Fig. 4.18.

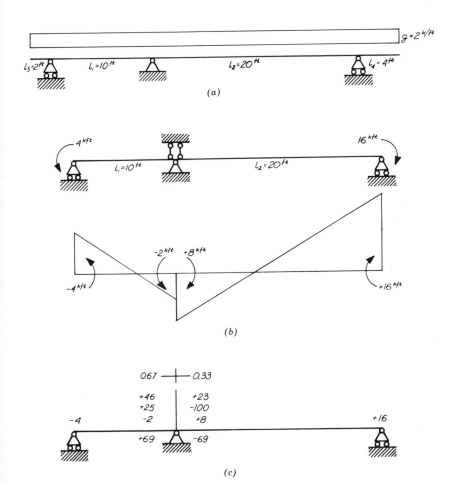

(a)

(b)

(c)

FIGURE 4.18

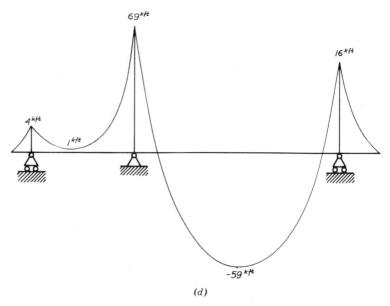

(d)

FIGURE 4.18. *(Continued)*

4.1.3. Using an equation of compatibility, find the moment transferred by the slide in Fig. 4.19*a*.

Solution.   Figures 4.19*b* and *c* show the principal structures and
their conjugates loaded by the diagrams of *EIg**.
The rotations on the left and right sides of the slide are thus

$$EIV_L^* = \frac{-Gl^2}{8} + lM,$$

$$EIV_R^* = \frac{gl^3}{6} - lM,$$

where counterclockwise rotations have positive sign. Equating the
preceding rotations gives

$$2lM = \frac{gl^3}{6} + \frac{Gl^2}{8},$$

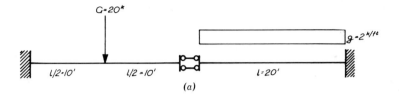

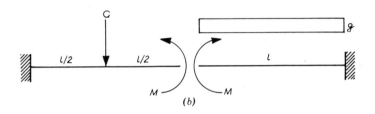

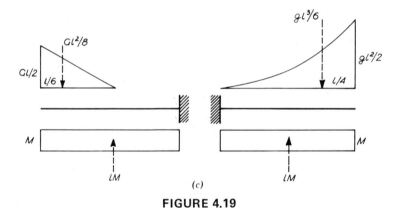

(c)

FIGURE 4.19

from which

$$M = \frac{gl^2}{12} + \frac{Gl}{16} = \frac{2}{12}(20)^2 + \frac{20}{16}(20) = 91.7 \text{ k-ft.}$$

4.1.4. Perform the task in Problem 4.1.3 using the principal structure in Fig. 4.19*d*, with the uniform load *g* replaced by a concentrated force *gl* = 40 k.

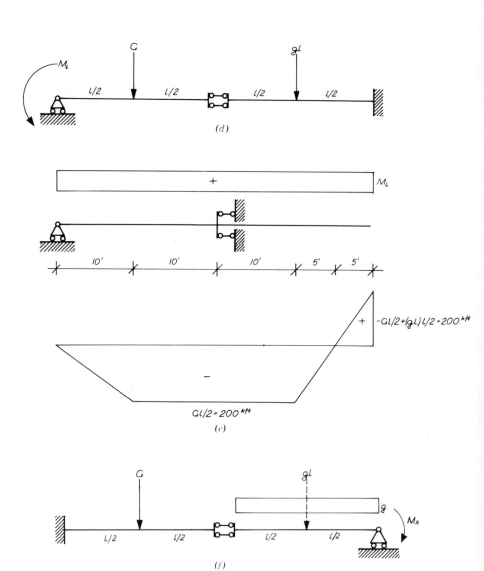

FIGURE 4.19. (*Continued*)

Solution. Figure 4.19e shows the conjugate of the principal beam, loaded by the moment diagrams (loads EIg^*). The shear force at the left end of the conjugate beam is

$$EIV_L^* = 2lM_L - \left(\frac{Gl}{2}\right) l - \frac{1}{2}\left(\frac{Gl}{2}\right) \frac{l}{2}.$$

Clearly the left end roller is the only vertical support and carries all of the loads EIg^*. The positive and negative triangles at the right end of the moment diagram due to the known loads cancel each other out. The preceding reaction of the conjugate beam vanishes, for the real beam does not rotate at its left end. Thus

$$EIV_L^* = 2(20) M_L - 20(10) 20 - \frac{1}{8}(20)^2 20 = 0,$$

from which

$$M_L = 125 \text{ k-ft.}$$

The moment transferred by the slide is then (Fig. 4.19d, e)

$$M = 200 - M_L = 200 - 125 = 75 \text{ k-ft.}$$

We note that this value of M is different from that obtained in Problem 4.1.3. This is because the uniform load is replaced with its resultant, as can be verified by solving Problem 4.1.5.

4.1.5. Perform the task in Problem 4.1.3, but replace the uniform load with a concentrated force $gl = 40$ k.

4.1.6. Perform the task in Problem 4.1.3 using the principal structure in Fig. 4.19f and with the uniform load g replaced by a concentrated force $gl = 40$ k.

4.1.7. Find the shear V transferred by the hinge in Fig. 4.20a with an equation of compatibility. Use the principal structure in Fig. 4.20b.

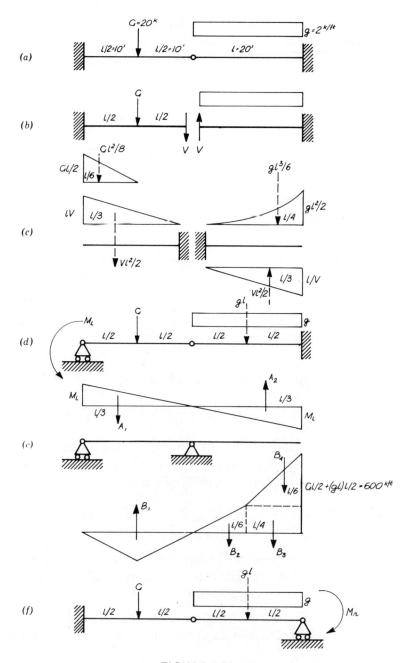

FIGURE 4.20

Solution. Figure 4.20c shows the conjugate of the principal structure loaded by the diagrams of EIg^*. The deflections on the left and right sides of the hinge are

$$EIM_L^* = \left(\frac{5l}{6}\right)\frac{Gl^2}{8} + \left(\frac{2l}{3}\right)\frac{Vl^2}{2} = \frac{5}{48}Gl^3 + \frac{Vl^3}{3},$$

$$EIM_R^* = \left(\frac{3l}{4}\right)\frac{gl^3}{6} - \left(\frac{2l}{3}\right)\frac{Vl^2}{2} = \frac{1}{8}gl^4 - \frac{Vl^3}{3},$$

where downward deflections have positive sign.

Equating the preceding deflections gives

$$\frac{2}{3}Vl^3 = \frac{1}{8}gl^4 - \frac{5}{48}Gl^3,$$

from which

$$V = \frac{3}{16}\left(gl - \frac{5G}{6}\right) = \frac{3}{16}\left(40 - \frac{100}{6}\right) = 4.375 \text{ k.}$$

4.1.8. Perform the task in Problem 4.1.7 using the principal structure in Fig. 4.20d and with the uniform load g replaced by a concentrated force $g = 40$ k.

Solution. Figure 4.20e shows the conjugate of the principal beam, loaded by the moment diagrams (loads EIg^*). The numerical values of the moment areas in Fig. 4.20e are

$$A_1 = A_2 = \frac{l}{2}M_L = 10M_L \text{ k-ft}^2,$$

$$B_1 = \frac{Gl^2}{8} = 1000 \text{ k-ft}^2,$$

$$B_2 = \frac{Gl^2}{16} = 500 \text{ k-ft}^2,$$

$$B_3 = \frac{Gl^2}{8} = 1000 \text{ k-ft}^2,$$

$$B_4 = \frac{Gl^2}{16} + \frac{gl^3}{8} = 500 + 2000 = 2500 \text{ k-ft}^2.$$

The reaction V_L^* of the conjugate beam, that is, the rotation of the principal beam, is obtained with an equation of moment equilibrium about the intermediate support of the conjugate beam:

$$-lV_L^* + \frac{2l}{3} A_1 - \frac{l}{2} B_1 - \frac{l}{3} B_2 + \frac{2l}{3} A_2 - \frac{3l}{4} B_3 - \frac{5l}{6} B_4 = 0.$$

Multiplication by 6 and substitution of symbols with numbers give

$$-6(20) V_L^* + 4(20) 10M_L - 3(20) 1000 - 2(20) 500$$

$$+ 4(20) 10M_L - 4.5(20) 1000 - 5(20) 2500 = 0,$$

from which

$$120V_L^* = 1600M_L - 420,000.$$

The left end rotation of the principal beam vanishes, for the real beam is fixed locally. Thus

$$0 = 1600M_L - 420,000,$$

from which

$$M_L = \frac{420,000}{1,6000} = 262.5 \text{ k-ft.}$$

Then

$$V_L = \frac{G}{2} + \frac{M_L}{l} = 10 + \frac{262.5}{20} = 23.125 \text{ k,}$$

and the shear V transferred by the hinge is

$$V = V_L - G = 3.125 \text{ k}.$$

We note that the preceding value is different from that obtained in Problem 4.1.7 because the uniform load is replaced with a concentrated load $gl = 40$ k. This can be verified by solving Problem 4.1.9.

4.1.9. Perform the task in Problem 4.1.7, but replace the uniform load with a concentrated load $gl = 40$ k.

4.1.10. Perform the tasks in Problem 4.1.7 using the principal beam in Fig. 4.20f and replacing the uniform load with a concentrated force $gl = 40$ k.

4.1.11. Find the moment at the left end of the beam in Fig. 4.21a. The beam is elastically fixed at its left end with spring constant s, that is, the ratio between the local moment M_L and rotation ϕ_L,

$$s = \frac{M_L}{\phi_L}.$$

Physically s is the moment that produces a unit elastic rotation.

Use an equation of compatibility to perform this task.

Solution. Figure 4.21b shows the principal beam and its conjugate loaded by the curvature diagrams (loads g^*). The rotation ϕ_L is the shear V_L^* of the conjugate beam. Thus

$$V_L^* = \phi_L = -\frac{2}{3} \frac{M_L l}{2EI} + \frac{Gl^2}{16EI} = \frac{M_L}{s},$$

from which

$$M_L = \frac{Gl^2/16EI}{(1/s) + (l/3EI)}.$$

4.1.12. Find the horizontal reaction at the left end of the beam in Fig. 4.21a when G is removed and the temperature rises by ΔT. The horizontal constraint of the beam's left end is elastic with a spring constant s_h; that is, the ratio between the local reaction H_L and the local horizontal displacement u_L is

$$s_h = \frac{H_L}{u_L}.$$

Use an equation of compatibility to perform this task.

Solution. The thermal expansion is $\alpha l \Delta T$, where α is the coefficient of thermal expansion. The contraction due to H_L is $H_L l/EA$. Their difference equals the penetration u_L of the bar in the wall:

$$u_L = \alpha l \Delta T - \frac{H_L l}{EA} = \frac{H_L}{s_h},$$

from which

$$H_L = \frac{\alpha l \Delta T}{(1/s_h) + (l/EA)}.$$

4.1.13. Find the vertical reaction at the left end of the beam in Fig. 4.21a. The vertical constraint of the beam's left end is elastic with a spring constant s_v; that is, the ratio between the local reaction V_L and the local vertical displacement w_L is

$$s_v = \frac{V_L}{w_L}.$$

Use an equation of compatibility to perform this task.

4.1.14. Find the moment at the left end of the beam in problem 4.1.11, when the gravity load G is removed and a counterclockwise moment M_R is applied to the beam's right end.

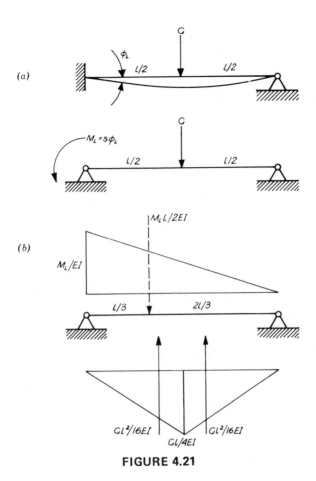

FIGURE 4.21

Solution. On the conjugate beam the reactive moment M_L of the spring at the left end produces the load g^* in Fig. 4.21b. The applied moment M_R produces a similar load g^*. The moment areas are $-M_L l/2EI$ and $+M_R l/2EI$. The rotation ϕ_L (shear V_L^* of the conjugate beam) is

$$\phi_L = V_L^* = \frac{M_L}{s} = -\frac{2}{3}\left(\frac{M_L l}{2EI}\right) + \frac{1}{3}\left(\frac{M_R l}{2EI}\right)$$

from which

$$M_L = \frac{M_R\, l/6E}{(l/3E) + (1/s)}$$

When the left end is rigidly rather than elastically fixed, then

$$\frac{M_L}{s} = \phi_L = 0$$

which means

$$s = \infty, \quad M_L = \frac{1}{2}\, M_R.$$

4.2.1. Using the method of deformations, obtain the moments of the beam and the column of the frame in Fig. 4.22a at their connection. Draw the complete moment diagram of the frame.

Solution. The moment M_3 on the overhang at the beam-column connection is

$$M_3 = 6 \times 6 = 36 \text{ k-ft.}$$

For the equilibrium of the joint in rotation, the sum of the beam moment M_1 and column moment M_2 must neutralize M_3 (Fig. 4.22b):

$$M_1 + M_2 = M_3.$$

The rotations of the bar ends at their connection are obtained as shear forces V^* on the conjugate bars. For this task, we list the moment areas in Fig. 4.22c:

$$A_1 = \frac{M_1 l_1}{12} = 2M_1 \text{ k-ft}^2,$$

$$A_2 = \frac{M_1 l_1}{3} = 8M_1 \text{ k-ft}^2,$$

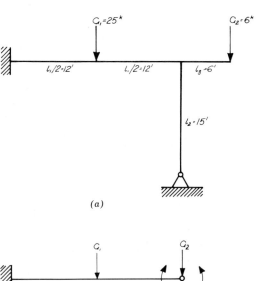

(a)

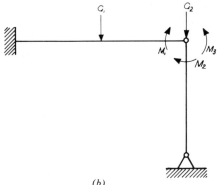

(b)

FIGURE 4.22

$$B_1 = \frac{18}{704} G_1 l_1^2 = 368.2 \text{ k-ft}^2,$$

$$B_2 = \frac{12.5}{704} G_1 l_1^2 = 255.7 \text{ k-ft}^2,$$

$$B_3 = \frac{5}{128} G_1 l_1^2 = 562.5 \text{ k-ft}^2,$$

$$C = M_2 \frac{l_2}{2} = 7.5 M_2 \text{ k-ft}^2.$$

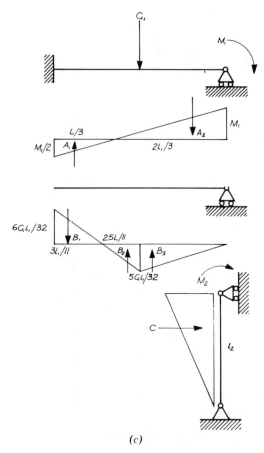

(c)

FIGURE 4.22. (*Continued*)

Thus on the beam

$$E_1 I_1 \phi = +A_1 - A_2 - B_1 + B_2 + B_3 = -6M_1 + 450,$$

where clockwise rotations are negative, and on the column

$$E_2 I_2 \phi = \frac{2}{3} C = -5M_2.$$

We assume for simplicity that $E_1 I_1 = E_2 I_2$. Thus

$$M_1 = \frac{1}{6}(-EI\phi + 450),$$

$$M_2 = \frac{-EI\phi}{5}.$$

With the preceding moment expressions, the equilibrium equation is

$$-EI\phi \left(\frac{1}{6} + \frac{1}{5}\right) + \frac{450}{6} = 36.$$

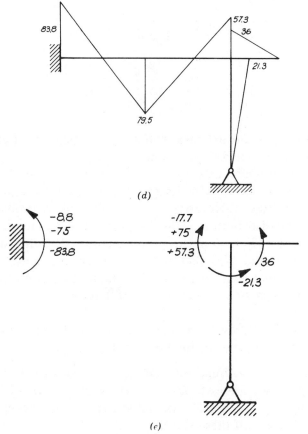

(d)

(e)

FIGURE 4.22. (*Continued*)

Consolidating, we obtain

$$\frac{11 EI}{30} \phi = 39,$$

from which

$$\phi = \frac{106.4}{EI}.$$

We substitute ϕ in M_1 and M_2 to obtain

$$M_1 = \frac{450}{6} - 106.4 = 57.3 \text{ k-ft,}$$

$$M_2 = - \frac{106.4}{5} = -21.3 \text{ k-ft.}$$

The negative result for M_2 means that this moment is counterclockwise rather than clockwise, as assumed.

We do not propose additional problems to be solved with the method of deformations, for its physical principle is analogous to that underlying the distribution methods. Indeed, in Problem 4.3.1 we perform the distribution of the 39 k-ft unbalanced moment (same as the moment $11 EI\phi/30$ in this problem) using the same stiffnesses of the bars $EI/6$ and $EI/5$ that appear in M_1 and M_2 in this problem. This implies equal rotations ϕ of all bars at their connection, the same point of departure as the method of deformations.

4.3.1.   Use the Hardy Cross method to find the moments at the ends of the bars of the frame in Fig. 4.22a.

Solution.   The fixed end moments on the loaded bars are shown in Fig. 4.22e. They are as follows: on the span, $G_1 l_1/8 = 75$ k-ft; on the overhang, $G_2 l_3 = 36$ k-ft. Assuming equal EI for beam and column, the stiffnesses of these bars are

$$\frac{4EI}{l_1} = \frac{EI}{6} \quad \text{(beam)},$$

$$\frac{3EI}{l_2} = \frac{EI}{5} \quad \text{(column)}.$$

The relative stiffness (distribution coefficients) are

$$\frac{1/6}{(1/6) + (1/5)} = \frac{1}{1 + (6/5)} = \frac{5}{11} \quad \text{(beam)},$$

$$\frac{6}{11} \quad \text{(column)}.$$

The total initial moment at the joint, with reversed sign, is -39 k-ft. The beam's share of this moment is

$$\frac{5}{11}(-39) = -17.7 \text{ k-ft.}$$

The column's share is

$$\frac{6}{11}(-39) = -21.3 \text{ k-ft.}$$

Figure 4.22d shows the final moments.

We note in this case how this approach is simpler than that in Problem 4.2.1.

4.3.2. Find the moment on the intermediate support of the continuous beam in Fig. 4.17a. Use the Hardy Cross distribution method.

Solution. The initial moments (fixed end moments) at the support are

$$M_{i1} = \frac{gl_1^2}{8} = 25 \text{ k-ft,}$$

$$M_{i2} = \frac{gl_2^2}{8} = -100 \text{ k-ft} \quad \text{(counterclockwise)}.$$

The stiffnesses of the two spans in Fig. 4.17b are

$$\frac{3EI}{l_1} = \frac{3EI}{10},$$

$$\frac{3EI}{l_2} = \frac{3EI}{20}.$$

The relative stiffnesses (distribution coefficients) are

$$\frac{3/l_1}{(3/l_1) + (3/l_2)} = \frac{3/10}{(3/10) + (3/20)} = \frac{1}{1 + (1/2)} = \frac{2}{3},$$

$$\frac{3/l_2}{(3/l_1) + (3/l_2)} = \frac{1}{3}.$$

Figure 4.17d shows the initial moments $gl^2/8$, the distribution moments, and the final moments.

4.3.3. Find the moments on the supports of the continuous beam in Fig. 4.18a.

Solution. The moment on the left support is

$$\frac{g}{2}(l_3)^2 = \frac{2}{2}(2)^2 = -4 \text{ k-ft},$$

clockwise on overhang l_3 but counterclockwise on span l_1. The moment on the right support is

$$\frac{g}{2}(l_4)^2 = \frac{2}{2}(4)^2 = 16 \text{ k-ft}.$$

When the rotation of the beam on the intermediate support is frozen (Fig. 4.18b), these end moments transfer (to the fixed opposite end of the spans) moments according to the table of transfer coefficients in this chapter. The initial moments on the intermediate support are thus

$$M_{i1} = \frac{g}{8}(l_1)^2 - \frac{1}{2}\left(\frac{g}{2}\right) l_3^2 = 25 - 2 = 23 \text{ k-ft},$$

$$M_{i2} = -\frac{g}{8}(l_2)^2 + \frac{1}{2}\left(\frac{g}{2}\right) l_4^2 = -100 + 8 = -92 \text{ k-ft}.$$

Their imbalance with reversed sign is

$$-(23 - 92) = +69 \text{ k-ft}.$$

This is distributed according to the relative stiffnesses obtained in Problem 4.3.2.

Figures 4.18c and d show the distribution chart and the final moments. To obtain the largest moments near the midspan, we calculate the span end shear:

$$V_{1L} = \frac{gl_1}{2} - \frac{(M_{1R} - M_{1L})}{l_1} = 10 - \frac{65}{10} = 3.5 \text{ k},$$

$$V_{1R} = \frac{gl_1}{2} + \frac{(M_{1R} - M_{1L})}{l_1} = 10 + 6.5 = 16.5 \text{ k}.$$

Then

$$M_1^{\max} = \frac{V_{1L}^2}{2g} - M_{1L} = \frac{3.5^2}{4} - 4 = 3.0625 - 4 = -0.9375 \text{ k-ft},$$

$$M_1^{\max} = \frac{V_{1R}^2}{2g} - M_{1R} = \frac{16.5^2}{4} - 69 = -0.9375 \text{ k-ft}.$$

Analogously,

$$V_{2R} = \frac{g}{2}(l_2) - \frac{(M_{2R} - M_{2L})}{2} = 20 - \frac{53}{20} = 17.25 \text{ k-ft},$$

$$M_2^{\max} = \frac{V_{2R}^2}{2g} - M_{2R} = 59.26 \text{ k-ft}.$$

4.3.4.   Find the moments M_A, M_B, M_C, M_D on the beam in Fig. 4.23a.

Solution.   Initial moments (fixed rotations at B and C) are

$$M_D^i = \frac{Gl_3}{8} = \frac{5}{8}(24) = 15 \text{ k-ft} = M_{C3}^i,$$

$$M_{C2}^i = \frac{Gl_2}{8} = \frac{5}{8}(16) = 10 \text{ k-ft} = M_{B2}^i.$$

To find M_A^i, we set equal to zero the shear V_{1L}^* at the left end of the conjugate of the principal beam of span 1 (Fig. 4.23b):

$$M_A^i l_1 - \frac{G}{8} l_1^2 = 0,$$

from which

$$M_A^i = \frac{G}{8} l_1 = \frac{5}{8}(24) = 15 \text{ k-ft} \quad (\text{clockwise}),$$

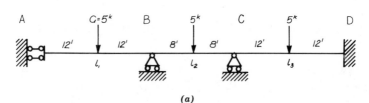

(*a*)

FIGURE 4.23

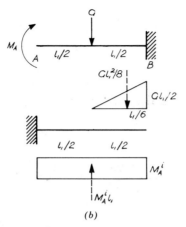

FIGURE 4.23. (*Continued*)

Then

$$M_{B1}^i = -M_A^i + \frac{G}{2} l_1 = -15 + 60 = 45 \text{ k-ft} \quad \text{(clockwise)}.$$

The stiffnesses (see the table of stiffnesses) are as follows:

Left of B,

$$\frac{EI}{l_1} = \frac{EI}{24}.$$

Right of B,

$$\frac{4EI}{l_2} = \frac{EI}{4}.$$

Left of C,

$$\frac{4EI}{l_2} = \frac{EI}{4}.$$

Right of C,

$$\frac{4EI}{l_3} = \frac{EI}{6}.$$

The distribution coefficients (relative stiffnesses) are as follows:

Left of B,

$$\frac{1/24}{1/24 + 1/4} = \frac{1}{1 + 6} = \frac{1}{7}.$$

Right of B,

$$\frac{6}{7}.$$

Left of C,

$$\frac{1/4}{1/4 + 1/6} = \frac{1}{1 + 2/3} = 0.6.$$

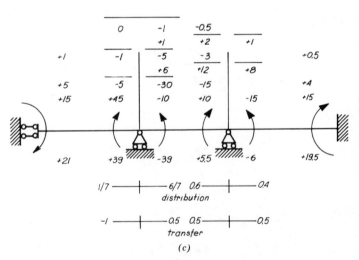

FIGURE 4.23. (*Continued*)

Right of C,

$$0.4.$$

The transfer coefficients are as follows:

Left of B, -1.
Right of B, 0.5.
Left of C, 0.5.
Right of C, 0.5.

Figure 4.23c shows the distribution chart and, below the beam, the final moments.

4.3.5. Find the moments at the ends of all bars of the frame in Fig. 4.24a.

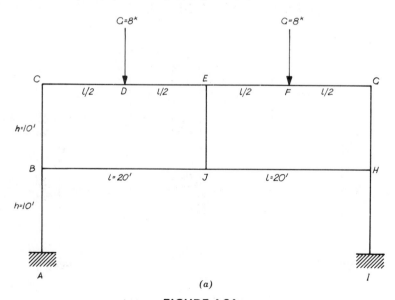

(a)

FIGURE 4.24

Solution. Due to symmetry, the beams of the frame do not move horizontally. The middle column, however, moves vertically. We start blocking this move with a roller at J and the rotations of all joints with slides at B, C, E, G, H, and J. Under these conditions the loads produce the initial moments $Gl/8$ in Fig. 4.24b:

$$\frac{Gl}{8} = \frac{8}{8} (20) = 20 \text{ k-ft.}$$

Assuming for simplicity an equal EI for all bars, the distribution coefficients at joints B and H are

$$\frac{4/h}{[2(4/h)] + 4/l} = \frac{4/10}{8/10 + 4/20} = 0.4 \quad \text{(columns),}$$

$$0.2 \quad \text{(beams).}$$

At joints C and G,

$$\frac{4/h}{4/h + 4/l} = \frac{1/10}{1/10 + 1/20} = \frac{2}{3} \quad \text{(column),}$$

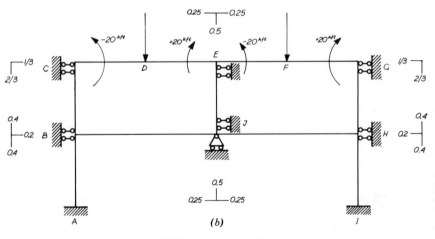

FIGURE 4.24. (*Continued*)

$$\frac{1}{3} \quad \text{(beam)}.$$

At joints E and J

$$\frac{4/h}{4/h + [2(4/l)]} = \frac{1}{1 + [2(h/l)]} = 0.5 \quad \text{(column)},$$

$$0.25 \quad \text{(beams)}.$$

```
    + 0.4          + 0.2      - 0.2              - 0.4
    + 6.7          + 3.9      - 3.9              - 6.7
    - 20.0         +20.0   i  - 20.0         i   +20.0
    - 12.9         +24.1   Σ  - 24.1         Σ   +12.9
```

Left column values (top): -0.1, $+0.9$, -1.3, $+13.3$, $+12.8$

Left side second level: -0.2, $+0.5$, -2.7, $+6.7$, $+4.3$

Right side (top): Σ -12.8; $+0.1$, -0.9, $+1.3$, -13.3 and $+0.1$, -0.9, $+1.3$, -13.3

Right side second level: Σ -4.9; -6.7; $+0.2$, -0.5, $+2.7$, -6.7

```
      - 0.1                          + 0.1
      - 1.3                          + 1.3
      - 1.4                      Σ   + 1.4
            - 0.7      + 0.7
```

Bottom left: -0.2, -2.7, -2.9

Right bottom: Σ $+2.9$; $+0.2$, $+2.7$

Lower left column: -0.1, -1.3, -1.4

Bottom right: Σ $+1.4$; $+0.1$, $+1.3$

i = initial moments
Σ = summation (final moments)

(c)

FIGURE 4.24. (*Continued*)

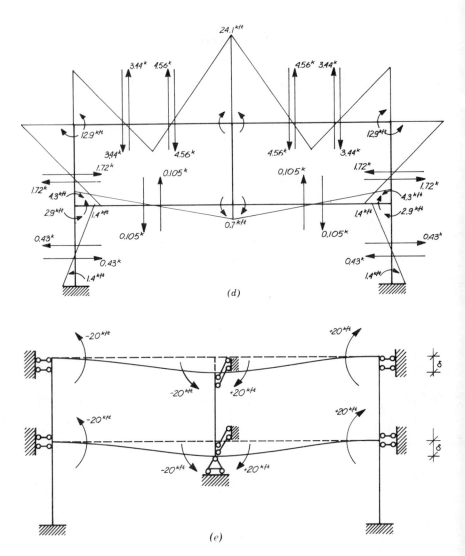

FIGURE 4.24. (*Continued*)

These distribution coefficients are shown in Fig. 4.24*b*. All transfer coefficients are 0.5.

In this symmetric case it is convenient to relax the rotation's constraints (slides) symmetrically, that is, starting at joints *C* and *G* simultaneously, and then, after blocking *C* and *G*, at *B* and *H*, and so

− 0.9	− 0.4	+ 0.4	+ 0.9
+ 6.7	+ 3.9	− 3.9	− 6.7
− 20.0	− 20.0	i +20.0	i +20.0
− 14.2	− 16.5	Σ +16.5	Σ +14.2

− 0.2
− 1.8
+ 2.7
+13.3

+14.4

M −14.4

−13.3 | − 2.7 | + 1.8 | − 0.2

+ 0.4
− 0.9
+ 5.3
+ 6.7

+11.5

+ 2.7	+ 1.4	− 1.4	− 2.7
− 20.0	− 20.0	i +20.0	i +20.0
− 17.3	− 18.6	Σ +18.6	Σ +17.3

+ 0.4
+ 5.3

+ 5.7

M −11.5

− 6.7 | − 5.3 | + 0.9 | − 0.4

M −5.7

− 5.3 | − 0.4

+ 0.2
+ 2.7

+ 2.9

M −2.9

− 2.7 | − 0.2

i = initial moments
Σ = summation (final moments)

(*f*)

FIGURE 4.24. (*Continued*)

on. The distribution procedure, the final moments, and the shear forces with the roller in place at J are shown in Figs. 4.24c and d. We see in Fig. 4.24d that the roller supports the central column with a reaction

$$R = 2(4.56) - 2(0.105) = 8.91 \text{ k.}$$

We now replace all the slides, remove the roller, and move the column down by an amount δ. This produces fixed end moments in the four beams (Fig. 4.24e). We choose δ so that the initial moments in Fig. 4.24e are arbitrarily

$$M_i = \frac{6EI\delta}{l^2} = 20 \text{ k-ft.}$$

We replace the roller and gradually relax the slides; that is, we distribute the fixed end moments. The distribution chart and the final moments and shears are shown in Figs. 4.24f and g. We realize from Fig. 4.24g that the displacement δ and its related moments are produced by a vertical force on the central column:

$$F = 2(1.54) + 2(1.795) = 6.67 \text{ k.}$$

Thus the removal of the roller in Figs. 4.24b and c, which coincides with the application of a downward force equal and opposite to its 8.91 k reaction and reestablishes the true state of the frame, is associated with moments given by those in Fig. 4.24g times the ratio:

$$\frac{R}{F} = \frac{8.91}{6.67} = 1.335.$$

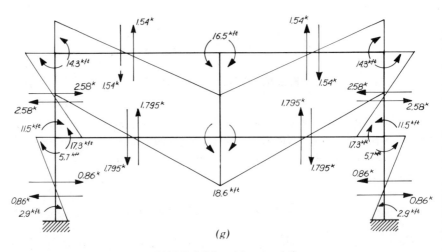

(g)

FIGURE 4.24. (*Continued*)

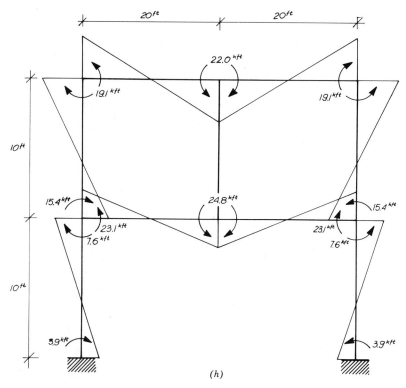

(h)

FIGURE 4.24. (*Continued*)

These moments (Fig. 4.24h) are algebraically summed with those in Fig. 4.24d to obtain the true and final moments in Fig. 4.24i. This figure also shows the shear forces on the beams, from which we realize that the central column is in equilibrium—evidence that the solution is correct.

4.3.6. Perform the task in Problem 4.3.1 using Young's moduli and moments of inertia as follows:

Beam	Column
E_b	$E_c = 0.5E_b$
I_b	$I_c = 0.5I_b$

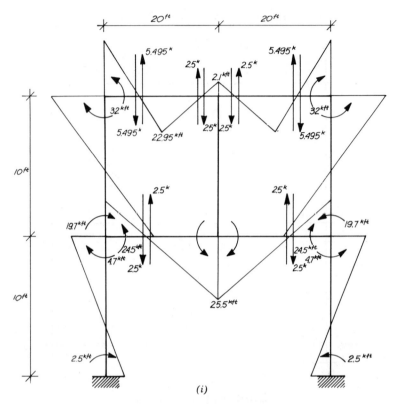

FIGURE 4.24. (*Continued*)

4.3.7. Perform the task in Problem 4.3.2 with Young's modulus $E_2 = 2E_1$ and moment of inertia $I_2 = 2I_1$.

4.3.8. Perform the task in Problem 4.3.4 using Young's moduli $E_1 = 4000$ k/in.^{2}, $E_2 = 2500$ k/in.^{2}, $E_3 = 3000$ k/in.^{2} and moments of inertia $I_1 = 4I_2$ and $I_3 = 2I_2$.

4.3.9. Perform the task in Problem 4.3.3 with $I_2 = 2I_1$.

4.3.10. Perform the task in Problem 4.3.5 with beams three times as rigid as the columns ($E_b I_b = 3E_c I_c$).

4.4.1. The roof beam in Fig. 4.25a is heated by the sun. The temperature increases 50°F at the top face and 10°F at the

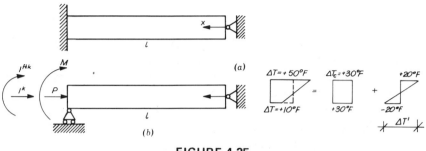

FIGURE 4.25

bottom face, with a linear variation in between. Find the horizontal reaction and the reactive moment using the principle of virtual work.

Solution. The diagram of temperature rise is replaced by a 30°F uniform rise, the same as that of the beam axis, and a linear variation through the depth of the beam that amounts to $\Delta T' = 40°F$ from top to bottom (Fig. 4.25b). The uniform rise $\Delta T_c = 30°F$ only prompts the reaction P. The linear variation only prompts the reactive moment M. To find P, we use a unit axial load, its associated reaction, and its internal force as a system of equilibrated virtual forces (Fig. 4.25b), and the true axial deformations as a system of coherent deformations. In this case the external virtual forces do not work, for the beam ends do not move horizontally. The internal virtual unit axial force does work for the real extension of a typical element dx of beam due to P and ΔT. Thus the virtual work equation is

$$0 = \int_0^l 1\frac{P\,dx}{EA} - \int_0^l 1\alpha\Delta T\,dx.$$

Integrating gives

$$\frac{Pl}{EA} = \alpha l \Delta T,$$

from which

$$P = \alpha E A \Delta T.$$

To find the reactive moment M, we use a unit left end moment, its associated vertical reactions, and internal moments as a system of virtual equilibrated forces, and the true deformations of the beams as a system of coherent deformations.

In this case the work of the virtual external forces vanishes, for the left beam end, where the unit moment is applied, in reality does not rotate, and neither beam end, where the vertical reactions are, moves vertically. The internal virtual moments $(1/l)x$ do work for the rotations $d\phi$ due to the real internal moments $(M/l)x$ (Fig. 4.25c):

$$d\phi = \frac{1}{EI} \left(\frac{M}{l} x\right) dx,$$

and for the rotations $d\phi$ due to $\Delta T'$

$$d\phi = \frac{\alpha \Delta T' dx}{D},$$

where D is the depth of the beam. Thus the equation of virtual work is

$$0 = - \frac{1}{EI} \int_0^l \frac{1}{l} x \left(\frac{M}{l} x\right) dx + \int_0^l \frac{1}{l} x \left(\frac{\alpha \Delta T'}{D}\right) dx.$$

Integrating gives

$$\frac{(M)}{EIl^2} \left(\frac{l^3}{3}\right) - \frac{(\alpha \Delta T')}{lD} \left(\frac{l^2}{2}\right) = 0,$$

from which

$$M = \frac{3}{2} \left(\frac{\alpha EI \Delta T'}{D}\right).$$

Then the vertical reactions are

$$\frac{M}{l} = \frac{3\alpha EI \Delta T'}{2 lD}.$$

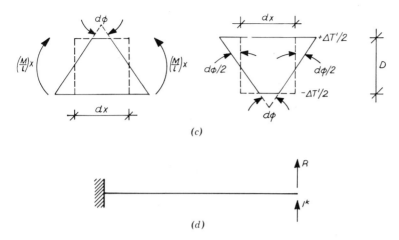

FIGURE 4.25. (*Continued*)

Problems of lack of fit are not different in principle from those of the thermal variations

4.4.2. The hinge of the beam in Fig. 4.25a moves down by an amount δ due to a foundation settlement. Find its reaction using the principle of virtual work.

Solution. We use a unit vertical force at $x = 0$, its associated reactions and internal forces as a system of virtual equilibrated forces, and the real deformations as a set of coherent deformations (Fig. 4.25d). The virtual external forces at the fixed end do not work, for this end does not move in reality. The virtual unit force at $x = 0$ does work for the real settlement δ. The virtual internal moments $1(x)$ do work for the real elemental rotations $xR \, dx/EI$. Thus the virtual work equation is

$$1(\delta) - \frac{1}{EI} \int_0^l 1(x) \, xR \, dx = 0.$$

Integrating gives

$$\delta - \frac{R}{EI} \frac{l^3}{3} = 0,$$

from which

$$R = \frac{3EI}{l^3}\,\delta,$$

and the reactive moment is

$$lR = \frac{3EI\delta}{l^2}.$$

4.4.3.   The top chord of the truss in Fig. 4.26a is heated by the sun. The temperature rise is $\Delta T = 50°F$. Find the reaction of the roller with the principle of virtual work.

Solution.   We use a unit vertical load placed at the tapered end of the truss, its associated reactions and internal forces as set of virtual forces, and the true deformations as a system of coherent deformations. The virtual external forces do not work, for their points of application do not move in reality. The virtual axial forces P_1 (Fig. 4.26b) do work, for the true deformations of the bars produced by the true axial forces P and in the top chord also by ΔT. The true axial forces P are the same as the products of the forces P_1 in Fig. 4.26b, with the magnitude R of the reaction:

$$P = P_1 R$$

The equation of virtual work is thus

$$\sum P_1 \left(\frac{P_1 R l}{EA}\right) + \sum P_1 \alpha l \Delta T = 0,$$

where the first summation covers all bars, and the second summation covers only the bars of the top chord. The magnitude of the reaction is thus

$$R = -\frac{\sum P_1 \alpha l \Delta T}{\sum P_1^2 l / EA}.$$

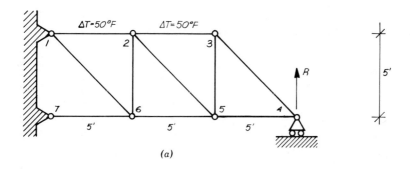

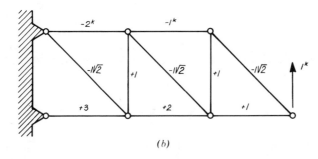

FIGURE 4.26

We assume for simplicity $E = 30,000$ k/in.^{2}, $\alpha = 65/10^7$, and $A = 1$ in.^{2} for all bars. The following table lists for each bar the following:

Terminal joints.
Length l.
Cross-sectional area A.
Inverse spring constant l/EA.
Virtual axial force P_1.
Thermal data $\alpha\Delta T$.
Numerator $P_1\alpha l\Delta T$.
Denominator $P_1^2 l/EA$.

Bar	l (in.)	A (in.^{2})	$10^3 l/EA$ (in./k)	P_1 (k)	$10^3 \alpha \Delta T$	$10^3 P_1 \alpha l \Delta T$ (k-in.)	$10^3 P_1^2 l/EA$ (k-in.)
1-2	60	1	2	-2	0.325	-39	8
2-3	60	1	2	-1	0.325	-19.5	2
3-4	$60\sqrt{2}$	1	$2\sqrt{2}$	$-1\sqrt{2}$	0	0	$4\sqrt{2}$
4-5	60	1	2	$+1$	0	0	2
5-6	60	1	2	$+2$	0	0	8
6-7	60	1	2	$+3$	0	0	18
3-5	60	1	2	$+1$	0	0	2
2-5	$60\sqrt{2}$	1	$2\sqrt{2}$	$-1\sqrt{2}$	0	0	$4\sqrt{2}$
2-6	60	1	2	$+1$	0	0	2
1-6	$60\sqrt{2}$	1	$2\sqrt{2}$	$-1\sqrt{2}$	0	0	$4\sqrt{2}$
						$\Sigma = -58.5$	$\Sigma = 59.97$

With the summations at the bottom of the last two columns in the table, we obtain

$$R = 1.008.$$

4.4.4. The roller of the truss in Fig. 4.26a settles by an amount

$$\delta = 1 \text{ in.}$$

Find the reaction of the roller using the principle of virtual work.

Solution. We use a unit vertical load at the tapered end of the truss, its associated reactions and axial forces as a system of virtual forces, and the true deformation of the truss as a set of coherent deformations. The virtual reactions do not work, for the left end constraints of the truss do not allow any local movement. The unit virtual load works for the settlement δ. The virtual axial forces P_1 work for the real extensions Pl/EA of the bars of the truss. Thus the virtual work equation is

$$1 \cdot \delta - \sum P_1 \left(\frac{P_1 Rl}{EA} \right) = 0,$$

where the real axial forces P are shown as products of the forces P_1 in Fig. 4.26b with the magnitude R of the reaction. Thus

$$R = \frac{\delta}{\sum P_1^2 l/EA}.$$

With the data and table in Problem 4.4.3 and the summation at the bottom of the last column, we obtain

$$R = \frac{1}{-0.0585} = -17.1 \text{ k},$$

which shows that the roller pulls the truss down when the ground settles, rather than push it up, as assumed.

FIVE

RESERVE OF STRENGTH
IN PLASTIC STRESS RANGE

The stress-strain diagrams of structural materials show an interval, between first yield and collapse, that suggests the possibility of extended performance of a structure's load-carrying function beyond first yield. This possibility is greater or lesser for various materials: steel and other ductile materials can tolerate considerable plastic deformation before the breaking point; concrete and other brittle materials fail soon after first yield. However, due to the lower value of the bending stresses away from the extreme fibers of a cross section, even brittle structures do not fail when the extreme fibers on a critical section yield. Rather, an increase of bending moment can be balanced by an increase of resisting moment through greater stresses in the fibers that have not yielded. As more and more fibers in proximity to the extreme fibers yield, the distribution of bending stresses progressively takes the forms in Figs. 5.1a, b, c, and d, where the bending stress diagram on a rectangular cross section is shown (from a to d) in the elastic range, at first yield, at advanced yield, and at complete yield. These diagrams are theoretical approximations of real stress distributions; any transition in the real, physical world would occur more smoothly than assumed by convenient theoretical simplifications.

We now calculate the values of the various resisting moments in Fig. 5.1 to show the reserve of strength of rectangular cross sections between first yield and complete plasticization; that is, when all fibers are stressed to capacity and an increase of bending moment, not balanced by an increase of resisting moment, produces rotation. This explains the name *plastic hinge* given to a section with a stress distribution as in Fig. 5.1d.

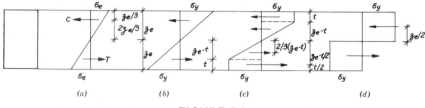

FIGURE 5.1

The average bending stress in Fig. 5.1a is $\sigma_e/2$, both on the tensile and compressive zones. The area of either zone is bz_e. Thus the compressive and tensile resultants have the value $\sigma_e bz_e/2$. Their mutual distance is $2(2z_e/3)$; hence the resisting moment is

$$M_R^a = \frac{\sigma_e bz_e}{2}\left(\frac{4z_e}{3}\right) = \sigma_e\left(\frac{2}{3}\,bz_e^2\right).$$

The resisting moment in the case in Fig. 5.1b is obtained by replacing σ_e with σ_y:

$$M_R^b = \sigma_y\left(\frac{2}{3}\,bz_e^2\right).$$

In Fig. 5.1c the resultant of the compressive plastic stresses is $bt\sigma_y$. Its distance from the neutral axis is $z_e - t/2$. The same holds true for the tensile resultant. Thus the resisting moment of the plastic stresses is $2bt\sigma_y(z_e - t/2)$. The average tensile or compressive elastic stress in Fig. 5.1c is $\sigma_y/2$ on an area $b(z_e - t)$. Thus the compressive or tensile resultant of the elastic stresses is $\sigma_y b(z_e - t)/2$, and the resisting moment of the elastic stresses is

$$2\left(\frac{\sigma_y}{2}\,b(z_e - t)\,\frac{2}{3}\,(z_e - t)\right) = \sigma_y\,\frac{2}{3}\,b(z_e - t)^2,$$

which can also be obtained by replacing z_e with $(z_e - t)$ in M_R^b. The total resisting moment in Fig. 5.1c is then

$$M_R^c = 2b\left[t\left(z_e - \frac{t}{2}\right) + \frac{(z_e - t)^2}{3}\right]\sigma_y,$$

which equals M_R^b when $t = 0$. The resisting moment in Fig. 5.1d is the product of the compressive or tensile resultant $\sigma_y bz_e$, with their mutual distance z_e. Thus

$$M_R^d = \sigma_y bz_e^2.$$

The ratio of the resisting moments in cases d and b is

$$\frac{M_R^d}{M_R^b} = \frac{z_e^2}{(2/3)(z_e^2)} = 1.5,$$

which shows that between first yield and occurrence of plastic hinge a rectangular cross section can carry moment increases up to 50% of the first yield moment.

For example, the resisting moment of a $2'' \times 4''$ joist at first yield is obtained from M_R^b with width $b = 2$ in. and extreme fiber coordinate $z_e = 2$ in.:

$$M_R^b = \frac{2}{3}(2)^2 2\sigma_y = \frac{2}{3}(8)\sigma_y.$$

The resisting moment of the same joist when its critical section becomes a plastic hinge is

$$M_R^d = 2(2)^2 \sigma_y = 8\sigma_y,$$

that is, 50% greater than M_R^b. The resisting moment M_R^c in elastic-plastic condition with a depth t of the plastic zone equal to one half of z_e is

$$M_R^c = 2(2)\left[1(2 - 0.5) + \frac{1}{3}(2 - 1)^2\right]\sigma_y = 7.33\sigma_y,$$

a value much closer to M_R^d than M_R^b. Indeed, the increase of bending stresses in the fibers close to the neutral axis does not add considerably to the resisting moment, for these fiber stresses lack a large lever arm about the neutral axis.

We now investigate the reserve of strength of cross sections other than rectangular. The section of the I beam in Fig. 5.2 has moment of inertia

$$I = \frac{B}{12}(2z_e)^3 - \frac{(B-b)}{12}(2z_e - 2t)^3 = \frac{6}{12}(12)^3 - \frac{5}{12}(10)^3 = 447 \text{ in.}^4$$

Its resisting moment at first yield is thus

$$M_R^y = \sigma_y \frac{I}{z_e} = \frac{447}{6}\sigma_y = 74.5\sigma_y.$$

At the formation of a plastic hinge, the resultants of bending stresses in the flanges are

$$C_f = T_f = tB\sigma_y.$$

Their distance from the neutral axis is $z_e - t/2$; their contribution to the resisting moment is thus

$$C_f\left(z_e - \frac{t}{2}\right) + T_f\left(z_e - \frac{t}{2}\right) = \left(z_e - \frac{t}{2}\right)(C_f + T_f) = 2tB\sigma_y\left(z_e - \frac{t}{2}\right).$$

The compressive and tensile resultants of the stresses in the web are

$$C_w = T_w = b(z_e - t)\sigma_y.$$

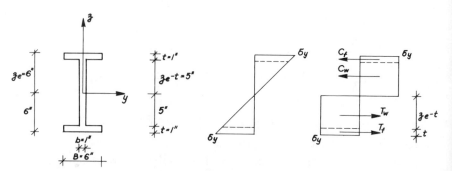

FIGURE 5.2

Their contribution to the resisting moment is

$$C_w \frac{(z_e - t)}{2} + T_w \frac{(z_e - t)}{2} = \frac{(z_e - t)}{2}(C_w + T_w) = b(z_e - t)^2 \sigma_y.$$

The total plastic resisting moment is thus

$$M_R^p = \sigma_y \left[2Bt\left(z_e - \frac{t}{2}\right) + b(z_e - t)^2 \right].$$

With the dimensions in Fig. 5.2 the preceding moment has the value

$$M_R^p = \sigma_y[12(6 - 0.5) + (6 - 1)^2] = 91\sigma_y.$$

The ratio

$$\frac{M_R^p}{M_R^y} = \frac{91}{74.5} = 1.22$$

is smaller than the ratio of plastic and first yield resisting moments of rectangular sections. The reason for a lower reserve of strength in this case is explained by the smaller amount of resisting material between the flanges, so that when these yield, there is little material left to carry a further increase of the bending moment.

Figure 5.3 shows the opposite case of a cross section with more material near the neutral axis than near the extreme fibers. In this case the moment of inertia is

$$I = 2\left(\frac{Bz_e^3}{12}\right) = \frac{1}{6}(4.24)^3 8.48 = 108 \text{ in.}^4$$

The resisting moment at first yield is

$$M_R^y = \sigma_y \frac{I}{z_e} = \left(\frac{Bz_e^2}{6}\right)\sigma_y = \frac{108\sqrt{2}}{6}\sigma_y = 25.45\sigma_y.$$

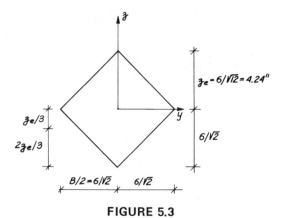

FIGURE 5.3

At the formation of a plastic hinge, the compressive and tensile resultants have the value

$$C = T = \frac{1}{2} B z_e \sigma_y = \frac{1}{2}\left(\frac{12}{\sqrt{2}}\right) \frac{6}{\sqrt{2}} \sigma_y = 18\sigma_y.$$

Their mutual distance is

$$\frac{2}{3} z_e = \frac{2}{3}\left(\frac{6}{\sqrt{2}}\right) = 2.33 \text{ in.;}$$

thus the resisting moment is

$$M_R^p = \frac{1}{3} B z_e^2 \sigma_y = \frac{1}{3}\left(\frac{6}{\sqrt{2}}\right)^2 \frac{12}{\sqrt{2}} \sigma_y = 50.9\sigma_y.$$

The ratio of the preceding resisting moments is

$$\frac{M_R^p}{M_R^y} = 2,$$

which is greater than the same ratio in the case of rectangular section.
    When a cross section does not have a symmetrical shape, as in Figs.
5.1, 5.2, and 5.3, the coordinates z_e of the extreme compressive and

tensile fibers are different. In the case of a linear distribution of bending stresses (Mz/I), these different coordinates z_{top} and z_{bot} are measured from the centroidal axis that coincides with the neutral axis. In the case of a uniform distribution of plastic bending stresses σ_y, the coordinates of the extreme fibers are measured from the median axis. Actually the neutral axis must coincide in this case with the borderline between two equal areas A_c in compression and A_t in tension; otherwise, the compressive resultant,

$$C = A_c \sigma_y,$$

and the tensile resultant,

$$T = A_t \sigma_y,$$

would be different and the axial equilibrium impossible.

As an example, we find the elastic neutral axis (centroidal) and the plastic neutral axis (median) of a cross section of a T beam, as well as its plastic resisting moment. Figure 5.4 shows such a section with its dimensions. Its partial and total areas are

$$A_f = 2(9) = 18 \text{ in.}^2,$$

$$A_w = 1(10) = 10 \text{ in.}^2,$$

$$A = A_f + A_w = 10 + 18 = 28 \text{ in.}^2$$

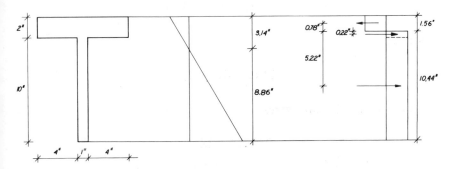

FIGURE 5.4

The neutral axis of linear stress distribution (centroidal) is given by the equality of moments of the partial areas and of the total area about a reference line, for instance, the top line:

$$\sum_i A_i z_i^{\text{top}} = z^{\text{top}} \sum A_i.$$

In this case

$$A_f z_f^{\text{top}} + A_w z_w^{\text{top}} = z^{\text{top}} (A_f + A_w).$$

Replacing symbols with their values,

$$18(1) + 10(7) = z^{\text{top}} (18 + 10),$$

from which

$$z^{\text{top}} = \frac{88}{28} = 3.143 \text{ in.}$$

The neutral axis of plastic stress distribution (median) is given by the equality of the tension and compression areas. Since in this case the flange area A_f is larger than the web area A_w, then the compression area A_c is only a fraction fA_f of the flange area. The tension area (A_t) is made of the web area (A_w) and the remainder $(1 - f)A_f$ of the flange area. Equating A_c and A_t gives

$$fA_f = A_w + (1 - f)A_f,$$

from which

$$2fA_f = A_w + A_f.$$

Use of numerical values gives

$$2(18)f = 28,$$

from which

$$f = \frac{28}{36} = 0.78.$$

Thus 78% of the flange area is in compression zone and the depth of the plastic neutral axis is

$$z_p^{top} = 0.78(2) = 1.56 \text{ in.}$$

The values of A_c and A_t are

$$A_c = 9(1.56) = 14 \text{ in.}^2 = \frac{1}{2}(28),$$

$$A_t = 9(0.44) + 10 = 14 \text{ in.}^2 = \frac{1}{2}(28).$$

The moment of inertia about the centroidal axis is

$$I = \frac{9}{3}(3.14)^3 - \frac{8}{3}(1.14)^3 + \frac{1}{3}(8.86)^3 = 321 \text{ in.}^4$$

Thus the first yield resisting moment is

$$M_R^y = \sigma_y \frac{I}{z_{bot}} = \frac{321}{8.86}\sigma_y = 36.23\sigma_y.$$

In calculating M_R^y, we have used z_{bot} because the bottom fibers yield first. To evaluate the plastic resisting moment, we need the lever arms of the compressive and tensile resultants about the median axis. The arm of $A_c\sigma_y$ measures 0.78 in. The tensile resultant $A_t\sigma_y$ is made of the two parts. The flange's share is given by

$$(1 - f)A_f\sigma_y = 0.44(9)\sigma_y = 4\sigma_y.$$

Its lever arm measures 0.22 in. The web's share of A_t is given by

$$A_w\sigma_y = 10\sigma_y,$$

with an arm of 5.44 in. Thus the plastic moment is

$$M_R^p = 14\sigma_y(0.78) + 4\sigma_y(0.22) + 10\sigma_y(5.44) = 66.2\sigma_y.$$

The plastic efficiency of this T section, that is, the ratio between plastic and first yield moments, is

$$\frac{M_R^p}{M_R^y} = \frac{66.2}{36.23} = 1.83.$$

Our discussion of yielding of structures has focused to this point on one critical cross section. We must now consider the effect that the occurrence of plastic hinges has on the safety of a whole structure.

If the original structure is statically determinate (i.e., constrained by a strictly necessary number of external and internal connections) the destruction of continuity at any one section makes the structure unstable under loads equal to or exceeding the load that produces the plastic hinge. However, the structure is still stable under smaller loads, despite a permanent rotation at the plastic hinge. These permanent rotations usually are functionally or aesthetically unacceptable. The bending moment at a plastic hinge is not zero as at a formal hinge, rather it remains constant with value M_R^p if the load is further increased. Only this increase in load makes the plastic hinge rotate and the structure a kinematic chain.

For example, the simply supported beam in Fig. 5.5 has a plastic hinge at midspan when the bending moment $Gl/4$ equals the resisting plastic moment M_R^p, that is, when

$$G = \frac{4M_R^p}{l}.$$

If the beam is unloaded after the formation of the plastic hinge, a permanent rotation remains at midspan, but the beam can be reloaded by a midspan force less than $4M_R^p/l$ without moving rigidly. Under any load G equal to or exceeding $4M_R^p/l$ the beam behaves like the dashed two-link chain in Fig. 5.5.

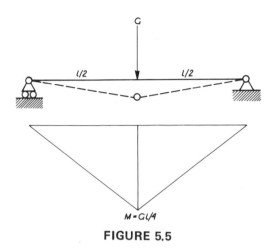

$$M = Gl/4$$

FIGURE 5.5

When the original structure is statically indeterminate, that is, constrained by a number of external and internal connections greater than that strictly required to prevent kinematic chain behavior, formation of a plastic hinge does not produce failure. This occurs rather when the number of plastic hinges offsets the redundant constraints. Thus the plastic efficiency of the structure (ratio of failure load and first yield load) exceeds that M_R^p/M_R^y of a typical cross section and depends on the number of redundant connections. A manifold redundant structure has a great reserve of strength in the plastic range.

For example, the threefold indeterminate beam in Fig. 2.6 forms two simultaneous plastic hinges (due to symmetry) when the fixed end moments $gl^2/12$ equal the plastic resisting moment M_R^p, that is, when

$$g = \frac{12M_R^p}{l^2}.$$

However, the beam hinged at both ends is still stable and can carry additional load despite the failure of the end sections. If the additional load produces a third plastic hinge at midspan, then the beam fails.

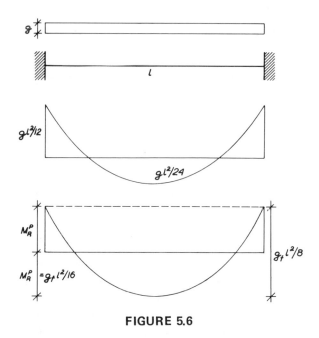

FIGURE 5.6

The failure load g_f is obtained by equating the midspan moment to M_R^p. With the values of the end moments fixed at M_R^p, the midspan moment is given by the sag of the parabola $gl^2/8$ minus M_R^p (Fig. 5.6). Thus the condition for failure is in this case

$$g_f \frac{l^2}{8} - M_R^p = M_R^p,$$

from which

$$g_f = \frac{16 M_R^p}{l^2},$$

a greater load than that of the first hinge formation. The plastic efficiency of the beam in Fig. 5.6 is thus

$$\frac{16}{12} = 1.33,$$

without taking the shape of the cross section into account. If the cross section is defined, then the total plastic efficiency of the beam is

$$1.33 \, \frac{M_R^p}{M_R^y}.$$

Particular loading conditions can produce simultaneous formation of a number of plastic hinges sufficiently large to prompt failure of a statically indeterminate structure at first hinge formation. For example, the beam in Fig. 5.7 has equal bending moments at midspan and at the fixed ends. When these moments equal M_R^p, the beam behaves like the dotted two-hinge chain in Fig. 5.7. Thus the failure load G_f is given by

$$\frac{G_f l}{8} = M_R^p,$$

from which

$$G_f = \frac{8 M_R^p}{l}.$$

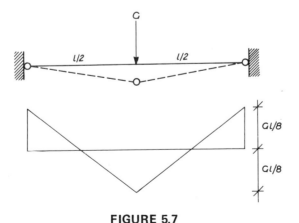

FIGURE 5.7

More complex structures with more complex loading conditions can fail in a variety of modes. Actually the prediction of particular failure loads and modes is not as direct as in the cases of Figs. 5.6 and 5.7 but rather a task of statistical analysis.

For example, the portal frame in Fig. 5.8a can fail in the beam mechanism mode (Fig. 5.8b) with three plastic hinges at beam ends and midspan. It can also fail in the sideway mechanism mode (Fig. 5.8c) with four plastic hinges at the top and bottom sections of the columns. A third failure mode is shown in Fig. 5.8d, with plastic hinges at the bottom of the columns, under the gravity load and at a beam end. We now evaluate the range of loads that produce the preceding modes of failure. When the horizontal load is small, failure will occur in the first mode. The value of the gravity load that produces the three plastic hinges on the beam can be obtained with the virtual work principle. With the simplified notations in Fig. 5.8b the

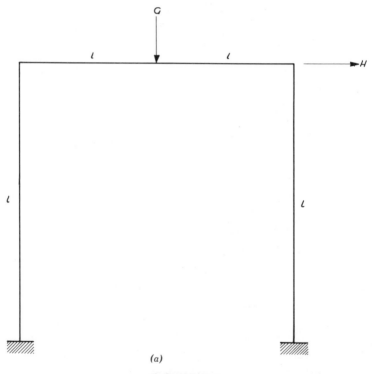

(a)

FIGURE 5.8

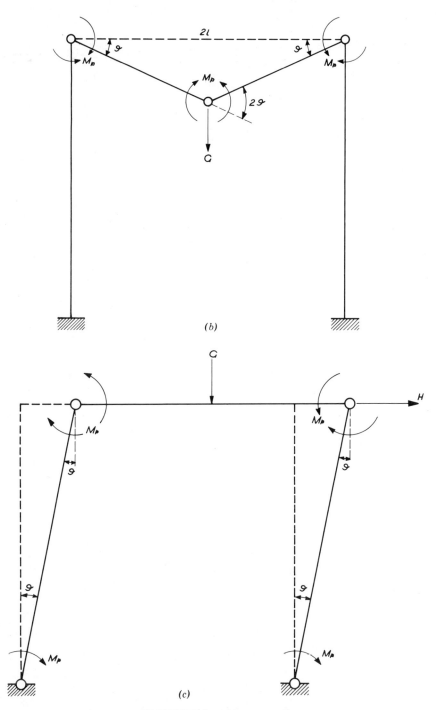

FIGURE 5.8. (*Continued*)

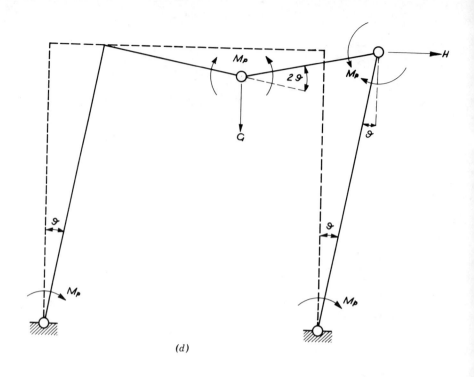

(d)

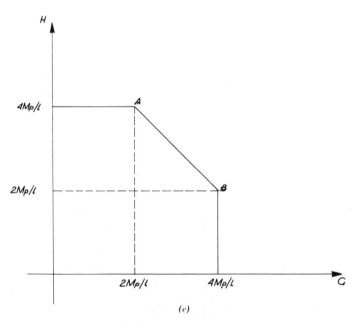

(e)

FIGURE 5.8. (*Continued*)

external work in the first failure mode is $Gl\theta$; H does not move and thus does not work. The work of the internal moments is $M_p\theta$ at both beam ends and $M_p(2\theta)$ at midspan. Thus the equation of virtual works is in this case

$$Gl\theta - M_p\theta - M_p\theta - 2M_p\theta = 0,$$

from which

$$G = \frac{4M_p}{l}.$$

When the gravity load is small, the portal fails in the second mode. In this case (Fig. 5.8 c) the external work is $Hl\theta$, and the work of the internal moments at the column ends is $4M_p\theta$. The equation of virtual works is thus

$$Hl\theta - 4M_p\theta = 0,$$

from which

$$H = \frac{4M_p}{l}.$$

When both H and G are important, but neither load reaches the value $4M_p/l$, the portal fails in the third mode (Fig. 5.8 d). The work of the outer forces in this case is

$$E_0 = Hl\theta + Gl\theta.$$

The work of the internal moments is

$$E_i = 6M_p\theta.$$

The virtual work equation is thus

$$Hl\theta + Gl\theta - 6M_p\theta = 0,$$

from which

$$H + G = \frac{6M_p}{l}.$$

The diagram in Fig. 5.8 e shows the range of pairs of values H and G that produce failure in the third mode. These are the pairs of coordinates of all points on segment AB except its end points A and B. Indeed, the coordinates of A not only add to $6M_p/l$ but the H coordinate equals $4M_p/l$, which produces a fifth plastic hinge at the top of the left column. Similarly, the sum of the coordinates of B equals $6M_p/l$, but the G coordinate equals $4M_p/l$, which produces a fifth hinge at the beam's left end. Thus points A and B produce a mode of failure other than that in Fig. 5.8 d. All other points of AB between A and B have coordinates less than $4M_p/l$ and their sum equals $6M_p/l$. Thus these pairs of coordinates belong to the load range that produces failure in the third mode (Fig. 5.8 d).

5.1. PLASTIC RESISTING MOMENT OF NONHOMOGENEOUS CROSS SECTIONS

Structures made of materials with negligible tensile strength, such as concrete and masonry, are reinforced with steel rods near the extreme tensile fibers to give them bending carrying capacity. When the tensile stress on sections of these structures equals their low tensile strength, the material cracks, and the steel reinforcement alone carries the resultants of tensile stresses. A typical cross section of a flexural member in this condition is therefore made of a compressive zone (in which stresses are transferred by concrete) and by a tensile zone which under a bending moment close to the plastic moment M_p is made only of the area of the reinforcing steel rods. Thus the section is not homogeneous, being made of materials with different physical properties in tension and compression zones.

The evaluation of the tensile and compressive resultants and, therefore of the plastic resisting moment, requires knowing the distribution of stresses on the respective zones. Since steel has a great stress-carrying capacity and is used in the form of thin reinforcing rods, it is correct to assume that the tensile stress f_y is uniform on the small area A_s of a rod, and therefore the tensile resultant $A_s f_y$ is applied along a rod's axis. The precise compressive stress distribution and even the precise strength are unknown, for concrete is not a material produced according to precise industrial standards, but rather according to widely varying procedures of mixing, pouring, and curing, which give different physical properties to every different batch. Building Codes like that of the American Concrete Institute (ACI) must therefore intervene to establish standard investigative approaches to reduce individual interpretations and approximations of the real physical events. Thus the ACI specifies that the distribution of stresses on rectangular compressive zones of cross sections of reinforced concrete be uniform, with value $0.85 f_c'$ over a depth a given by $\beta_1 c$ (Fig. 5.9). The preceding notations have the following meaning:

f_c' = the compressive strength of concrete ascertained by crushing cylindrical specimens 12 in. tall and 6 in. in diameter cured in standard conditions,

β_1 = a coefficient that varies with f_c' according to the table

f_c' (k/in.²)	$\leqslant 4$	5	6	7
$\beta_1 = \dfrac{a}{c}$	0.85	0.80	0.75	0.7

c = the depth of the real neutral axis of stresses and strains, measured from the extreme compressive fibers.

The value of c can be obtained in conditions of balanced failure (simultaneous yielding of steel and concrete) by considering the linearity of the strain distribution (Fig. 5.9), which gives

$$\frac{d - c}{c} = \frac{\epsilon_s}{\epsilon_c},$$

from which

$$\frac{d}{c} = 1 + \frac{\epsilon_s}{\epsilon_c} = \frac{\epsilon_c + \epsilon_s}{\epsilon_c}.$$

The strain of steel ϵ_s at yielding is the ratio f_y/E_s of steel's yield stress and Young's modulus ($E_s = 29{,}000$ k/in.²). The concrete strain ϵ_c at yield is fixed by the ACI code as 0.003. Thus the preceding equation can be written as

$$\frac{c}{d} = \frac{\epsilon_c}{\epsilon_c + \epsilon_s} = \frac{0.003}{0.003 + (f_y/29{,}000)} = \frac{87}{87 + f_y},$$

from which we obtain the depth of the real neutral axis in balanced yielding condition

$$c = \left(\frac{87}{87 + f_y}\right)d.$$

Given the grade of steel used (f_y) and the strength f_c' of concrete, we can obtain c, β_1, and $\beta_1 c$, that is, the depth of the codified uniform stress distribution approximating the unknown true distribution in Fig. 5.9. Then the compressive resultant is

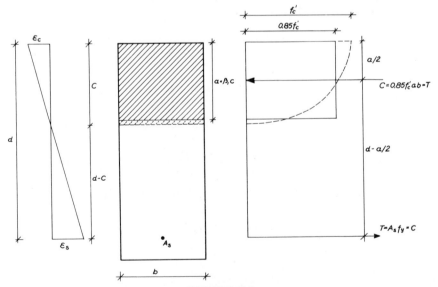

FIGURE 5.9

$$C = 0.85 f_c'(ab);$$

the tensile resultant is

$$T = A_s f_y;$$

and the plastic resisting moment, called the ultimate moment M_u in the ACI code, is

$$M_u = T\left(d - \frac{a}{2}\right) = A_s f_y\left(d - \frac{a}{2}\right),$$

or, using the compressive resultant

$$M_u = C\left(d - \frac{a}{2}\right) = 0.85 f_c'\left[ab\left(d - \frac{a}{2}\right)\right].$$

Actually the code requires a 10% reduction of the preceding ultimate moment, which is done by using a prefix $\phi = 0.9$. All the notations used in this section are standard notations of the ACI code.

Another code notation is obtained from the equality of the tensile and compressive resultants. Thus from

$$A_s f_y = 0.85 f_c'(ab),$$

we obtain the ratio A_s/bd called ρ.

$$\rho = \frac{A_s}{bd} = 0.85 \frac{f_c'}{f_y} \beta_1 \frac{c}{d}.$$

In balanced yield condition this becomes

$$\rho_b = 0.85 \frac{f_c'}{f_y} \beta_1 \frac{87}{87 + f_y}.$$

Using the notation ρ, the code's depth of the neutral axis can be written as

$$a = \frac{1}{0.85} \frac{f_y}{f_c'} \rho d.$$

Then the two expressions of the ultimate moment become

$$M_u = A_s f_y d \left(1 - 0.59 \frac{f_y}{f_c'} \rho \right),$$

and

$$M_u = b f_y \rho d^2 \left(1 - 0.59 \frac{f_y}{f_c'} \rho \right).$$

The two preceding expressions in which ρ appears explicitly are useful in the design and investigation of cross sections of reinforced concrete according to an ACI specification that limits the value of ρ to the range

$$\frac{200}{f_y} \leqslant \rho \leqslant 0.75 \rho_b.$$

The lower limit of the range prevents the under-reinforcing of concrete flexural members, and the upper limit prevents the opposite practice, which favors failure by crushing of concrete rather than yielding of steel. This type of failure is even less desirable because it occurs somewhat explosively, without warning.

The design and investigation of rectangular cross sections of reinforced concrete flexural bars is illustrated in the following example.

Example

A rectangular beam of reinforced concrete must carry an ultimate bending moment of 240 k-ft. Dead and live loads contribute to this moment, as indicated by the specifications of the American Concrete Institute in the next chapter. Other data are as follows:

Concrete strength, $f_c' = 3$ k/in.^{2}
Steel strength, $f_y = 60$ k/in.^{2}
Width of cross section, $b = 12$ in.
$\rho = \rho_{\max} = 0.75 \rho_b.$
$\rho_{\min} = 200/f_y.$

Solution.

$$\beta_1 = 0.85,$$

$$\rho_b = 0.85(0.85)\frac{3}{60}\left(\frac{87}{87+60}\right) = 0.02138,$$

$$\rho = \rho_{max} = 0.016,$$

$$M_u = bf_y\rho d^2\left(1 - 0.59\frac{f_y}{f'_c}\rho\right) = 12(60)0.016(1 - 0.189)d^2.$$

We equate the preceding moment with the ultimate bending moment

$$240(12) = 9.34d^2,$$

from which

$$d = \left(\frac{240(12)}{9.34}\right)^{1/2} = 17.6 \text{ in.}\quad(\text{use 18 in.}),$$

$$a = \frac{1}{0.85}\frac{f_y}{f'_c}\rho d = \frac{1}{0.85}\left(\frac{60}{3}\right)0.016(18) = 6.78 \text{ in.}$$

From

$$M_u = A_s f_y\left(d - \frac{a}{2}\right),$$

we obtain

$$A_s = \frac{240(12)}{60(18 - 3.39)} = 3.3 \text{ in.}^2$$

If four steel rods with 9/8 in. diameter and 1 in.^{2} cross section are used, the actual A_s is 4 in.^{2} This is adequate.

SIX

SAFETY COEFFICIENTS
AND SAFETY EQUATIONS

The task of structural analysis is ascertaining that a structure can carry the design loads with adequate strength and rigidity. The strength requirement is obvious, for a structure insufficiently strong does not exist for very long and collapses as soon as the full design load is imposed on it. The rigidity requirements are less definite in their wide range but equally important. A roof deck carrying heavy, vibrating air-conditioning equipment needs more rigidity than the roof of a tent structure. A tall building rising in a zone of hurricane hazard but free of earthquake hazard (like the Texas coast) needs rigidity as much as a California building needs resilience. In any case compliance with rigidity requirements is verified by comparing actual deflections of a structure with tolerances specified by building codes. This is an external criterion, for it is based on measurements of visible effects of loads.

Two possible criteria exist to verify compliance of a structure with strength requirements: one *internal* and one *external*. Traditionally, the values of actual extreme stresses on critical cross sections are compared with safe stresses specified by the building codes as fractions of the yield stresses. The inverse of such a fraction is called a safety coefficient, that is, the number of times design loads are to be exceeded before any yielding occurs. This is an internal safety criterion, for it is based on invisible effects of the loads. It is consistent with the use of elastic theories of structural analysis, for it confines the internal stresses everywhere in a structure within upper limits that guarantee elastic behavior and thus the validity of the design assumptions.

As an example, the allowable bending and shear stresses of laterally braced flexural members of steel and concrete are shown in the following table:

Stress	Yield	Allowable Bending	Allowable Shear
Steel	F_y	$0.66F_y$	$0.4F_y$
Concrete	f_c'	$0.45f_c'$	$1.1\sqrt{f_c'}$ [a]

[a] Beams without web reinforcement.

Analogous specifications limit the values of axial compression and tension, bearing stresses, and bond stresses in different materials. Variable limit stresses are specified for columns and unbraced compression flanges of flexural members, depending on slenderness ratios. The great number of variables affecting the strength of wood (botanical species, growth zone, moisture content, duration of load, treatments, defects, direction of stresses with respect to direction of grain, curvature, lamination, etc.) require lengthy tables of allowable stresses, and the reader is referred to the manual of the American Institute of Timber Construction (AITC) for their inspection. The complete tables of allowable stresses in steel and concrete are to be found, respectively, in the manual of the American Institute of Steel Construction (AISC) and the code of the American Concrete Institute (ACI).

The case of combined bending and axial stresses (beam-column case) is dealt with by summing algebraically the separate ratios of actual and allowable axial and bending stresses (possibly in two planes) and limiting the sum to 1. With the notations of the AISC and AITC manuals, the safety equation is thus

$$\frac{f_a}{F_a} + \frac{f_{bx}}{F_{bx}} + \frac{f_{by}}{F_{by}} \leqslant 1.0,$$

where the stresses in the numerators are actual axial and bending stresses and the stresses in the denominators are the corresponding allowable stresses for axially loaded bars (F_a) and for the tension or compression flange (whichever rules) of flexural bars (F_b).

A similar equation is also used to investigate concrete beam columns. However, the AISC and ACI codes provide more elaborate safety investigation means for the cases where the beam column exceeds established thresholds of hazard. For steel members, the hazard is greater with large axial loads; for concrete members, the hazard is greater with large bending. This is because the great strength of steel permits using thin framing elements that are prone to buckle. Concrete's moderate compressive strength requires stouter columns less prone to buckle but more ready to fail in tension, for this material lacks tensile strength. Readers are referred to the steel and concrete manuals for detailed information.

The preceding internal criteria fail to investigate the real safety margin of a cross section, for failure does not occur when the extreme stresses equal the yield stress of a structural material but rather when all the fibers yield. Moreover these criteria fail to reveal the safety margin of a whole structure, for it generally does not collapse with the yield of a critical section but rather when a sufficiently large number of sections are unable to sustain an increment of load and the structure becomes collapsible. For this reason an external criterion has been preferentially used for the design of concrete structures since the 1971 issue of the ACI code. This safety criterion assumes that all structural material on a critical cross section has yielded and that therefore the section's strength capacity has been fully utilized. The resisting capacity of the section is calculated under this assumption. For instance, the resisting moment of a plastic, rectangular reinforced concrete section as a function of the steel strength f_y or concrete strength f_c' (Chapter 5) is

$$\phi A_s f_y \left(d - \frac{a}{2} \right), \quad \text{or} \quad \phi 0.85 f_c' ba \left(d - \frac{a}{2} \right).$$

The resisting capacity is compared with the moments or forces produced on the critical section by the design loads amplified by safety coefficients. For example, the preceding resisting moments of a plastic, rectangular reinforced concrete section are compared with a bending moment (called the ultimate moment) given by

$$M_U = 1.5 M_{DL} + 1.7 M_{LL},$$

where

$$M_{DL} = \text{the dead load bending moment,}$$

$$M_{LL} = \text{the live load bending moment.}$$

We note the judicious use of two different safety coefficients for dead and live loads. Dead loads can be rather accurately predicted, and their changing during the lifespan of a structure is unlikely. (Obviously, since the dead load is the weight of the structure itself, it changes only if the structure changes.) This justifies a lower safety coefficient to cover the possibility of defective construction and erroneous calculations. Live loads are more uncertain and deserve a greater safety coefficient. The old-fashioned criterion specifies indiscriminately equal safety margins for both dead and live loads by applying one safety coefficient to the internal stresses rather than different coefficients to different external loads.

The newer external safety criterion commendably considers the full strength capacity of a cross section. However, it does not account for the difference between the load that produces the first plastic section and that which produces a collapsible mechanism. Except for the most elemental structures, the prediction of such loads is an extremely arduous task, for the number of possible collapse mechanisms increases rapidly with the number of framing elements and connections. To each collapse mechanism corresponds a different amplification of each load. Statistical analysis helps define load ranges that favor various modes of failure (Chapter 5), but they are to be tailored to each individual structure; this makes the generalization of code specifications impossible. It is foreseeable that sophistication of computational aids may soon permit the use of external safety criteria that consider the true ultimate load of entire structures rather than of critical cross sections.

SEVEN

EXCEPTIONAL LOADS

The order of steps in the design and investigation of structures, discussed in my previous book, *Statics of Structural Components* (Wiley, 1983), and reviewed in Chapter 1 of this book, changes considerably when strong random loads from gusty winds and earthquakes must be considered. Not only the ground acceleration during earthquakes and the wind gusts' velocity (unlike gravity acceleration) are unknown, but their dynamic interaction with a structure conditions the intensity of loads. These are therefore unknown until materials, geometries, and constraints of the structure, as well as nonstructural components such as partitions, curtain walls, and fireproofing encasements, are defined. These building features in turn cannot be designed without assessment of loads. It is thus necessary to resort to a trial-and-error design approach.

The initial structure is designed with the intuitive ability that derives from previous design experience and painstaking scrutiny of successful buildings as well as collapsed ones in similar environmental hazard conditions. The effect of wind or earthquake on the trial structure is then investigated. The results of the investigation provide clues for the modifications to be made. The following discussion provides an insight into the complexity of the task of evaluating available data, using the conclusions in the design case at hand, performing a reliable dynamic analysis of the trial structure, interpreting the design improvement clues from those results.

7.1. EFFECTS OF EARTHQUAKES ON BUILDING SITES

Earthquakes are produced by faulting of the earth's crust (mantle), which floats on the molten core. The rupture is occasionally due to volcanic explosion. More often, however, stresses build up in a slab

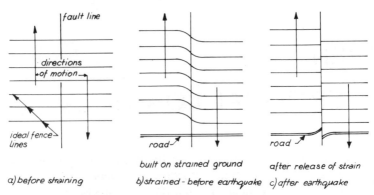

a) before straining   b) strained - before earthquake   c) after earthquake

FIGURE 7.1. (Taken from reference [3].)

of the mantle when two parts of it tend to displace independently. The line of stress concentration which divides the two parts is called a *fault* (Fig. 7.1). One example is the San Andreas Fault, which extends over a considerable length of California (Fig. 7.2). Its west side

FIGURE 7.2. The San Andreas Fault in California is an active fault, not typical of all faults. In 1906 it moved 22 ft horizontally; however, since then, it only shifts about 2 in. per year.

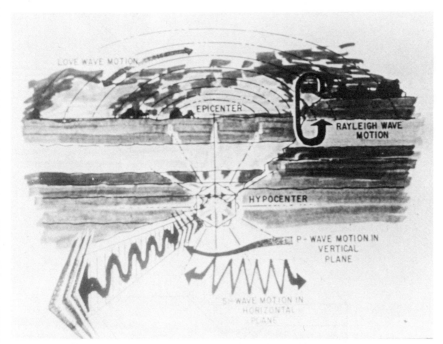

FIGURE 7.3. The hypocenter, epicenter, primary (P) waves, and shear (S) waves. These are not to be confused with the slower-moving visible surface or ground waves.

tends to separate with northwesterly motion from the east side. The motion averages 2 in. per year. Thus a state of stresses and strains builds up in the rock of the local earth crust. When the stress exceeds the strength of the rock, rupture occurs. The point where the crack originates deep in the crust is called the ipocenter of the earthquake (Fig. 7.3). The point on the surface directly above the ipocenter is called the epicenter. The rupture propagates from the ipocenter in all directions on the fault's plane. Thus two separate slabs of rock slip horizontally with respect to one another (Fig. 7.4). This is called a strike-slip fault. Mutual displacements of up to 21 ft could be observed over a 200 mile stretch of the San Andreas Fault after the 1906 San Francisco earthquake. The relative motion of one side of a fault with respect to the other can also be vertical (Figs. 7.5a and b), in which case it is called a dip-slip fault. This occurs when the two sides of the fault tend to move toward one another, and one of the

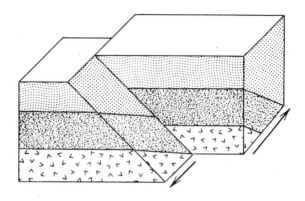

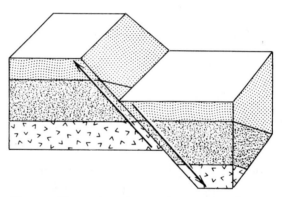

FIGURE 7.4.   The top illustration shows a lateral slip of a fault. The bottom illustrates normal faulting which appears as either vertical lifting or ground settlement. Most faulting is a combination of these two examples.

two parts undermines or lifts the other. Scientists believe now that such a westward motion of the South American continent prompted the lower, denser crust under the Pacific Ocean to raise the Andean chain and that a northward motion of India raised in similar manner the Himalayan chain.

   Slippage of a fault produces earthquakes, during which energy is released from the ipocenter in the form of waves of stress and strain (Fig. 7.3). Two kinds of waves are most important: P waves and S

FIGURE 7.5a. This is an example of vertical offset in Dixie Valley, Nevada (1954). Notice that little damage occurred in the framed structure only a few feet away.

FIGURE 7.5b. This is an example of ground settlement which occurred in a school in Anchorage, Alaska, in 1964. The amount of the slip seems to be about 10 ft vertically and horizontally.

waves. They propagate in the earth's crust with approximate velocities of 5 mph and 3 mph, respectively.

The strains associated with P waves have the same direction of wave propagation. In order to visualize P waves, we may think of a steel bar fixed at both ends and set in tension by moving the bar ends apart in the direction of the bar's axis (Fig. 7.6a). If the bar is suddenly severed at its midspan point C, each of its halves previously in tension becomes free to return to an undeformed state. This happens as if a compression force P applied at point C neutralized the local tensile force (Fig. 7.6b). The neutralization of tension propagates with a strain equal and opposite to the initial tensile strain, from point C to the beam end, that is, in the direction of the strain. The length (thus the volume) of a half bar changes, but the right angle between the axis of the bar and a typical cross section does not change. This justifies the dilatational and irrotational attributes given to P waves (P as in primary waves and pressure waves). Once set in motion, the molecules of the bar continue to move even after the bar has reached its undeformed state, for their kinetic energy is not instantly dispersed in intermolecular friction, heat, and so forth. From this point therefore the bar starts shrinking, and its kinetic energy turns into potential energy of expansion. As all available kinetic energy is transformed into potential energy, the bar starts expanding again, and the wave of tensile strains propagates from the fixed to the free end. These oscillations of positive and negative

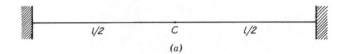

(a)

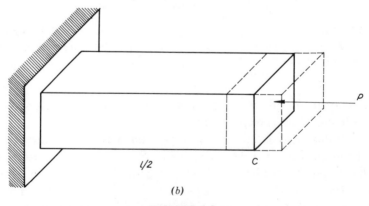

(b)

FIGURE 7.6

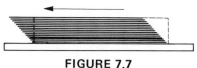

FIGURE 7.7

strains and stresses continue until all energy is dispersed. Similarly, P waves propagate from the ipocenter through a plate of the earth mantle.

The displacements associated with S waves are at right angle to the direction of wave propagation. This can be observed when the top of a deck of playcards, resting on a table, is moved by hand so that each card slides on the next (Fig. 7.7). The cards move in a direction parallel to the table, but the sliding motion propagates from the top to the bottom card in the deck at 90° to the table. We may also visualize S waves with a horizontal steel bar (Fig. 7.8a) fixed at both ends and deformed by giving the bar ends a relative vertical displacement. If the bar in this state is suddenly severed at its bending-

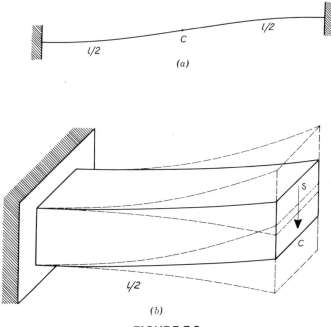

FIGURE 7.8

FIGURE 7.9.   A structure riding *S* waves alternately tilts right or left according to its position with respect to the wave crest. This pendular motion may shatter the structure.

free midspan point *C*, each half bar becomes free to return to an undeformed shearless state, as if a shear force *S* applied at *C* were transferred along the bar from *C* to the fixed end and on each cross section neutralized the local shear force (Fig. 7.8*b*). As in the dilatational case, the kinetic energy that is not dispersed reaches its largest value when the deformation of the bar vanishes, and it carries the bar past this position. From this point the available kinetic energy turns into potential energy of deformation, and at the time the transformation is complete, the bar starts the second leg of its oscillatory cycle. These cycles continue until all energy is dispersed. The shear deformation, better displayed by the deck of cards in Fig. 7.7, occurs without change of volume but with a change in the angle between a typical playcard (or cross section of the bar) and the axis of the deck (or that of the bar). This justifies the univoluminal and rotational attributes given to *S* waves (*S* as in secondary waves and shear waves). Figure 7.9 exemplifies the effect of *S* waves on structures.

The risk of earthquake effects on structures cannot be entirely eliminated. Indeed, risk is produced by hazard and exposure. Earthquake hazards exist in many geographic areas of our planet. Often the natural beauty of these areas is enhanced by volcanic activity or continental drift, with which earthquakes are associated. These activities create mountain backdrops that mitigate the climate by deflecting strong winds and favoring accumulation of rain-ripe clouds. The natural fertilizers provided by volcanic ashes conjure with the moisture and milder temperatures a conducive environment for luxuriant vegetation and natural comfort. Then humans provide the exposure by building in areas of earthquake hazard. Trying to prevent this would be equivalent to preventing settlements around the Mediterranean Sea, on the west coast of the North and South American continents, in the Far East and South Pacific (Figs. 7.10*a* and *b*). If this had ever been attempted, spirit of gambling and desire for challenge would have given humans the incentive to violate the ban. (Currently, the nuclear energy industry even resists opposition to construction of reactors in seismic areas.) The sensible alternative is to design structures that can endure the shock of an earthquake with minimal loss of life and property.

Assuming a structure is built or is going to be built in a seismic zone, it will be exposed to one, several, or all of the following hazards:

The crossing of an underground fault.

The quickening of the foundation ground due to a landside, consolidation, liquefaction, or lurching.

Earthquake aftereffects such as tidal waves (tsunami), fires, air, water and land pollution.

Strong vertical and horizontal vibrations.

We discuss these hazards individually.

A building that spans a fault will most likely be destroyed when the fault slips, unless the foundation structures are exceptionally strong and remain monolithic while the ground shifts. This has occurred, for instance, in the 1972 earthquake in Nicaragua, where the Banco Central building in the capital city of Managua survived a devastating earthquake (Fig. 7.11). The fault slippage circumvented the massive concrete foundation of the building, which contained the bank's safe vaults.

Quickening of the foundation ground can occur in several forms. A large wedge of soil can get loose from a hillside when the ground

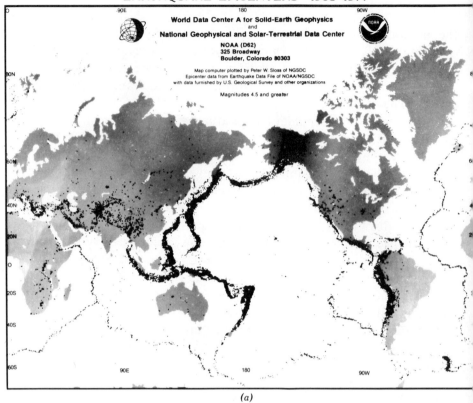

(a)

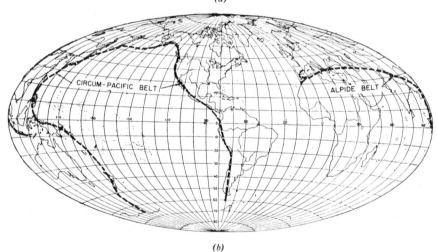

(b)

FIGURE 7.10. (a) Earthquakes 1963–1967. (b) Principal Earthquake Belts of the World. (Taken from reference [3].)

FIGURE 7.11.   This is an aerial view of Managua, Nicaragua, in 1972. Note the standing high-rise building and the fires in the background.

FIGURE 7.12.   Clay soils leading to a collapse in Anchorage, Alaska, 1964.

shakes. Frictional resistance of structural materials is improved by compression and reduced by tension; it is indeed more difficult to slide two bricks on one another while pushing them together. The vertical acceleration of the ground due to earthquakes takes alternating signs. When it has a sign opposite to that of the gravity acceleration, the layers of ground "lose weight," and the benefit of gravity pressure on the frictional resistance of the ground vanishes. An upper layer may then slide on a lower one and carry downhill a structure built on it (Fig. 7.12). The conditions that favor landslides may be mitigated by creating barriers with retaining walls, or networks of vegetation roots, and by drainage of the groundwater which acts as a lubricant among the grains of earth.

Consolidation of the ground occurs when an earthquake shakes particles of soil that are in a state of unstable equilibrium due to buoyancy in groundwater or to increased frictional strength under pressure over limited contact areas (Figs. 7.13a and b). When these conditions are disturbed, the ground particles resettle like dry beans in a jar when the jar is shaken and dropped. If the foundation of the structure is monolithically built, the structure itself will resettle as one, without much damage. This is the case when columns, piers, or bearing walls rest on a general foundation mat or on footings connected by a network of strong tie beams. If, however, differential settlements of the foundations occur, extensive damage will result and the structure could collapse. The prevention of damage from ground consolidation is thus obtained with monolithic foundations or with piles and caissons reaching deep into stable layers of soil. Another technique is preconsolidation of the ground with injections of cement grout.

Liquefaction of the ground occurs when the particles of soil are in the state of unstable equilibrium described earlier, and the shaking of the ground produces resettlement with sinking of the particles into the deeper reaches of the unstable layer. The superficial zone becomes thus mostly liquid, as in a jar of beans in brine that is dropped several times on a countertop (Fig. 7.14a and b). Buildings erected on such a layer sink and overturn, as in Fig. 7.15 which shows the effect of ground liquefaction during the 1964 earthquake

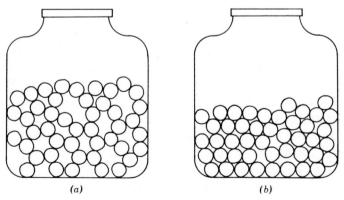

(a)   (b)

FIGURE 7.13

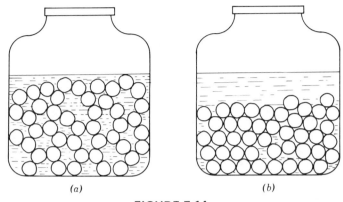

(a)   (b)

FIGURE 7.14

in Niigata, Japan. Prevention of damage by liquefaction of the ground is obtained with the same devices mentioned in the preceding case.

Lurching is a split in a foundation layer similar to that observed in a bowl of gelatin that is shaken abruptly. This earthquake effect is not necessarily devastating, provided that the foundations are solidly interconnected and differential displacements do not occur.

Tidal waves are set in motion far at sea when an earthquake shakes the deep ocean floor. These waves can move with speeds of up to 500 or 600 mph. Their originally small amplitude can be consider-

FIGURE 7.15.   One form of ground failure during an earthquake is liquefaction. Buildings in Niigata, Japan (1964), literally settled intact into the liquefied sand.

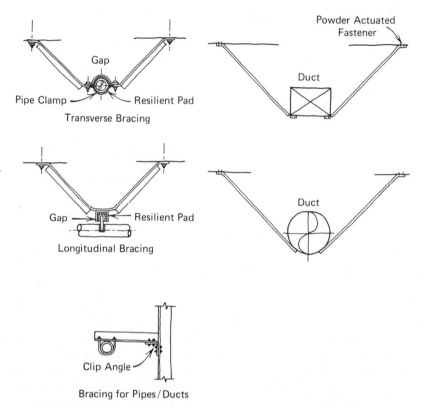

FIGURE 7.16a.   Details for bracing or anchoring pipes and ducts.

ably increased near shore by a combination of depth and shore geometries with respect to the direction of motion. As the huge swelling falls on a coastal area and then withdraws, trees, beaches, and man-made structures are wiped out. Tidal waves can hit repeatedly at intervals of several minutes, or even hours.

Fires frequently follow earthquakes, as the 1906 San Francisco earthquake exemplifies. The rupture of gas mains, shorted circuits in electric lines, and arson by looters, are typical triggers of ignition. The loss of pressure in broken water mains, the darkness due to failure of electrical power, and the debris littering streets and firestairs, all complicate the rescue and extinguishing operations.

Air, water, or land pollution is caused by smoke, fuels from ruptured mains, sewage running from treatment plants, and debris.

These devastating effects of earthquakes can be reduced by designing pipelines, sewage mains, and utility plants according to sound structural concepts—namely, by reducing the rigidity of pipelines with strategically placed loops and flexible connections (Figs. 7.16*a* and *b*) by erecting utility plants on reliable foundations, as indicated in the preceding discussion, and by intelligent city planning, including rules for correct construction of seism-resistant structures.

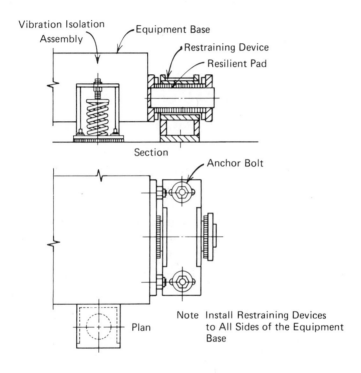

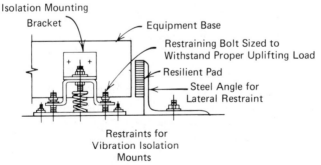

FIGURE 7.16*b*. Architectural details for vibration isolators. These deal with the possibility of lateral as well as vertical displacement.

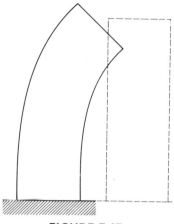

FIGURE 7.17

7.2.   SEISMIC EFFECTS ON THE STRUCTURES
OF BUILDINGS

When the ground on which a building is erected moves during an earthquake, the building foundation moves with it. By inertia, the mass of the higher tiers of the building tends to keep its state of rest. If the building is sufficiently flexible, the initial motion of the foundation is therefore greater than that of a typical higher tier (Fig. 7.17).

In a like manner the action of wind bends the frame of a structure while the foundation ground remains stationary. The similarity of the deflection in the two cases indicates that earthquakes as well as wind are causes of horizontal loads on buildings. Whereas the wind load at any given instant is the product of the instantaneous wind pressure with the area of the invested side of the building, the earthquake load is the product of the building mass with its instantaneous acceleration. If the building is tall, the acceleration of its center of mass is generally different from the ground acceleration, whereas the considerable rigidity of a low-rise building makes it move as one with the ground. A single instantaneous displacement of the foundation, preceded and followed by rest, would produce the deflection of a tall building shown in Fig. 7.17, followed by a free oscillation during which the structure would return to its undeformed state, then deflect in the opposite direction, return once again to a rest position and start a second cycle of oscillation.

If at the beginning of a new oscillatory cycle the ground again moves away from the center of mass of the building, the deflection of the building is even greater, for the ground is moving, for instance, to the left while the building is moving to the right. The recurrence of this condition at every cycle or integer number of cycles (resonance) would produce a deformation exceeding the bounds compatible with the integrity of the structure. Since the variety of the periods of free oscillation of buildings is as great as the number of buildings, it is possible, at least theoretically, that some structures will vibrate in resonance with the ground and therefore collapse. Moreover structures that cannot adequately resist dynamic loads, or even static loads as great as those produced by some earthquakes, will collapse with or without resonance. It is therefore necessary for architects and engineers who undertake the design of buildings in seismic zones to be acutely aware of the risks and of the structural features that minimize those risks. In the following discussion we are going to emphasize these features after a review of the specifications of building codes for a standard approach to quantitative estimates of earthquake loads.

These specifications are a necessary control on individual engineering calculations frequently flawed by simplifications necessary to overcome the complexity of the task and by lack or uncertainty of the data they are supposed to elaborate. Although the acceleration of ground vibrations has both vertical and horizontal components, our discussion concentrates on the effects of the horizontal acceleration because the conventional design of buildings for gravity loads and the safety coefficients used in that design are often adequate for the safety of structures shaking vertically.

7.2.1. The Total Earthquake Load on a Building

When seismograms from preceding local earthquakes are available, the calculations of earthquake loads on buildings in the same zone are both easier and more reliable. Seismograms give a time history of the ground acceleration during earthquakes. They show a consistent similarity in a zone, for instance, California, where the recurrence of

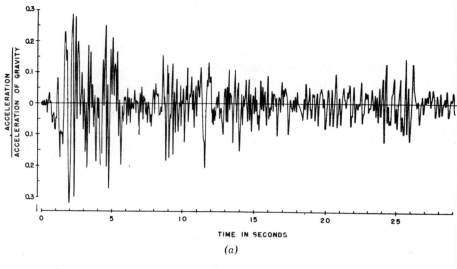

TIME IN SECONDS

(a)

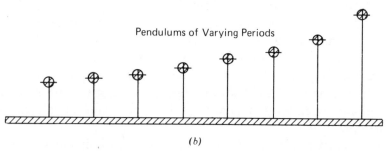

Pendulums of Varying Periods

(b)

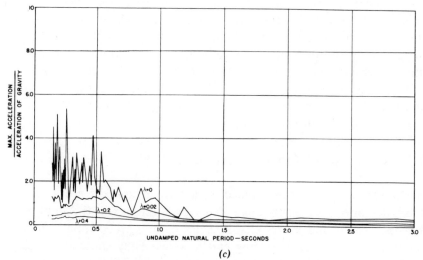

UNDAMPED NATURAL PERIOD—SECONDS

(c)

FIGURE 7.18. (Taken from reference [3].)

earthquakes is associated with the activity of the local fault of the earth mantle. These ground-acceleration history charts are used as input to evaluate the response of the computer simulation of a series of buildings with various periods of free oscillation. The response is the maximum acceleration of a building with a given period associated with the ground acceleration recorded during an earthquake.

Figure 7.18b shows schematically a series of buildings (pendulums) with increasing periods of free oscillations, ranging from about one-tenth of a second (one-story structures) to several seconds (high-rise buildings). The computerized values of the maximum north–south accelerations of these sample buildings during the May 18, 1940, earthquake in California is plotted in Fig. 7.18c. The graph of the ground acceleration recorded during the quake at El Centro, California, is shown in Fig. 7.18a.

We see from these figures that the greatest acceleration occurred two seconds after the start of the earthquake, with a magnitude of approximately 30% of the gravity acceleration. Figure 7.18c indicates that without damping ($\lambda = 0$), the preceding ground acceleration could produce accelerations exceeding five times the gravity acceleration on buildings with a period of oscillation close to 0.25 sec (low-rise) and an acceleration equal to the gravity acceleration in high-rise buildings with a period of free oscillation close to 1.2 sec. Under this condition the horizontal loading would be the same as the gravity load, as if the building cantilevered horizontally from a mountain cliff rather than vertically from the ground. This is a condition for which buildings erected with ordinary structural materials, construction techniques, and budgets would be utterly unsuited.

The effect of various degrees of damping is shown by the lower curves, in Fig. 7.18c, but even with considerable damping, the acceleration and associated loading are by no means vanishing, and for buildings oscillating with a 0.5 sec period it still remains as high as 20% to 30% of gravity. Damping dissipates the earthquake energy in permanent deformation or destruction of nonstructural building components (like infill walls), as well as structural elements and connections. In a building designed to survive earthquakes, the structural elements and connections that fail early must be redundant so that their destruction reduces the earthquake energy without impairing the stability of the structure. Energy dissipation by damping is unlike

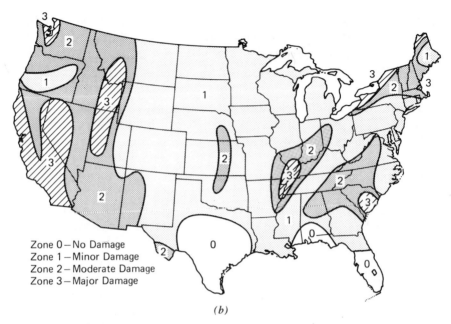

Zone 0 — No Damage
Zone 1 — Minor Damage
Zone 2 — Moderate Damage
Zone 3 — Major Damage

(b)

FIGURE 7.19.   Hazard Map. (After Algermissen.)

that associated with the elastic deformation of a structure, since the
latter is only temporarily absorbed and is returned when the elastic
deformation of the building vanishes. Actually this energy produces
the free oscillation of the structure, and, if it becomes concordant
with that of new ground shakings (resonance), it produces most likely
the collapse of the building. Ductility—that is, the ability to sustain
large and permanent deformations without breaking—is a very important requisite of structures in seismic zones.

A typical curve, such as that shown in Fig. 7.18c, is called an acceleration spectrum, and it is used as base for an evaluation of earthquake loads on buildings in the seismic zone where the curve has
been recorded. Local building codes provide smoothed-out versions
of spectra or equivalent analytical expressions for these curves for
use in seismic design. When this function C of the period T is known,
the total earthquake load on a building with known period is the
product

$$V = CW,$$

where W is the weight of the building. The Uniform Building Code specifies the shares and types of superposed dead load and live load to combine with dead loads in the determination of W. In fact the code formula for V includes other factors which we are going to consider next, and the complete formula is, rather,

$$V = CZIKSW.$$

In the preceding product the various coefficients have the following meaning and values: Z is the hazard zone coefficient used to reduce the design earthquake load in low-hazard areas. A map of earthquake hazard zones in the United States is shown in Fig. 7.19; it is based on the records of damaging earthquakes rated according to the Modified Mercalli Intensity Scale in Table 7.1. The values of Z according to zone are

Zone	4	3	2	1	0
Z	1	$\frac{3}{4}$	$\frac{3}{8}$	$\frac{3}{16}$	$\frac{1}{8}$

I is the occupancy importance factor. It is used to design on the safer side structures whose collapse may cause great losses of lives due to the number of occupants or interference with directing and executing rescue operations. The values of I are given in Table 7.2. The highest value 1.5 is used for essential facilities, that is, hospitals, fire and police stations, government offices, communication centers, and so on. The K factor is used to increase or reduce the design earthquake load according to the type of framing. Structural systems with a record of better performance during earthquakes are designed with a lower coefficient K, and vice versa. The specific values are given in Table 7.3.

The soil coefficient S accounts for the possibility of resonance of the building's oscillation with that of the site. Using the notation T_s for the oscillation period of the site, the code formulas for S are as follows:

	$T/T_S < 1$	$T/T_S > 1$
S	$1 + T/T_S - 0.5(T/T_S)^2$	$1.2 + 0.6(T/T_S) - 0.3(T/T_S)^2$

TABLE 7.1. Modified Mercalli Intensity Scale[a]

1. Not felt. Marginal and long period of large earthquakes. [Rossi-Forel (RF–I)]

2. Felt by persons at rest, on upper floors, or favorably placed. (RF–I to II)

3. Felt indoors. Hanging objects swing. Vibration like passing of light trucks. Duration estimated. May not be recognized as an earthquake. (RF–III)

4. Hanging objects swing. Vibration like passing of heavy trucks; or sensation of a jolt like a heavy ball striking the walls. Standing motor cars rock. Windows, dishes, doors rattle. Glasses clink. Crockery clashes. In the upper range of 4, wooden walls and frames crack. (RF–IV to V)

5. Felt outdoors; directions estimated. Sleepers wakened. Liquids disturbed, some spilled. Small unstable objects displaced or upset. Doors swing, close, open. Shutters, pictures move. Pendulum clocks stop, start, change rate. (RF–V to VI)

6. Felt by all. Many frightened and run outdoors. Persons walk unsteadily. Windows, dishes, glassware broken. Knickknacks, books, and so on, off shelves. Pictures off walls. Furniture moved or overturned. Weak plaster and masonry D cracked. Small bells ring (church, school). Trees, bushes shaken visibly, or heard to rustle. (RF–VI to VII)

7. Difficult to stand. Noticed by drivers of motor cars. Hanging objects quiver. Furniture broken. Damage to masonry D including cracks. Weak chimneys broken at roof line. Fall of plaster, loose bricks, stones, tiles, cornices, unbraced parapets, and architectural ornaments. Some cracks in masonry C. Waves on ponds; water turbid with mud. Small slides and caving in along sand or gravel banks. Large bells ring. Concrete irrigation ditches damages. (RF–VIII)

8. Steering of motor cars affected. Damage to masonry C; partial collapse. Some damage to masonry B; none to masonry A. Fall of stucco and some masonry walls. Twisting, fall of chimneys, factory stacks, monuments, towers elevated tanks. Frame houses moved on foundations if not bolted down; loose panel walls thrown out. Decayed piling broken off. Branches broken from trees. Changes in flow or temperature of springs and walls. Cracks in wet ground and on steep slopes. (RF–VIII to IX)

9. General panic. Masonry D destroyed; masonry C heavily damaged, sometimes with complete collapse; masonry B seriously damaged. General damage to foundations. Frame structures, if not bolted, shifted off foundations. Frames racked. Conspicuous cracks in ground. In alluviated areas sand and mud ejected, earthquake fountains, sand craters. (RF–IX)

TABLE 7.1.   (*Continued*)

---

10. Most masonry and frame structures destroyed with their foundations. Some well-built wooden structures and bridges destroyed. Serious damage to dams, dikes, embankments. Large landslides. Water thrown on banks of canals, rivers, lakes, etc. Sand and mud shifted horizontally on beaches and flat land. Rails bent slightly. (RF–X)

11. Rails bent greatly. Underground pipelines completely out of service.

12. Damage nearly total. Large rock masses displaced. Lines of sight and level distorted. Objects thrown into the air.

---

[a] Abridged and rewritten by C. F. Richter.

In conditions of resonance ($T = T_S$), S attains its largest value 1.5, to be used also when the ratio T/T_S is unknown. According to the code, S shall be not less than 1.0, T not less than 0.3 sec, T_S not less than 0.5 sec nor larger than 2.5 sec. The coefficient C is discussed in greater detail next.

7.2.1.1.   The Relative Acceleration According to Various Codes.

The ratio C between the maximum acceleration of a building during recorded earthquakes and the gravity acceleration g is a function (called "spectrum") of the period of free oscillation. A few examples of this function are shown in Figs. 7.20 through 7.23. The first of these was proposed in 1943 for the city of Los Angeles and for buildings not exceeding the height of 13 stories, formerly the local limit to building rise. This function differs from those in the other charts, for it relates the ratio C of a given tier of a building directly to the number of stories above that tier and indirectly to the period T of oscillation. Thus it provides the distribution of the total earthquake load among the various tiers, a task not attempted by the other curves proposed for the function C. The coefficient of the Los Angeles code is intended for multiplication with dead load only. The second example is a simplified spectrum proposed in 1951 by a committee of the Structural Engineers Association of Northern Cal-

TABLE 7.2. Values for Occupancy Importance Factor I [a]

Type of Occupancy	I
Essential facilities[b]	1.5
Any building where the primary occupancy is for assembly use for more than 300 persons (in one room)	1.25
All others	1.0

[a] "Reproduced from the Uniform Building Code, 1982 edition, copyright 1982, with permission of the publisher, the International Conference of Building Officials."
[b] See Section 2312 (k) for definition and additional requirements for essential facilities.

TABLE 7.3. Horizontal Force Factor K for Buildings or Other Structures[a]

Type or Arrangement of Resisting Elements	Value of K
1. All building framing systems, except as hereinafter classified	1.00
2. Buildings with a box system as specified in Section 2312(b)	1.33
EXCEPTION: Buildings not more than three stories in height with stud wall framing and using plywood horizontal diaphragms and plywood vertical shear panels for the lateral force system may use $K = 1.0$.	
3. Buildings with a dual bracing system consisting of a ductile moment-resisting space frame and shear walls or braced frames using the following design criteria:	0.80
a. The frames and shear walls shall resist the total lateral force in accordance with their relative rigidities, considering the interaction of the shear walls and frames	
b. The shear walls acting independently of the ductile moment-resisting portions of the space frame shall resist the total required lateral forces	
c. The ductile moment-resisting space frame shall have the capacity to resist not less than 25% of the required lateral force	
4. Buildings with a ductile moment-resisting space frame designed in accordance with the following criteria: the ductile moment-resisting space frame shall have the capacity to resist the total required lateral force	0.67
5. Elevated tanks plus fill contents, on four or more cross-braced legs and not supported by a building	2.5
6. Structures other than buildings and other than those set forth in Table 7.4	2.00

[a] "Reproduced from the Uniform Building Code, 1982 edition, copyright 1982, with permission of the publisher, the International Conference of Building Officials."

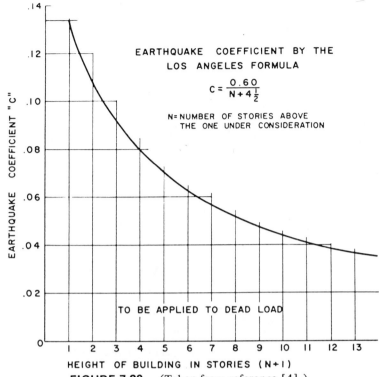

FIGURE 7.20. (Taken from reference [4].)

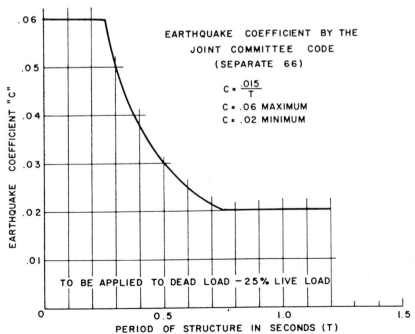

FIGURE 7.21. (Taken from reference [4].)

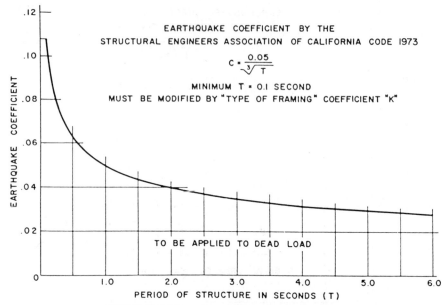

FIGURE 7.22. (Taken from reference [4].)

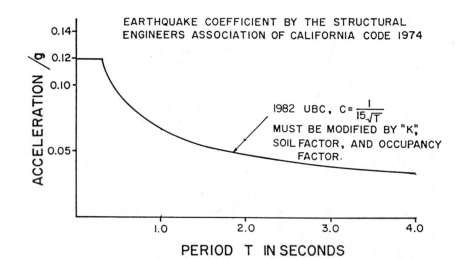

FIGURE 7.23. (Taken from reference [4].)

ifornia (SEAOC) and the San Francisco Chapter of the American Society of Civil Engineers (ASCE). In this case the coefficient C is intended for multiplication with a total weight that is the sum of the building dead load and 25% of all the live loads. The third example is the function C proposed by the Structural Engineers Association of California in 1957, and it is intended for multiplication with the total dead load of a building. The 1973 Uniform Building Code (UBC) used this function. The 1982 Uniform Building Code adopted the formula proposed by SEAOC in 1974:

$$C = \frac{1}{15(T)^{1/2}}.$$

This constitutes the fourth example in Fig. 7.23.

7.2.1.2. The Period of Oscillation According to Various Codes.
When the acceleration spectrum is known from existing earthquake records, the next problem is the determination of the period T of free oscillation of a building. T depends on variables that are practically unknown, for it is difficult to estimate accurately the mass and stiffness of a building that is only at the design stage. The mass of a building includes that of the occupancy, nonstructural walls, and fireproofing encasements. These nonstructural components also influence the rigidity of the building on which T depends.

The UBC proposes for T the formula

$$T = 0.05 \frac{h_n}{D^{1/2}},$$

where h_n is the structure's height above its base and D is the horizontal dimension of the structure, in feet, in the direction of the earthquake forces. Another UBC formula for T is

$$T = 2\pi \sqrt{\left(\sum_{i=1}^{n} w_i \delta_i^2\right) \div g\left(\sum_{i=1}^{n-1} F_i \delta_i + (F_t + F_n)\delta_n\right)},$$

where

F_i = the fraction of V assigned to tier i,

F_n = the analogous fraction assigned to uppermost tier n,

F_t = the fraction of V considered to be concentrated at the building's top, in addition to F_n,

w_i = the weight of tier i,

δ_i = the building's deflection at level i relative to the base,

δ_n = the analogous deflection of the uppermost level n.

These deflections should be calculated using the rigidity of the earthquake-resisting structure.

The problem with the preceding formula for T is that it should serve to evaluate C and then V, but it uses the fractions F_i, F_t, and F_n of the earthquake load V that we are trying to determine. It requires therefore trial-and-error routines. Moreover measurements of the oscillation period of existing structures reveal considerable errors in the theoretic values of T obtained by computers without accounting for the contribution of nonstructural components to the rigidity of the frame.

Experimental values of T obtained by the U.S. Coast and Geodetic Survey from measurements on more than 500 buildings are shown in Fig. 7.24 as functions of the ratio between the square of a building's rise H and its dimension b in the direction of the earthquake forces. The solid curve in Fig. 7.24,

$$T = 0.06 \left(\frac{H^2}{b} \right)^{1/2},$$

is a reasonable representation of the results. However, the more conservative dashed curve,

$$T = 0.05 \left(\frac{H^2}{b} \right)^{1/2},$$

recommended by the SEAOC is on the safe side of 80% of the results. On the unsafe side, it limits the error on 10% of the results to 25% and the error on the remaining 10% of the results to the range 25% to

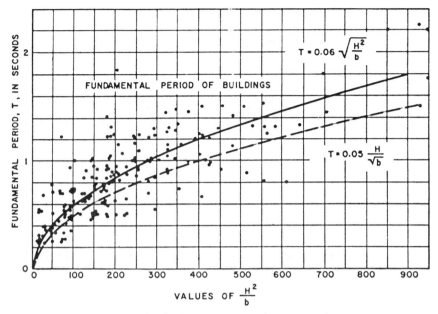

FIGURE 7.24.   (Taken from reference [4].)

40%. Here the expressions "safe" and "unsafe" indicate T values on the curve

$$T = 0.05 \left(\frac{H^2}{b} \right)^{1/2}$$

respectively shorter or longer than those actually measured by the U.S. Coast and Geodetic Survey. Indeed, the preceding spectra examples show greater values of acceleration and more proximity to resonance for buildings with short periods of oscillation. Thus attributing a longer period T to a building is equivalent to underestimating the earthquake load.

Other formulas of the period of oscillation have been proposed for moment-connected steel frames and strongly reinforced concrete frames. The UBC formula

$$T = 0.1N$$

links T to the number of stories N. The empirical formula proposed by the Applied Technology Council

$$T = C_T h_n^{3/4}$$

links T to the rise h_n of the structure above the foundation and is derived from measurements of T during the San Fernando earthquake of 1971. The coefficient C_T takes the following values:

	Steel Frames	Concrete Frames
$C_T =$	0.035	0.025

The two preceding formulas for T are not valid for frames stiffened by braced bents or shear walls.

7.2.2. Distribution Diagram of the Total Load

Assuming that the total earthquake load V on a building has been determined, it is necessary next to distribute this load to the various tiers according to a realistic diagram so that the shear at a typical level (the sum of the shares of V attributed to tiers above that level) may be correctly calculated. The true share of V for a typical tier depends on the tier's share of the total mass of the building and on the instantaneous acceleration with which that tier vibrates. Since a building vibrates simultaneously in different modes, the instantaneous acceleration of any tier is the sum of all the modal accelerations. However, only the first few modes are relevant.

The modes of vibration of a model structure can be experimentally observed by coupling the model to a base vibrating with continuously variable frequency and identifying deflection curves and stationary points (nodes) of the structure every time the acceleration of the base is resonant with one of the modes of free vibration of the model. This is another impossible task to perform on a real structure, let alone one in the design stage, and we have already discussed the flaws of theory-based computerized values.

The code specifications for the distribution of V among the various tiers of a building set aside a fraction F_t of V to be concentrated on top of the building:

$$F_t = 0.07TV,$$

where T is the period of free oscillation of the building. If T is less than 0.7 sec, F_t is neglected. The value of F_t shall not exceed 25% of V. The remainder of V is distributed among the n tiers of the building (including the top tier to which F_t is assigned) according to the ratios

$$\frac{w_x h_x}{\sum_{i=1}^{n} w_i h_i},$$

in which w_x is the weight of the xth tier and h_x its elevation in feet on the base of the building. The preceding distribution coefficients produce a triangular load on a building of uniform mass from base to top (Fig. 7.25). They correctly emphasize the mass of a given tier

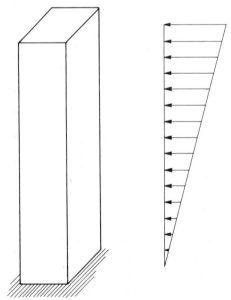

FIGURE 7.25. (Taken from reference [4].)

and also its distance from the ground, for top-heavy buildings are more severely tested during earthquakes. Across the floor plan of a typical tier x, the local load (share F_x of V) is distributed according to mass concentration.

The shear force at the level of tier x, that is,

$$F_t + \sum_{i=x}^{n} F_x,$$

is distributed among the earthquake-resistant frames in the building according to their relative shear rigidity. This rigidity has an analogous definition for frames and for individual bars (Chapters 3 and 4).

When eccentricity of the center of mass (thus of the earthquake load) with respect to the resisting structural framing produces torsion on the planes of the floors, the effects of shear and torsion are combined, provided they are concordant. Otherwise, torsion is neglected.

7.2.3. Other Code Specifications

Individual structural and nonstructural elements, portions of structures, and their connections must be designed for earthquake loads consistent with the load V used for the entire system, in order to remain coherent with it during the shaking. The UBC proposes for this task the formula

$$F_p = ZIC_p SW_p.$$

The symbols in the preceding formula are the same as in the expression for V. The subscript p indicates that the values of C_p and W_p are those related to a specific part. The values of C_p for various building parts are given in Table 7.4; I and S have the same values as in V, but they can be limited to 1 when the value of C_p in Table 7.4 equals or exceeds 1.

Every portion of a structure is required to be effectively connected to the entire assembly to prevent vibration with a period different from that of the complex. This would produce separation of the parts (Fig. 7.26), and then the possibility of collision (pounding), if the displacements of the separate parts have opposite signs. Portions

TABLE 7.4. Horizontal Force Factor C_p for Elements of Structures[a]

Part or Portion of Buildings	Direction of Horizontal Force	Value of C_p
1. Exterior bearing and nonbearing walls, interior bearing walls and partitions, interior nonbearing walls and partitions—see also Section 2312(j)3C. Masonry or concrete fences over 6 ft in height.	Normal to flat surface	0.30
2. Cantilever elements:		0.80
a. Parapets	Normal to flat surface	
b. Chimneys or stacks	Any direction	
3. Exterior and interior ornamentations and appendages.	Any direction	0.80
4. When connected to, part of, or housed within a building:	Any direction	0.30
a. Penthouses, anchorage and supports for chimneys, stacks and tanks, including contents		
b. Storage racks with the upper storage level at more than 8 ft in height plus contents		
c. All equipment or machinery		
5. Suspended ceiling framing systems (applies to Seismic Zones Nos. 2, 3, and 4 only)— see also Section 4701(e)	Any direction	0.30
6. Connections for prefabricated structural elements other than walls, with force applied at center of gravity of assembly	Any direction	0.30

[a] "Reproduced from the Uniform Building Code, 1982 edition, copyright 1982, with permission of the publisher, the International Conference of Building Officials."

FIGURE 7.26. If this stairtower at Olive View Hospital in California had been tied to the main structural system, it would not have separated from the building.

that cannot be effectively connected should be completely separated by a gap sufficiently large to avoid pounding.

Incremental deflections of a building from one tier to the next are required to be limited to the value

$$(0.005 h_x)\ \frac{1}{K}.$$

This is called "drift" in code language. The symbol h_x represents the story height, and K is the same coefficient used for the evaluation of V. The preceding requirement tends to limit the desirable flexibility of a seismic structure, and such inconveniences to the occupants as alarming swaying even during minor quakes or simple wind gusts; cracking of partition walls, plaster finish, parapets, and so on (Fig. 7.27); shattering of window and door glass panels (Fig. 7.28).

Structures rising above 160 ft are required to fit the description of type 3 or 4 in Table 7.4. Type 4 buildings ($K = 0.67$) have solely steel or concrete ductile, moment-resisting space frames for resisting

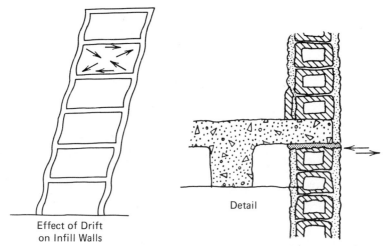

Effect of Drift
on Infill Walls

Detail

FIGURE 7.27. Building drift during an earthquake causes major failure of infilled exterior walls.

FIGURE 7.28. Broken windows due to the deformation of the glass and window mullions.

401

earthquake loads. Type 3 buildings feature space frames in association with shear walls designed so that the backup space frame can resist at least one-fourth of V and the shear wall can resist the entire
load V (calculated with $K = 0.8$). The actual shares of V absorbed by
space frames and shear walls in type 3 buildings depend on the relative rigidity of each system with respect to the total rigidity of the
assembly.

In zone 1 ($Z = \frac{3}{16}$) buildings rising above 160 ft may fit the description of type 1 in Table 7.4; that is, they may have concrete shear
walls for earthquake-resisting structure, in which case a K value of
1.33 must be used in design.

In zones 2, 3, and 4 concrete frames designed to resist either horizontal or gravity loads are required to have geometries and reinforce-
ments adequate to classify them as ductile moment-resisting space
frames. In zones 2, 3, and 4 portions of structures not included in
the earthquake-resisting system are required to withstand not only
the internal forces due to gravity loads but also those associated with
lateral deformations coherent with those of the earthquake-resistant
structure. These deformations are calculated with the codified earthquake loads amplified by the coefficient $3/K$. The preceding requirement promotes compatible deformability of all the parts of a building to keep it coherent under large deformations and to prevent failure
of the parts carrying the ever-bearing gravity loads.

The rigidity of ductile moment-resisting space frames may be improved by adjoining them and even enclosing them with more rigid
systems, such as shear walls or braced frames (which lack flexibility).
In this case, however, the space frame must be so designed that it
can independently carry the earthquake loads even without the help
of the rigid systems. Moreover the formula $T = C_T h_n^{3/4}$ for evaluating
the period of free oscillation is not applicable in this case.

In seismic zones 2, 3, and 4 all the bars of a braced frame must be
able to carry axial forces 1.25 times larger than those calculated with
the earthquake load V. This is equivalent to an amplification of the
1.33 value of the K coefficient applicable to braced frames and all
rigid buildings of type 2 in Table 7.4. The extra safety is required by
the instabilizing effect that buckling of the compression bars produces. Connections of the bars must have a least the same strength as
the bars themselves.

Nonstructural elements on the exterior of the building, such as precast panels, are required to be adequately connected to the structure to tolerate its deformations without separation. For this purpose connections must be by mechanisms that allow those movements or by ductile materials. The UBC specifies the least displacement between two contiguous stories that these connections must endure, as the largest of the following values:

Twice the story "drift" due to the design wind.

$3/K$ times the story "drift" due to seismic loads.

$\frac{1}{4}$ inch.

Individual footings, pile caps, and caissons must be connected to neighboring ones by means of tie beams able to carry a tensile or compressive axial force equal to 10% of the larger gravity load on its terminal footings.

Every structure must be designed to resist the overturning moment due to wind or earthquake, whichever is greater. Separate and simultaneous application of gravity and earthquake loads must both be considered in structural design. Indeed, the worst loading condition in a typical framing element may be due to gravity load alone, earthquake load alone, or both acting jointly. In the range of plastic deformations the principle of superposition and Hook's law are not valid, and the effect of simultaneous action of gravity and earthquake loads is not the sum of their separate effects. These two sets of loads must therefore be considered as simultaneously applied to structures for a realistic evaluation of stresses and deformations. The UBC, however, allows for neglecting the live load of the roof.

7.3. LIMITATIONS OF THEORETICAL SEISMIC DESIGN AND CODE SPECIFICATIONS

The code requirements for seismic design, discussed under the preceding two headings, are useful guidelines to architects and engineers. They are not, however, a substitute for the correct intuition and specification of the structural characteristics (materials, geometries, and connections) that make a building fit for survival in earthquake zone. They neither reduce the professional liability of architects and engineers or that of builders. There is not any assurance that a building in full compliance with the codes will endure an earthquake without damage or even collapse and that a building not in compliance with the codes will necessarily be damaged. Code requirements only set a minimum standard of uniform seismic design. Similarly, theoretical calculations, even at the highest level of sophistication presently attainable, do not offer any guarantee of safety.

The reasons for this lack of reliability are many. The most important datum needed to begin any calculation or estimate of a building's response to earthquake loads is the ground acceleration associated with the load. Only few records exist of ground acceleration during earthquakes of the past, and they have been used to obtain the spectra proposed by the codes. However, the records available are not those of devastating earthquakes, and they are only an indication of possible ground motion during future earthquakes caused by new slippage of the same ground fault. Even in this event the distance of a building from the epicenter and the geological features of the building site will influence the local ground motion so that it will not duplicate that on record. In most earthquake zones of the world, records of ground acceleration are not available at all.

The second most important datum is the period T of a building's free oscillation. We have already discussed the inadequacy of the theoretical values of T given by computers. The problem is the difference between the ideal structure considered in these analyses, that is, the earthquake-resistant framing, and the real vibrating structure that includes the building enclosures, partitions, and any other stiffening element that is not a part of the seismic structure.

A third uncertain datum is the instantaneous value of Young's modulus of a structure during an earthquake. In the case of concrete buildings, the true Young's modulus is not uniform throughout the structure, and its average value determined by tests on standard specimens is not the same as that of concrete batches poured in different amounts and cured in different conditions. For steel as well as for concrete the slope of the stress-strain curve (Young's modulus) varies in the plastic range with the stress level (Fig. 7.29). Moreover, due to

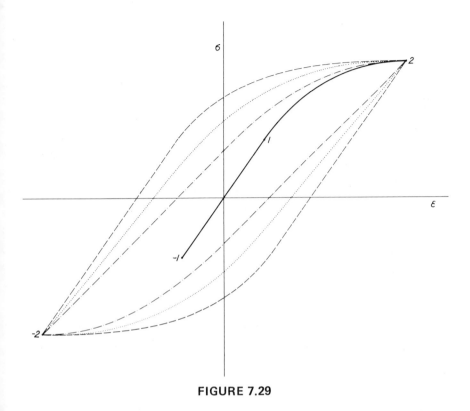

FIGURE 7.29

the degrading hysteresis effect of cyclical loading in the plastic range, the curve's slope is lower when the same stress level is reached in subsequent cycles of oscillation. This is shown in Fig. 7.29. Cyclical reversal of the signs of stresses in elastic range makes a typical point $P(\sigma, \epsilon)$ on the solid straight line move between positions 1 and -1. If, however, point P returns to the ϵ axis after an excursion in the plastic range, it does so following the dash line from position 2. As the stress vanishes, a permanent strain remains. The reversal of the stress sign in this case first eliminates the residual strain and then produces strains of opposite sign according to the dash line in Fig. 7.29. Another similar half-cycle takes point P from position -2 back to position 2. The area limited by the dash line, the sum of elemental areas $\sigma d\epsilon$, is proportional to the work done on the structural material.

Indeed, the product of σ with an elemental cross-sectional area $dydz$ is the elemental force $\sigma dydz$, and the product of $d\epsilon$ with an elemental fiber length dx is the displacement of the preceding elemental force. Thus the elemental work done by the internal stresses is obtained by multiplying $\sigma d\epsilon$ with the infinitesimal volume $dxdydz$ of structural material. This explains the advantage of ductility in seismic structures: materials lacking plastic deformability do not disperse earthquake energy since the curve of elastic deformations (between position 1 and -1 on the straight line) does not include hysteresis areas, and the material crumbles when deformations exceed the elastic range. Continued cyclical reversals of the sign of stresses change the hysteresis curves as shown by the early (dash) and later (dash and dot) typical curves in Fig. 7.29. It is readily seen that repeated bending of a steel bar with alternate signs of the curvature gradually softens the material, and the bar can be bent with gradually less effort. On the stress-strain curves this is equivalent to progressively lowering the coordinates σ corresponding to the same coordinate ϵ and to progressively reducing the area inside the hysteresis curves (less work is needed for the same deformation). In sum, Young's modulus gradually decreases, and this index of stiffness constitutes another element of uncertainty in seismic design.

An additional unpredictable and insidious earthquake effect is the runaway motion of the base from under the building's mass (Fig. 7.30). This effect, called "crawling," is prompted by repeated abrupt ground motions in one direction with slow return or no return in the opposite direction. If the deformation of the building is elastic, it vanishes after several oscillations with decreasing amplitude. If the abrupt motions of the base in one direction produce permanent deformations all with the same sign, the eccentricity of the center of mass of the building on its base becomes sufficiently large to produce $P\delta$ effect.

We have discussed this effect in Chapter 3, in an example of application of the principle of virtual work to the case of a cantilever column, loaded by gravity and horizontal forces, in the range of plastic stresses and large deformations. As the seismic deformation of the building (Fig. 7.30) produces non-negligible arms of the gravity load W with respect to the structure, the additional bending due to

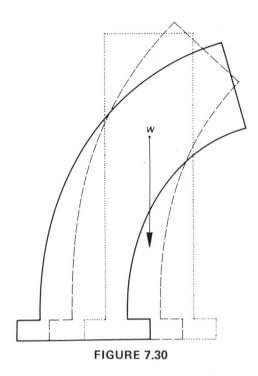

FIGURE 7.30

W increases the deformation of the building possibly beyond safe boundaries. Crawling and $P\delta$ effects are more likely to occur during earthquakes of long duration. This is related to the magnitude of the quake and thus to the extension of fault slippage. Table 7.5 shows an example of the relationship between length of the slipped fault and earthquake magnitude. Major seisms tend to shake the ground with greater duration, for a greater fault slippage materializes over a longer lapse of time. In sum, the difficulty in predicting magnitude of a seism and duration of ground shaking makes estimating crawling and $P\delta$ effect difficult.

Applying to a structure the static equivalent V of the dynamic loads and specified shares of V to each tier, the further subdivision on a floor plan of its share of V according to mass concentration, and the distribution of a floor's shear to the various resisting structures according to relative stiffness, all result in concordant seismic actions on a building. When the building shape, strength, and mass

TABLE 7.5.   Idealized Relation between
Magnitude and Length of Slipped Fault[a]

Magnitude	Length (miles)
8.8	1000
8.5	530
8.0	190
7.5	70
7.0	25
6.5	9
6.0	5
5.5	3.4
5.0	2.1
4.5	1.3
4.0	0.83
3.0	0.33
2.0	0.14(735 ft)
1.0	0.05(270 ft)
0	0.018(100 ft)

[a] From G. W. Housner, *Strong Ground Motion*, Chapter 4.

lack uniformity and symmetry in plan and elevation, the various parts do not vibrate concordantly. Thus a static application of the seismic load yields unrealistic results. Only dynamic analysis can in this case reflect the true state of stresses in the structure and the stress concentration effects of discontinuities. This is a complex undertaking with large and irregular structures, which are therefore often reduced to simplified models for the purpose of analysis. Incorrect modeling can in turn produce unreliable results.

For example, in tall shear walls with wide piers and shallow spandrels (Fig. 7.31), modeling vertical bands in the fashion of thin columns produces diagrams of bending moments under horizontal loads similar to those in Fig. 4.10*h*, that is, with reversal of the moment sign near a column's mid-height. In reality this condition occurs only at the upper floors, while the moments on the columns of the lower floors do not change sign and reach values several times greater than those obtained with the thin column model. Similarly, the modeling of the horizontal bands in Fig. 7.31 in the fashion of beams produces

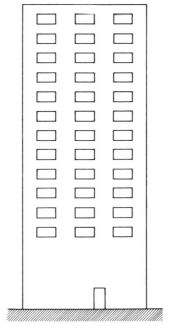

FIGURE 7.31

on them moment diagrams similar to that in Fig. 4.10*h*, that is, with an inflection point at midspan. Experimental tests have shown that a typical horizontal band in Fig. 7.31 behaves rather like the two adjoining cantilever beams in Figs. 7.32*a* and *b*; thus tension is produced both at the top and bottom fibers of a typical horizontal band by earthquake loads of either sign. As a result horizontal bands extend and bend, with a wedging action between vertical bands.

In large and complex structures the application of the most reliable method of calculation currently available, the finite element method, can be extremely laborious and costly, both in terms of professional-hours and computer time. Moreover the complexity of calculations is increased by the impossibility of applying the principle of superposition in the range of plastic stresses and deformations. The UBC requires, for good reasons, that gravity and seismic loads be simultaneously applied in order to obtain realistic results from the stress analysis. For example, horizontal and gravity loads on the

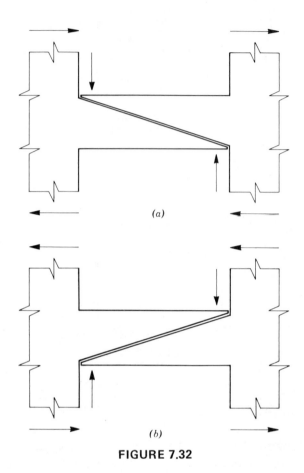

(a)

(b)

FIGURE 7.32

hinged portal in Fig. 7.33*a* produce separately the moment diagrams in Figs. 7.33*b* and *c*. The three bars of the portal have equal cross sections and a plastic moment capacity

$$M = 40 \text{ k-ft.}$$

Superposing moment diagrams *b* and *c* gives the combined diagram in Fig. 7.33*d*. This diagram is unrealistic because a plastic hinge is formed at joint *D* as soon as the local moment reaches the value 40 k-ft, which then remains constant. Moreover it may appear from Fig.

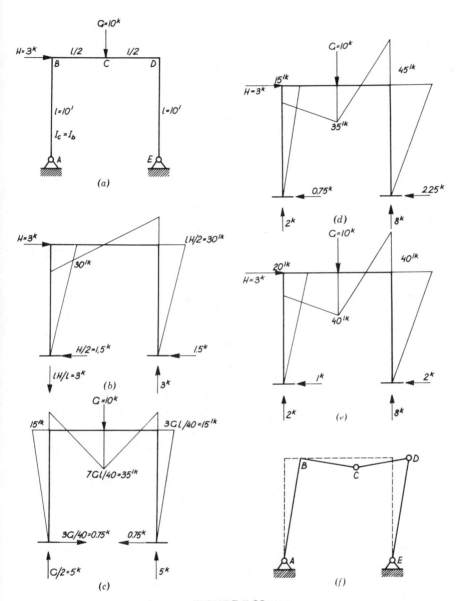

FIGURE 7.33

411

7.33*d* that the portal remains stable with the formation of only one hinge at *D*. Simultaneously applying gravity and horizontal loads produces instead the true moment diagram in Fig. 7.33*e*. Under this condition the portal collapses (Fig. 7.33*f*), for plastic hinges are actually formed at *C* and *D*.

The preceding discussion of the shortcomings of theoretical stress analysis of seismic structures emphasizes the importance of correct preliminary design, that is, choosing geometries, materials, and connections with an acute awareness of their role in conditioning the earthquake load, the dissipation of seismic energy, and the flow of stresses. Lacking secure means of investigating earthquake effects, we must be aware of and resort to all available means for mitigating them. In the following sections we review the behavior of structural materials and systems available to architects and engineers with the aim of recognizing those best fit for survival in seismic zone.

7.4. SEISMIC PERFORMANCE OF STRUCTURAL MATERIALS AND SYSTEMS

Few key words summarize the attributes of materials and systems that have exhibited endurance through earthquakes: lightweight, resilient, ductile, continuous. Few others describe the geometries of well-designed seismic structures: multidirectional, smooth, multiconnected. We discuss these attributes as we review individual seismic behavior of materials and systems.

Steel is the principal structural material for building in seismic zones. In the range of elastic stresses, steel structures are strong but flexible and light, because the stress capacity of steel permits its use in the form of slender framing elements that, like bamboo canes in a windstorm, bend rather than snap. The comfort of a building's occupants and the integrity of nonstructural building components, such as partition walls, door frames, and curtain walls, during minor earthquakes and gale winds, require that the flexibility of steel structures be controlled. This is achieved by giving the preceding nonstructural building components sufficient strength to provide stiffening diaphragm action during moderate seisms and strong windstorms. Under

extreme loading conditions, as in a major earthquake, these diaphragms fail and in the process absorb part of the seismic energy.
Another feature of steel, ductility, provides additional capacity to
dissipate energy (damping) and withstand large deformations without global collapse. The area within the hysteresis curve of a ductile
structure indicates the energy absorbed or work done on the structural material in a cyclical plastic deformation (Fig. 7.29).

The capacity of tolerating large deformations without breaking is
best shown by steel's stress-strain plot (Fig. 2.2) which has an extended plastic branch. As in Oriental martial arts, ability to yield
without collapse reduces the impact of a foe's blows, so in the case
of steel structures, the impact of an earthquake. Indeed, a hypo-
thetical unyielding material should be able to resist the stress σ^* in
Fig. 2.2, which is much greater than steel's yield stress σ_y, to survive
a deformation ϵ^* without collapse. Thus a structure built with such
a material would be hit by much greater earthquake force proportional to stress σ^* rather than σ_y.

Brittle construction materials such as unreinforced masonry and
concrete are most unsuitable for seismic structures. Their low stress
capacity results in rather massive, heavy, and rigid building blocks
that vibrate with high frequency closer to resonance with the ground.
Another cause of rigidity can be found in their low strain values
under working stresses. For concrete, for instance, a typical value
would be

$$\epsilon_c = \frac{\sigma_c}{E_c} = \frac{1.5}{3000} = \frac{1}{2000},$$

that is, only one half of a typical steel strain

$$\epsilon_s = \frac{\sigma_s}{E_s} = \frac{30}{30000} = \frac{1}{1000}.$$

Their lack of a reserve of strength in plastic range prevents the dis-
persal of the great seismic forces generated by their mass and rigidity,
and failure follows as soon as first yield occurs.

Strongly and uniformly reinforcing masonry and concrete produces construction systems with greatly improved seismic performance. In cast-in-place construction all the joints are naturally monolithic. However, the detailing of the reinforcement of the joints must be carefully designed and executed, possibly with welding of spliced reinforcing bars (Figs. 7.34 through 7.37). Unlike reinforcement for gravity loads, that produce tension on one side only of the centroidal axis, shear and bending reinforcement of a typical cross section of seismic structure must be symmetric due to expected reversal of the load. Stiffening diaphragms such as exterior and partition walls that are not part of a reinforced concrete earthquake-resisting frame may have strength comparable to that of the structure proper, and their cracks may extend across adjoining framing members. The distinction between sacrificial framing elements and primary structure becomes uncertain.

We do not expand on the use of timber in seismic construction since the advantages of its light weight, flexibility, and tensile strength are neutralized by its unsuitability for large structures and vulnerability to fires that often follow earthquakes.

Continuous steel space frames are by far the best structural system to resist earthquake loads. During World War II German bombing knocked out framing members and portions of British steel buildings without causing their collapse. Redundant sacrificial framing elements and connections dispersed blast energy as they failed, while others provided alternate routes of stress flow. Continuity and high statical indeterminancy are realized in steel structures by welding. A limited amount of welding can be performed in the shop during prefabrication of individual components or portions of structures. The large amount of welding to be performed in the field is one of the drawbacks of moment-connected steel space frames, for field welding is costly and less reliable than shop welding. Indeed, some field welding is done overhead and cannot be X-rayed for detection of entrapped air bubbles and electrode coating. Joining thick steel plates with equally heavy welding tends to transform the physical properties of steel and make it brittle. Engineers and builders attempt to reduce the amount of field welding by selecting only parts of the framing as earthquake-resistant structure and by shear-connecting the framing that is carrying only gravity loads. This practice is the beginning of a dangerous trend in reducing continuity and statical

FIGURE 7.34. Proper splicing of masonry reinforcement would have prevented the failure of this exterior wall.

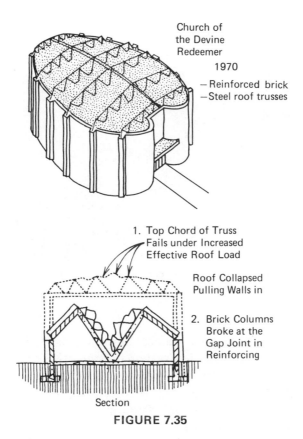

Church of
the Devine
Redeemer

1970

—Reinforced brick
—Steel roof trusses

1. Top Chord of Truss
Fails under Increased
Effective Roof Load

Roof Collapsed
Pulling Walls in

2. Brick Columns
Broke at the
Gap Joint in
Reinforcing

Section

FIGURE 7.35

415

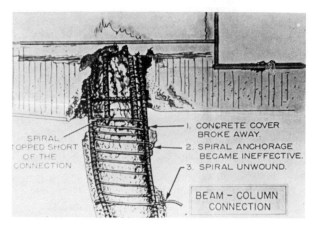

FIGURE 7.36.   An example of the need for proper reinforcement in a beam-column connection.

FIGURE 7.37.   An example of the need for proper reinforcement of a slab-column connection.

indeterminacy of steel space frames, those very assets that assure the superiority of this construction system over all other seismic-resistant structures and that justify the code specification of the value 0.67 for the coefficient K. Another drawback of moment-connected steel space frames is their considerable flexibility. An exceedingly flexible building may require costly replacements of cracked partition walls, shattered window glass, and distorted curtain-wall frames. It may also sway alarmingly during minor quakes and strong windstorms, causing panic among the occupants. Additional rigidity, however, can be provided by solid exterior and interior walls that also increase the damping effect of the system's ductility by absorbing the energy of major earthquakes that cause their early failure.

Reinforced concrete ductile space frames are considered by the UBC equally effective in resisting seismic loads, and their K coefficient is given the same value 0.67 as in steel frames. To qualify, however, as ductile, these frames must comply with reinforcing criteria for which the code sets minimum standards. Moreover the joints must be carefully designed and executed to avoid discontinuity. Whenever possible, discontinuity of cross-sectional shape and size as well as that of other geometries and stiffness, must be minimized to avoid stress concentrations and to favor a uniform, smooth stress flow throughout the structure.

Reinforced concrete shear walls forming boxed earthquake resistant structural cores, similar in shape to steel beams commercially available, feature great rigidity and vibrate with a frequency close to that of the foundation ground. They generate greater earthquake loads than flexible structures, and the UBC specifies a 1.33 value for their coefficient K which is twice as large as that of ductile space frames. The code also limits their height to 160 ft, an additional indication of disthrust. Shear walls can be erected around vertical duct work and circulation shafts or on the outlines of buildings. In the former case they have a few perforations for horizontal circulation and are therefore solid but slender. In the latter case various patterns of fenestrations reduce the solidity of the walls; their horizontal dimensions, however, are much closer to their height. The slender shear walls of the former case are subject to bending stresses more important than their shear stresses, and have a very poor record of seismic performance. Indeed, brittle rigid materials like concrete are not suited for flexible bladelike structural shapes, above all when the thinness does not permit adequate reinforcement of the extreme fibers. The disastrous seismic performance of the structure of the Four Seasons residential building (Fig. 7.38) during the 1964 earthquake of Anchorage, Alaska, confirms this. Outer shear walls performance records vary according to their fenes-

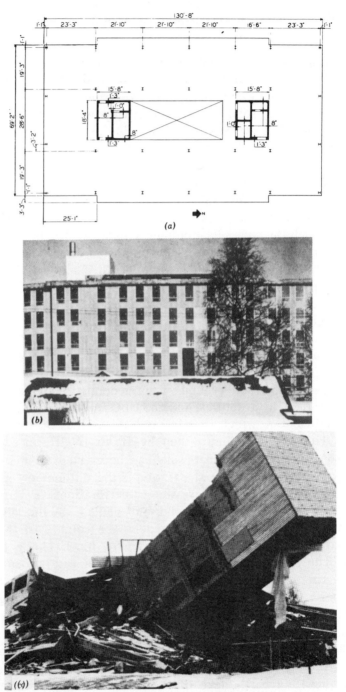

FIGURE 7.38. Four Seasons apartment building before and after earthquake. (*a*) Building plan, (*b*) building before earthquake, (*c*) after earthquake, looking SW. (Taken from reference [3].)

FIGURE 7.39.   These heavy spandrels transferred their load to the thinner columns and caused failure of the structure.

tration patterns. The thin-pier–deep-spandrel pattern (Fig. 7.39) has the poorest performance record. The limited resistance of a pier's small cross section and the pier's inflexibility due to its short axis conjure inevitable collapse. In 1968 several buildings on the campus of the Hakodate College in Tokachi-oki, Japan, failed in an earthquake. Their structure featured thin-pier–deep-spandrel shear walls, which collapsed. At 90° to these walls solid shear walls between classrooms survived the earthquake. We have already mentioned behavioral features of wide-pier–thin-spandrel shear walls in Section 7.3 (Fig. 7.30). Although there are no records of catastrophic collapse, earthquake damage of these structures has been considerable.

The solid external shear wall with small windows, wide piers, and deep spandrels is the safest of all. Finite element approach is in this case the only reliable means of investigation, since the size of vertical and horizontal members and that of their joints does not give beam-column frame modeling any realistic validity.

Staggered truss frames, staggered wall beam frames, and braced

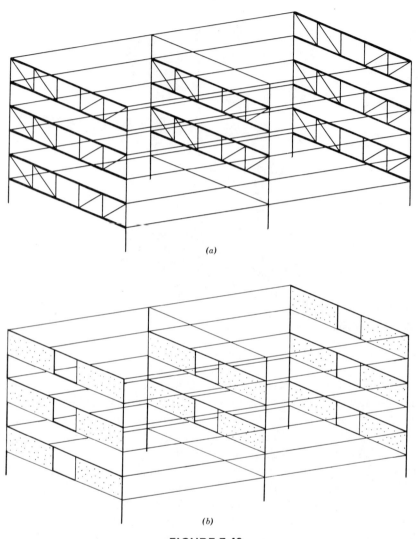

(a)

(b)

FIGURE 7.40

(c)

FIGURE 7.40. (*Continued*)

frames (Figs. 7.40a, b, and c) have the same high rigidity of boxed shear walls; thus the same value 1.33 is mandated for their load coefficient K. The thin short horizontal bars framing the double-loaded corridors of staggered trusses and wall beams are liable to fail like piers of thin-pier–deep-spandrel shear walls, and for the same reasons. Indeed, any abrupt variation of geometries and rigidity is a liability in seismic structures. Braced frames can be given greater flexibility by avoiding concurrence of diagonal bracing at the beam-column joints (Figs. 7.41a, b, and c).

Combination of shear walls with backup ductile moment-connected space frames is an ideal structural system for seismic zones. In principle, it is not different from the ductile moment-connected frame stiffened by nonstructural infill, but in this case the infill is structural. Roles and responsibilities of the two partner systems are precisely defined by the UBC which assigns a K value of 0.8 to these combination structures. The code requires that the shear wall be sufficiently strong to resist the total earthquake load (calculated, however, with $K = 0.80$ rather than 1.33). Indeed, the flexible steel frame may not offer much resistance before the shear wall fails. It can still play, however, the important role of reinforcing the concrete walls which play the main load-carrying role. The steel frame must be able to carry alone at least 25% of the total earthquake load, as it is the code's assumption that 75% of the earthquake impact is dispersed in the destruction of the shear walls. However, the actual share of V

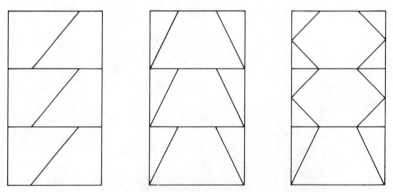

FIGURE 7.41. (Taken from reference [4].)

attributed to the steel frame must be in accordance with its relative rigidity, that is, its percentile share of the total rigidity of the system.

Intermediate building systems that do not fit the description of the preceding types are given by the UBC a K value 1.00, under the assumption that their seismic performance will also fall between that of very rigid and very flexible buildings.

Top-heavy structures on slender supports, such as elevated tanks, are considered the most threatened by earthquakes and assigned a K value 2.5. Structures other than buildings, not fitting specific code descriptions, are given a K coefficient 2.0.

A very important role in the seismic performance of structures is that of their geometric configuration. We have already mentioned this in discussing geometric details of shear walls and braced frames. The overall geometric configuration of a building, however, is as important in conditioning its seismic performance as the choice of structural material and detailing of connections. Figure 7.42 shows a SEAOC summary of the geometrical irregularities of buildings that invite trouble during earthquakes. The captions in Fig. 7.42 and the rationale for avoiding faulty geometries given on various occasions in this chapter should suffice to raise an awareness of good and bad seismic geometries.

We briefly review some of the problems caused by faulty geometries. Lump building masses tend to vibrate with frequencies other than that of the main part of the building. Depending on the direction of ground motion, this may cause a wing of a building with irregular plan (first row in Fig. 7.42) to pull away from or pound against the rest of the building (Fig. 7.26) unless the various parts are effectively connected. A wing may also be sheared off from the other building parts. The horizontal shear at the joint, being eccentric with respect to the wing's center of mass, produces torsion as well (Figs. 7.43 and 7.44). Torsion also occurs in buildings with "outwardly uniform appearance but nonuniform mass distribution or converse" (Fig. 7.42). In buildings with setbacks and split-levels the lower mass tends, so to speak, to hit the higher mass in the belly, or to pull its guts out. The rigidity but not the strength of buildings with unusually high or low stories abruptly changes at those levels. As a result exceptional deformations or stress concentrations are produced. The

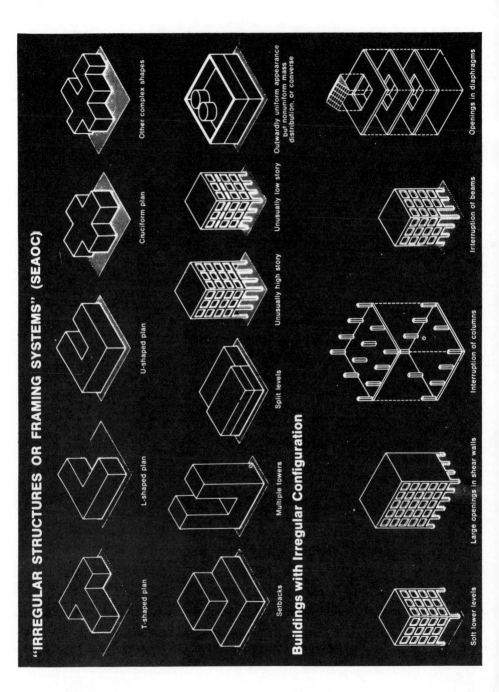

"IRREGULAR STRUCTURES OR FRAMING SYSTEMS" (SEAOC)

T-shaped plan

L-shaped plan

U-shaped plan

Cruciform plan

Other complex shapes.

Setbacks

Multiple towers

Split levels

Unusually high story

Unusually low story

Outwardly uniform appearance but nonuniform mass distribution, or converse

Buildings with Irregular Configuration

Soft lower levels

Large openings in shear walls

Interruption of columns

Interruption of beams

Openings in diaphragms

424

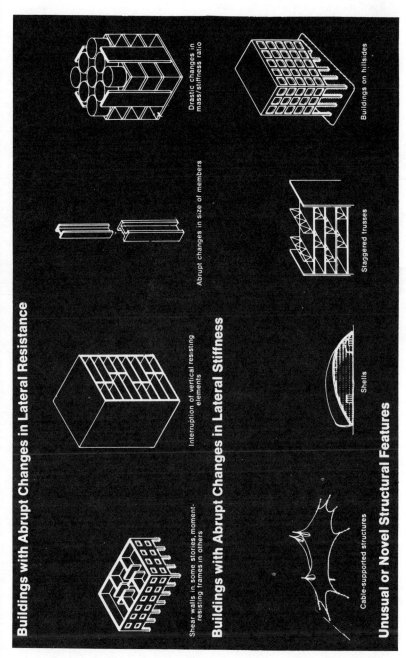

Buildings with Abrupt Changes in Lateral Resistance

Drastic changes in mass/stiffness ratio

Abrupt changes in size of members

Interruption of vertical resisting elements

Shear walls in some stories, moment-resisting frames in others

Buildings with Abrupt Changes in Lateral Stiffness

Buildings on hillsides

Staggered trusses

Shells

Unusual or Novel Structural Features

Cable-supported structures

FIGURE 7.42

425

FIGURE 7.43. Shear cracks due to torsional problems created by an unsymmetrical building configuration.

FIGURE 7.44. The San Francisco earthquake of 1906 caused this house to experience torsion. Note the location of separation in the facade.

FIGURE 7.45. Earthquake forces pushed the second story out of the column line.

426

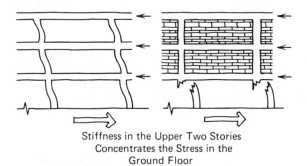

Stiffness in the Upper Two Stories
Concentrates the Stress in the
Ground Floor

FIGURE 7.46. The use of rigid structural systems on top of a more flexible one results in failure of the first story.

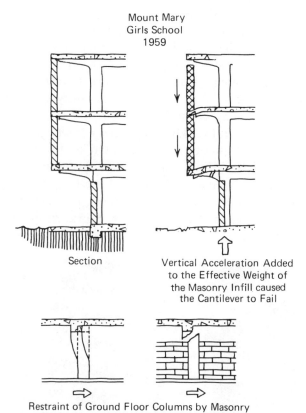

Mount Mary
Girls School
1959

Section

Vertical Acceleration Added
to the Effective Weight of
the Masonry Infill caused
the Cantilever to Fail

Restraint of Ground Floor Columns by Masonry
Walls Changed What Might Have Been an
Acceptable Amount of Bending
into a Shean Failure

FIGURE 7.47. In-fill panels can impose a short-column effect, causing shear failure.

same effects are produced by the simultaneous changes of stiffness and strength exemplified in the remaining cases in Fig. 7.42. Records of seismic performances or irregular buildings consistently verify the preceding statements. Figures 7.45 and 7.47 are used here as evidence.

7.5. SAFETY PRECAUTIONS FOR NONSTRUCTURAL BUILDING COMPONENTS

The permanent deformation and even the destruction of nonstructural building components during strong earthquakes is beneficial to the safety of the main earthquake-resistant structure of a building because it adds to the damping effect. Precautions are necessary, however, to harness the behavior of nonstructural building components and prevent damage from their failure as vast as that of structural failure. Unreinforced nonstructural masonry enclosing a building or its stairwells may crumble on fleeing occupants and obstruct means of egress (Fig. 7.48). The same effect can be produced by the fall of precast panels incorrectly connected to the building's spandrels (Fig. 7.49). Utility lines may rupture and release poisonous and combustible fuels or water sorely needed for fire sprinklers. Broken water mains are also open to contamination. Live electric wires may be exposed, with risk of shock and fire. Elevators can get loose of

FIGURE 7.48. Reinforcement in the masonry would have lessened this damage.

FIGURE 7.49. This concrete sunscreen fell from the facade of a building in Caracas, Venezuela, in 1967 and killed several people.

FIGURE 7.50. This ceiling damage would have injured many people had the auditorium been in use.

their rails, as can heavy roof-top cooling units. Furniture, hanging soffits, and fixtures can fall if ill-connected to walls and ceilings (Fig. 7.50). Structural design of joints, rails, connections, and supports of nonstructural building components is therefore another important branch of seismic design (Figs. 7.16a and b). Architects and engineers must be aware of risks and remedies to protect property and lives from the effect of failure of structural as well as nonstructural building components (Tables 7.6 and 7.7).

TABLE 7.6. Property Damages in Major United States Earthquakes, 1865-1975

Year	Locality	Actual Damage ($m)[a]	Damages 1974 ($m)[b]
1865	San Francisco, Calif.	.5	1.6
1868	San Francisco, Calif.	.4	1.5
1872	Owens Valley, Calif.	.3	1.2
1886	Charleston, S.C.	23.0	125.1
1892	Vacaville, Calif.	.2	1.1
1898	Mare Island, Calif.	1.4	7.6
1906	San Francisco, Calif.	524.0	2851.2
1915	Imperial Valley, Calif.	.9	4.4
1918	Puerto Rico (tsunami damage from earthquake in Mona Passage)	4.0	13.1
1918	San Jacinto and Hemet, Calif.	.2	.65
1925	Santa Barbara, Calif.	8.0	22.5
1933	Long Beach, Calif.	40.0	151.8
1935	Helena, Mont.	4.0	14.3
1940	Imperial Valley, Calif.	6.0	21.0
1941	Santa Barbara, Calif.	.1	.33
1941	Torrance-Gardena, Calif.	1.0	3.3
1944	Cornwall, Canada-Massena, N.Y.	2.0	5.6
1946	Hawaii (tsunami damage from earthquake in Aleutians)	25.0	62.8
1949	Puget Sound, Wash.	25.0	51.5
1949	Terminal Island, Calif. (oil wells only)	9.0	18.5
1951	Terminal Island, Calif. (oil wells only)	3.0	5.7
1952	Kern County, Calif.	60.0	111.2
1954	Eureka-Arcata, Calif.	2.1	3.8
1954	Wilkes-Barre, Pa.	1.0	1.8
1955	Terminal Island, Calif. (oil wells only)	3.0	5.5
1955	Oakland-Walnut Creek, Calif.	1.0	1.8
1957	Hawaii (tsunami damage from earthquake in Aleutians)	3.0	5.3
1957	San Francisco, Calif.	1.0	1.8
1959	Hebgen Lake, Mont. (damage to timber and roads)	11.0	18.6
1960	Hawaii and U.S. West Coast (tsunami damage from earthquake off Chile coast)	25.5	42.4

TABLE 7.6. (*Continued*)

Year	Locality	Actual Damage ($m)[a]	Damages 1974 ($m)[b]
1961	Terminal Island, Calif. (oil wells only)	4.5	7.4
1964	Alaska and U.S. West Coast (includes tsunami damage from earthquake near Anchorage)	500.0	794.1
1965	Puget Sound, Wash.	12.5	19.5
1066	Dulce, N. Mex.	.2	.3
1969	Santa Rosa, Calif.	6.3	8.4
1971	San Fernando, Calif.	553.0	675.0
1973	Hawaii	5.6	6.2
1975	Aleutian Is.	3.5	3.2
1975	Idaho/Utah (Pocatello Valley)	1.0	.9
1975	Hawaii	3.0	2.7
1975	Humboldt, Calif.	.3	.27
1975	Oroville, Calif.	2.5	2.3
	Total	1878.0	5077.25

[a] These damage estimates are at the time of the earthquake. They do not include the effects of inflation. They are not estimates of the likely damage if a similar earthquake occurred today.

[b] Corrected to 1974 dollar values by O. Clarke Mann, P. E., 271 Shrine Building, Memphis, TN 38103.

TABLE 7.7. Lives Lost in Major U.S. Earthquakes, 1811–1975

Year	Locality	Lives Lost
1811	New Madrid, Mo.	Several
1812	New Madrid, Mo.	Several
1812	San Juan Capistrano, Calif.	40
1868	Hayward, Calif.	30
1872	Owens Valley, Calif.	27
1886	Charleston, S.C.	60
1899	San Jacinto, Calif.	6
1906	San Francisco, Calif.	700[a]
1915	Imperial Valley, Calif.	6

TABLE 7.7.   (*Continued*)

Year	Locality	Lives Lost
1918	Puerto Rico (tsunami from earthquake in Mona Passage)	116
1925	Santa Barbara, Calif.	13
1926	Santa Barbara, Calif.	1
1932	Humboldt County, Calif.	1
1933	Long Beach, Calif.	115
1934	Kosmo, Utah	2
1935	Helena, Mont.	4
1940	Imperial Valley, Calif.	9
1946	Hawaii (tsunami from earthquake in Aleutians)	173
1949	Puget Sound, Wash.	8
1952	Kern County, Calif.	14
1954	Eureka-Arcata, Calif.	1
1955	Oakland, Calif.	1
1958	Khantaak Island and Lituya Bay, Alaska	5
1959	Hebgen Lake, Mont.	28
1960	Hilo, Hawaii (tsunami from earthquake off Chile coast)	61
1964	Prince William Sound, Alaska (tsunami)	131
1965	Puget Sound, Wash.	7
1971	San Fernando, Calif.	65
1975	Hawaii	2

[a] Earthquake and fire.

7.6.   EFFECTS OF WIND ON STRUCTURES

An object submerged in a fluid in motion is pushed with a force given by

$$F = \frac{k\gamma A V^2}{2g},$$

where

A = the cross section of the object on a plane at $90°$ to the direction of flow,

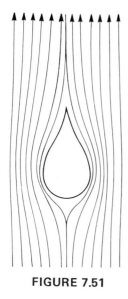

FIGURE 7.51

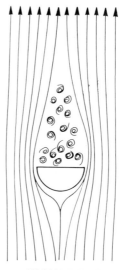

FIGURE 7.52

V = the velocity of the fluid,

γ = the unit weight of the fluid,

g = the gravity acceleration,

k = the drag coefficient that depends on γ, V, the fluid viscosity v, and on the width d of the object through Reynold's number $N = V\gamma vd/g$.

For a given value of N, k also depends on the shape of the object. Indeed, in a given fluid current, formation of eddies behind the submerged object depends on its shape. When the flow of fluid around the object turns from viscous (Fig. 7.51) to turbulent (Fig. 7.52), static pressure on the area surrounded by vortices is lesser than that on the area surrounded by smooth flow. Indeed, the total energy of a fluid current is, according to Bernouilli's principle, the constant

$$h + \frac{p}{\gamma} + \frac{V^2}{2g},$$

where (in units of distance)

h = the potential energy of position such as the potential of a mass of water to do work by falling a distance h,

p = the hydrostatic pressure,

γ = the unit weight of fluid,

V = the velocity of fluid,

g = the gravity acceleration.

With h being equal, in the downstream zone of turbulence (V large) the kinetic energy $V^2/2g$ is very large, and the static pressure p (potential energy) is low; in the upstream zone, where the liquid particles come to a halt against the object, V is small and p large; in the side zones, where the liquid rushes around the object with intermediate velocity, p is also intermediate.

Thus a shape that favors formation of eddies produces a static pressure difference between upstream and downstream surfaces of the submerged object in addition to dynamic pressure. A rain drop is molded in a shape that minimizes resistance to its fall (Fig. 7.51). In like manner designers of vehicles and aircraft strive to minimize the resistance of air to motion with aerodynamic shapes that reduce fuel consumption at a given speed or increase the speed attainable with a given fuel consumption. The shape of tall buildings as well should be optimized for least wind resistance in strong wind zones. Another effect of the high wind velocity and low pressure on the leeward and side elevations, and on the roof of a building, is the tendency of windows to pop out and of the roof to lift off. Indeed, the pressure p inside the building where the air is still ($V = 0$) is greater than its counterpart on the preceding surfaces and is even increased by the high pressure on the windward surface, above all if openings allow penetration of wind.

It is thus evident that wind forces are another set of random dynamic loads with which engineers have to be concerned in designing large buildings, above all in zones exposed to windstorms such as hurricanes, tornados, downslope winds, thunderstorms, and extratropical cyclones. We briefly describe the distinctive characteristics of these windstorms.

A hurricane wind may spin a volume of air as large as 300 miles in diameter and 9 miles high with a core, or eye, 30 to 40 miles in diameter. The tangential velocity of the wind may range from 75 to 200 mph in the eye, but it decreases rapidly toward the edge. The storm travels usually with a speed not exceeding 50 mph. As it passes over cool or rough terrain, a hurricane loses speed and expands. Its encounter and merging with a front of cold air above the equator may generate an extratropical cyclone. The hurricane season lasts from June to November, but it may be as long as May to December, with its most frequent occurrence in September.

Tornados are trumpet-shaped vortices of air seldom exceeding 16 miles in height and $\frac{1}{4}$ mile in diameter. The tangential speed of wind is, however, as high as and possibly higher than that in the eye of a hurricane. The traveling speed also is similar to that of hurricanes. The high wind velocity reduces the air pressure in the center of a tornado to a fraction, as little as one-tenth, of the atmospheric pressure. As a result tornados over the sea draw huge masses of water skyward. On land, the great pressure difference between the inside of buildings caught in a tornado and their exterior surfaces makes the buildings explode.

Downslope winds are caused by the sinking of cold, dense air masses, emerged from the windward side of a mountainous chain, into a lighter medium of warmer air along the leeward slope. Their duration is limited to a few hours and their range to a narrow band at the foot of the mountains, where they vanish by blending with warmer air.

Thunderstorms, caused by the rising of air from warm ground and sinking of colder air masses from high levels during summer months, produce strong but not widespread winds, which in nontropical zones are the main causes of windloads on buildings.

The effects of windstorms on important structures and on their parts, such as roofs, infill panels, curtain walls, and windows, should be determined by wind tunnel tests. Several models at different scale must be tested for a thorough investigation of wind effects.

The topographic model duplicates in scale (usually 1:2000) an area of approximately three square miles of the terrain or cityscape at the building site. The roughness of the wind tunnel floor is regulated to produce wind conditions corresponding to a 10 mile fetch (the unobstructed path along which a wind approaches the building). The vertical gradient of wind velocity and the intensity of turbulence at the building site are measured under these conditions, with various orientations. The measurements give the characteristics of the model wind to be produced in the tests of the aeroelastic model, of the pressure model, of landing conditions on the roof, and comfort conditions on the street level around the building.

The aeroelastic model duplicates in larger scale the building under study and the neighboring buildings for the purpose of investigating its structural response to winds from various directions. The roughness of the tunnel floor is adjusted to reproduce the model wind of the topographic model.

The pressure model is used to evaluate wind effects on roofs, curtain walls, large lobby glass plates, etc., by means of pressure gauges. Integration of pressures over the surface of the model also allows calculation of the overturning moment for comparison with results of tests on the aeroelastic model. A large scale model (usually 1 : 100) is used for studying wind patterns over roof-top helicopter pads and on plazas surrounding the building under study.

Wind analysis of buildings is facilitated by specifications in American National Standard Minimum Design Loads for Buildings and Other Structures, ANSI A58.1-1982. The following is a brief summary of that standard's procedure for determining the wind load against the main wind-resisting structure of a building. It, as well as Figures 1, A8, A6, and A7, are reproduced with permission from American National Standard A58.1-1982, copyright 1982 by the American National Standards Institute. Copies of this standard may be purchased from ANSI at 1430 Broadway, New York, NY 10018.

1. The category of a building is obtained from Table 1* according to the nature of its occupancy.

2. With the input from step one, the importance factor I is selected from Table 5.

3. The category of exposure is obtained from Section 6.5.3.1 in ANSI A58.1-1982.

4. The velocity pressure exposure coefficient K_z is selected from

---

*The numbers of tables mentioned in this summary are those in the ANSI publication A58.1-1982, where the tables are to be consulted.

Table 6 or, for buildings taller than 500 ft, calculated with the formula

$$K_z = 258 \left(\frac{z}{z_g}\right)^{2/\alpha}$$

Table A6 gives the values of α and z_g according to the exposure category from step three.

5. The basic wind speed V is obtained from Fig. 1 in ANSI A58.1-1982 (see Fig. 7.53) or, for Hawaii and Puerto Rico, from Table 7. These give the extreme fastest-mile wind speed statistically evaluated in a 50-year mean recurrence interval. The statistically elaborated data are collected by anemometers (weather vanes) placed 10 m (approximately 33 ft) above ground in open country. To measure the fastest-mile wind velocity, an anemometer trips an electrical switch with the passage of each mile or air and records the time that elapses during such passage.

The ANSI publication A58.1-1982 also provides tables of extreme fastest-mile wind speeds in 25 and 100 years intervals.

For special wind regions (mountainous terrains, gorges, ocean promitories, some of which are shown on the map in Fig. 7.53, the basic wind speed must be determined from reliable regional climatic data and approved by the authority having jurisdiction locally.

6. With the input from steps two, four, and five, the velocity pressure is calculated using the formula

$$q_z = 0.00256 \, K_z (IV)^2$$

in which the constant is justified by the equation

$$\gamma \frac{v^2}{2g} = \frac{(0.0756 \text{ lb/ft}^3)}{2(32.2 \text{ ft/s}^2)} \left(V \frac{\text{mi}}{\text{h}}\right)^2 \left(5280 \frac{\text{ft}}{\text{mi}}\right)^2 \left(\frac{1}{3600} \frac{\text{h}}{\text{s}}\right)^2$$

$$= 0.00256 \, V^2$$

The symbols for the preceding equation have the following meanings:

$$\text{lb} = \text{pound force}$$
$$\text{ft} = \text{foot}$$

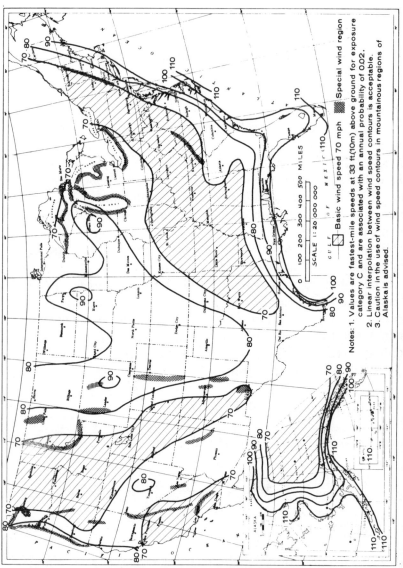

FIGURE 7.53. Basic wind speed in miles per hour. Annual extreme fastest-mile speed 30 ft. above ground. 50-year mean recurrence interval. This material is reproduced with permission from American National Standard ANSI, A58.1-1982, copyright 1982 by the American National Standards Institute. Copies of this standard may be purchased from the American National Standards Institute at 1430 Broadway, New York, N.Y. 10018

Notes: 1. Values are fastest-mile speeds at 33 ft(10m) above ground for exposure category C and are associated with an annual probability of 0.02.
2. Linear interpolation between wind speed contours is acceptable.
3. Caution in the use of wind speed contours in mountainous regions of Alaska is advised.

Basic wind speed 70 mph ▨ Special wind region

SCALE 1: 20 000 000

0 100 200 300 400 500 MILES

$$mi = mile$$
$$s = second$$
$$h = hour$$
$$v = \text{wind velocity in ft/s}$$
$$V = \text{wind velocity in mi/h}$$
$$\gamma = \text{air density}$$
$$g = \text{gravity acceleration}$$

In conditions other than the "standard atmosphere" (temperature 59°F = 15°C, sea level pressure 29.92 in. of mercury) the air density γ must be obtained from Table A5.

7. The wall pressure coefficient C_p is obtained from a table in Fig. 2.

8. A gust response factor G_z is selected from Table 8. The values in this table are calculated with the formula

$$G_z = 0.65 + 3.65\,T_z$$

where

$$T_z = \frac{2.35(D_0)^{1/2}}{(z/30)^{1/\alpha}}$$

The surface drag coefficients D_0 are listed in Table A6. When the building's height z exceeds 500 ft, a different gust response factor $\bar{G}$ must be calculated as shown in step 9.

9. The gust response factor $\bar{G}$ accounts for the effects of dynamic amplification of wind loads and is dependent on dynamic properties and size of the structure. It is given by

$$\bar{G} = 0.65 + \left(\frac{P}{\beta} + \frac{(3.32\,T_1)^2\,S}{1 + 0.002c}\right)^{1/2}$$

where the symbols have the following meanings:

β = the building's damping coefficient (% of critical). Lacking substantiated test data, use $\beta = 0.01$ for steel and $\beta = 0.002$ for concrete structures.

c = the average width of the building in ft on a plane at 90° to the wind flow [shown as B in Fig. 2 (upper right)].

S = the structure size factor to be found in Fig. A8, here Fig. 7.54 as a function of the building height $z = h$.

T_1 = the value of T_z in step 8 with z = building height h.

$P = \bar{f} J Y$

$\bar{f} = 10.5 f(h/sV)$

f = the building's fundamental natural frequency in hertzs.

$h = z$ = the building height

s = parameter in Table A9

V = basic design wind speed in miles/hour

J = pressure profile factor (a function of γ) from Fig. A6, here Fig. 7.55.

γ = parameter in Table A9

Y = resonance factor (a function of γ, c/h, and $\bar{f}$) from Fig. A7, here Fig. 7.56.

The following example from ANSI publication A58.1-1982 shows how $\bar{G}$ is calculated in a given case. Data:

V = 90 miles/hour

B = exposure

f = 0.15 hertzs

$z = h = 600$ ft

$c = 100$ ft

$\beta = 0.002$

Operations:

$s = 1.33$ (from Table A9)

$\bar{f} = 10.5(0.15)600/1.33(90) = 7.89$

$c/h = 100/600 = 0.167$

$\gamma = 3.28/600 = 0.00547$ (from Table A9)

$J = 0.0105$ (from Fig. 7.55)

$Y = 0.96$ (from Fig. 7.56)

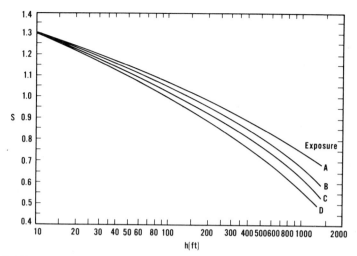

FIGURE 7.54. Structure size factor, S. (Taken from reference [15].)

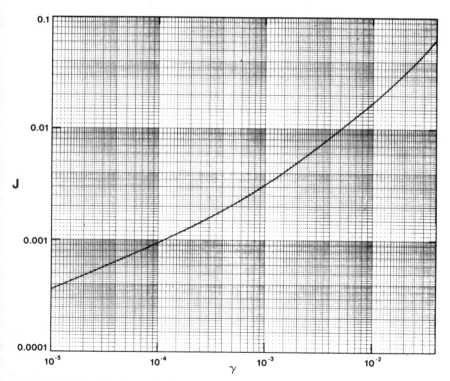

FIGURE 7.55. Pressure profile factor, J, as a function of γ. (Taken from reference [15].)

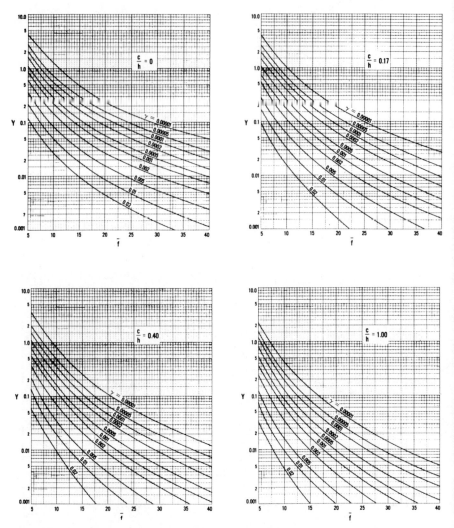

NOTE: The four sets of curves correspond to four different values of the ratio c/h.

FIGURE 7.56. Resonance factor, Y, as a function of γ and the ratio c/h. (Taken from reference [15].)

442

$$P = 7.89(0.0105)0.096 = 0.00795$$
$$\alpha = 4.5 \text{ (from Table A6)}$$
$$D_0 = 0.01 \text{ (from Table A6)}$$
$$T_1 = \frac{2.35(0.01)^{1/2}}{(600/30)^{1/4.5}} = 0.13$$
$$= 0.78 \text{ (from Fig. 7.54)}$$
$$\bar{G} = 0.65 + \left[\frac{0.00795}{0.012} + (3.32)^2(0.13)^2 \frac{0.78}{1+(0.002)100}\right]^{1/2} = 1.37$$

10. Finally, the wind pressure (p) against the building is calculated as shown in Table 4.

The design of individual building components and cladding proceeds analogously. The ANSI code has all the detailed information for this task.

The determination of wind loads on buildings with unusual geometric shapes and response characteristics, or in regions not covered by available documentation, should be pursued with properly conducted wind-tunnel tests.

APPENDIX

The preceding discussion of earthquake effects on buildings intentionally lacks a systematic presentation of a dynamic analysis procedure for the determination of seismic loads. Indeed, the limited scope of this book would make such a presentation preposterous, even more so in consideration of the discussed credibility gap that flaws many such analyses. However, in an attempt to show an interested reader how ground motion, mass, stiffness, and damping (the elusive parameters that influence a building's dynamic behavior and its seismic load) interplay, we briefly review the principles of dynamic analysis with a summary and an example from reference [3].

When the base of a plane frame with a single mass W/g (Fig. 7.57) moves during an earthquake, inertia tends to keep the mass at rest. Thus the columns bend with a lateral deflection u, and the displace-

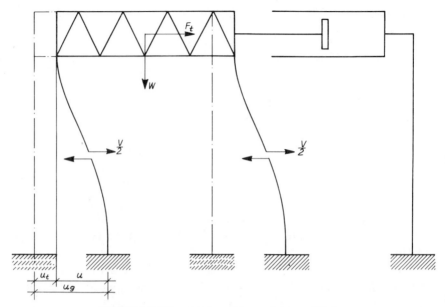

FIGURE 7.57.   (Taken from reference [3].)

ment u_t of the mass is the difference between ground displacement u_g and u:

$$u_t = u_g - u.$$

The acceleration of the mass is the second derivative $\ddot{u}_t$ of u_t, different of course from the ground acceleration $\ddot{u}_g$. The velocity of the building's deformation is the first derivative $\dot{u}$ of u. Using the preceding notations and the symbols k for the building's lateral stiffness (force required for a displacement $u = 1$), and c for the damping constant (force required to deform the frame with velocity $\dot{u} = 1$), the forces acting on the mass are as follows:

$$\text{Inertial force} = \frac{W}{g}\,\ddot{u}_t.$$

Spring force (sum of column's shears), $V = ku$.
Damping force $= c\dot{u}$.

These forces are related as impulse and response. Thus at any instant their sum vanishes:

$$\frac{W}{g}\ddot{u}_t - c\dot{u} + ku = 0.$$

The signs in the preceding equation are in accordance with Fig. 7.57. Replacing $\ddot{u}_t$ with $\ddot{u}_g - \ddot{u}$, the equation becomes

$$\frac{W}{g}\ddot{u} + c\dot{u} - ku = \frac{W}{g}\ddot{u}_g,$$

the same as if the foundation were stationary and a force $(W/g)\ddot{u}_g$ were applied to the mass. As an example of the frame's response to impulsive forces, we write the expression of the displacement u_{max} (from the solution of the preceding differential equation) due to an harmonic excitation:

$$\frac{W}{g}\ddot{u}_{g0}\sin\frac{2\pi}{T_p}t,$$

where

$\ddot{u}_{g0}$ = the amplitude of ground acceleration,

T_p = the period of the impulse,

$$u_{max} = \frac{W}{gk}\ddot{u}_{g0}\left\{\frac{1 + [2\lambda(T/T_p)]^2}{[1 - (T/T_p)^2]^2 + [2\lambda(T/T_p)]^2}\right\}^{1/2},$$

where $\lambda = c/c_c$ is the ratio of viscous damping c to reference or critical damping c_c and T is the fundamental period of the frame.

It appears from u_{max} that, lacking damping ($\lambda = 0$), the deformation is infinitely large when the period T_p of the impulsive load equals the fundamental period T of the frame (resonance), and that the deformation vanishes (the frame moves as one with the ground) when

TABLE 7.8.   Typical Values of Damping[a]

Stress Level	Type and Condition of Structure	Damping (% critical)
Low, well below, proportional limit, stressed below ¼ yield point	Steel, reinforced or prestressed concrete, wood; no cracking; no joint slip	0.5–1.0
Working stress, no more than about ½ yield point	Welded steel, prestressed concrete, well reinforced concrete (only slight cracking)	2
	Reinforced concrete with considerable cracking	3–5
	Bolted and/or riveted steel, wood structures with nailed or bolted joints	5–7
At or just below yield point	Welded steel, prestressed concrete (without complete loss in prestress)	5
	Reinforced concrete and prestressed concrete	7–10
	Bolted and/or riveted steel, wood structures with bolted joints	10–15
	Wood structures with nails	15–20
Beyond yield points, with permanent strain greater than yield point limit strain	Welded steel	7–10
	Reinforced and prestressed concrete	10–15
	Bolted and/or riveted steel, and wood structures	20

[a] Taken from reference [16].

the stiffness k is very large (braced frame). Table 7.8 compiled by Newmark and Hall lists values of λ for various building materials and stress levels.

Earthquake impulses vary randomly rather than harmonically, as shown by the ground acceleration history in Fig. 7.18a. Thus the solution of the preceding equation cannot be obtained in closed form.

Rather, it is given, when λ is not large, by the Duhamel integral

$$u(t) = \frac{W}{gk} \frac{2\pi}{T} \int_0^t \ddot{u}_g(\tau) e^{-\lambda(2\pi/T)(t-\tau)} \sin \frac{2\pi}{T} (t - \tau) \, d\tau,$$

where τ is the dummy time variable,

$$0 \leqslant \tau \leqslant t,$$

and $\ddot{u}_g(\tau)$ is the ground acceleration history from an available seismogram, like that in Fig. 7.18a.

The product

$$ku(t) = V(t)$$

is the instantaneous earthquake load (same as the total shear on the base) at the time t. Evaluation of the preceding integral for only one given instant t can be performed numerically, but repeating the task for all the instants t during an earthquake duration would be a tedious and interminable task without a computer.

The frame in the preceding example has only one degree of freedom, that is, one possibility of motion of the mass W/g. Indeed, the columns prevent vertical displacement w and rotation dw/dx of the mass, while lack of earthquake load at 90° to the x, z plane of the frame excludes any other displacement or rotation. A more general plane frame with several masses at several levels has several degrees of freedom, and its dynamic analysis is considerably more complex. Indeed, a multistory frame can vibrate with as many different deflection shapes (modes) as many masses. In the first mode all n masses displace. In the second mode one mass is practically stationary (vibration node), and $n - 1$ masses displace. In the third mode two of the n masses are practically stationary, and $n - 2$ masses displace. To each vibration mode there corresponds a different set of displacements $u_{zn}(t)$ that is, the displacement of the mass at level z, in mode n, at time t.

Also, to each oscillatory mode corresponds a different active building mass, since the stationary masses are not contributing to the dynamic action. An effective mass can be defined for each mode so that a multistory frame can be treated as a single mass oscillator in each particular mode. This mass must be smaller in the higher modes, since in the highest mode all but the top mass are idle and therefore ineffective. This also indicates that only the first few modes are relevant since the oscillator is nearly massless in the highest modes. The expression of the effective mass in mode n is

$$\frac{1}{g} W_n = \frac{\left(\sum u_{zn}W_z\right)^2}{\sum u_{zn}^2 W_z},$$

where W_z is the weight of the story at level z. With the effective modal masses available, the instantaneous base shear in mode n, $V_n(t)$, is obtained from

$$V_n(t) = \frac{W_n}{g} \frac{2\pi}{T_n} \int_0^t \ddot{u}_g(\tau) e^{-(2\pi/T_n)\lambda(t-\tau)} \sin \frac{2\pi}{T_n} (t - \tau) \, d\tau,$$

and the instantaneous total base shear, sum of all the modal base shears, is

$$V(t) = \sum V_n(t).$$

The distribution of the total earthquake load $V_n(t)$ in mode n to the various stories is obtained with the use of distribution coefficients as follows:

$$F_{zn}(t) = V_n(t) \left(\frac{u_{zn}W_z}{\sum u_{zn}W_z} \right).$$

Thus the total force at level z and at time t is

$$F_z(t) = \sum F_{zn}(t).$$

We note that the UBC distribution coefficients

$$\frac{h_z W_z}{\sum h_z W_z}$$

coincide with the former ones in a first mode shape (Fig. 7.59), with displacements increasing linearly from base to top.

Summarizing the analysis of a multiple mass oscillator starts with the evaluation of the mode shapes and, for each mode, of the effective mass W_n and period of vibration T_n. Next the modal base shears $V_n(t)$ and their fractions $F_{zn}(t)$ at the levels of the floors are calculated. All the modal loads $F_{zn}(t)$ are then superposed to obtain the total earthquake-load diagram. It is not possible to calculate the maximum base shear V_n^{max} in each mode, superpose the maxima, and

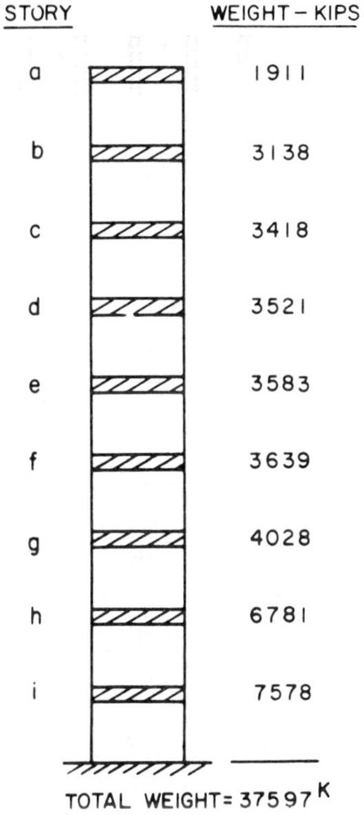

STORY		WEIGHT – KIPS
a		1911
b		3138
c		3418
d		3521
e		3583
f		3639
g		4028
h		6781
i		7578

TOTAL WEIGHT = 37597 [K]

FIGURE 7.58.   (Taken from reference [3].)

TABLE 7.9.[a]

Tier	a	b	c	d	e	f	g	h	i
a	26	-50	25	-1	0	0	0	0	0
b	-50	128	-105	27	0	0	0	0	0
c	25	-105	165	-112	27	0	0	0	0
d	-1	27	-112	117	-118	27	0	0	0
e	0	0	27	-118	186	-122	27	0	0
f	0	0	0	27	-122	194	-130	30	1
g	0	0	0	0	27	-130	220	-149	31
h	0	0	0	0	0	30	-149	230	-141
i	0	0	0	0	0	1	31	-141	235

[a] Taken from reference [3].

distribute the sum because the maxima in the various modes occur at different times. The task is monumental indeed, and it cannot be performed without a computer. In the following example from reference [3] the foundation of the nine-story oscillator in Fig. 7.58 is subject to the ground acceleration (Fig. 7.18a) of El Centro, California, during the 1940 earthquake, the strongest quake for which a seismogram is available. The building is assumed founded directly on rock. If a soft layer or piles existed between the building and rock, they should be treated as parts of the building. Table 7.9 lists the elastic properties of the building in the form of reactions of rollers (in kips) constraining the horizontal displacement at all floors but one when the free floor is displaced by 0.01 in. For example, the values in the first column represent the forces needed to displace the top floor by 0.01 in. and keep all other tiers still. Thus if a 26 k horizontal force pulls the top floor to the right while all other floors are constrained with rollers, the top floor moves 0.01 in., the roller at level b reacts with -50 k (pushing left), the roller at level c reacts with 25 k (pushing right), and so on. If level b is to be displaced 0.01 in. to the right, a 128 k force at b is needed, while the rollers at a, c, and d react with forces -50 k, -65 k, +27 k, respectively. These forces are evaluated by statically indeterminate analysis, as in the example of the two-story frame in Fig. 4.11a.

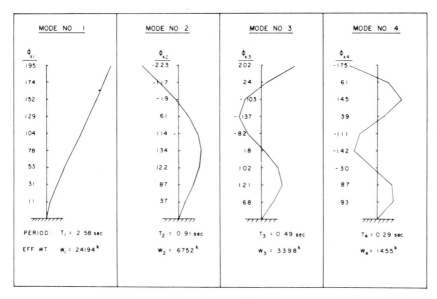

FIGURE 7.59

With the preceding elastic properties and the story weights in Fig. 7.58, the computer output values of modal periods, effective weights, and deflection curves are shown in Fig. 7.59 for the first four modes. We note how the sum of the effective weights in the first four modes,

$$W_1 + W_2 + W_3 + W_4 = 24{,}194 + 6752 + 3398 + 1455 = 35{,}799,$$

represents 95% of the sum of all nine modal effective weights, that is, 37,597 k which is the same as the building's total weight. This is an indication of the negligible importance of the modes 5 through 9 in this case. The modal periods are considerably longer than in typical nine-story buildings, but this frame is only a theoretic case without actual resemblance to typical buildings. The computer output of the base shear $V_n(t)$ in modes 1 and 2 is plotted in Fig. 7.60 and is calculated according to a damping ratio $\lambda = 0.05$ (the same as the value in the Los Angeles code). The distribution among the floors of the maximum base shear in modes 1, 2, 3, and 4 is shown in Fig. 7.61a with the time at which the modal shear is maximum. The diagrams of

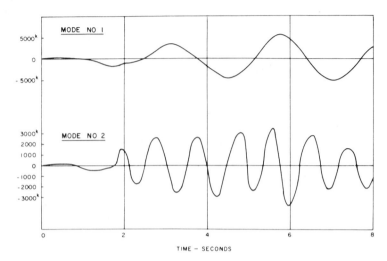

FIGURE 7.60

shear forces on the frame due to the preceding loads are shown in Fig. 7.61*b*. These shear diagrams cannot be superposed, since they occur at the different times shown in Fig. 7.61*a*. The largest base shear is obtained by superposition of the four modal shears at $t = 2.75$ sec, to which the shear diagram in Fig. 7.62 is related. This diagram, however, does not produce the worst floor shear at every floor. This is rather obtained with the "envelope" of shear diagrams in Fig. 7.63, in which the shear at each floor is the worst for that floor during the earthquake regardless of the time when it occurs. The maximum base shear in the preceding example is 19% of the building weight.

The preceding procedure can be approximated and simplified by the use of acceleration spectra, which for any period T give the ratio of the maximum ground acceleration to gravity acceleration g for the duration of an earthquake. With an appropriate spectrum available, the maximum base shear in mode n is thus

$$V_n^{\max} = W_n C,$$

where

W_n = the effective mass in mode n,

C = the ordinate of the spectral curve at $T = T_n$ for the appropriate damping λ.

As previously noted, the maxima of the modal shears cannot be summed to obtain the total maximum base shear because they occur

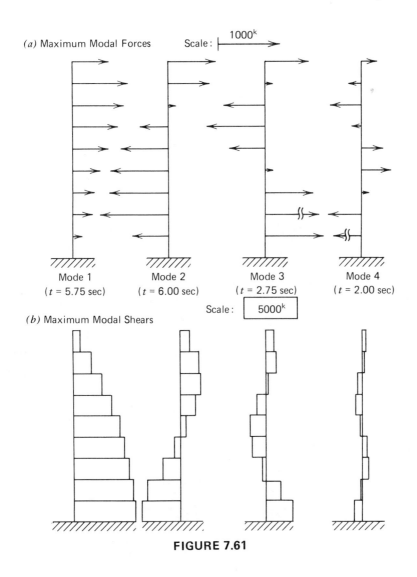

FIGURE 7.61

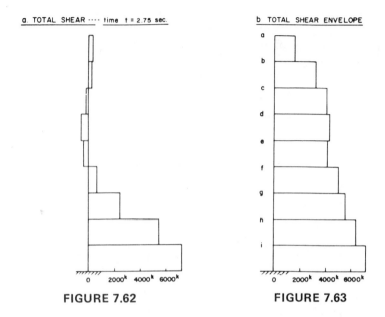

FIGURE 7.62   FIGURE 7.63

at different times. This problem is overcome by using the square root
of the sum of the squares of the modal maxima as the maximum total
base shear.

Table 7.10 from reference [3] presents a comparison of computer
output values and approximate values of the maxima of modal base
shears for the nine-story frame under discussion. The values of the
coefficients C are not listed in the table; they are rather obtained as
products of $2\pi/gT$ with the listed spectral velocities that are the
maxima (for given modal periods T_n and damping ratios λ) of the
Duhamel integrals. Indeed, such an integral gives the value, at any
time t, of the expression

$$\frac{ku(t)}{W} \frac{gT}{2\pi},$$

that is, a velocity. Table 7.13 also shows the value of the total maximum base shear from the computer output and its approximate value

TABLE 7.10.   Response Spectrum Analysis of Example Building[a]

Mode	Period (sec)	Spectral Velocity (ft/sec)	Maximum Base Shear (kips)	
			Spectral Value	Computer Solution
1	2.58	3.1	5660	5779
2	0.91	2.6	3770	3663
3	0.49	2.5	3380	2498
4	0.29	1.0	980	819

Total maximum:

$$V = (V_1^2 + V_2^2 + V_8^2 + V_4^2)^{1/2} = 7660 \text{ kips}$$

Total maximum from computer solution = 7244 kips

[a]Taken from reference [3].

obtained as square root of the sum of the squared modal maxima. In consideration of the uncertainty surrounding the values of mass, stiffness and therefore period, as well as damping, the degree of approximation evident in the table is not unsatisfactory.

REFERENCES

The author gratefully acknowledges the contribution of information and figures from the following publications:

1. Clough, R. W. "Dynamic Effects of Earthquakes." *Proc. ASCE*, Vol. 87, No. ST4 (April 1960).
2. Alford, J. L., Housner, G. W., and Martel, R. R. "Spectrum Analysis of Strong Motion Earthquakes." Report of Office of Naval Research. Earthquake Research Laboratory, California Institute of Technology, August 1951.
3. Clough, R. W. "The Agadir, Morocco, Earthquake, February 29, 1960." A report in *Earthquakes*. A publication of the American Iron and Steel Institute, 1975.
4. Degenkolb, H. J. "Earthquake Forces on Tall Structures." Bethlehem Steel Booklet 2717-B.
5. Weigel, R. L. (Ed.). *Earthquake Engineering*. Englewood Cliffs, N.J.: Prentice-Hall, 1970.
6. Anderson, James C., and Bertero, VitelmoV. "Seismic Behavior of Multi-Story Frames Designed by Different Philosophies." Report No. EERC-69-11. University of California Earthquake Engineering Research Center.
7. Proceedings of the U.S.-Japan Seminar on Earthquake Engineering with Emphasis on the Safety of School Buildings, Sendai, Japan, September 1970.
8. Degenkolb, H. J. "Limitations and Uncertainties of Present Structural Design Methods for Lateral Force Resistance." Proceedings of the Fourth World Conference on Earthquake Engineering, Santiago, Chile.
9. Degenkolb, H. J., and Loring, A. W. "Improving the Seismic Response of Braced Frames." Proceedings of the Sixth World Conference on Earthquake Engineering, New Delhi, India, January 10–14, 1977.
10. Yucel, O., Sendil, U., and Tall, L. (Eds.). "Bibliography on Tall Buildings." Report No. 8C, ASCE-1ABSE. Joint Committee on Planning and Design of Tall Buildings, Fritz Engineering Laboratory, Lehigh University, Bethlehem, Pennsylvania, 1973.
11. Proceedings, Wind Effects on Buildings and Structures, Third International Conference, Tokyo, 1971.

12. Davenport, A. G. "Gust Loading Factors." *J. Structural Div. ASCE*, Vol. 93, No. S73 (1967).

13. Robertson, L. E. "Wind Engineering of Tall Buildings." Proceedings of the Symposium on Tall Buildings, Nashville, Tennessee, Novermber 14–15, 1974.

14. Uniform Building Code, 1982.

15. American National Standard Building Code Requirements for Minimum Design Loads for Buildings and Other Structures, ANSI A58.1-1982.

16. Newmark, N. M., and Hall, W. J. "Seismic Design Criteria for Nuclear Reactor Facilities," Proc. Fourth World Conference on Earthquake Engineering, Santiago, Chile, January 1969.

Additional references can be found in the Bibliography of *Earthquake Engineering*, by E. P. Hollis, 1971 available through Earthquake Engineering Research Institute, 2620 Telegraph Avenue, Berkeley, CA 94704.

INDEX